THE
MILLENNIUM
OF
EUROPE

OSCAR HALECKI

THE
MILLENNIUM
OF
EUROPE

With a Foreword by

HENDRICK BRUGMANS

UNIVERSITY OF NOTRE DAME PRESS

*Publication of this volume
was assisted by a grant from the
Ford Foundation, which is gratefully acknowledged.*

UNIVERSITATI CRACOVIENSI

ALMAE MATRI MEAE VENERABILI

ANNO PROXIMO SESCENTENNIUM SUUM CELEBRATURAE

Foreword

THERE IS a great deal of truth in Marx's remark that "our social situation determines our mental consciousness." People of different nationalities, surroundings, generations, will take a different view, both of the past and the present. As long as history remains "unfinished"— which means, as long as the Last Judgment has not been declared— new events will cast new light on previous ones.

Take the French Revolution as an example. As long as political discussion in Europe went on between the so-called Left and Right, this dividing line also set historians of these two schools in opposition to one another. It was not by chance that Taine, as the author of *Les Origines de la France contemporaine,* was at the same time a Conservative, nor that the "Robespierrist" Mathiez should later sympathize with Communism. For the same reason, it is only natural that, to see a Jewish historian like Professor J. L. Talmon write a book on *The Origins of Totalitarian Democracy,* we should have to await the rise of messianistic political regimes in our own time. The words, "totalitarian democracy," would have been incomprehensible to any nineteenth-century historian.

Along the same line, it is hardly surprising that modern historiography should have been influenced by recent attempts to federate the nations of western Europe. There is not only subject-matter to be studied here; events such as the Marshall and the Schuman Plans have already become new fields of scholarly research in themselves. But the increased intercourse between neighboring countries has induced their peoples to reconsider their cultural backgrounds and to discover that their basic ideas and ideals, their institutions and structures, are always comparable and sometimes even similar or identical. In undertaking this "collective psychoanalysis," peoples of the various countries were forced to conclude that their common civilization springs from the same sources, and that they underwent the same experiences, the same ordeals, the same expectations and despairs.

This discovery of European togetherness does not mean, however, that the existence, or the positive value, of historic nationalism should be henceforth ignored. Nationalism is, in fact, one of the principal features of European history. At the end of the Middle Ages, it gave rise, not only to sovereign nation-states, but also to coherent groups, "families within the family," that were justly proud of their original characters and their distinctive personalities. It would be intellectually dishonest—and for that matter, a poor service to the European cause—should we attempt to explain away this essential phenomenon out of Europe's past.

However, we should state two other facts, which are equally undeniable.

First, nationalism itself is an international movement—sometimes liberal, sometimes authoritarian—which, as such, has had its historians.

Second, one of the greatest periods of European history—the "classical" twelfth and thirteenth centuries—was able to develop its immense vitality long before the modern nation-state came into being.

In other words, while nothing was more European than nationalism, still, Europe existed long before nationalism triumphed. Very briefly summarized, these are the basic discoveries which European historians have made in the past thirty years.

These European scholars belonged to various nationalities. Most of the time they worked without foreknowledge of one another's work, and they confronted each other's conclusions only after they had been published in book form.

The older generation of historians included a Swiss like Gonzague de Reynold and a Belgian like Henri Pirenne, whose European orientation became more and more notable at the end of his life, when he dominated more forcefully the historical material he had been struggling with in earlier years. There were also Italians like Gaetano Salvemini and his great compatriot, Benedetto Croce, who envisaged the

European past in the light of his very personal, liberal Hegelianism. There was a Dutchman like Huizinga, who painted *The Waning of the Middle Ages* in colorful, impressive chapters, and where the whole of Europe appeared around the splendor of fifteenth-century Burgundy. There was an Englishman, Christopher Dawson, who threw new light on the "dark ages," and called his book *The Making of Europe*. Even more ambitiously, a German, Hans Freyer, wrote his *Weltgeschichte Europas* in two volumes, while a brilliant French scholar, Paul Hazard, analyzed *"la Crise de la Conscience Européenne,"* and thereby gave us one of the most delightful works of learning, a classic on the early Enlightenment. In short, the concept of Europe as-a-whole had entered the realm of historiography, even before it became accepted as a political ideal or a key to economic prosperity.

Of course, the list of specifically "European" historians could be considerably expanded. For today, however, we will concentrate on the author of the present book.

He is a Pole by birth and by deeply-rooted attachment, but he bore the idea of free Poland with him while crossing the Atlantic Ocean to live and teach in freedom on American soil. Possessing a universal mind by virtue of his broad genius and his Catholic conviction, he rightly thinks that his long-oppressed fatherland deserves the special concern and affection of all those who believe in the rich variety of languages, landscapes and ways of life that make Europe so fascinating. He never believed that men must become less patriotic in order to be loyal to the larger European community. This devoted Pole rejects the pagan nationalism of "blood and soil." As a Christian with a free mind, he is now more at home on this side of the Iron Curtain—and especially in Rome—than under the rule of communist absolutism, where he would no longer be able to spread his message. He therefore embodies the tragedy of a nation and a century.

The present book is an inspiring synthesis. Such works are often looked upon with distrust by so-called specialists. Fortunately, Professor Halecki has proved on numerous occasions that he does not employ second-hand sources and that he draws his conclusions from a life-long career of carefully detailed research. He for one knows the joy every serious historian has experienced when contact with historic reality is established—the feeling which Huizinga described so well in these words: "Yes, thus it must have been. . . ." But even in his attempts to search out basic data, Halecki has constantly been a man with the courage to reach conclusions. His image of good historiography is not the old curiosity shop, nor even the museum; it is the resurrection of mankind in evolution.

Professor Halecki describes the "millennium of Europe," which means that he considers the beginning of European history, as such, to have occurred approximately during the second half of the tenth century.

Of course, this is not a beginning *ex nihilo,* as the different elements of western civilization had already developed into a cultural synthesis during the fourth century, when the Roman Empire had adopted Christianity. But that empire had been short-lived, at least so far as its western half was concerned. Outside the realm of Byzantium, the onslaught of the "barbarians" seemed to have engulfed once and for all a state, an economic system, and a culture and ecclesiastical organization that had borne the mark of Christendom.

And still, the fall of Rome did not bring to an end this promising, Roman "pre-Europe." In fact, it survived the catastrophe. Western monasticism and western rational theology, western feudalism and western trade, were strong enough to prevent the Continent from falling prey to total disruption. In spite of inner anarchy and outside aggression, the fire under the ashes was not extinguished. Half a millennium after Romulus Augustulus' abdication, the great millennium of Europe could begin. Even the Moslem attack on the Mediterranean had not prevented this Renaissance. Indeed, it had rather inspired it, and Henri Pirenne was undoubtedly right in pointing to the link between "Mahomet et Charlemagne."

The history of Europe is something of a miracle. Surely Professor Halecki, as a Christian, will not reject the word. Of course, that does not mean that God would have been more merciful to this continent than to others. But it so happened that the history of Christendom coincided for many centuries with Europe's. Only in the present day, when prelates of all races and colors meet at the Second Vatican Council, does this begin to change spectacularly. Today, therefore, Christian philosophers ask themselves, what is the deeper sense of that twin contemporary phenomenon: Europe's "dwarfing" (as Professor Toynbee has called it), even in the universal Church, and, at the same time, the trend toward unity which characterizes contemporary European history.

Be that as it may, Professor Halecki is correct in putting the Gospel and the Church in the center of his work. He does so, not solely because he is faithful to the Truth with a capital "t," but because honest analysis has taught him that we cannot understand Europe otherwise, any more than Arabian society can be understood without a constant reference to Islam. It is true that today Islam is in a process of "dis-Arabization," just as Christianity is losing its overwhelmingly European overtones. But the past millennium has seen a constant coexistence between Europe's Christian churches and Europe's states, since, until recently, Christianity and Europe were nearly identical on the world's map. This is the European's pride and tragedy, a source both of great inspiration and deep humility.

The Americas are an offspring of this historic society. From Europe, they received their institutions and their languages, their religion and their style of life. True, they soon developed a history of their own, and when Napoleon sold Louisiana, a new Continent took up its own destiny. The epic of "the frontier" began, and there is no word in European history to translate such a concept. Yet, "greater Europe" remained attached to the civilization from which it sprang. All countries around the Atlantic share the values arising from common sources, and nobody can understand one half of this community, without knowing the other.

Europe is America's "old testament." America should understand this, in order to understand itself. What Professor Halecki offers, is, therefore, a textbook for mutual Atlantic comprehension. May it find its way to many minds and hearts, on both sides of the modern Mediterranean.

Hendrik Brugmans
Rector, College of Europe
Bruges, Belgium

The Origin and Method of the Present Study

Twelve years ago, in the middle of this century, I published a brief study of European history,[1] which tried to determine the limits and divisions of that history in time and space, but it was only in a concluding chapter that I touched on some problems regarding the content of the history of the European community. Now, at the beginning of the century's seventh decade, there appear two different reasons for re-examining that content, not by giving once more a survey of the rather well-known facts, but by trying to discover the meaning of European history for the Europeans themselves and for mankind as well, and to establish its record through an examination of the European conscience.

On the one hand, the last ten years have certainly evidenced an almost unexpected economic recovery of western Europe, thanks mainly to American aid but also to the efforts and abilities of its peoples. However, in spite of the progress of western Europe's integration—a process much more successful in the economic than in the political field—it has become evident, too, that not only the German center, but all of Europe will probably remain divided for a long time, since the liberation of East Central and Eastern Europe, which in 1956 seemed just around the corner, is presently a rather distant hope.

Nothing makes us better realize Europe's critical situation than the contrast between the denial of self-determination to so many formerly independent historical nations of that part of the world, and the emancipation, in the name of self-determination of a whole series of Asiatic countries, old and new, and quite recently of one after the other of the peoples of Africa, even the underdeveloped. In the so-called Cold War, which after a few years of illusion has been resumed with even greater intensity, the position of Europe's free nations, defended by the United States and threatened by Soviet Russia, is more dependent than ever before on the policies of the two extra-European super-powers. And in view of the development of atomic and nuclear research in the last fifteen years, the outbreak of a real war would mean an even more certain annihilation for the comparatively small European area, placed between these two powers, than for the rest of the world. It is, therefore, high time to appraise the values of the European heritage and the chances of its preservation in our technological age; in spite of its European origin, this technological age has now created a world united from the material but divided from the spiritual point of view, where Europe could be easily submerged if not lost.

Under such conditions, another, much less conspicuous phenomenon of the present moment, is highly significant. Individual European nations are turning from that present and its truly overwhelming issues to the memories of their earliest past, celebrating as usual not only the various anniversaries of events that occurred fifty or a hundred years ago, but also the millennia which take them back from the middle of the twentieth to the middle of the tenth century.

It is hardly surprising that the Poles, ever historically-minded, are leading in that respect, since they have special reasons for recalling the early origin of their membership in the European community, as well as the continuity of their part in European history through the last thousand years. But the commemorations of the Polish millennium, which for reasons to be explained later, had already started in 1960—that is six years in advance—made it immediately obvious to historians that the Polish case cannot be studied in isolation. Other millennia of European nations, both western and eastern, exercise a similar appeal, after being anticipated long ago. In 1962, it was a thousand years since an empire, supposedly supranational, came into existence in the center of Europe, and in spite of its dissolution after less than eight and a half centuries, that empire left behind a fascinating tradition. Therefore, the study of history has to consider now, in the second half of the twentieth century, the millenium of a Europe which in the second half of the tenth was finally constituted as an integral whole.

The Polish example makes the historian aware not only of the timeliness of such a study, but also of its difficulty as far as the scholarly method of research and presentation is concerned. Strange as it may seem, the celebration of the Polish millennium and the historical investigations which are needed for that purpose are sponsored and encouraged by Poland's present communist regime no less than by the anti-communist Polish emigration in the free world. This can be explained not only by reasons of expediency—the concern with public opinion and the quest for popular support—but also by the frequently overlooked fact that Communism, a socioeconomic doctrine which seems to imply a total break with the past and its tradition, is based upon a philosophy of history, which, through the reinterpretation of the past by Marxist scholars, wants to give to the masses a certainty of victory in the struggle against capitalism. Hence the controversies between Marxist and non-Marxist Polish historians regarding the interpretation of the millenium of their country, and the instructive character of these controversies for all historians, especially for those interested in the millennium of Europe. For they show that such a problem cannot be fully grasped without taking a position with respect to the basic issues of the philosophy of history.

The Marxist historians are better prepared to meet the challenge than their opponents, who do not have a common, generally accepted philosophy of history and are doubtful as to the utility or even the possibility of such a philosophy.[2] It is obviously not enough to take such a negative attitude, simply to use a method opposed to the Marxist one, and to limit the story to the bare facts without any judgments of value based upon general principles. It is no solution of the problem, either, merely to disregard the alleged laws, similar to those of nature, which are supposed to determine in advance the historical process, in particular the unavoidable, regular succession of the various forms of production: slavery, feudalism, capitalism, and socialism. A positive approach, replacing the Marxist, is badly needed, and the experience of the discussions about the Polish millennium can be helpful in that respect.

In the case of Poland the principal controversial issue is clear. According to the Marxists,[3] the national millennium ought to be the commemoration of the origin of the Polish state, a state which, as a matter of fact, existed long before the middle of the tenth century. But in the sixties of that century, (soon after 960) it was mentioned for the first time in contemporary sources, and succeeded in using the organization of the Catholic Church for consolidating the feudal structure of the body politic and its socioeconomic basis. According to the traditional, non-Marxist interpretation,[4] the conversion to the Catholic faith, which before 966 had only a very limited impact on some of the Polish tribes, in that crucial year was formally and finally accepted by Poland's ruler and people. For these non-Marxists, this was the basic event leading to the full integration of the country with the western Christian community, the decisive turning point in its destiny which deserves to be commemorated as such.

That alternative is indeed of general significance, because independently of the individual case under discussion it raises the question whether the Christian interpretation of history and the emphasis of the religious, purely spiritual element in the evolution of mankind is not the best answer to the claims of historical materialism. And it suggests the method which, rather than that of the Marxist, ought to be used in approaching a problem like the millennium of any nation, region, or even larger, continental community. Furthermore, these conclusions are closely connected with important trends in present-day historiography.

It so happens that in these last years Arnold Toynbee and Gonzague de Reynold, whose standard works, even before being completed, proved so suggestive for the study of the limits and divisions of European history, have stressed in the latest volumes of these works the basic and decisive importance of religion for the study of universal history and of the formation of Europe. There is, indeed, a very great difference in the approaches to religion of the English historian,[5] who seems to favor more and more some kind of syncretism reconciling all great religions, and of the Swiss writer, who remains unreservedly devoted to the Catholic Church which put "the Christian roof" on Europe's structure.[6] But an even more recent discussion among representatives of practically all religions of the Occident and Orient on the role of these religions in the lives of the various peoples[7] resulted, in spite of the profound doctrinal differences which were sincerely admitted, in a general agreement on moral principles and the primacy of spiritual values. It is interesting to note that it was only the spokesman for Catholicism who explained its impact on the peoples of the West, who included in his survey the whole background of the last two thousand years, and who examined the contemporary civilization under what he called the historical context. And shortly before that meeting, two outstanding Catholic philosophers, Jacques Maritain[8] and Father M. C. d'Arcy,[9] proved the possibility of a Catholic philosophy of history, fully adapted to the needs of our time. There is, however, no doubt that all religious minds, whatever their specific beliefs and the degree of their interest in the study of history might be, consider the development of mankind from the point of view not of socioeconomic laws or rather necessities but of moral laws or rather divine commandments on whose observance any real progress depends.[10]

It is from such a viewpoint that the problem of Europe's millennium will be studied in the following pages. But before this is done, the different meanings of the term "millennium" will require a few introductory comments in order to determine the extent, in addition to a truly objective historical method, to which the leading ideas of the Christian philosophy of history must be applied in the interpretation of any millennium.

The writing of this book would have been impossible without two grants which I received for research and study in Europe: one in 1957, from the John Guggenheim Memorial Foundation, the other one in 1961, from the Program on East Central Europe of Columbia University, thanks to its Director, Professor Henry L. Roberts.

I am also very grateful to Notre Dame University, in particular to the Chairman of the Committee on International Relations, Professor Stephen D. Kertesz, for recommending my manuscript, and to the Director of the University Press, Miss Emily Schossberger, for preparing it for publication with the greatest possible care.

Rome, December 1962.

Contents

[xix]

The Three Meanings of
the Millennium

Tнᴇ ʜɪꜱᴛᴏʀɪᴄᴀʟ ꜱᴄɪᴇɴᴄᴇꜱ, whether included in the humanities or in
the social sciences, should not and cannot be assimilated to the exact and
natural sciences as far as their method is concerned. However, by making their terminology more precise and unequivocal, they should and
can be made more exact and penetrating as to the nature of things past.[1]
A typical example in this respect is the term "nation," along with words
like "nationality" and "nationalism" which are derived from it.[2] These
terms are used continually by historians and will be frequently used in
the present study as well, and yet there is no universally accepted definition of their meaning, or rather there are different meanings, in various
periods and regions, with a great deal of misuse and confusion resulting.
The term "millennium," not as frequently used, seems to be a much
simpler case, but nevertheless a close examination reveals three different
meanings of that expression which have to be distinguished and defined.

The usual meaning is, of course, similar to that of terms like "centennial" and analogous designations of anniversaries. Just as a centennial
or centenary is the commemoration of an event which occurred one
hundred years ago, a millenium or millenary is an evocation of something that happened a thousand years ago. In all such cases there is danger of exaggeration, of celebrating too many anniversaries, and though
they all contribute to a deeper interest in history and stimulate scholarly
research in sometimes neglected directions, they can be misused for propaganda purposes and for anachronistic interpretations of the past from

the viewpoint of the present. Therefore, such commemorations should be limited to the celebration and clarification of really important events which deserve to be made a living past. This is particularly true for the millennia that take us far back into ages of which so little can be said with full certainty.

An objective criterion of the importance of such a distant fact and of the changes connected with it is the simultaneous occurrence of other significant events in or about the same year, a phenomenon which is rarely fortuitous. In any case, the background, origin, and consequences of the basic fact itself and of those accompanying it must receive careful attention, and no single date should be overemphasized. Returning for an illustration of that theoretical statement to the example of Poland's millennium, it is entirely legitimate to consider, besides the basic event of the Christianization in 966, not only the first description of the country by a foreign traveller who visited it about the same time,[3] but also the first recorded clashes with the Germans in 963 and 967, if only the attention remains focused on the central issue, its intrinsic, independent significance and its casual connection with the others.

As to the general importance of the epoch which a millennium is supposed to evoke, the best criterion seems to be the simultaneous appearance of basic changes in several countries belonging to the same cultural community. In such a comparative study the individual dates of particular years lose even more completely their exceptional place, at least a whole generation's lifetime has to be examined, and even the entire century, separated by a thousand years, more or less, from our own time, requires due attention. The place of the tenth century in European history can serve as an appropriate illustration of such a requirement, since in the light of recent research in various lands the exceptional part of that century in the formation of Europe can no longer be questioned.[4]

Despite such an enlargement of the millennium conception even in its first and simplest meaning, a study limited to that meaning alone would not be too difficult in the case of Europe. It is true that the sources seem comparatively scarce to the historians of later centuries, and that alarming gaps will consequently always remain in our knowledge of the facts, especially if the countries of Eastern Europe are included. But by the very fact that so few records exist, they are easy to exhaust, they have been published and commented upon long ago and many times, and they are therefore familiar to all specialists. More difficult to exhaust than the primary sources are, indeed, the statements of the secondary authorities, and more disconcerting than the unavoidable repetitions in their writings are their contradictory hypotheses, almost unconsciously influenced by national bias. However, the historian who wants only to study what happened a thousand years ago can limit himself to the traditional task of his profession: to the discovery and description of how things have really been.[5] No philosophy of history seems necessary, and concern with the problems of such a philosophy might even seem dangerous in that first phase of any millennium study.

The situation changes drastically as soon as the second meaning of the term "millennium" is taken into consideration. In order to discover that meaning, it is advisable to return to the general problem of historical anniversaries. For example, celebrating a centenary means not only to recall what happened one hundred years ago, but also to connect these memories with the present and to survey the development between the two dates: the historical one and the year of commemoration. The necessity of such an approach is particularly obvious whenever the birth of a great man or the origin of an important institution is recalled. Much more meaningful than the circumstances of such a birth or foundation is the evolution which followed: the whole life and mature achievements of the given person, which sometimes cover almost the whole century, or the subsequent growth of what had been organized at the beginning of that period of one hundred years, including the repercussions up to the present.

In the case of a millennium the situation is naturally different. The life of a person born a thousand years ago constitutes only a small part of that period, even if its posthumous impact is considered. And rare are the creations which, even in an evolved form, have persisted throughout or influenced ten centuries. But such events as the birth of a nation or of a community of nations gain their real momentum only when studied in connection with the whole life of such a collective, practically immortal, body, from its early origin, were it even in the remote tenth century, to its present stage of development. In such cases the millennium means, in addition to the commemoration of the origin, the study of a continuity of existence through a thousand years along with a synthetic view of this long, still unfinished experience. And historical synthesis is, as a matter of fact, at least a first step in the direction of a philosophy of history, even if that more ambitious term is avoided.[6]

All countries which celebrated or are preparing to celebrate their millennium did or will do it in the second sense more than in the first, usually combining both approaches without clear distinction. And the second one is by far the more important and more difficult. The same is true of the millennium of Europe, requiring an even higher-level synthesis, which is hardly possible without a philosophy of history.

The second meaning of millennium is more important than the first, because it implies that the events of the past which are singled out have inaugurated a new, long period in the history of a nation or of a civilized society. Sometimes it even appears that such a history has started with those events, not suddenly indeed but after a pre-historic introduction, a period of preparation which was perhaps equally long. The millennium, if interpreted as the summing up of that history to the present day, is supposed to show that basic problems have dominated all ten centuries, and that ideas of lasting power have created a link between all the thirty generations which lived through that period.

How may one discover these problems and these ideas? The period which has to be considered is so long that no single scholar can have a sufficient first-hand knowledge of all the sources nor even be familiar with all that has been written about it. In contrast to the millennium in its first meaning the question now is not to exhaust the material, even if this were possible, but to select the facts which give evidence of the unity and continuity of the millennium in its second meaning, and of the importance of its heritage. This is even more difficult, because it presupposes not only extensive information but the thoughtful application of objective criteria. Some of them will be similar to those which had to be considered in the study of the millennium as an anniversary. Furthermore, facts will have to be singled out which were typical of a given nation or group of nations in the whole course of ten centuries, clearly distinguishing them from other nations or communities. But all this is insufficient guidance, since the scholar who is making the necessary selections will always remain influenced by his own philosophical interpretation of history.[7]

What is the basis and what is merely the superstructure of the historical process? Which are the truly constructive values that contribute to the progress of mankind? All the selections which must prepare the synthesis of a millennium in the second sense depend on the answers which the scholar gives to such questions. The contrast between the spiritualistic and the materialistic interpretation is, of course, the most conspicuous. But as soon as the heart of the matter is approached, the historian has also to take a definite position on the perennial opposition between nationalism and internationalism, authority and freedom, evolution and revolution. And he is placed before difficult alternatives, not only when he has to decide what should be included in his synthesis but even more when he feels the necessity of evaluating what he has included.

It is here that the Christian interpretation of history and its primary concern with moral values prove eminently helpful for the study of any period in any part of the world, because for the Christian these moral values are universally objective. But in the case of the millennium of any European nation, or of Europe as a whole, that approach offers a special advantage in that it corresponds with the whole climate of a history which for such a long time practically coincided with that of Christendom.[8] Furthermore, such an interpretation corresponds with the beliefs of the majority of those whose destinies are to be interpreted—a majority which was overwhelming in the earlier centuries of the millennium and remained considerable even among the more recent generations—provided those persons are included who in spite of their turning away from the orthodox Christian doctrine were and are deeply influenced by the laws of Christian ethics. This even remains true if the extra-European extensions of the western world, which continue to be influenced by their European heritage, are, as they ought to be, included in the picture.

Should there still remain any doubt as to the role of the philosophy of history in the study of the millennium problem, the third meaning of the term would finally remove it. For that meaning, which seems merely symbolic, is rather metaphysical. In order to understand it, it is advisable to compare again the millenary with the centenary, and to ask why the idea of a century has such a strong appeal that we celebrate it rather than the anniversary of what happened ninety or one hundred and ten years ago. Obviously, it is not because one hundred years are supposed to be the maximum lifetime of an individual, nor because a century corresponds to the period of creative activity of three generations, each of which has been in contact with the preceding and following one. Though supported by scientific genealogy, such an explanation seems quite artificial, and nobody thinks of it when speaking about a century. Instead, that term has, particularly in its Latin form *saeculum*,[9] a strange appeal, creating the impression that one hundred years are a decisive step on the road which leads through time to eternity. Appearing first in pagan Rome, such interpretations are also familiar to Christian

thought and liturgy.[10] In mediaeval Latin,[11] *saeculum* was even identified with this world, limited in time, as opposed to the other world
which is eternal. Hence the origin of such well-known expressions as
"secular" institutions and "secularism."

Returning now to the millennium, a similar question arises as to why
the number of ten centuries is considered significant, and why, for example, the much more symbolic number of twelve, or any other, is not
considered. Even more than in the case of the individual century an explanation of a mathematical character, possibly connected with the deci-
mal system, would be meaningless from the viewpoint of history. But
there appears once more the symbolic meaning of a chronological term,
which even in modern languages remains Latin, a meaning which in the
case of the millennium is typically Christian.

At the root of that interpretation, certainly, is the image used in Holy
Scriptures: in trying to convey to the human mind the idea of eternity,
the Scriptures say that a thousand years are like one day in the eyes of
God.[12] But more important than such a vision of timelessness for the
historian is something that has never been included in the official doctrine of the Church and has even led to heretical ideas. It was a mistake
to conclude from the symbolic reference to the thousand years of Christ's
reign, that His second coming and the end of this world should be expected in the year one thousand of the Christian era. Recent research has
shown that such an expectation was not at all general when the end of
the first Christian millennium was approaching.[13] There remained,
however, the so-called chiliastic idea, which, using the millennium as a
symbol of a long period with specific characteristics, would predict the
coming of another such period, possibly a better one. Mystics of the
later Middle Ages, especially Joachim of Fiore,[14] would go further;
they hoped that just as the incarnation of the Son had inaugurated a
period superior to that when the Father alone was known to Man, so
the next period, that of the Holy Spirit, would be even more perfect,
something like a golden age of the future.

Though similar ideas reappeared in modern philosophy,[15] they never
found acceptance either in secular opinion or in ecclesiastical teaching.
Yet they expressed a deep longing of the human mind, understandable
in times of crisis. And in the particularly severe crisis of our time, the
millennium of Europe, if defined as the sense of European history in the
last one thousand years, unavoidably raises two questions which only a
sound philosophy of history can answer. What was the sense, or the place

in history, of the preceding period of more or less the same length, which
was already Christian and prepared the formation of the European community? And what might be the impact of the millennium of Europe,
which we are now commemorating, upon the next period of history—
perhaps again one of a thousand years—which is just starting?

The first of these questions will be briefly touched upon in the prologue to the present study. A few comments regarding the second one
will serve as its epilogue.

The First Millennium of Christianity

CHAPTER I

The Twofold Dualism of the European Tradition

Europe as a historical community has been erected on two main pillars: Graeco-Roman humanism and Christianity. Both remained the two chief components of Europe's tradition and heritage. To recall this at the beginning of a study of the millennium of Europe is neither an oversimplification nor the superfluous repetition of a commonplace. It is no oversimplification, because it does not at all exclude the contributions of the so-called barbarians[1] who, however, were integrated with the European community only after coming in contact with Graeco-Roman culture and accepting Christianity. Nor does it exclude the due consideration of the geographical factor, because the integration of Europe was not achieved before the whole Continent with the adjacent islands—an area comparatively small but filled with exceptional diversity —came under the constructive impact of that culture and that religion.

It is not superfluous to repeat all this: first, because it has been and is still denied by the totalitarian ideologies which originated within the geographical limits of Europe but from the outset rejected the basic European ideas; and secondly, because it is an urgent warning against a dangerous misconception—the identification of Christianity with Western culture.[2] That culture, though definitely Christian, came into existence by a historical association of Christianity with what survived of Graeco-Roman civilization, and similar associations of the same religion with other cultural traditions are entirely possible and are already starting. Last but not least, the twofold character of Europe's origin

[3]

explains a momentous fact which is at the root of the almost permanent tensions in the European community, of the crises which occurred time and again in the last millennium. The two constituent elements of historical Europe, which were not always easy to reconcile, resulted in a sometimes dangerous dualism of the European tradition.

Furthermore, before considering that dualism of the Graeco-Roman and the Christian element, it must be realized that this is not the only dualism which is typical of Europe, a source of both greatness and trouble. There is, indeed, another dualism inherent in the first of these two elements. As indicated by its designation, it has two different roots: one of them Greek, the other Roman. It is true that at the time when Christianity entered the field, the Greek and Roman cultures were already merged in the Mediterranean world in what seemed to be one civilized society. To that society, distinguished scholars would even give a single name, calling it simply Hellenic, after the older and more brilliant of its constituent parts. But such a unifying terminology has been rightly criticized by specialists.[3] And the clear distinction of Europe's Greek and Roman origins is indispensable if the difference between its eastern and its western part, the conflicts between Greeks and Latins and between the European peoples influenced by either of them, are to be correctly understood in the study of later European history—which cannot be arbitrarily limited to western Europe only.

Another apparent commonplace: the statement that at the dawn of the Christian era the Greeks, politically conquered by the Romans, had already culturally conquered their victors, makes us realize that although in the unified Mediterranean world Rome was supreme in power, nevertheless the Greek root of the European tradition must be studied first, be it only for chronological reasons. For similar reasons the combined Graeco-Roman heritage has to be studied before the Christian, although the latter not only proved victorious, but for those who believe in its divine origin is also considered spiritually superior.

The very name of Europe first appeared in Greece and is of Greek linguistic origin. But the remote origin of that name, which independently of its mythological implications[4] was probably first used by navigators as a designation of Greece's coastal areas, should not make us believe that the subsequent extension of the name to the whole Continent, of which Greece is a peninsula, was merely artificial, nor that the concept of Europe's unity, in opposition to the much larger Asiatic Continent to which Europe itself is attached as a peninsula, was merely a misleading fancy.[5] The very fact of the gradual geographical extension of Europe's name, and its connection with what might be called the European idea, makes us understand, better than anything else, that ancient Greece was the nucleus of the Europe of the future, a kind of proto-Europe[6] or a European microcosm.

This is important for at least two reasons. First, it suggests to the historian seeking the origin of the European community of the last millennium, that he consider not only the preceding millennium which started with the foundation of the "universal" Roman Empire, but also the earlier period of the Mediterranean world, even before the conquest of Greece by the Romans. Only by so doing can he trace back to their earliest origin some of the distinctive features of the European tradition. It also appears, thanks to such an approach, that some of the most significant of these features have a purely Greek rather than Graeco-Roman origin. It is an exaggeration to say that the religion of the ancient Greeks was a preparation for the Christian revelation,[7] but there is indeed a continuous development leading from the various trends of Greek thought to the philosophical schools of Christian Europe. To no other minds are these schools more indebted than to Plato and Aristotle, and equally uncontroversial is the lasting influence of Greek art and literature, older than the Roman. That influence has not only exercised itself through a Byzantine intermediary upon Eastern Europe, but has proved so important for western Europe as well that even those historians who minimize the role of the eastern part of the continent in the general development of European civilization feel obliged to give due attention and appreciation to the outstanding contributions of that oldest part of eastern Europe that was Greece.[8] Finally, of Greek origin, too, are the basic political conceptions of Europe, all with Greek names, to mention only autocracy, aristocracy, and democracy. The same is true of the most inspiring ideas which the European community tried to put into practice with no more success than that of the ancient Greeks: ideas such as freedom and federalism. The Greeks were the first to fight for these ideas, not only in their unfortunate fratricidal wars but in wars of defense against their obliteration by the aggressive imperialism of the Asiatic East.

In view of all these facts it is not surprising that Hellenic antiquity was revived in the Renaissance period not only in the Byzantine Empire, making it more Greek than ever before and contributing to its last intellectual flowering on the eve of its fall,[9] but also by the western humanists who realized that the heritage of ancient Rome needed such a Greek implementation. The survival of Hellenism—meaning not the semi-Asiatic culture of the so-called Hellenistic period of decline, but the authentic spirit of the age of Pericles, rightly considered one of the greatest in the history of mankind—was until our time an inspiration for all of Europe, not only for modern Greek nationalism.[10] It is true that in recent days Greek studies were the first to suffer from the crisis of classical studies and of humanistic culture in general. But it is surprising, anyway, that for such a long time the "dead" language of ancient Greece, altered as it is in the modern Greek tongue, was taught in so many European schools and is still taught in some of them and in America as well. It survived along with Latin, which in the West had never ceased to be practiced, even if only as the supranational language of the Catholic Church.

The difference between these two so-called classical languages, which use different alphabets and reflect different mentalities, leads us to the question as to the extent that Roman culture, though profoundly influenced by the Greeks at an early stage of its development, nevertheless remained different as a whole. The linguistic difference, important as it was in its far-reaching consequences, ought not to be overrated. At the beginning of the first Christian millennium both Greek and Latin were "international" languages in the Mediterranean world united under the Roman Empire. Latin was the official language of the eastern Roman, i.e., the Greek Empire, until the sixth century A.D.[11] While later the knowledge of Latin disappeared in the East even more than the knowledge of Greek in the West, so that in all negotiations, political or religious, between Rome and Byzantium that ignorance created additional obstacles, such difficulties were not much greater than those which appeared inside the western world when Latin ceased to be generally used as a medium of communication among the various nations of the same civilized society. Even today these nations suffer from that linguistic problem.

Among the deeper reasons for the persistent dualism in Graeco-Roman culture, one is generally acknowledged: while the Greeks amidst all their political concerns were particularly creative in the intellectual field, the Romans, though their original achievements in that field should not be minimized, contributed chiefly to the legal and institutional foundations of the public order. However, if this had been the only important difference, the two cultures would simply have supplemented one another, leading to a sound balance in a common society.

The problem was complicated by a difference between the Greek and the Roman attitudes in the same field of politics, and of what we would call today international relations.

Greece, though small as a country, established within that limited area a comparatively large number of independent political units, each jealous of its autonomy, and it was to these city-states that the first loyalty of the individual Greek had always gone. There were among the political and social systems of these states striking contrasts, with that between Athens and Sparta being the most conspicuous, and even the expansion of the Greek sphere of influence—the emergence of a "Greater Greece"—though of obvious cultural and economic importance, did not result in the creation of any great power and even less of an empire. When the Macedonian Alexander conquered such an empire, he rather distorted the course of Greek history, and his achievements were in turn distorted by the various successor-states.[12] On the contrary, Rome, originally an even smaller state than Greece, was from the outset anxious to extend her political control, first over all of Latium, then over all of Italy, and eventually over the whole Mediterranean basin.[13] Determined to become a great power and to destroy her opponents in the game of power politics, Rome proved eminently successful, and absorbed into one unified body politic not only Greece proper but even a large part of what had belonged to the empire of Alexander the Great outside of Europe.

These events of a distant, pre-Christian past are at the root of the opposition between two political ideologies. They bore serious cultural implications, which were to influence European history until our days: one of them, of Greek origin, stressing the rights and contributions of small states and nations; the other one, of Roman origin, taking for granted the predominance of the great powers, finding their leadership justified and favoring the creation of empires.

That political dualism of the European tradition, deriving from its Graeco-Roman origins, does not coincide with the opposition between eastern and western Europe, which has a similar background. The opposition between the claims of large and small states was to manifest itself in both geographical sections of Europe, and when their unification in one all-European empire proved impossible, the imperial idea found enthusiastic supporters and concrete realizations in both parts. It is also true that this idea, considered from the viewpoint of universal history, was not specifically nor primarily Roman. It can be correctly understood only against an oriental background which is not Greek, indeed, nor East European, but Asiatic, and this is connected with an entirely different problem which explains another profound difference between Greek and Roman culture.

Long before Alexander, empires which lasted much longer than his had been created entirely outside Europe though in its neighborhood: the oldest one, the Egyptian, in Africa, the others in southwestern Asia, where the Egyptians also temporarily penetrated, in what we now call the Near and Middle East. The uninterrupted succession of four empires, Babylonian or Assyrian, Medean or Persian, Macedonian, and Roman was considered the main trend of history even by the Fathers of the Church[14] and by the Chroniclers of Christian Europe, although the Persian, reborn in Roman times, seriously threatened Europe. From the beginning those most threatened were their immediate Greek neighbors, and the same "father" of European history, Herodotus, who glorified the struggle of his Greek people against the Persians, studied with extreme interest all these non-European peoples and states, and their impact upon his own. Ancient Greece was more opposed to Asia than were the Romans, whose empire, after all, had to "co-exist" with the later Persian. However, it is equally obvious that the Greeks, much more than the Romans, were exposed to the influence of Asiatic powers and cultures, at least those of the Near East. It was this non-European oriental impact which more than anything else made Greek culture different from the Roman, thus contributing to the dualism of the classical heritage.

Strangely enough, however, the Romans, though in general much less affected by Asiatic influences than the Greeks, adopted the imperial idea, which appealed to their lust of power in spite of its Asiatic origin and which for a few centuries served their purposes so well. And that idea was to remain part of the heritage which Rome, rather than Greece, left to all of Europe, though the imperial claim to universalism proved impossible to reconcile with the dualism of the Graeco-Roman tradition. That dualism resulted in divisions of the Empire, rivalries between its two parts, and attempts of each to dominate the other.

When these consequences became apparent in the period of transition from the disintegrating Mediterranean to the rising European community, another dualism had already originated in the whole region which the Roman Empire had tried to integrate. That much deeper dualism resulted from the appearance of Christianity. The very existence of the Roman Empire facilitated the propagation of the new religion to the extent that it appeared providential to the Christians. And the same could be said about the spread of Graeco-Roman culture all over the Mediterranean world.

In that culture there were basic elements which could be easily reconciled with Christianity. Antiquity's moral ideals, whether the Greek καλοκαγαθία or the Roman *virtus* were certainly in agreement with the Christian ethics, since they likewise aimed at the perfection of man and stressed the dignity of the human person. The respect of the best Greeks and Romans for spiritual values and achievements prepared them for the Christian approach to life; and in view of a growing dissatisfaction with their own traditional religious beliefs and practices, as well as with those recently imported from Asia, the new doctrine could appeal to many of them.[15] Soon, however, the differences appeared between their anthropocentric humanism, turned towards this world, and the Christian doctrine, which placed the one God and Creator in the center of the universe and turned the human mind towards eternity. Notwithstanding all the respect for legitimate secular authority which that new doctrine professed and recommended to its followers, their first loyalty was to God, and not to the Greek city-state nor to the Roman Empire; they had to distinguish between the things which were God's and those which were Caesar's. This was the root of a conflict which Europe was to inherit with the dualism of its traditions: the Graeco-Roman and the Christian.

That conflict seemed irreconcilable as long as the empire remained pagan, under rulers who claimed divine authority for themselves and persecuted the Christians who would not recognize such a claim. But, strangely enough, the problem, far from being solved, became even more involved when the emperors were converted and the Church could freely develop. The controversies about the relationship of ecclesiastical and secular power, which started in the Christianized Roman Empire, were to continue through the first and to increase during the second millennium of Christianity, influencing the history of all European and non-European Christian nations until the present time. The attitude of the individual Christian towards the two authorities to whom he would owe allegiance also remained subject to conflicting interpretations.

After many earlier statements of the Fathers of the Church—who did not always agree in these matters—one of the greatest among them, St. Augustine, gave to those vital issues so much attention that his famous work *De civitate Dei,* arraying them against the whole historical background,[16] can be considered the first philosophy of history. It was for a long time the only one in the Christian world, while outside of that world nothing similar was conceived.

In order to understand the real meaning of that philosophy, the usual translation of the key word *civitas* into city—and translations into languages other than English, including the French *cité,* are hardly better— ought to be corrected. This is particularly necessary in view of the opposition between two different *civitates,* the leading idea of the whole work, which was to reappear in so many later writings on "the two cities." The Latin *civitas* means much more than *urbs* or *oppidum,*[17] much more than our notion of a city or town. It means the community to which a *civis* or citizen belongs and which in most cases is so much larger than just an urban center. Furthermore, different communities may not be of a similar character, and therefore a translation of the word *civitas* into state, more correct from a philosophical viewpoint, would not be appropriate, either, in the case of St. Augustine's two *civitates. His civitas Dei* is distinguished by its very essence from any human community, from all that remains outside. It is the community—and this is the best possible translation—of all those who are fully and primarily loyal to God, of the citizens of His invisible kingdom which is not of this world. In addition to that community of a mystical and yet very real character, there are in the visible world several other communities and societies. Of these the state is the most powerful and so, many centuries later, another Father of the Church, St. Thomas Aquinas, called it a *societas perfecta.* St. Augustine, too, did not deny at all the legitimate existence nor even the necessity of the perfectly organized secular state or states. He would even appeal to their authority in his struggle against the aggressive heresies of his time, thus creating a dangerous precedent, badly misused in later periods.[18] Why, then, did he not hesitate to compare the *regna,* the usual term for states, to *magna latrocinia,* or organized robberies?[19] Did he mean to oppose them all—a *civitas terrena* or even a *civitas Diaboli* an earthly or diabolic community—to the *civitas Dei?*

In order to answer such questions, it must be remembered that for St. Augustine and for Christianity in general these were not questions of power or organization, but of morals. The "community of God" was, of course, under His moral law and whoever obeyed that law was its citizen, no matter to what secular community he belonged. As long as these communities, in particular the states, respected that same law and were ready to defend it, citizenship in and loyalty to such a community was no obstacle to belonging to the *civitas Dei*. When, on the contrary, secular rulers violated God's moral law, they were no better than ordinary criminals, and their realms deserved to be called *latrocinia,* since they and their followers had placed themselves outside the community of God, thus forming a community of His opponents, of the world or even of the devil.

It must be remembered at the same time, that St. Augustine's original purpose in writing about these problems and in discussing the making of history was to refute a charge made against Christianity by the most devoted adherents of the Graeco-Roman tradition. In his time, when that tradition was still the only cultural heritage of the Mediterranean world, and the empire seemed to be the only guarantee of its survival, many saw in Christianity the decisive reason for the empire's disintegration and fall—which in the West was already threatening. To show the bias of such an interpretation was then a comparatively easy task, and modern science has arrived at similar conclusions, whether emphasizing the internal, social and economic, causes of Rome's decline or the external causes, the invasions of the "barbarians."[20] In both respects the Augustinian explanation was of lasting significance, because the internal crisis of the empire could have been avoided or overcome, and the defense against external aggression made more efficient, if the moral forces of the Romans had been stronger.

For historians of Europe as a whole and of individual European states as well, the issue studied by St. Augustine remains vital: whether the decline and fall of any community—a civilized society or a single country—is mainly caused by internal or by external factors. This will always be an object of controversy in historiography, and St. Augustine's contribution, that is, his emphasis on the moral aspect of such problems, deserves serious attention today, particularly on the occasion of millennium commemorations.

This is even more true inasmuch as the author of *De civitate Dei,* though chiefly interested, as most theologians are, in individual morality,[21] considers also the application of Christian ethics, of God's laws, to the relations between communities, including, of course, the states. His conception of peace decisive for the appraisal of such relations, is indeed universal: he wanted a peace *rerum omnium,* and only such a peace can be a real *tranquillitas ordinis.*[22] In "all things" the relations between one body politic and another are obviously included, and therefore it can be said that what we call today international peace and cooperation was already for St. Augustine a prerequisite condition in establishing a true "tranquillity of order" which would favor the extension over the whole world of the "community of God." According to one of his occasional references, a step in that direction would be the creation in the secular sphere of a larger, perhaps universal community, which was certainly not to be erected in opposition to the *civitas Dei* but rather as its image here on earth, facilitating the implementation of its ideals.[23]

The conclusion is clear. There was from the beginning, and always will be, a possibility of harmonious synthesis, embracing both the Christian revelation and the well understood humanistic tradition of Greece and Rome. But this was and is a possibility only, requiring repeated efforts by men of good will and genuine understanding from each generation. For in the Christian interpretation of history there are no inescapable laws of development, and nothing is predetermined in the historical process except its ultimate outcome: the triumph of the kingdom of God at the end of time. In the meantime, on the long road towards the great goals of harmony, order, and peace, there have been and will be, in the case of Europe's destiny as in any other, recurrent tensions and occasional conflicts reflecting the dualism of the Christian and the Graeco-Roman heritage in addition to the original dualism of the latter. However, even in the midst of a particularly alarming crisis, both political and cultural, when it was still impossible to foresee that the Catholic Church would help to restore the empire and to save the lasting values of ancient culture, a mind as far from optimistic illusions as was St. Augustine's, was able to shed an inspiring light on the whole controversial issue from the apparent darkness of his age.

It is, therefore, understandable that so many of those who in the course of history considered it their most important duty to work for a real peace, based upon justice and charity, and to preserve the European heritage for the benefit of the whole world, were looking back time and again to the author of *De civitate Dei*. In our time, which is even more critical than was his, the example of Pope Pius XII is particularly instructive in that respect.[24] The historian who is looking back at the entire evolution of the issue which St. Augustine had to face, certainly has the right and even the duty to stress in his survey the continuity of all the efforts to overcome the discrepancies between Christianity and humanism, even more than the contrast between West and East in the ancient and European tradition.

It will be easier to study in that spirit the millennium which is ending today, the millennium of the European community, if the antecedents of the problem which appeared in the first millennium of Christianity, when Europe was only in the making, are considered first from that twofold viewpoint. Rome must naturally occupy the center of the story: the Rome of Caesar as well as that of Peter, and the new Rome, transferred to the Greek cradle of Europe, as well as the original one. Such a prologue to the interpretation of the subsequent European age will perhaps contribute to a better understanding of three equally important questions. First, why did the making of Europe, as outstanding historians see it today,[25] take no less than a thousand years? The two other questions, which are more specific, concern the initial and the final phase of the process: why was *pax Romana,* the earliest attempt at an integral solution, nothing but an illusion? and why did the first attempt at restoring the Christian empire by a western ruler of Charlemagne's prominence end in failure in spite of papal support?

CHAPTER II

The Rome of Caesar

WHEN CAESAR WAS BORN, Macedonia and Achaea had already been Roman provinces for almost half a century. Ten years before his death the conquest of Gaul was near completion, and the invasion of Britain extended Roman rule over practically all of western Europe along the shores of the Atlantic Ocean. The conquest of Greece had assured Rome's control of the Mediterranean world. Now, thanks to Caesar, Roman expansion reached far beyond the Mediterranean basin, and it became apparent that the center of gravity of the empire into which the Roman Republic was being transformed, would shift toward the northwest. It was also obvious that vast transalpine regions with almost unlimited prospects for further extension would be included in the new body politic as well as in its cultural sphere of influence.

This was indeed a decisive step toward the formation of Europe.[1] Thus started the integration of the main part of the Continent and even of the islands off its northern coast with the southern peninsulas where European history had originated. It was not yet a turning away from the possible expansion of the Graeco-Roman community farther and farther into the Asiatic and African parts of the Mediterranean area. But two alternatives appeared: an easterly and southerly expansion, following the traditions of Alexander the Great and of the Punic wars; or a new expansion in an opposite direction—the question being which was more desirable. And there also appeared the chance of compensation for an eventual retreat from non-European lands by extension of Roman leadership over all Europe.

This was to be a very long process, typical of the millennium after Caesar, a process which could not have been anticipated in his day. Nor could it be foreseen that old Celtic Gaul, where fierce resistance had to be broken before Vercingetorix was finally defeated, would turn into an unconquerable center of Latin culture, second only to Italy herself.[2] Even more difficult and modest were the beginnings of Roman penetration into the British Isles—which Caesar had merely initiated—and his first moves through what was to be the future Switzerland and Belgium, into western Germany. But here too, in both directions, prospects for the next generations were opened, thus making the last century B.C. a decisive transition period in the course of a history which was no longer exclusively Mediterranean, though not yet fully European. Neither the British Isles nor Germany were ever to be totally occupied by the Romans, and especially in the case of the latter the subsequent limitation of Roman expansion, started by Caesar under rather promising auspices, was to have lasting consequences for the problem of European unity. Nevertheless, neither Britain, in spite of her geographical isolation, nor Germany, in spite of the lasting traces of the *limes Romanus,* could ever remain outside the emerging European community whose early origin can be traced back to Caesar's bold initiatives. A first "new" Europe had definitely been added to the old Mediterranean Europe before the first Christian millennium even began. Another similar addition, that of the northeastern part of the Continent, was not to come before the end of that millennium.

It is true that Rome's subsequent attempts to enlarge Caesar's hold on the Germanic tribes by pushing ahead from the Rhine to the Elbe ended in failure hardly half a century after his death. And in contrast to this early setback in western Europe, Roman rule in eastern Europe, at first limited to Greece proper and Macedonia, with only a narrow land connection with Italy through the Illyricum, was soon to cover the whole Balkan peninsula and even the Pannonian plain as far as the Danube. That river, which formed the frontier of Roman domination in Central Europe when the whole Alpine region had been occupied, was also crossed in the eastern section of its course when Dacia was temporarily added to the Roman provinces. However, the Roman withdrawal from that eastern European territory left behind a vacuum where the continuity of the Latin tradition is rather doubtful in spite of its revival more than a thousand years later,[3] while the almost simultaneous and similar withdrawal from Britain did not break her connection with the Latin world[4] which was to survive all the later invasions from other sides.

This is clear evidence that the integration of northwestern Europe with the Latin part of southern Europe proved much more durable than the extension of the Roman-controlled but basically Greek eastern part beyond the Balkans. This was to be of lasting significance for Europe's structure in the future. And so was the rather artificial character of the division of the Continent along the final frontier of Roman expansion. Geographically, it could be considered a natural frontier, since it was following the Channel, the Rhine, and the Danube. But at least in Central Europe that line, based mainly on military considerations, was cutting in two areas which, like southwestern Germany or the Danubian plain in Pannonia, were really one. Thus the impact of Roman rule on half of them could not permanently separate those sections from the other half. These are just examples showing that the complete integration of Europe, though to a large extent prepared by the Romans, remained to be achieved through different means in the Christian era.

In any case, it is surprising that the integration of northwestern with southern Europe was by comparison rapidly and permanently achieved, though it had started under Caesar and was continued immediately after him by means of ruthless conquest. This ruthlessness explains why any further advance of the Roman legions was so strongly and, in general, successfully opposed. This presents a problem intimately connected with the second aspect of Caesar's place in early European history, an aspect that was to influence Europe's whole future as decisively as did his foreign policy.

That policy can be rightly called imperialistic[5] and has its counterpart in the internal development of the Roman state, where Caesar's virtual dictatorship was a transition from the republic to the empire. That momentous change, which just like the shift of the territorial basis of the state, took place on the eve of the appearance of Christ, was to have equally momentous consequences not only for the first but even for the second millennium of Christendom. To the dualism in Europe's heritage which resulted from the contrasts between its Christian and its ancient elements, and between the Greek and the Roman components of the latter, there was now added another dualism, this one within the scope of the strictly Roman tradition: the contrast between its republican and its imperial aspects. Less fundamental than the others, that third dualism was to be nevertheless an additional source of tension in European history.

Formally, the Roman Empire did not come into existence before Augustus, almost exactly at the time of the Incarnation. Yet it was Caesar who laid the empire's foundations not only in the territorial but even more in the institutional and ideological sense. His very name, which in the later Roman Empire itself was used as the title of only a co-regent and presumptive successor of the *imperator,* survived in the German and Slavic languages as translation of the title of the emperor himself. And much earlier the name of Caesar in Christian terminology became the symbol of the emperor's secular power in opposition to divine and ecclesiastical authority. Therefore, in order to understand the difference between Rome's republican and imperial traditions, the question must be raised as to what extent the Rome of Caesar altered the heritage of the earlier course of Roman history.

In a study which tries to interpret the subsequent history of Europe, it seems advisable to approach that problem not so much as part of ancient history, but rather from the viewpoint of the Europeans of later centuries who wanted to rediscover the roots of their Graeco-Roman heritage. It is obvious that their interpretation of that heritage depended largely on their own political philosophy. Typical in that respect is the contrast between the Poles and the Russians, or rather the Tsars of Moscow, of the sixteenth century. The former, strongly influenced by their Renaissance interest in ancient Rome, but also by their traditional hostility against any empire and by their fear of *absolutum dominium,* would look to the Roman Republic as a source of inspiration for both their humanistic ideals and the constitution of their commonwealth.[6] Ivan the Terrible, not satisfied with his claim to the heritage of the Eastern Roman Empire, would pretend descent from a brother of Emperor Augustus himself.[7] But according to recent studies[8] there appeared even earlier in that very center of Italian Renaissance culture which was Florence—a reaction against the glorification of the Roman Empire, in spite of the high authority of its admirer Dante. Instead of being proud of the foundation of their city by Caesar, the Florentines, interpreting their own past as a history of civic liberty, would stress that before Rome's imperial expansion Italy had been a freer world of independent city-states.

This reminds us of the statement that by conquering the world the Romans lost their republic.[9] However, it ought to be remembered, too, that even in the Republican period Rome had not been just another city-state satisfied with its own independence, similar to those of Greece. Long before Caesar, a policy of conquest had been started,[10] not a utopian conquest of the world which as a whole never came under Roman control, but of a systematically extended area, the annexation of one territory leading, usually, to the desire or even the apparent necessity of occupying the next. Imperialism existed in Rome, as elsewhere, long before an empire was formally constituted, just as in history colonialism quite frequently precedes the organization of real colonies. It can even be said that Caesarism appeared in Rome long before Caesar, whether that term is supposed to indicate an aggressive foreign policy depriving other peoples of their freedom, or the suppression of truly "republican" liberty in the people's internal life. It was, in effect, the replacement of the concept of a state serving the common good by the arbitrary personal rule of a dictator.

But in addition to these obvious facts which today, at the end of the millenary experience of European history, we all understand better than ever before, it must also be recalled that Caesar alone cannot be held responsible for the turn from Rome's long republican tradition to new, entirely different forms of government. Rome had known dictators well before him, and the development leading through the *triumviratus* to the *principatus* was not completed before Augustus. Furthermore, soon after Augustus' "golden age," his exceptionally noble vision of the Roman Empire was distorted by an almost uninterrupted succession of tyrants whose rule is the best evidence of how difficult, or rather, impossible, it was to reconcile the genuine virtues and the sense of legal order of the old Romans with an imperial idea which was more and more influenced by its Asiatic antecedents and examples.

Last but not least, the Rome of Caesar, or rather, of the Caesars, is a serious warning against a justification of absolute power, often used in the later course of European history, which would have us believe that such power can be a protection of the interests of the people at large against a privileged ruling class. Patrician ambition and selfishness had indeed violated plebeian rights only too frequently in the days of the Roman Republic. But under the empire Roman society still continued to be based upon the institution of slavery, and in spite of the gradual extensions of the rights of the *civis Romanus,* none of them could ever be sure that his freedom would be respected by the autocratic might of the ruler, tempted to misuse the quasi-divine character which was attributed to his authority. This was, much more than any economic crisis, the most deepseated reason for the empire's rapid decline, anticipated from the outset by the gloomy interpretation of Tacitus, not only Rome's greatest historian, but also the staunchest defender of her original spirit, who deplored the servitude imposed upon the senate and the plebs alike.[11]

All this was but too soon forgotten under the impression of the even darker days which followed the fall of the Roman Empire in the west. The idea of the renovation of that empire—accompanied by an uncritical exaltation—which appeared at the end of the first Christian millennium, gave to the second millennium, that of the European community, a misleading start which made the organization of that community exceedingly difficult. There was, however, another misconception connected with the memory of the man who completed Caesar's achievements, Augustus, which throughout European history influenced the noblest minds and continues to do so even today. It was and is the belief, widely held in historiography and political science, that at the price of a strong and far-reaching imperial leadership, controlling external as well as internal opponents, something had been guaranteed for a comparatively long time that responded to the well-justified aspirations of all men of good will: universal peace—a peace not only envisaged in theory, as it was by St. Augustine, but realized in practice. It is on the appraisal of the so called *pax Romana* in that historical, generally accepted sense that the historian's verdict on the Rome of Caesar must ultimately depend.

The Roman Empire, whose establishment was made possible and prepared by Caesar, was indeed the universal state which the Graeco-Roman civilized society, similar in that respect to many others, if not to all of them, produced in the final phase of its development. And to such a universal state, according to many historians,[12] a *pax oecumenica* would correspond. However, both the state and the peace were, in the Roman case as in any other known to history, ecumenical only in a sense limited to one civilized society. Therefore, the word "universal," when used in that connection, does not correspond at all to its generally accepted sense, meaning the whole world, nor even to the sense of the Greek word οἰκουμένη, meaning the world known to the Greeks and later to the Graeco-Roman community. It is true that the Roman Empire in the time of its greatness did include large and important areas where other civilizations once had flourished and even established their "universal" empires. The birth of the Roman one almost coincided with the conquest of Egypt, the oldest of all, and when Christ was born, not only Palestine but also Syria had already been under Roman rule for more than half a century. However, that rule was only much later and for a very short time extended over Mesopotamia, the cradle of the Babylonian and Assyrian empires of the past, while Persia, now the Parthian Empire, always remained outside as a challenge to Roman power and Roman peace.

The fact that this peace was enjoyed for a long time by at least the major part of the world known to them—which the Romans had succeeded in uniting in one body politic—was indeed no mean achievement. It is hardly necessary to point out once more how much it meant for cultural and economic intercourse among so many peoples, which gave to Caesar what was Caesar's. But can it really be said that all these peoples enjoyed that *ordo Romanus,* and that real peace, that Augustinian *tranquillitas ordinis,* both internal and external, was assured to them for a long time?

Even for the Romans themselves, the conquerors of the major part of what they called the world, the price for such a triumph was rather high. But all the non-Romans, whether they were Greeks whose culture had unprecedented possibilities of expansion all over the empire, or peoples of various other tongues and traditions, suffered not only from the general limitations of freedom, but even more from the loss of their independence, of which they had been deprived by sheer force. Their resistance to foreign conquest, whether by a republican or an imperial Rome, was unforgotten all the time; even in the case of a small people whose independence had always been precarious, the Jews, it led to a tension which was quite apparent in the days of Christ and was to lead in the next generation to a catastrophe which He had predicted and deplored in advance.[13]

The revolt in Judea, with the destruction of Jerusalem as a consequence, coming barely a century after Caesar and scarcely fifty years after Augustus, is a striking example that even in the early, most glorious days of the empire, internal peace was by no means well established. This is only natural, since those rather artificial boundaries included so many heterogeneous populations awaiting an opportunity to throw off the Roman yoke. Even in Gaul, which eventually became well integrated with the Latin world, revolts broke out in the first century A.D., before and after that of the Jews which was repeated in the second. The frequent revolts among the Roman legions had, of course, another character, but they were particularly dangerous for both internal and external peace when they broke out in the border regions of the empire. They were usually connected with the struggles for succession to the imperial throne, those civil wars between rival candidates which became almost matters of routine in the later empire until they led to its division in two or even four parts.

It would, therefore, be an illusion to believe that permanent peace was assured even in the *orbis Romanus,* that part of the world—a large one indeed—which Rome had politically united. Such a peace was even less assured in what we would call today international relations:[14] in the relations between the empire and its unconquered neighbors. In addition to the permanent hostility with Persia, a source of endless conflicts, there was an equally permanent tension along the whole long European border. Even the reign of Augustus, which started with the symbolic closing of the temple of Janus and the dedication of the *ara pacis* in 9 B.C., was troubled in 9 A.D. by the disastrous defeat in the German war. In the following centuries all the "barbarians" on the other side of the border were not only making impossible any further expansion of the empire and forcing the Romans to withdraw from temporarily occupied territories; but through their continuous excursions deep into the Roman provinces they were creating a feeling of insecurity long before they definitely crossed the exposed frontiers in the so-called great migrations, seriously threatening the eastern half of the empire and destroying the western.

As conditions of life in subsequent centuries became much worse, and almost all parts of the once powerful empire suffered from uninterrupted warfare and destruction as a consequence of invasions and penetrations, the bygone age of the *pax Romana* seemed almost an ideal situation to which men would look back in times of even greater troubles. Furthermore, following the Roman precedent, all conquerors of future ages who had established their dictatorial rule at home and tried to force it upon one foreign country after the other, were to justify their imperialistic policies by pretending that they would create a new and better order, putting an end to the rivalries among the troublesome smaller states and unifying large areas to the economic advantage of the populations. That fallacy reached a climax in the days of Hitler, whose Third Reich wanted to continue for the next millennium the imperial tradition which the first German Empire had inherited from the Roman. And a similar misconception is behind the present foreign policy of the Soviet Union: its goal of world domination, inherited from the Russian idea of Moscow being the Third Rome—the last and final empire—and dialectically justified by the Marxist periodization of world history, is supposed to be at the same time a realization of the idea of universal peace.

Today the free world is well aware that such a *pax Sovietica,* like any other allegedly universal peace under the control of a particular power, would be a peace not of justice but of enslavement. However, it still is quite insufficiently realized that the idea of the *pax Romana,* the first of these distorted conceptions of peace, is at the root of all such dangerous illusions. Under Caesar and his imperial successors, conditions were certainly much better than under the totalitarian regimes of the twentieth century, but this does not necessarily mean that they created a sound foundation for the making of Europe nor for the organization of the European community.

It is, therefore, highly instructive to reconsider the apparently very well-known origin and character of the Rome of Caesar. Her unquestionable greatness and her amazing achievements in the first one or two centuries of the Christian era must not make us overlook the fact that the imperial tradition is the most questionable part of our Graeco-Roman heritage, different from its highest, truly humanistic ideals, and that it is at the same time the part which is most difficult to reconcile with our Christian heritage.

It is certainly true that Caesar's conquests in the northwestern section of the European Continent were a first and decisive step in the direction of its integration. But it was accomplished by violence, and for that very reason was limited geographically and not followed for a long time by any similar advances of the Graeco-Roman world toward the heart of Europe. They remained in any case the most constructive contribution of the Rome of Caesar to the molding of Europe's future. The other consequence of his policy, the replacement of the republican by the imperial form of government, was a serious setback on the road toward greater freedom and greater respect for the human person. It thus delayed an advance which had started in pre-Christian days, particularly in ancient Greece, and was to remain in European history a basic criterion of any real progress, second only to that moral perfection which Christianity was to emphasize.

Even more questionable than the change in internal status of the leading power of the Mediterranean world was the erection of the customary Roman imperialism in her relations with other peoples into a principle according to which Rome was destined to dominate the civilized world[15] and to give to that world an arbitrarily conceived peace. When in spite of that enforced unification the Mediterranean community disintegrated, that principle was all too readily adopted by the European powers which considered themselves the heirs of the Roman Empire. Such a political philosophy could only retard the solution of the problem of how to organize the new community which was emerging in the European part of the Mediterranean.

It has been shown that the foundations of that European community which can be traced back to Caesar influenced, to a large extent, the continuous development of Europe's culture until Charlemagne,[16] that is, through most of the first Christian millennium. If, in spite of the shortcomings of these early foundations and in spite of all the crises which accompanied the decline and fall of the Roman Empire, that development was not altogether unsuccessful, it was thanks to the fact that soon after Caesar there appeared besides his imperial Rome another, entirely different Rome which was to save the most valuable part of the Graeco-Roman heritage and to supplement it by new constructive elements. And it was thanks to that unexpected and long-neglected contribution that the first millennium after Caesar could prepare for the outstanding achievements of the following one.

CHAPTER III

The Rome of Peter

Religion, that is the belief in God and the concern with the relations between God and man, is a universal phenomenon, common to all mankind, and the decisive factor in world history if that history is interpreted not from the materialistic but from the spiritual viewpoint. However, there is in the field of religion an extreme diversity, a surprising variety of doctrines and even of moral conceptions. Philosophy can explain that striking fact by distinguishing between different sources of both morality and religion, trying at the same time to simplify the problem by dividing all forms of religious life into two great categories.[1] The study of primitive societies which survived until our time in prehistoric conditions can shed some light on the earliest origins of religion's multifold expressions.[2] For the historian it is most important to discover which religions contributed most to the spiritual and moral progress of their followers and, therefore, deserve to be considered the really great religions, and which of these great religions were most universal, influencing the largest areas of the world and uniting peoples of all races and tongues.

It can be safely said that universalism is more characteristic of Catholic Christianity than of any other religion. "Catholic" is, in fact, a qualification which in its original Greek form means, precisely, universal. When Christianity was divided into various churches only one officially retained the name "catholic," and is generally so designated, although the dis-

sident Christian churches also claim to preserve the truly catholic
heritage.

Universal indeed was the message of the founder of that religion, of
Christ Himself who ordered His disciples to preach His gospel to all
peoples of the earth. He made it clear that His divine Father was the
father of all, and that He wanted to save them all by His death on the
cross. And the Holy Spirit whom He sent a little later to His followers
manifested Himself by giving them the ability to talk in all languages.
It was, therefore, only natural that the man who was most active in
propagating the new religion, St. Paul, did it through journeys to all the
countries which he could possibly reach, and deserved to be called the
doctor gentium.

Yet, from the historical point of view two striking facts seem to con-
tradict the universal character of Christianity, so emphatically stressed by
its theologians and so persistently claimed by its leaders. One of these
facts, the intimate connection and, sometimes, even identification of
Christendom with one part of the world and one civilization, is of special
importance for a study of the millennium of Europe as a distinct community, and even for an introductory survey of the first Christian millennium since that connection and identification appeared before Europe
was fully integrated. But before turning to that big problem, another
fact, which chronologically comes first, must receive due attention: the
original connection of Christianity with a much older religion which
was not universal at all and the link of continuity between the two.

Christ was born in Asia and His doctrine originated there, too, on that
Continent so much older and larger than its European peninsula, in that
part of the world which was the cradle of all religions recognized as
great in history. And Christianity originated in that part of Asia—the
southwestern, the Near East if looked upon from Europe, near indeed to
both Europe and Africa—where appeared the other great religions which
were to spread far beyond the limits of Asia: the religion which preceded
Christianity and afterwards had to give up its local character, and the
religion which followed the two with world conquest as its goal.

All three, Judaism, Christianity, and Islam, would justify, at least in
the eyes of their faithful, the saying: *Ex oriente lux*. And, in general, it is
true that, time and again, from that same Asiatic East which so frequently
was a threat to Europe's political security and freedom, issued religious
conceptions, mostly of a mystical character, which exercised a deep in-

fluence.[3] Even if they did not lead, as did the three great religions which came from the Near East, to any durable organization of spiritual life in the spheres of their respective influence, and even if their influence was more destructive than constructive, such beliefs and attitudes of the mind contributed to intellectual contacts between Asia and the Europe of the future and to a curiosity in religious matters which to a certain extent facilitated the early spread of Christianity.

At the very time of Christianity's appearance in the Graeco-Roman world the religious life of that world was in the midst of a profound crisis.[4] Among many peoples, mysteries of Asiatic origin were replacing the Hellenic mythology. While this mythology was no longer taken seriously, it could not generally be replaced by philosophies which appealed only to the most cultivated minds and which were in disagreement with each other. In such an atmosphere the search for a god, still unknown, possibly the only real God, was readily comprehensible and a preparation for the acceptance of a new oriental doctrine which would satisfy both the intellect and the heart—a real *lux in tenebris*.

That Christianity was such a light was made clear by Christ's apostles and disciples through the emphasis they placed upon something which was indeed unique and unprecedented in the new religion: the basic conviction that the founder was God Himself made man, who by His incarnation, death, and resurrection, witnessed by the preachers of the Gospel, had changed the destinies of mankind. This basic dogma of the Christian religion had far-reaching consequences for the interpretation of history. For all believers it meant not only that God had personally and directly interfered with historical evolution but also that all history had been clearly divided into two great periods: before and after the coming of Christ. This has been pointed out by prominent historians and philosophers of all ages;[5] but surprisingly enough, this periodization of history, which is logical only from the Christian point of view, has never been accepted in the practice of writing and teaching history, though gradually all Christian nations adopted a chronology which replaced earlier systems of dating—for example, starting with the creation of the world at an arbitrarily chosen date—and distinguished the years "B.C." and "A.D." That example has been followed by most non-Christian peoples.

That such a system of chronology has not influenced those who for practical reasons have to divide history into periods, is more than an inconsistency. It was and still is an obstacle to any presentation of the past which would correspond to its Christian interpretation. And since it has become clear in the light of historical materialism that periodization is basic for any philosophy of history,[6] that inconsistency of Christian historians is also one of the obstacles to an elaboration of a Christian philosophy of history. Particularly objectionable is the inclusion of the pre-Christian era and the first four or five centuries "A.D." in one and the same period called "ancient history," an arbitrary practice which makes it so difficult to determine when European history really started and what its relation to Christian history is.

Before approaching these questions it must be admitted that notwithstanding the fundamental division of history by the coming of Christ—whatever the exact date of His birth may be—there is a continuity between pre-Christian and Christian history, thanks to the place occupied in the former by the people to which Christ Himself belonged as a man. Not only for the Jews but also for the Christians, the exceptional destiny of that small people, chosen by God for a very special role, is part of the real light coming from the East and of a tradition which frequently is called Judaeo-Christian.[7] The New Testament is indeed inseparable from the Old. Christ did not come to abolish the laws of the Old Testament when He lived for thirty-three years in the country where Israel had settled after Moses' death. Nobody has more definitely opposed the prejudices of "anti-Semitism"—a very misleading term since the Jews are only a small part of the Semitic race, opposed by most of the others—than the popes of our time: Pius XI, who did not hesitate to say that spiritually the Christians can also be considered "Semites"; Pius XII, who protected the Jews in their darkest hours; and John XXIII, who changed certain expressions in Catholic liturgy which could offend them. For similar reasons it is a mistake from the Christian point of view if the Jewish element in the Gospel is singled out for criticism and held responsible for Christian shortcomings in following the Savior's commandment of love. Such attempts could easily lead to arbitrary interpretations of the role of Christianity in history and to the rejection of parts of the Christian doctrine which seem difficult to accept.

On the other hand, it is a decisive fact that this doctrine has been rejected as a whole by the overwhelming majority of Jews, who refused to recognize Jesus as the Messiah expected by their prophets, and who accepted the terrific responsibility for His condemnation to death. The place of the Jewish people in the history of the Christian era remained indeed exceptional, as it had been before, but in an entirely different sense. It was no longer the privileged position of the people who had preserved the original faith in one God as opposed to the distortion of religion by so many others. It was, on the contrary, the tragedy of those who had failed to carry out a truly unique mission, and amidst humiliation and even persecution had to look for a new destiny. For the first two millennia of Christianity that destiny was a Diaspora of the Jews in foreign lands, mostly among Christians and only too frequently in opposition to them; thus Jewry unwillingly became an almost international community in contrast to its original character. Closely associated with, and occasionally even assimilated by various European nations of the western world, the Jews eventually found themselves divided between those who continued that association and the Jewish nationalists who toward the end of the millennium of the European community succeeded in regaining their homeland in Asia.

In that homeland of Israel, which at the same time was the cradle of Christianity, the Church of Christ could hardly have developed, because even that small part of the Jews who accepted Jesus as their Messiah was slow to realize that He was not the royal leader who would liberate them and restore their worldly power, and that in His heavenly kingdom there would be more gentiles than sons of Abraham. Therefore, Jerusalem, which Jesus loved so much but whose destruction He anticipated, could not possibly be the center of Christendom. Had the apostles all remained there, they would scarcely have reached all those foreign peoples who had to be converted as soon as possible. However, the question of where to transfer the center of their activity and where to erect the lasting structure of the Church which was to be built on the rock of the Prince of the apostles, was certainly difficult for them to decide. For the believing Christian, it is beyond doubt that the same divine Providence which had planned the work of the Redemption decided this as well.

However, even from a purely human point of view, it could be said that the choice was practically limited to two places which were the main centers of that Mediterranean world in which Christ was born at the time of its greatness. These places were Athens and Rome, both situated in the European part of the Mediterranean community and to the west of Jerusalem. Therefore, in any case the center of Christianity was to be moved in the western direction and to Europe.

Again, from a human viewpoint, Athens would have been perhaps the first choice; even St. Paul seemed to be specially interested in that old, glorious city, though he was not particularly successful there.[8] It is true that Athens' power and political leadership were then things of the past. But precisely because it did not represent political concerns any longer, but only a great, spiritual heritage, a tradition which even in the religious field had much in common with Christian ideals, and a brilliant philosophical thought which Christian theology could utilize and adapt in later ages, that Greek city could have served as a convenient basis for the Church of the Apostles. Last but not least, it was much nearer than Rome, nearer to Jerusalem and the Holy Land, and in general, to Asia. It is another question, however, whether the closeness to Asia and, accordingly, to Asiatic influences, always important but also confusing as far as religious matters were concerned, would have been an unqualified asset. And this leads to the arguments in favor of Rome.

The political center of the empire offered different but truly unique opportunities. The very existence of the ecumenical state that united the Mediterranean world facilitated the spread of any new doctrine which was to be universally known and accepted. For similar reasons, the capital of such an empire, a large city which had a cosmopolitan and supranational character, could serve as a perfect center for Christian action and propaganda. The conquests of Rome, which through their very method shocked the Christian conscience,[9] could be considered by that same conscience as something of a *felix culpa;* and the political and military domination exercised by the Romans could be replaced in the future by the spiritual domination of the same area by the new religion, to which were opened at the same time unlimited possibilities of further expansion, patterned after the advance of the Roman legions.

In which direction that expansion would develop most successfully was the decisive question for a future which the human mind could hardly anticipate in the first century of the Christian era. As far as the extension of the Roman Empire was concerned, it was already obvious that a substantial advance of its frontiers on Asiatic soil was hardly possible, while the conquests of the last century B.C. were definitely pointing in the northern direction: from the Mediterranean Sea to the heart of the European Continent and beyond. It was much less obvious that the spread of Christianity and the organization of its ecclesiastical centers would proceed in a similar direction; on the contrary, it was significant that the earliest patriarchates, which always remained proud of their apostolic origin, were founded outside Europe, in Africa, as at Alexandria, and in Asia, as at Antioch and Jerusalem, in the southeastern frontier regions of the Roman Empire. Yet it was Rome herself which was to occupy the first place in the Church of Christ just as she had in the empire of Caesar, with the attention of both of them more and more turning toward Europe.

The city where this happened was, strictly speaking, no longer the Rome of Caesar nor even of Augustus, under whose rather benevolent rule Christ was born. It was the Rome of the imperial tyrants who succeeded them and more specifically, at the hour of decision, the Rome of the worst of them, of Nero. Nevertheless, through a development which to the human mind could seem paradoxical, precisely at the time when pagan Rome was burning before Nero's admiring eyes, an entirely different Rome was born out of blood and tears, the Rome which long after the fall of the other, apparently reconstructed in new splendor, would survive through one millennium after the other, convinced that it would last as the spiritual center of mankind, until the end of time. This was the Rome of Peter.[10]

The fisherman whom Christ had chosen as His first vicar on earth had another hour of weakness—similar to that when he thrice denied his Master—when he had to face the horrors of the Rome of Nero where he was supposed to found another Rome. It was also then that he had to face Christ Himself once more and to hear the answer to his question: *Quo vadis, domine?* As if one cross on Jerusalem's Calvary had not been enough for the Redemption, Christ was ready to be crucified for a second time in Rome, if Peter had not accepted his destiny. So it was Peter's cross, erected upside down in order to be distinguished from the Savior's, which marked the city of Caesar and his successors as the capital of the *civitas Dei,* of the Christian community.

The Rome of Peter was at first a *Roma subterranea.* Even today no part of the Eternal City—eternal in spite of the historical evolution of its very character—has a stronger and more moving appeal than the buried Rome of the catacombs. It was there, in obscurity, that the obscure leaders of a small, condemned group which was to develop into the universal Roman Church, inaugurated that Church's history. And it was there that a power was founded which, though it never wielded a physical might comparable to that of the successor states of the quasi-universal Roman Empire, was to represent a continuity unique in history, and particularly in the history of Europe with which the history of the Church was so closely associated for the next two thousand years. Not a single one of the states which existed in Europe during the first of these two Christian millennia, neither the empire western or eastern nor the creations of the so-called barbarians inside or outside the empire's frontiers, survived until the present time. And even the most fortunate of those states which were formed or re-formed at the end of that millennium and which constituted the European community of the next had a history full of discontinuity during these last ten centuries. That lack of continuity is best evidenced by the facts that none of the dynasties survived as the ruling house of its country of origin and that no republican governments continued without interruption through Europe's millennium. The only uninterrupted line was that of the successors of Peter, who continued through the ages to govern the Church of Christ and to symbolize the historical continuity of Europe as a whole.

It is true that the line of the first Roman pontiffs, most of them martyrs like Peter, all of them saints of the Church like the apostles, is not easy to establish with full chronological accuracy, and that very little is known about those first popes.[11] But even if some of them may have been rather insignificant personalities from the human point of view, this would only be an early confirmation of the fact that the Church of Christ developed independently of any human weaknesses or shortcomings of its leaders, a fact that is interpreted with good reason as a proof of its divine character.

It is equally true that the revolts against imperial authority soon corresponded to various heresies within Christianity, leading to the separation of dissident groups from the Church of Rome. More dangerous than the divisions of the empire were the first schisms, fortunately only temporary ones, which opposed eastern to western Christendom. But just as occasional appearances of anti-popes did not interrupt the continuous line of the legitimate successors of Peter, so the continuity of their rule in and from Rome survived even the transfer of the capital of the empire and the imperial residence to Byzantium, called Constantinople. In that new place, called a new or second Rome, there continued the line of legitimate rulers bearing the title of Emperors of the Romans, though they were, as a matter of fact, rather Emperors of the Greeks, a designation which they resented. That strange situation lasted from the middle of the first to the middle of the second Christian millennium. But all the while, in contrast to that fiction of imperial Roman continuity, soon to be disregarded by the West, the continuity of papal Rome survived—in spite of a brief transfer of the papal residence to Avignon—not only to the fall of the new Rome in the East but until the present. The Rome of Peter, well established at the site of the old first Rome, where no emperor, even after the restoration of a western empire, would ever reside again, was to remain the only real one.

It was from this center where the tradition of Peter triumphed over that of Caesar, that there started a missionary activity which, strangely enough, even in imperial days could reach peoples never conquered by the Romans. Even in the days of Peter, when the Church still had to remain underground, there were among the unfortunate slaves who had been the first adherents, captives from distant lands belonging to diverse ethnic groups. It was something more than the product of a writer's imagination when the Polish novelist, Henryk Sienkiewicz, inspired by the *Quo Vadis* problem, placed among Peter's first disciples, ready for martyrdom, such hostages and prisoners of war brought to Rome from border regions of the Slavic world.[12]

When finally the Roman Church was granted, first, tolerance and then status as the official religion of the empire, that gradually declining empire began to be threatened particularly in the area where it had originated: in the Roman and Latin West. Far from being responsible for the alarming situation, the greatest popes of that period of crisis, long considered by the historians as the transition from the "ancient" to the "mediaeval" world, were at the same time the most courageous defenders of the abandoned imperial city against "barbarian" invaders. It was because it was the Rome of Peter that the Rome of Caesar was saved.

But more had to be saved and preserved than just one city, a symbol of old glory. What was threatened in the western part of the once-powerful empire was a civilization which is called ancient because of its Graeco-Roman origin in old, pre-Christian days, and which for a long time was contrasted by most historians with a different civilization, that of mediaeval times. The Middle Ages were called "dark" because they were considered a long interruption between the flowering of the Graeco-Roman world and the rebirth of that world's humanistic heritage in the Renaissance. Today it is almost universally admitted that there was no break separating Antiquity and Middle Ages but rather a gradual, continuous evolution, a long and slow transition from the Hellenic or rather Graeco-Roman to the so-called western civilized society, which from its beginning in the mediaeval form, was so closely connected with the former that the term of affiliation has been rightly used.[13] There are two main differences between these societies. The first is a geographical one, since the Graeco-Roman was primarily Mediterranean, and the western, originally European. Second—what is much more important—there is a religious difference: the former was pagan, the latter Christian and penetrated by Christianity to such an extent that it would be most appropriate to call it not simply western but a western Christian society.

This is particularly advisable and natural if the other civilized society which is affiliated with the Hellenic is called eastern Christian. The difference between these two—besides the obvious fact that the western is based upon the Latin part and the eastern on the Greek part of the pre-Christian heritage—is mainly that in the East the continuity of the historical evolution could not possibly be questioned, evidenced as it is by the survival of the Eastern Empire which suffered much less than the Western from "barbarian" invasions.

In western Europe there was indeed no empire during the three centuries between Romulus Augustulus and Charlemagne, and seemingly there had been a destruction or disruption not only of the political but also of the cultural heritage of the Rome of Caesar. Even in Italy its rule was replaced by Germanic successor-states of a different cultural background, while papal Rome—not yet the capital of a papal state—was apparently nothing but an isolated, continuously threatened island in a new, alien world.

It was, however, much more than that and, in general, much more than a city in the sense of a Latin *urbs*. It was the center of a *civitas,* of a vast, though merely spiritual community, externally based upon an ecclesiastical organization which soon was reaching beyond the boundaries of the former Western Empire—to mention only the Christianization of Ireland, which herself became a center of extraordinary missionary activities[14]—and which remained in contact with the ecclesiastical organization within the limits of the Eastern Empire. There, in spite of occasional tensions and rivalries, the primacy of papal Rome was still recognized.

The impact of that Christian Rome on Graeco-Roman culture started in the days of Peter. It is true that the first Christians, persecuted and hidden in underground Rome, were mostly of humble origin, living outside the refined world of philosophical thought, literature, and art, which seemed to them, and generally still was, a world of paganism in both beliefs and morals. But there were conversions to Christianity even in that world which was passing through a profound spiritual crisis and that process of gradual penetration continued through the next three centuries; when the empire itself became officially Christian, the Christianization of its culture was achieved to such an extent that any attempt, like that of Julian the Apostate, to restore the pagan character to both empire and culture was doomed to failure.

The origin of Christian culture in the Mediterranean and European world—both of them still inseparable and to a large extent identical—must therefore be traced. This search must not halt at an imaginary dividing line between Antiquity and Middle Ages somewhere in the middle of the first millennium of Christianity, but to the beginnings of that millennium, if not to the day when Christ's miracles converted the first Roman centurion, at least to that day when St. Peter transferred the center of Christendom to Rome.

From the outset, that early Christian culture employed the basic elements of the so-called ancient culture: the same language or rather languages—Latin and Greek; the way of life in the same artistic environment; the same social structure which even in its most objectionable features—to mention only the institution of slavery—was not affected by immediate revolutionary changes but only subject to a progressive moral influence. A prerequisite condition of the survival and further development of Roman culture in the West was, of course, the assimilation of the barbarian, mostly Germanic, invaders who settled there permanently in much larger numbers than in the East. However, this was by no means a new problem. The pagan Romans had faced a similar task whenever they occupied territories with non-Latin populations, for example Gaul. It was certainly no easier to Romanize the Celtic tribes of that large area than, a few centuries later, to Latinize the Franks or the Burgundians who conquered the same country. On the contrary, it was rather easier to gain these newcomers for a Latin culture which now was accepted along with Christianity, while in the past the Romans had little to offer in the religious sphere that would have been superior to the creed of the natives. Only so long as Arianism exercised an anti-Catholic influence upon many of the converts, did papal Rome encounter obstacles in integrating them with the universal Church and its culture.

New problems appeared indeed in the field of literature. The level of Latin writing had declined after the "golden age" of Augustus, but not because of the new trends inspired by Christianity. These trends, as soon as they manifested themselves in literary production, added much that was of lasting value to the Roman heritage. This was especially true of the writings of the Church Fathers, which even when inferior in formal elegance were so much superior as far as the content was concerned.

Though influenced by earlier models—another element of continuity in intellectual life—the great Christian theologians were naturally not without prejudice against the pagan literature of the past, which was so deeply penetrated by philosophical and ethical conceptions impossible to reconcile with Christianity. However, as soon as there was no longer any reason to fear that these conceptions would be taken too seriously, the new Christian writers did not hesitate to take from their pagan predecessors whatever was uncontroversial and really valuable, to preserve the manuscripts of their works and even to copy them for the use of posterity.[15]

This was done most frequently in the monasteries, and no less than in the East, monasticism in the West—though in different forms and with more variety—was one of Christianity's greatest contributions to the constructive evolution of Graeco-Roman culture in the formative centuries of the European community.[16] In the first Christian millennium, it was the Benedictine order which proved outstanding in that respect. Its earliest monasteries in the neighborhood of Rome put into practice the principle of adding work to prayer, and while the manual work of the monks favored material progress, their inspiring intellectual labor was to be one of the pillars of Christian culture erected on its ancient foundations and to be instrumental in influencing the noblest minds of all the countries which eventually joined the new community under the leadership of papal Rome.

In the really dark centuries of political confusion, Romans and Romanized Celts or Teutons had to defend themselves against Asiatic invasions like that of Huns and Avars from the East or that of the Arabs through northern Africa. These invasions penetrated deep into the heart of western Europe, but the Rome of Peter, in spite of all material destruction, succeeded in preserving, sublimating, and augmenting the cultural heritage of the Rome of Caesar. Thus was made possible the first of the various "renaissances"[17] which from the later part of the first Christian millennium to the middle of the second revived that heritage and adapted it to the changing conditions of European history.

Before that happened and before the Arabs had advanced through Spain as far as Gaul, threatening the very existence of western Europe's culture, the expansion of Islam had permanently cut off from Europe the Near Eastern and African parts of the Mediterranean world and made very difficult the sea communications between Europe's west and east. In the latter direction, the Byzantine Empire was menaced by the same danger from another side. Therefore, that empire was less than ever in a position to assist the West, where it retained only its Italian foothold, and western unity depended exclusively on papal authority.

That unity was much looser than it had been at the time when imperial Rome still was a powerful political center, and the new, poorly organized states which emerged during and after the great migrations were in endless struggles among themselves even after their conversion to Christianity. But the variety which developed in western Europe, similar to that which had existed in the Greek nucleus of Europe and in the whole Mediterranean area before the Roman conquest, was not necessarily a setback nor a liability for the future. As long as it was a diversity tempered by a common religion and a common Latin culture, enriched both by the Church and the tradition of the non-Latin peoples, it could add to the vitality of the West. It was to be typical of the European community when such a community came into existence after the integration of those parts of Europe which never had been under Roman rule.

Before that integration was accomplished through the missionary activity and expanding influence of the Roman Church, the question was raised whether it would not be possible and advisable to reunite politically the whole or at least the major part of western Europe. It was, of course, out of the question to include in such a body politic the whole Iberian peninsula, almost completely occupied by the Arabs, or the islands of Britain and Ireland,[18] which were geographically isolated. But at least three regions, all of them under the rule of Germanic peoples but subject to strong Latin influence, seemed ripe for a close association when the last quarter of the first Christian millennium started: Italy, the nucleus of the Latin world; Gaul, whose role in that world was so rapidly growing; and the western part of Germany which had been since the beginning of the Christian era under Roman control. There remained, however, two difficulties: one of them resulted from the continued existence of a unified Roman Empire in the southeast, the other, from the unsettled situation in the still pagan lands of the northeast. All depended on the question whether the support of papal Rome would suffice to overcome these obstacles.

CHAPTER IV

The New Rome

THE UNIFICATION of the whole Mediterranean world in the Roman Empire at the time of its early greatness seemed to remove one of the two dualisms of the European tradition: the difference and even opposition between its Greek and its Roman elements. The divisions of that same empire, beginning at the end of the third century A.D., especially the basic division into a western, predominantly Latin, and an eastern, predominantly Greek part, proved that the short-lived unification had been more apparent than real, and reaffirmed the old dualism. The transfer of the capital to the Greek center of the eastern part made the chances of lasting unification particularly doubtful, since it could hardly be expected that the Latin part, which had conquered the Greek even before the empire was founded, would abandon its claims to leadership or to separate existence. Nor could it be expected that the West would accept Greek political supremacy, in addition to Greek predominance in the cultural field. The old Rome would never yield to the new Rome, in spite of that rather artificial and pretentious designation of the city founded by Constantine and solemnly inaugurated as capital of the whole empire.

Yet, it was equally certain that the emperors residing in Constantinople would never give up the claim to rule over the whole heritage of Caesar and Augustus. Their attempts at a real reconquest of the West had no chance of total and lasting success even under Justinian.[1] But nobody could deny that these emperors, and they alone, represented the legitimate and never-broken continuity of imperial succession and authority. Their dynasties would frequently change, were frequently of neither Roman nor Greek origin, and violent palace revolutions would repeatedly decide controveries in the matter of succession. But all this had happened also at the time when West and East were united under emperors residing in the old Rome.

Most important, however, was the fact that for a long time no emperors resided in the old Rome at all—an interruption which never occurred in the new one. And when the western empire was restored for the first time, only to be discontinued once more after being rather arbitrarily subdivided, it was much too late to have such a decision recognized by the new Rome.

The original dualism of the Graeco-Roman world reappeared, therefore, before the comparatively brief unification at the beginning of the Christian era could produce lasting results. The old tension, intensified first by the Roman conquest of Greece and then by the fiction of Constantinople's ruling over Rome, continued for the next two millennia and from the start was aggravated by many tensions in the spiritual field.

These tensions had nothing to do with the second basic dualism of the European heritage: that which opposed Graeco-Roman humanism to Christianity. That dualism continued both in the Latin West and the Greek East. But what was new and particularly alarming was the dualism within Christianity which resulted from the differences of opinion in matters of ecclesiastical organization and even of doctrine. These differences, opposing West and East soon after their conversion, were connected with the differences in general culture and mentality which were inherited from the pagan past.[2] This contributed to the tragedy which was to affect the whole future of Christendom and the process of the making of Europe, a tragedy which could hardly be foreseen when it was decided at the time of the apostles that the center of Christendom would be not in Greece but in Rome.

Strangely enough, it seemed that in spite of the continued papal residence in Rome and the recognition of papal primacy, Constantinople, as soon as it became the residence of the emperor, had assumed leadership in ecclesiastical matters also. Was not the first Council of the Church in 325 held in nearby Nicaea, and did not all the eight councils of the first Christian millennium meet in the East, four of them in Constantinople? While the Roman popes were represented at these councils only through their legates, imperial influence was strong at all these meetings from the day when the first had been presided over by Emperor Constantine. And though we know today that the so-called caesaro-papism of the Byzantine Empire has been overrated,[3] there is no doubt that even the most prominent patriarchs of Constantinople were dependent on the emperors, certainly more than on the faraway popes.

The interpretation of papal authority was, under such conditions, one of the most important sources of misunderstanding between the old Rome and the new, where gradually the conception developed that the Church was to be led not by one head but by a pentarchy of patriarchs four of whom were in the East, the patriarch of the West enjoying only a primacy of honor. But this was not the only reason for repeated breaks between western and eastern Christendom. Here again exaggerations, based upon legend rather than history, ought to be avoided. It has been shown[4] that the date of 867 did not have the decisive significance which it received in a long tradition, and that the conflict between Rome and Patriarch Photius which reached a climax in that year, was, to a large extent, caused by internal troubles in Constantinople. After being appeased, it was not followed by any second Photian schism a few years later. But at the height of the dispute when the patriarch did not hesitate to condemn the pope, he not only created a dangerous precedent for the future, but revived and intensified the memory of much longer breaks which in the past had disrupted the unity of the Church. The most recent of these, the iconoclast controversy, lasted almost a century and ended only a score of years before Photius.

Before the crisis of 867 the periods of disagreement between Rome and Constantinople were almost as long, if taken together, as those of normal relations.[5] And some of those earlier schisms set the old Rome at odds not only with the new one but also with other dissident Churches of the East which remained separated from both of them. It is highly significant that these were Christian communities outside Europe. This shows clearly that even before the missionary expansion of Christendom all over the world it would be objectionable to identify it with the Continent, where the main body of the Church was established.[6] It was in particular the early heresies of Nestorianism and Monophysitism which, in spite of the Muslim conquest, have survived until now in the African and Asian parts of the Mediterranean area, and which, at the turn of the first Christian millennium, spread far into Asia, counting numerous followers. Yet, they did not succeed in converting whole peoples who, as in Europe, would base their whole way of life upon a specifically Christian culture, and their rather isolated groups were largely absorbed or at least reduced by the progress of other religions, especially Islam.

In Europe there appeared an entirely different danger. It appeared as if during the first Christian millennium, even before Greek Orthodoxy finally broke with Roman Catholicism, two different Christian cultures were developing, perpetuating in a new form the original dualism inherited from the Graeco-Roman world, coexisting side by side and competing each other. And though the unity of the Church was maintained until the end of that millennium, through reconciliations which followed each of the temporary breaks, even dogmatic differences appeared: besides the problem of defining papal primacy the question of the procession of the Holy Ghost was raised, when the West started to add the word *filioque* to the Nicaean creed.[7] The Greeks not only considered any addition to that text illicit but also raised objections to the doctrine that the Holy Spirit proceeded from both Father and Son, a question which touched the most delicate dogma of the Holy Trinity and could revive Christological disputes.

It is, however, obvious that such purely theological issues, important as they were, could not justify the distinction between two cultures. More significant in that respect, though rather futile from the religious point of view, were differences of a formal character, reflected in rite and liturgy, and only too frequently overemphasized in occasional discussions. For they were an external expression of differences in mentality which, more than subtle philosophical distinctions, interested and sometimes even impassioned the masses of the people, leading to prejudice and antipathy. This, in turn, was connected with the difference of language which always had separated Greeks and Latins, and now contributed to the difficulty of clarifying controversial points. A typical example which appeared in the discussions regarding the *filioque* was the uncertainty whether that term was identical or not with the formula διὰ τὸν υἱόν, used by the Greek Fathers of the Church, which literally should be translated by the Latin *per filium*.[8]

But difference of language was something more. How important it would prove in later European history, when each nation started considering its vernacular a basic, if not the essential, element of its culture and an expression of its political independence, could not be anticipated at a time when the universal use of the Latin language corresponded to the supranational Roman Empire. For centuries that language had been universally used in administrative practice, not only in the West where no other tongue had reached literary maturity, but also in the East. There, in spite of the old and splendid tradition of the Greek language, Latinization was so successful that, for example, Justinian's famous code, though the achievement of an eastern emperor, was composed in Latin. It was not until the end of his century, the sixth A.D., that Greek became the official language of the Byzantine Empire.[9]

Now it may seem artificial to continue calling this empire Roman and its emperor a βασιλεὺς τῶν 'Ρωμαίων, though that title was maintained to the end for political reasons. The νέα 'Ρώμη was now really quite different from either the Rome of Caesar or that of Peter, was becoming proud of her Hellenic heritage.[10] That growing consciousness of the cultural continuity linking Byzantium with old Greece had proved stronger than the official continuity of the Roman Empire in the East. It made the Byzantines look down upon the Latins, just as the Greeks had done after the Roman conquest when a feeling of cultural superiority was their comfort. The same feeling was to be typical of the Byzantine attitude toward the West in that last century of the first Christian millennium when there was no religious schism at all, but when western power was growing again.

Much earlier, the old and new dualism in the Mediterranean world had repercussions in the respective spheres of influence of its Greek and Roman parts. This was unavoidable when imperial territory originally neither Latin nor Greek became an object of controversy where the limits, both political and ecclesiastical, between West and East had to be determined. The case of the Illyricum, the important region which on land was the only link between an extended Italy and an even more extended Greece is typical in that respect. No less notable is the case of one of the foreign peoples who permanently settled within the limits of the Eastern Empire, the Bulgarians, who hesitated whether they should accept Christianity from distant Rome or from nearby Constantinople. It has been clearly shown how much that controversy contributed to the tension between the papacy and Photius as well as the Greek Church in general.[11] And since culturally the Bulgarians were assimilated not by the Greeks but by the Slavs who had penetrated far into the Balkan peninsula before that, their case was part of the larger issue of which influence, Latin or Greek, would prevail among the numerous Slavic peoples within and outside the old imperial frontiers.

It is an exaggeration to say that in the field of missionary activities the Greeks showed less initiative than the Latins. Only the extraordinary scope of the Irish missions—which did not even come directly from Rome—was unequalled in the East. But it was no later than the days of Photius that Constantinople, too, started systematic efforts to convert all peoples which its influence could possibly reach. For the Europe of the future the fact that Christianity spread from two different centers was of lasting importance, though that twofold process started before the final break between those centers. But the consequences of that fact for the integration and constitution of the European community manifested themselves only at the turn of the first Christian millennium to the second. Therefore, before considering the trend toward the division of the European community—similar in that respect to the Mediterranean—into a western and an eastern half, it must be recalled that in both cases the division would not have been so profound, if the eastern part had not been exposed so decisively to Asiatic influences.

In that respect, as in so many others, Byzantium was the heir of ancient Greece, continuing both her struggle against, and her peaceful relations with the extra-European neighbors. It was not without serious consequences that the capital of the Eastern Roman Empire, practically a Greek Empire, was established, not somewhere in the heart of Greece proper, but at the straits, which separated but also connected Europe and Asia and where the crossing from one Continent to the other was so very easy. Placed, therefore, right at the border between them, the new Rome had inherited from the old one large Asiatic possessions which extended far beyond the colonial expansion of ancient Greece, but which included, of course, Asia Minor, a constituent part of the Greater Greece of the past, with a largely Greek population, at least along the shores.

It has been pointed out time and again,[12] and not without good reason, that the Anatolian peninsula through which Asia approached Europe was one of the main sources of Byzantine power, politically and even more, economically, and that the empire declined when that territory was gradually lost after the loss of the more distant and less essential Asiatic possessions. But it can also be said that all these possessions, without excluding Asia Minor, which, after all, was never completely Greek, were at the same time a source of weakness. With an eastern frontier that was always difficult to defend and never definitely fixed, even at the height of Roman power, these non-European extensions of a European state—they could well be called its colonies—invited attacks by Asiatic peoples, so that the Byzantine Empire was never able to concentrate on its European interests. On the other hand, the more that empire was in control of Asiatic territories, the more it became ambiguous in its own character. Asiatic influence, which had already been strong in the old Roman Empire when it included the whole Mediterranean world with its center in Italy, was naturally much stronger in an empire limited to its eastern half with its center at the border between Europe and Asia. There was a danger that Byzantine culture, which was no longer under a simultaneous Latin influence, would be Hellenistic rather than truly Hellenic, as happened in the successor-states of the empire of Alexander the Great.

But without even considering such possibilities, it must be pointed out that Asiatic influence manifested itself particularly in two important spheres which, as a matter of fact, had been already affected by that influence in the undivided Roman Empire at the dawn of the Christian era. Now they were even more exposed to such a penetration. The very character of imperial power, emphasized by the divine worship which the monarch was supposed to receive, had been largely Asiatic from the outset, alien to the tradition of both the Roman Republic and free Greece. And Byzantine autocracy, with its elaborate ceremonial, had even more in common with Asiatic despotism. On the other hand, it is true that the Christian character of the Eastern Roman Empire, precisely from the time its capital was established in Constantinople, was a counterbalance which had not existed before. But even Christianity was subject in the East to an impact of Asiatic beliefs and practices which, while not so confusing as they had been in the last period of Roman paganism, contributed nonetheless to the differences and tensions between Eastern and Western Christendom.

It has been rightly stressed[13] that in so far as the Greek Church was strictly orthodox, in the literal sense of that word, it was much less opposed to the Latin than when it was troubled by internal religious controversies which very frequently had an Asiatic origin. Even such heresies as Nestorianism, which eventually broke with Constantinople and survived only in distant non-European areas, had affected earlier relations between Constantinople and Rome. And the longest breaks between the two before Photius, at the time of the iconoclastic emperors, were the result of the temporary triumphs in Constantinople of a trend which seemed more opposed to the eastern than to the western rites of the Church and can be explained only by Asiatic, particularly Islamic, attitudes.

In spite of all this it must never be forgotten that the same Byzantine

Empire was from its origin a continuous, frequently heroic, and sometimes successful defender of Europe against Asiatic aggression, exactly as ancient Greece had been. Much more than in old pagan days, that defense was inspired by religious motives and was part of the struggle between Christendom, whether eastern or western, and Islam. While in the West that struggle was exclusively defensive until the end of the first Christian millennium, the East did not limit itself to the defense of Constantinople against the Arabs in the first of the many sieges of the imperial city which preceded its fall. Long before the West, the East undertook expeditions with a view to liberating the Holy Land. Even the Latin crusaders of later centuries, who certainly were not prejudiced in favor of the Greeks, would praise Emperor Heraclius six hundred years after the event as the first crusader.[14] What has been called the "Byzantine epics"[15] was indeed a series of wars in and against Asia, conducted at a time when in the West the European community was only being prepared, when the problems of Europe's eastern borderlands hardly received adequate attention there, and when no cooperation with their defenders was considered.

Without being fully conscious of it themselves, they were, however, the defenders of all of Europe and of a civilization which in spite of all the elements of dualism, old and new, was basically one, founded, as it continued to be, on the Graeco-Roman heritage and on Christianity. Though there was apparently no connection between the fight against the Arabs in the southwest and southeast sections of Europe, it was, after all, a fight against the same invaders who in a wide pincer movement threatened the European part of the Mediterranean world after conquering the non-European. It also was a rivalry between two entirely different civilizations: the Christian and the Islamic. Compared with the basic difference between these two, the internal differences between Latins and Greeks were really insignificant.

There appeared at the same time an entirely new problem, affecting both these internal differences and the relations between Christendom, or what remained of the Mediterranean community, and the outside world. That outside world continued to exercise a pressure not only from the south, where the new civilization of Islam proved so aggressive and dynamic, but also from the north, the part of the European Continent which was still pagan and considered "barbarian." In addition to the assimilation and Christianization of those tribes which had already settled on imperial territory in consequence of the great migrations, there was the task, growing in importance, of opposing further attacks from the north and of possibly conquering and integrating areas and populations which never had been under Rome. And that great problem was a twofold one.

Particularly aggressive and dynamic were the peoples who had their original home in the extreme north of Europe and therefore, not with-standing the tribal differences among them, were all called Normans. Their outstanding role in the history of the later part of the first Christian millennium, leading to their definite entrance into the European community of the second, was again an issue which touched both the Latin West and the Greek East. It was another pincer movement, leaving aside or bypassing the center of the Continent but reaching by entirely different roads the Atlantic area on the one hand and the Black Sea basin on the other.

Normans such as those whose raids frightened western Europe were indeed the "Russians" whose first attack against Constantinople, in 860,[16] warned the Byzantine Empire that the southeastern, Arabic threat was not the only one which had to be faced. But the enigmatic name given these eastern Normans raises immediately another question, that of the Slavs across the border of the Eastern Empire and of the successor-states of the Western. For that same name, in the misleading form derived from the original "Rus'," would be given later, at least in the western languages, to all eastern Slavs. By those who would minimize the Norman impact on these Slavs, that name is even considered originally Slavic.[17]

For the Greeks, the difference between the Normans who approached Constantinople after a long advance from the Baltic region through the Slavic settlements in the Dvina and Dnieper basins, and the Slavic tribes themselves whose warriors would join the Norman leaders in their expeditions, was of no great importance nor interest, especially as long as both of them were pagans. But how all these tribes in the northeast of Europe, so much more numerous than those which had penetrated into the Balkan peninsula and created enough trouble there, would develop in the future was a serious concern for the Byzantine Empire. On the one hand, with the progress of political organization in the vast areas north of the Black Sea, the danger of losing the old Greek colonies on its shores, as well as the danger of new invasions across the Danube, could seriously increase. On the other hand, in that one direction which remained open there was a possibility of extending cultural and perhaps even political Byzantine influence, Christianization being, as usually on such occasions, the first step. For a long time it was not easy to foresee which alternative would materialize, and it was not before the end of the first Christian millenium that in northeastern Europe, Christianized from Constantinople, something like an "off-shoot" of Eastern Christian society began developing.[18] And it was only then that the integration of that remote part of the Continent with the European community could be attempted.

In spite of an obvious difference in geographical conditions and in the historical, or rather pre-historical, background, there appeared an analogous problem in western Europe, strictly speaking in the central part of the continent, between the two main roads of Norman expansion. Since the Danubian region of Central Europe, half of which had been conquered by the Romans, was, like the territory north of the lower Danube [that Dacia from which the Roman legions had to be withdrawn at an early date] a neighboring region of the Byzantine Empire, the problem was one more link between West and East. It was a problem of the relations with the western Slavs, not yet separated from the southern ones who were already connected in one way or another with the Byzantine Empire and had occupied the controversial Illyricum.

These western Slavs, whose gradual advance far into formerly Germanic or Celtic territory was rather unspectacular, were little known to the Graeco-Roman world, though some writers, from Ptolemy to Procopius and Jordanes, distinguished the *Venedi,* as they referred to them, from the *Sclaveni* and *Antes,* their southern and eastern kin.[19] Only the amber trade with the Baltic region made some western merchants cross Slavic territory and reach the even less known non-Slavic tribes, the Balts.[20] When one of these merchants, Samo, who probably was not a German but a Latinized Celt from Gaul, created a first Slavic state in the Danubian basin,[21] at the frontier of the Byzantine Empire, that development of the seventh century A.D. did not receive much attention, since very soon that state seemingly disappeared, overrun by another wave of Asiatic invaders, the Avars.

Under their rule the Slavs of that region could not have any direct contacts with the historical and cultural Europe of that epoch; and those north of them, who had advanced even beyond the Elbe-Saale line, were still separated from the Christianized and Latinized Germanic states of western Europe by Germanic tribes, in particular the Saxons and Bavarians, who had not yet been converted themselves and were even less organized in states on the Roman pattern. Nevertheless, the time was approaching when the whole Slavic world and not merely its fringes would be placed under able leaders and would meet the vanguard of both Christianity and Graeco-Roman culture. There the Slavs would join the other "barbarian" peoples of the Continent, who comprised the third constitutive element of the European community.

It remained to be seen by which methods they were to be integrated with that community, how much independence they would retain, what contributions they would make and, last but not least, whether all this would be decided and achieved by the new Rome alone, the one which first had to deal with the Slavs, or by the heirs and successors of the old Rome as well.

In order to understand that issue it must be remembered that in the opinion of the new Rome nobody except herself was nor could be a legitimate heir of the Rome of Caesar. For Byzantium, the unity of the *orbis Romanus* now under the leadership of Constantinople still continued, and for a long time the Rome of Peter shared that view, looking to the Eastern Empire for protection against the invaders who had destroyed the Western.

In 595 Pope Gregory the Great, writing to Emperor Mauritius, described the difficult position of the Church in western Europe, and complained that these lands had come under the domination of "the barbarians." Most of them had already been converted by that time, and on other occasions Gregory would praise the Frankish kings, the successors of Clovis in particular.[22] Those Merovingian kings of the sixth century themselves rejected any kind of Byzantine overlordship and the Greek interpretation of the continuity of the Roman Empire. And gradually the Papacy, too, receiving no assistance from Constantinople, would recognize that the kingdom of the Franks in the West had a providential mission to fight those peoples who still were "barbarians," similar to the mission which the emperors had in the East.

From that admission there was only one step to the conception of a separate western community under St. Peter, independent from Byzantium, and to what might be called the adaptation of the idea of imperial unity to the realities of the situation in western Europe. The repeated ecclesiastical conflicts between Rome and Constantinople contributed, of course, to such an evolution of the papal attitude. Even more decisive in that respect was the rise of Frankish power, which in the eighth century proved so helpful to Christendom in defeating the Arabs who had

penetrated from Spain deep into Gaul, and which could serve as a unifying force in the part of the old empire outside Byzantium's control.

The new dynasty of the Carolingians, which in many respects had to
face great difficulties, especially in the economic field, soon showed the
ambition to unite the whole *Occidens,* including even Britain and Spain,
in opposition to the Eastern Roman Empire. And papal Rome, which at
last found a protector in place of faraway Constantinople, was ready to
make Christian universalism benefit from Frankish policy. In 787 Pope
Hadrian I wrote to Empress Irene and her son Constantine about the
victories of King Charles over *omnis Hesperiae occiduaeque partis bar-
baras nationes,*[23] welcoming as defender of Christendom in the West the
son of that Pepin who thirty years before, by his Donation of the *Patrimonium Petri,* had made the Rome of Peter the capital of the Papal
States.

That Donation, confirmed by Charles on the occasion of his first visit
to Rome in 774, was made at the expense of what the New Rome still
possessed in Italy. At the same time it made the Papacy dependent on a
new power which seemed more qualified than Byzantium to organize
Europe on the basis of both Roman and Christian tradition. Such a development was, however, a threat to the political and, as demonstrated
later, to the religious unity of Christendom as well. The awareness of
these implications was certainly one of the reasons why the future Charlemagne, in spite of all his ambitions, is said to have felt some misgivings[24] when Pope Leo III crowned him as Emperor at St. Peter's, on
Christmas Day of the year 800, while in Constantinople the imperial
throne was for the first time occupied by a woman.

CHAPTER V

Carolingian and Byzantine Europe

A STUDY OF THE ANNIVERSARY of Europe's foundation and constitution will necessarily add another question to all the controversial ones which have been raised in historiography with regard to Charlemagne's coronation and first renovation of the Roman Empire in the West. This question, despite its formal character, is of decisive importance for the understanding of Europe: Is it justified to speak today, in the middle of the twentieth century, of a millennium of Europe, thus presupposing that Europe, as a historical community, originated only in the middle of the tenth century, or should not that origin be traced back to the beginning of the ninth century, to Charlemagne?

Among the various arguments in favor of such an interpretation which would imply that the millennium of Europe should have been celebrated, if at all, at the beginning of the nineteenth century, two are of special interest, because the first is based upon primary sources of Charlemagne's lifetime, and the second, upon a striking experience of the present.

There are indeed contemporaneous texts which seem to identify the realm of Charlemagne with the *Christianum imperium* and with Europe. A quarter of a century before his coronation as emperor, around 775, an Anglo-Saxon clergyman stressed that God had elevated him *in honorem gloriae regni Europae* and later, in an anonymous epical poem, the emperor is called *Europae venerandus apex, celsa pharus, pater Europae*.[1] Whatever we may think about the usual exaggerations in such statements, the fact that he could be called "father of Europe" certainly proved that for at least some of the contemporaries his reign seemed to be the beginning of a great destiny for Europe.

Before determining which area was so designated in these texts, it is interesting to point out that there is today an area which almost exactly corresponds to Charlemagne's empire in its final frontiers, with the exception of only the marches which he created in northern Spain and in the Austria of the future. That area is indeed a Europe, but it is rightly called the "small" Europe or the Europe "of the six" because in addition to the three "Benelux" states—the Low Countries of earlier centuries— it includes only France, West Germany to the Elbe river, and Italy. The only difference from the territory controlled by Charlemagne is the inclusion of the whole Appenninian peninsula, with the parts of Italy which in Carolingian days were still under the control of Byzantium. In any case, such an analogy reminds us that what was or is called Europe may not necessarily be the whole of the European community, whose integration or reintegration merely started on these occasions.

With that experience in mind, it is easier to turn to three interpretations of Europe's origin by great historians of the last generation, which, conflicting though they are, all support the idea that the celebration of Europe's millennium comes about one hundred and fifty years too late. If the foundations of Europe's cultural development have been laid in the period beginning with Caesar and ending with Charlemagne, as Alphons Dopsch tried to show so convincingly,[2] the conclusion could be that after Charlemagne Europe was already constituted and a new period was beginning. If the so-called Pirenne thesis is not rejected altogether, mainly because some of its economic implications have been questioned,[3] it would appear that the role of Charlemagne, which was a consequence of the disruption of Mediterranean unity by the Arab conquests, had in turn as its consequence the establishment of a new unity around the center of Europe. And if Gonzague de Reynold's comprehensive investigations of the formation of Europe go beyond the age of Charlemagne only in exceptional cases, it is because he definitely considers the emperor the founder of Christian Europe.[4]

However, all three scholars agree in general that there are no sudden cuts in the historical process and that no single event, even the most important, can constitute a dividing line between two great periods of history. On the contrary, there are between such periods shorter or longer times of transition. And such times are particularly long, if a really great change is to be accomplished and great achievements are to be implemented. Even the truly unique event of Christ's Incarnation, so much more important than any other, did not immediately change the face of the world, even only the Mediterranean world, either in the year of His birth, or in that of His death. There was a transition of more than a century between the establishment of the Rome of Caesar and that of the Rome of Peter, and neither of the two achieved at once its ultimate goal: the creation of the Roman Empire or the organization of the Roman Church.

A similar process is visible in the creation and organization of the European community under "the Christian roof," to use de Reynold's meaningful expression. Such an achievement was made possible by gradual developments which lasted through all the centuries of the first Christian millennium. Most of these developments were connected with the history of the empire in which Christianity had appeared and was propagated. Decisive, indeed, was the Christianization of that empire which took three centuries. Rich in consequences were the division of the Roman Empire and the disintegration of its western part. Therefore, the first attempt to restore the empire in the West was important, but it must be remembered that when such an attempt was made in 800, the losses outside Europe had not yet been substantially compensated for by the inclusion of new European territories. On the contrary, it proved impossible to recover even the Iberian peninsula for the time being, either for the restored empire or for Christianity, while the remarkable progress of Christian culture in the British Isles and particularly in Ireland began well before Charlemagne, and continued, in his time, outside the empire though in contact with it.[5] It must be remembered also that the Carolingian Empire lasted only to the end of the ninth century, that is, hardly one hundred years: the first restoration of the Roman Empire in the West failed even before the extinction of the Carolingian dynasty in the tenth century.

The conclusion seems clear, especially in the light of the last remarks. Charlemagne's coronation was indeed a significant precedent; but there is no continuity—only another crisis of the imperial tradition of the West—between the Carolingian Empire, whose success depended on the outstanding personality of its founder, and the next restoration or *renovatio imperii,* which independently of the more or less prominent personalities of its rulers was to last for eight centuries and a half. The Carolingian age was, therefore, only the last phase of the preparation for the Christian community of Europe, a preparation which took a thousand years—the prologue to the second Christian millennium, the real millennium of Europe.

However, in order to be more specific, such a general conclusion requires two supplementary comments. The first concerns the problem of the territorial extension of Europe. Under Charlemagne and his successors, the Europe of which Charlemagne was called the summit, light, and father was very small indeed, not only because the original, Greek nucleus was excluded—a problem which must be considered separately —but also because the eastern expansion in the heart of the Continent, the only one which was possible, made only slow and limited progress. Under the founder of the restored empire, even before his coronation, and under those of his successors who ruled in the East Frankish kingdom, that drive began toward the East which, reversing the westward trend of the great migrations, was later to be typical of German policy and colonization. But even the conquest, Christianization, and integration of the German tribes of Saxony and Bavaria, and the liquidation of the Avar pressure proved no easy task. The first moves against the Slavic neighbors not only failed to cross the Elbe, but hardly began the penetration of Bohemia. Through the Slovene settlements this drive established short-lived contacts with Croatia. With the exception of these border regions which, after all, the Romans had already reached prior to the Slavic advance, the Carolingian Empire included only that part of Latin and Celtic Europe which had come under Germanic rule. To identify that area with the European community is scarcely possible for historians, and if some contemporaries did it, it was conceived of as nothing but a program for a still distant future. Yet such an approach influenced western historiography for a long time.

This western historiography has even more frequently overlooked another factor which had appeared by Carolingian times. It is tempting to consider the empire proclaimed in 800 as one of the forms of the Christian Empire which succeeded one after the other, beginning with Constantine the Great.[6] But none of these empires, whether in the first or in the second millennium, inherited the ecumenical character of the first which, by continuing for a rather short time the tradition of the Rome of Caesar, was still the universal empire of the Mediterranean world. After the disintegration of that world no empire was ever universal so far as the new European world was concerned. They contributed, as the Carolingian did to a certain extent, to the integration of

that world into a Christian community which expanded in the direction of the geographical limits of the Continent, but that process of integration was by no means achieved by imperial conquest alone.

For the imperial idea was originally neither European nor Christian,
and while the succession of empires—even though none of them were
really world-wide—was, according to Christian tradition, supposed to
be the essence of pre-Christian history,[7] it failed not only to explain or
exhaust *that* history but actually proved most misleading as a key to the
understanding of Christian and European history too. What was necessary, whenever a new part of Europe was to become a rightful member
of the European community, was the Christianization of the peoples and
the penetration of Graeco-Roman culture into that area, but not the inclusion into any Christian Empire. On many occasions, especially in the
extreme north of Europe from Ireland to Scandinavia, this would have
been practically impossible for geographical reasons. In other cases,
especially in those of the Slavic and Baltic peoples, the resistance to imperial claims was to remain for centuries the main obstacle to their inclusion into the European community, an inclusion which usually was
achieved without their joining any empire. This was evident in Carolingian times, in the ninth century, because there were now not one but
two Christian empires, and because outside of either of them a Christianized state, recognizing the authority of papal Rome, succeeded in
surviving through that century: the state of Greater Moravia.

As to the empire, there had been situations before when two emperors
ruled simultaneously, one in the West and the other in the East. But this
had been the result of a division, based upon mutual agreement, of an
empire which always remained one. In 800, an emperor was crowned in
old Rome without any agreement on the part of the new Rome, as if
there should be henceforth two Christian empires,[8] independent from
each other, coexisting with each other just as the Roman had earlier
with the non-Christian and non-European Sassanian Empire in Persia.
In any case, this meant a loss of prestige for the Roman Empire in Constantinople, a challenge to its very title; and it could even mean a threat
to the Eastern Empire, in case the Western, restored with the blessing
of papal Rome, would also try to restore the traditional unity of the empire under western leadership.

This was certainly not the intention of the realistic statesman who
was Charlemagne—who was perhaps troubled even by the possibility of
such interpretations. Neither was it in the interest of Leo III that the

power of his protector should increase so tremendously. But in the political sphere there was a real danger that the Eastern Roman Empire might be encircled by the bonds which were forged between the independent Western Empire and the powerful Caliph Harun-al-Rashid[9] whose realm was, as a matter of fact, another empire controlling the non-European part of the Mediterranean world. It was, of course, unthinkable that Charlemagne, so closely associated with the Papacy, would actively cooperate with a Muslim power against eastern Christendom. But in the religious sphere there was another very serious danger: the political gesture made by Leo III in 800 necessarily contributed to the tension between the Holy See and the Greek Church,[10] a tension which had caused a temporary break during the first period of iconoclasm in Constantinople, and which was to enter into a new critical phase in view of the trend in the Latin Church to add the *filioque* to the Creed.[11] To the religious matters which were leading to the schism between Latin and Greek Christendom, was now added the resentment of Constantinople arising out of the papal initiative in a most delicate political matter, an initiative which was a challenge to the imperial authority of the new Rome.

For all these reasons the establishment of the Carolingian Empire, far from being a step in the direction of the integration of Christian Europe, rather increased the multifold dualism which was such a permanent obstacle to that integration. For the same reason there immediately appeared a desire to make the decision of 800, at least *post factum,* acceptable to the Byzantine Empire. The excuse that the throne of that empire was at that moment occupied by a woman and therefore could be considered vacant, suggested a first possibility of agreement: the marriage of Empress Irene to Charlemagne[12] would at once restore imperial unity under the two of them. It is, however, doubtful whether such a solution, very simple in theory, was seriously considered by either side, whether by the persons concerned or by their peoples. They were scarcely prepared for such a union, in which, thanks to Charlemagne, the West would have exercised supremacy in the eastern part of the Christian Empire. Such a situation would have recalled to the Greeks the Roman domination of the pagan empire before the transfer of the capital to Constantinople.

Another solution seemed, therefore, easier to achieve: the voluntary recognition by Constantinople that there were now two equal and independent Christian empires with their respective capitals in the two

Romes, one under Greek, the other under Frankish leadership. After long negotiations with the successors of Irene, whose deposition and death caused the matrimonial solution of the problem to vanish, peace was concluded in 803 between Charlemagne and Nicephorus; and finally, in 812, Michael I recognized Charlemagne as Emperor in the West, retaining Byzantine sovereignty over Venice, Istria and Dalmatia, thus determining the frontier between the two empires.[13]

At the given moment, this was a recognition of the *de facto* situation and corresponded to the real power of the western emperor. It was plain that he was much stronger than any of those who briefly occupied the throne of Constantinople amid internal and external troubles. That situation changed, however, after Charlemagne's death in 814: it soon became apparent that the restoration of the Western Empire, which depended on the truly great personality of its founder, was a rather unnecessary fiction; for the disintegration of the empire started almost immediately, its large area being divided time and again among Charlemagne's sons and grandsons, none of whom was equal to him. After the artificial partition of 843 which first recognized the ethnic and linguistic difference between the West Frankish and the East Frankish parts, with a controversial transition region in the middle, the division of that region in 870 made final the distinct position and rivalry of what was to be the France and the Germany of the future, leaving Italy separate also, but in a particularly confused situation. However, as late as 896, the East Frankish King Arnulf, an illegitimate scion of the dynasty, was crowned in Rome as emperor.[14]

That title no longer had any concrete significance, and that last imperial coronation of a Carolingian, only three years before his death, spelled the end of a process which prepared the lasting division of the Western Empire into individual, one could almost say national, states. In the meantime the Eastern Empire had recovered from the crises of the eighth and early ninth century and in 867, with the accession of the Macedonian dynasty which was to rule almost two hundred years, entered a period in which it reached the height of its power. Though we can no longer consider that same year the date of a decisive religious schism, it was no mere chance that about that time the relations between the Papacy and the Patriarchate of Constantinople deteriorated. The rivalry between two empires, which the agreement of 812 did not completely eliminate, made any rivalry in the ecclesiastical field more meaningful than before; and both the political and religious rivalries appeared not only in the direct relations between the two centers of Christendom but also whenever an extension of their influence appeared possible.

It was precisely in the ninth century that besides Rome and Byzantium there appeared a third force on the Continent: the Slavic and Slavicized peoples who had not yet been included in either of the two empires and were still pagan. They were open, more than before, to Christian influence, and the growing contacts with them, whether friendly or hostile, made it clear how urgent and desirable it was to make them enter, one way or another, into the community of Christian Europe which was being formed. Any extension of that community outside Europe being out of the question, each of the empires, realizing that it controlled only a part of western Europe or eastern Europe respectively, was naturally desirous to advance into the other part. There was, however, a twofold difference between the two planned expansions. That in the eastern half of Europe remained the expansion of an empire with its traditional Greek culture represented by the Greek Church. In the western part it was not the Carolingian Empire as such, which after Charlemagne hardly existed as a unit, but one of its components only, the East Frankish Kingdom—far from being culturally Latinized itself and rather distant from Rome—which conducted the drive into the Slavic world, conceived of as a Germanic conquest. Which part of that Slavic world was eastern or western, that is, in the Greek or Frankish sphere of influence, was not easy to determine, the frontier between an eastern and a western Europe being even more controversial outside than inside of what had been the one Roman Empire of the past.

That empire had penetrated deep into the Danubian region of Central Europe, but it had reached only up to the Danube river itself and prior to the settlement of Slavic tribes there. Now it was an important issue whether these tribes, after the destruction of Avar power by Charlemagne, would be connected with Carolingian or Byzantine Europe. The former seemed to have a better chance, especially since the East Frankish kingdom, after fighting the Croats[15] in the old, still controverted Illyricum, entered into relations with the distant but much stronger Bulgarian state on the lower Danube and in old Dacia. Here Byzantine interests were directly touched, and though the issue was mainly political, it also had ecclesiastical implications: the Latin Church was a rival of the Greek in the matter of the conversion of the Bulgarians; and the Frankish advance was accompanied by the missionary activity of the Bavarian clergy among the Slavs of old Pannonia.

These Slavs, the ancestors of the Slovaks and Slovenes, had created their own state under the native dynasty of the Moymirides early in the ninth century, perhaps a continuation of the state of Samo which had existed in approximately the same area two hundred years before.[16] Seeking to resist German penetration and threatened by encirclement through Frankish-Bulgarian cooperation, their ruler Rastislav in 862 attempted to secure Byzantine assistance at least in the ecclesiastical field. And in the following year the famous Greek "apostles of the Slavs," the future saints Constantine-Cyril and Methodius, started their remarkable missionary activities in the so-called Moravian state.

Few events of the ninth century, except the creation of the Carolingian Empire and the problem of the Photian schism, have received so much attention in modern historiography as has, especially in recent years, the story of that mission.[17] And with good reason. Painstaking research against the general background of European history, western and eastern, has demonstrated that possibilities were opened on that occasion which could have affected that history more decisively than the legendary tradition of the two saints would indicate. And though these possibilities materialized only temporarily and in small part, their study explains, on the one hand, why one more attempt toward a lasting organization of Europe in the Carolingian age ended in failure, and on the other hand, why this attempt had far-reaching consequences for that organization as it really developed from the next century onward.

In order to understand the favorable prospects for success which appeared on that occasion, it must be recalled once more that while there was a persistent tension between the two Christian empires, there was not yet any break between the Latin and the Greek churches, so that the apostles of the Slavs, in spite of their Greek origin, could be loyal to both the popes of Rome and the patriarchs of Constantinople. And if the Moravian state, fully Christianized through a cooperation of both religious centers of Christendom, and expanding beyond its original nucleus, could succeed in remaining outside and independent of either empire, though in peaceful relations with both, it could develop into a political center attracting the neighboring Slavic peoples and constituting an intermediary link between West and East. It is not correct to speak of a Moravian "empire." This title never appears in the sources and would not correspond to the contemporaneous conception which demanded a Roman origin for any Christian empire. Such a conception could, then, scarcely admit that two such empires could exist side by side. Yet the state of the Moymirides, or Greater Moravia, seemed, as long as it existed, a constructive extension of Europe's Christian community, implementing the role of both the Carolingian and the Byzantine empires, which were unable simply to conquer and annex the rest of Europe. In a Europe thus extended and integrated, the whole Slavic world could find not only its rightful place but prospects of cooperation with Teutons, Latins, and Greeks as well.

To the role of the Christianized Slavs, their Greek apostles wanted to make a lasting contribution by providing a liturgy in the Slavic language and an alphabet which would be appropriate to that language and would best serve their cultural progress on native grounds. It is, however, a question whether these two achievements, outstanding as they were, can be considered unqualified blessings. Even the invention of a new alphabet, related to the Greek but still different from it and even more from the Latin—was to prove the source of many unnecessary difficulties. That special alphabet, accepted by many Slavs and used by them until the present day, isolated them from the majority of Europeans who continued to use the Latin or the Greek alphabet, and since part of the Slavs favored the Latin, which proved quite adaptable to their needs, a cultural cleavage was created within the Slavic world, similar to the difficulties which resulted from the use of two alphabets in the Graeco-Roman world. The cultural integration of the Slavs with that world was certainly not made easier.

These troubles were to appear only in later centuries when one Slavic tongue or dialect after the other developed into a literary language and began to be used for administrative purposes also, and when cultural relations and exchanges were established both among the various Slavic peoples and between Slavs and non-Slavic Europeans. But the question of using the Slavic language in the Christian liturgy became at once a highly controversial problem. It is true that the use in ecclesiastical life of a language understandable to the people facilitated sincere conversions to the Christian faith. Yet the Slavic dialect of that region of Tessalonika from which Constantine and Methodius came and which therefore served as a basis for what was to be called the Church Slavonic was even in those early days different from the vernacular spoken by the various Slavic tribes of other regions, including that of Greater Moravia. In any case they preferred it, in general, to the Latin language. Latin was used by the German clergy and, therefore, was easily associated by the Slavs with German predominance. Furthermore, it was a practice of that Greek Church to which the two apostles of the Slavs belonged to tolerate the use of non-Greek languages in the liturgy, while Rome, recognizing the equal right of the Greek language in the East, preferred in the West the use of Latin only.

The visits of the two brothers to Rome and later, when Constantine died there, of Methodius alone, were quite successful insofar as they convinced one pope after the other that it was advisable to approve, possibly with some minor restrictions, the use of the Slavic language even in churches which were to be directly under Rome. One example of this was the archdiocese created for Methodius, although his see, Syrmium, was located at the border of the Eastern Empire. It appeared also in the interest of the Papacy to support a practice which would limit the influence of the Bavarian clergy, who were favorable to the development of a state Church without too much Roman control.[18] But for this very reason and for many others connected with the desire to bring the Moravian state under the control of the East Frankish kingdom, the whole activity of the Greek apostles of the Slavs met with the strongest possible German opposition, and the innovation which they introduced by the use of the Slavic liturgy offered to their enemies a welcome pretext for questioning their orthodoxy.

The question, therefore, arises whether it was wise to give them such a pretext, especially since Rome obviously hesitated and for centuries remained undecided in that linguistic matter. Many Slavs were unable or unwilling to resist the pressures in favor of the non-Slavic Latin language which was, after all, not the German but the traditional supranational language of the Western Church. Even the most prominent ruler of the Moravian state, Svatopluk, did not support the ecclesiastical policy of Methodius nor defend him against German persecution; the attitude of the Czech leaders, whose conversion was mainly achieved through German influence and with the use of Latin liturgy, wavered too. Methodius, in spite of his use of the Slavic liturgy, found it difficult to obtain the voluntary conversion of the ruler of the Polish people on the upper Vistula. We know today how long, notwithstanding such initial failures, the Slavic liturgy survived in both Bohemia and Poland, but the rivalry between the two liturgies continued to be a source of trouble even there.[19]

Obviously, the decisive reasons for the decline and fall of the Moravian state were not ecclesiastical but political, and since Carolingian power was declining at the same time, the final catastrophe did not come until German hostility was combined with the Hungarian invasion of the Danubian region. On that occasion, as on so many others in the past and in the future, the Slavs had to suffer from pressures coming simultaneously from the European West and from the Asiatic East. But in the case of Greater Moravia the consequences were particularly disastrous both for the Slavs themselves and for Europe, at least at the given moment. The state of the Moymirides disappeared forever; Slovaks and Slovenes were reduced for many centuries to the role of stateless peoples under foreign rule, therefore considered "non-historic"; and not only those two, hitherto close, neighbors, but in general, all the northern and the southern Slavs were permanently separated from each other, with the German advance through the Alpine region soon contacting the Hungarian settlement in the Pannonian plain.

The Moravian state was destroyed only a few years after the death of the last Carolingian Emperor—that Arnulf who had been its principal enemy—and a few years before the extinction of the East Frankish line of Charlemagne's dynasty, which had tried so hard to extend his Europe in the northeastern direction. It so happened that at exactly the same time the Bulgarians, who had threatened the Moymirides along with the Germans—though recently converted under Byzantine influence—turned against Constantinople. The idea of replacing the Greek Empire by a Bulgarian[20] in southeastern Europe proved utopian, but the extension of Greek influence into northeastern Europe was to a large extent blocked under these circumstances, notwithstanding a first trade agreement freshly concluded with that Kievan state which was then rapidly rising under Norman leadership. Blocked, too, was the advance of either Latin or Greek influence into the Danubian area, where instead of the promising Moravian state a pagan, non-European people was established, whose invasions were penetrating far into the former territory of the Roman Empire.

The restoration of that empire had failed in the West, after making the dualism within Europe's Mediterranean core even deeper than in the past, and only the dualism between Europe's Graeco-Roman and Christian heritage seemed gradually to disappear, as evidenced by the Carolingian Renaissance.[21] But even that cultural progress in the West, accomplished without much cooperation with the more advanced Byzantine East, did not endure after the breakup of the Carolingian Empire, when the Papacy was also entering a rather dark period of history. While the West Frankish kingdom declined under the last Carolingians, their East Frankish branch was replaced by the new Saxon dynasty, which, coming from the eastern part of Germany, was particularly interested in the drive toward the Slavic East, a drive which was supposed to extend Christianity and Latin culture in Europe. But as a matter of fact, it was rather a program of German conquest, evoking fierce resistance from the Slavic tribes east of the Elbe. Only in Bohemia did it seem possible to combine national survival with Christianization and recognition of German overlordship.

The tenth century, therefore, began with prevailing conditions which seemed rather unfavorable to the establishment of a Christian community which would unite most of Europe under the leadership of both old and new Rome and under the spiritual primacy of papal Rome, still recognized by all Christendom, western and eastern. That task was made particularly difficult by two circumstances: the perennial necessity of defending Europe, now practically identical with Christendom, against aggressions coming from the Asiatic, non-Christian East; and the new problem of integrating the parts of Europe which had been outside the Roman Empire in a way which would not be merely a violent conquest, but would respect the identity and love of freedom of its peoples. Such integration would then make it possible for them to develop into real nations similar to those which were originating among the "barbarians" settled on formerly imperial territory.

The preparations for such a solution, which had been made in the ninth century, chiefly in connection with Charlemagne's achievements but also because of the interesting experiment of the Moravian state, were certainly not without lasting value. But they proved inadequate, and new attempts in the same direction had to be initiated in the tenth century. Therefore, almost the whole first millennium of Christianity, including the Carolingian period, was nothing but a prologue to the European age which more or less coincides with the second millennium of our era. How a European community, far from perfect, but representing substantial progress and able to last for the next ten centuries, was founded toward the middle of the tenth, has to be studied in the first part of any scholarly, historical commemoration and analysis of the Millennium of Europe.

PART I

The Constitution of Europe
in the Tenth Century

CHAPTER VI

Northeastern Expansion

A T THE BEGINNING of the tenth century Christian Europe was in a situation of chaos and crisis. At the end of that same century Christendom included almost all European peoples, and the prospects for uniting them in a lasting community were unusually favorable. Early in the century the frontiers of the Christianized part of Europe hardly reached beyond the area once united in the old Roman Empire: in the extreme northwest, Ireland was added, but in the southwest almost the whole Iberian peninsula was lost, while in Central Europe all the German lands were finally integrated with the West, but the entire Danubian plain was conquered by Asiatic invaders. On the contrary, when the century approached its end, the frontiers of Christendom approached the extreme geographical limits of the European Continent both in the north and the east.

That extraordinary expansion was the result of a process which started in mid-century and proved much more successful than similar trends toward integration which had appeared in ninth-century Europe.

At the turn of that century it was already obvious that the Carolingian Empire had finally disintegrated. The second renovation of the Western Empire, in 962, was to last almost through the whole second millennium of Christianity, and imperial successor-states survived until the close of that millennium. It is true that the new empire, "transferred" as it was to the Germans, corresponded only to the East Frankish kingdom with the addition of a never clearly defined nor fully integrated part of Italy.

But in western Europe, well organized kingdoms, the leading one being the former West Frankish, were constituted and survived as truly national states longer than the empire itself, while the Christian reconquest of Spain started.

The greater part of the tenth century proved to be a critical age only for Italy whose divisions were to last almost to the end of the millennium. This was the case especially for papal Rome, formally and traditionally the center of the empire, where the emperor was supposed to be crowned by the Pope but not to reside with him. However, even here there was a definitive improvement toward its end, when the new power of Venice originated which was to persist for the next eight hundred years as one of the leading Italian states.

Greater Moravia, the first Slavic state with serious chances of a promising future, disappeared forever in the first years of the tenth century. But Bohemia, which had been connected with it, survived, and though her struggle for independence was rarely fully successful, remained one of the centers of western Slavdom. Another such center emerged around mid-century in Poland, whose continuity of national unity and independence was frequently threatened, but never fully destroyed in the next millennium. And what was more surprising, about the same time pagan and alien Hungary was transformed into a Catholic kingdom, as Latinized as was Poland and surviving along with her through that same millennium in spite of even earlier and longer periods of partition and foreign rule.

The Eastern Roman Empire remained indeed separated from the new Western one as it had been from the Carolingian. Thus, at the height of her power, Byzantium looked down upon the Saxon usurpers of the imperial dignity. But there was at least no new break between papal Rome and Constantinople, whose struggles against the Muslim world in this tenth century, more than in any other, were a defense of all Christendom. Therefore, in spite of occasional tensions the relations between Christendom's two centers were never interrupted in that century and at its end were even improving. Furthermore, when in spite of the continued troubles with Bulgaria the Eastern Empire succeeded in including the Kievan state in its sphere of influence, this marked a wide extension of Europe as a whole, with whose western part that state, though closely associated with Byzantium, also had direct relations.

This had little to do with the Norse origin of the leaders of Rus'. In eastern Europe the Varangians were, by that time, no less absorbed and assimilated by the Slavs[1] than were their Norman kin in western Europe by the populations which they conquered there. But what proved to be a lasting contribution to the geographical enlargement of the European community, achieved in the course of the tenth century, was the integration of the distant Scandinavian homeland of the Norman Vikings, where three kingdoms were definitely constituted and were to last for the next millennium.

The basic change which marked the passage from the first to the second Christian millennium and made the latter a real millennium of Europe is, therefore, determined by the striking fact that to the old Graeco-Roman Europe, once a part of the Mediterranean community, a new Europe was added in the northeastern part of the Continent. Equally large, that new Europe was, of course, culturally much less advanced than the other, but ready to catch up with its development, not only to share the heritage of the Christianized Graeco-Roman world, but also to make constructive contributions to that heritage in the future.

One immediate contribution to the civilization which from now on could rightly be called European was an increase in its variety, that variety in unity which had been typical of the small Hellenic nucleus of Europe two thousand years before and which was to remain the distinctive feature of European culture for the next ten centuries. The Carolingian Europe had been limited to the area of the Romance and Germanic peoples, not including even the Celts in the northwest nor the Greeks in the southeast. The integral Europe, constituted through the great northeastern expansion, included in addition to all the former almost all the Slavic peoples of their three main branches, each of them composed of numerous tribes, along with the Hungarians and all the non-German Teutonic peoples. As for the Slavs, there was only one exception: the group of tribes between the Elbe and Oder rivers remained in opposition to the forces which were creating the Christian community of Europe and eventually disappeared almost completely. Another exception was that of the Baltic peoples, showing similar resistance when at the end of the tenth century the first serious effort toward their integration was made. But that small and ethnically isolated group not only survived along with the Finnish tribes of the same area, but in the first centuries of Europe's millennium was gradually integrated with Europe through various means and in different forms.

This leads to the important question of how, in general, the northeastern expansion of the European community was achieved and which methods proved particularly successful in giving to that community its lasting constitution. Before studying any individual cases, one fundamental distinction must be made, a distinction and comparison between two alternatives. In view of the imperial tradition left behind by the first millennium of the Christian era, it would seem that the most efficient method would be the expansion of the Christian Empire. But it must not be overlooked, first, that the imperial tradition was originally a pagan one, and secondly, that soon after the empire's Christianization it was split in two, a process which because of the two restorations of the Western Empire resulted in the unavoidable but confusing coexistence of two rival Christian empires in Europe.

As to the first point, the pagan Romans had indeed been eminently successful in conquering one territory and people after the other. But that progress in political unification and in cultural assimilation and development was gained at a heavy price that involved a dangerous risk. The ruthless methods of subjugation used by a power whose principle was *parcere subjectis et debellare superbos* resulted in a profound resentment on the part of the vanquished who were deprived of their freedom, and in a stubborn resistance on the part of those who had fought in vain and who only awaited the opportunity to attack the empire and to break through its frontiers.

That was precisely what happened when the empire was declining, and therefore, soon after its Christianization, it had to pay for those aggressive policies of pagan times which St. Augustine so rightly blamed.[2] When, however, after a few centuries the destroyed Western Empire was restored by Charlemagne, similar policies were followed only too frequently, even in the relations with the Germanic Saxons.[3] And when in turn German kings of Saxon origin resumed the drive in the eastern direction, their treatment of the eastern neighbors, now all Slavic, was quite similar before and after the coronation of Otto I as Roman Emperor. There was, of course, no mass extermination and the spread of Christianity was supposed to justify the German conquests. But just because these two goals seemed inseparable, the Slavic tribes, threatened by foreign domination, resisted even more fiercely than the Saxons had before. Politically they were not so well organized as the Moravian state had been, in spite of the creation of a Veletian federation,[4] and could not turn to any other Christian power for support. Their fight for freedom was, however, so strong and so prolonged that after the great uprising of 981 most of what the Germans had gained before was lost again. Only the border region, where a series of German marches were organized, was permanently attached to the empire, while the final conquest of all Slavs between the lower Elbe and Oder rivers had to wait for the twelfth century. In the tenth, even the project of the first Saxon emperor to make the newly founded archbishopric of Magdeburg the center of an ecclesiastical organization in Slavic lands and, at the same time, a tool of his eastern policy, did not materialize.[5] And Otto the Great was even less prepared to match—in faraway Kievan Rus'—the growing influence of Byzantium.

The Eastern Roman Empire was neither able nor willing to make Christianization an instrument of imperial, in its case Greek, conquest and domination outside its frontier. The endless struggles with the Bulgarians inside these old frontiers were difficult enough and so were those with Asiatic aggressors in the East. The Greek mission in the Danubian region had been no threat to the independence of the Moravian state but on the contrary was meant to protect it against much more dangerous foreign influences. And when the disciples of St. Methodius, after their expulsion from Moravia, directed their missionary activities to the still pagan Slavic peoples in the northeast, there was even less danger that they would serve any political ambitions of Constantinople. On the other hand, the imperial city on the Bosphorus exercised an attraction for both Varangians and Slavs, who amidst their raids against the Byzantine Empire were anxious to establish trade relations with the Greeks and were impressed by the splendor of Greek culture and liturgy. The first Christians who appeared among these faraway peoples had been converted by the Eastern Church, thanks to contacts with either Bulgaria or Constantinople before any extension of the Eastern Empire's influence could be exercised in the political field or in matters of ecclesiastical organization.

However, the time was approaching when the Slavs and non-Slavs of the Kievan state, considering the advisability of integrating that state with the nascent European community and wishing to do so without giving up their freedom and independence, had to face the question whether relations with eastern or western Christendom would offer them better guarantees in that respect.[6] For them also, the German kingdom to which the Western Empire was transferred was far enough away not to be an immediate threat as it was to the western Slavs; and missionary activities coming from that distant West were penetrating as far as the Dnieper region without any apparent political implications. The possibility of accepting the Christian faith without coming under the control of any empire was therefore quite obvious. Furthermore, in western Christendom methods of propagating Christian faith and Latin culture independently of any political coercion were being developed to replace those which only too frequently combined Christianization with German conquest.

From the outset, such indeed had been the methods of the Irish missionaries, who coming from a distant island had no political views whatever when they first decisively contributed to the final conversion of all German tribes and then continued their activities in non-German areas.[7] Probably inspired by their example, there appeared also German missionaries who wanted to serve the cause of the faith in a spirit of Christian charity rather than in the interest of imperial power.[8] Such an approach opened prospects for an extension of the European community through peaceful conversion to Christianity and cultural assimilation with the Graeco-Roman world without any extension of imperial rule over peoples who wanted to remain free. On the contrary, such methods favored the development of these peoples into real nations and independent, equal members of the community which they willingly entered.

It is not surprising that before such possibilities appeared with regard to Slavic peoples—ethnically and linguistically quite different from the Germans and at the same time not separated from them by any natural frontier—these peaceful ways achieved slow but lasting results in the three Scandinavian kingdoms. These homelands of the Normans, who through their raids, trade routes, and settlements had penetrated into so many countries of western and eastern Europe, and were even to reach Sicily far in the south, remained for a long time in isolation, outside the nascent European community, and pagan like so many Slavs. One of these countries, Norway, seemed even to turn away from the European Continent by means of colonial expansion. After temporary conquests in Ireland and Iceland in the ninth century, in the tenth the Norse reached Greenland, and about 1000 A.D., they even attained the "Wineland" of the western hemisphere in what might be called a first discovery of America.[9] In that connection a millennium of European overseas expansion in the western direction could be celebrated, though these early successes were not followed up in any continuous process. And since, as early as 930 an assembly called Althing was established in Iceland, a millennium of parliamentary institutions on European soil could have been commemorated some thirty years ago,[10] if that initiative had not been completely isolated from the development of Europe proper in the tenth century. But in the course of that same century the integration of the whole Scandinavian region with the European community was gradually accomplished.

That process, the importance of which should not be underestimated for Europe's future, had indeed, just like similar development in the Slavic world, significant antecedents in the ninth century. At almost the same time—even somewhat earlier—when the Greek apostles of the Slavs appeared in central Europe, a monk from northern France, though possibly of Saxon origin, the future Saint Ansgar, started such promising missionary activities in Denmark and even in Sweden that he has been called the "apostle of the North."[11] The bishopric, which at his suggestion was founded in Hamburg, was to serve as basis for his efforts which, however, found no sufficient understanding among the German hierarchy: there was no problem of any non-Latin liturgy as in Moravia, but there simply was no interest in a project which, important as it was from the purely religious viewpoint, did not open any serious prospects of political expansion.

Such an expansion through German conquest, obviously impossible as far as Sweden and Norway were concerned, was attempted in relations with Denmark by that same tenth-century Saxon dynasty which followed a similar policy toward the Slavs.[12] But even in the Danish case the geographical situation was not favorable: the difficult access to the Jutland peninsula was still partly blocked by unconquered Slavic tribes east of the lower Elbe, and the Danes themselves not only strongly defended that narrow isthmus of Schleswig which was to be an object of controversy for a thousand years, but even appeared at the mouth of the Oder threatening both Germans and Slavs.

In view of such a situation it could seem surprising that Christianization was making steady progress among all Scandinavian peoples, probably because the process was kept separated from hopeless political claims of Germany, whether before or after the restoration of the Western Empire under the Saxon kings. That empire, in spite of the racial community of all Teutonic tribes, was never to include the Danes, Swedes, or Norwegians, who under their native dynasties, though frequently quarreling with each other, had even in pagan days established independent kingdoms and now spontaneously accepted the Christian faith.

In none of the three countries is that decisive event connected with any specific date or even with the rule of any individual king. Early initiatives in the Carolingian period, like the baptism of an exiled king of Denmark at the court of Emperor Louis the Pious even before Saint Ansgar's mission, had not left any lasting traces, and even in the tenth century some attempts of Scandinavian kings to Christianize their respective countries proved premature. In Denmark, nearest to the fully-converted part of Europe, Christianity was advancing under Harald Bluetooth soon after the mid-century, but Harald's son Sven, at the turn of the century, still can be considered the first Christian king of that country. The same can be said of his Swedish contemporary, Olaf Skutkonung, and of the Norwegian opponent of the latter, Olaf Trygvesson, the conqueror of Iceland and Greenland, who was baptized in England, while his successor, Saint Olaf, received his baptism in Normandy. These details are important[13] because they show that Christian influence coming from non-German countries was particularly efficient and did not provoke any pagan reaction similar to that which broke out in Denmark when the Germans, anxious to impose their overlordship, suffered setbacks both in Italy and in the Slavic borderlands.

In the next generation Canute the Great of Denmark was to conquer not only Norway but also England, and thus a Christian Scandinavian ruler appeared, like the pagan Normans of the past, as a dangerous aggressor. However, the very fact that in the early eleventh century he could create some kind of northern empire which was definitely part of the European state-system is the best evidence that in the tenth the integration of the Scandinavian region with the Christian community of Europe had been completed in a way which left to its peoples full opportunities for free national development. That on various occasions—to recall only the policies of Sweden in the seventeenth century—they could be aggressive in their relations with other European countries is another question connected with the only too-well-known fact that the millennium of Europe was by no means an era of undisturbed peace and order in international relations. In any case, the inclusion of Danes, Swedes, and Norwegians in the sphere of Europe's Christian culture—to which they were to later make so many valuable contributions—must be considered a weighty argument illustrating the significance of the tenth century in the history of Europe's growth and of the role of smaller nations in that evolution.

As far as the Scandinavian countries are concerned, that role is recognized to a large extent in general European history, though even they do not always receive sufficient attention in the study of that history, which usually emphasizes the role of the empires and of the great powers. Only when one of the Scandinavian nations tried to play the part of such a great power, did it seem necessary to all historians to include its policies in the treatment of the given period. The situation is much worse with regard to the Slavs. It is true that in view of their large number and the great variety among them they are sometimes called "a Slavic world." But that world, which seems to be strangely isolated,[14] and its destiny so often shared by non-Slavic peoples of the same area, frequently was and sometimes still is considered a secondary supplement to European history. Again, as in the Scandinavian case, an exception used to be made only for those Slavs who in a longer period of that history succeeded in creating an empire participating in European power-politics. Hence the special attention given to Russia in the last centuries of Europe's millennium and even the misleading trend to identify that Russian Empire with Slavdom as a whole. Yet long before modern Russia emerged as a great power, from the early beginnings of the millennium of Europe, the problem of the integration of all Slavs and of the non-Slavs who were inseparable from them, proved of truly decisive importance for Europe's constitution.

This is particularly clear if the geographical element of history is duly considered, not as a determining force, but as an entity of natural conditions influencing the populations of a given area and their creative achievements. When Scandinavia was integrated with historical Europe, only a small area was added, limited to two peninsulas of which the larger one was rather isolated and its northern part very scarcely populated. What is called the entrance of the Slavs into European history was an almost unlimited extension of that history, including the major part of the European Continent and possibilities of further colonial expansion, not in distant regions beyond the seas but in contiguous territories where even the geographical frontiers of Europe were difficult to determine.

Thus the whole intermediary sphere between the old nucleus of Europe and the gigantic land mass of Asia was added to Europe as a historical community, and at the same time the agelong pressure which Asiatic forces exercised upon Europe from the northeast, in addition to the parallel pressure through Asia Minor, was reduced. The gate to the heart of Europe through the plains north of the Black Sea could be closed only when the Slavic world was associated with Europe, whose defense against the non-European East was hardly possible as long as the European East did not contribute to that defense in cooperation with western Europe.

Equally important is the ethnographical aspect of the problem. Never was all eastern Europe populated exclusively by Slavs. But the Slavs always formed the great majority of the European population east of the Teutonic peoples. The tension between the two groups resulted in a long-lasting prejudice against the Slavs in a historiography which formerly was strongly influenced by German thought. It seemed as if the Slavs, whose very name was wrongly conceived to have some connection with that of slaves, were destined to be always dominated either by their Germanic or by their Asiatic neighbors,[15] being unable to organize their political life without foreign impact and leadership. On the other hand, it has been pointed out, first by Greek historians of the fifth and sixth centuries,[16] when contacts were established with the Slavs, that they were distinguished by their love of freedom and were more peaceful than the other "barbarians." This, too, should not be exaggerated as it was in modern times in Slavic historiography and even by the German Herder. It would be anachronistic to speak about democracy in the earliest days of Slavdom and one-sided to overlook the violence of Slavic invasions, similar to those of other "barbarians," in the territories of their western and southern neighbors. However, the Slavs were by no means inferior to those better known "barbarians," in particular to the Germanic tribes, who are rightly considered an important element in the making of Europe.[17] Recent archeological research has revealed that the original homeland of the Slavs was much larger and extended much farther toward the West than it has been admitted previously, and that even in prehistoric times their culture was on a fairly high level and included a well developed agriculture.[18] The Slavic migrations in western and southern directions usually followed those of the Germanic peoples, and their wars were predominantly of a defensive character, a resistance against foreign tribes which so frequently overran their territory.

Little is known indeed of what was going on in that vast territory, about which the ancient Graeco-Roman writers had comparatively little information.[19] But it seems that tribal federations, at least, trying to oppose foreign aggression, were created in the course of the first millennium of our era by both eastern and western Slavs. And even if those of them who penetrated farthest to the southwest, the Croats and Serbs, perhaps had Iranian leaders,[20] the Moravian state which was the first to establish regular relations with the Greek as well as the Latin world was not the only one which the Slavs themselves had created under native rulers in the Carolingian period. In addition to the Czech state of the Přemyslides, there already existed, in the very center of the Slavic home-land and therefore hardly in contact with the outside world, the state of the Piasts,[21] who had been preceded by an earlier dynasty and had grad-ually united most of the Polish tribes.

It was, threefore, of prime importance for Europe that after these early beginnings of a proto-historic, pagan existence, the free Slavic peoples were at last included in the European community, along with that seg-ment which under Norse leadership was forming a large, though loosely organized body politic farther to the East, reaching from the Baltic to the Black Sea region. The apparent vacuum between the western world and the Kievan state was thus being filled, and the question arose whether, besides the Slavs, the Hungarian and the Baltic peoples would also and at the same time become part of the European state system. As to the former, this happened more rapidly and completely than could have been expected, being accomplished by the end of the tenth century, while the Balts, cutting off the Slavs from a long sector of the Baltic coast —just as Turkish tribes prevented them from reaching the Black Sea— were to remain for a few more centuries outside the European com-munity, being the last and only gap in the integration of the Continent. Why this was so, since racially the Balts, the closest kin of the Slavs, had so much more in common with the European peoples than the Finno-Ugrian Magyars, cannot be explained by the geographical situation alone, but leads to the most decisive question of how the northeastern part of the Continent was connected with the southwestern so that they could form together one community or civilized society, including also the European peninsulas and islands.

Such a result was achieved, exactly as in the Scandinavian case, not by any conquest but by a peaceful process of Christianization whereby the people of that vast area voluntarily accepted the Catholic faith in a Church not yet divided by any final schism. And since that Church had assimilated and was preserving the heritage of Graeco-Roman culture, all the newly converted peoples participated henceforth in the develop-ment of that culture. They adapted it to their native tradition and sooner or later they made original contributions, following in all this the same pattern observable in the evolution of other "barbarians" converted at an earlier date.

In view of their geographical position, these newcomers to the European community, different in many respects from earlier members but contributing for that very reason to the constructive variety within Europe's basic unity, were affected, much more than those of western and northern Europe, by the original dualism of the European tradition. Most of them came in contact with both Rome and Constantinople, and the decision as to which of these two centers of Christian culture each of them should join was sometimes a difficult one, especially since in the whole area the final and official Christianization had been preceded by missionary activities inspired by both centers and conducted in different rites and liturgies. The problem of the conversion of the Slavs and non-Slavs of northeastern Europe is, therefore, connected with the instructive experience of the Slavs of the Moravian state in the Danubian region. But while that experience of the ninth century had ended in failure, the gradual achievements of the tenth finally completed the construction of Europe and thus inaugurated Europe's millennium.

The immediate results were particularly striking as far as the European Continent north of the Mediterranean peninsulas was concerned. In the Carolingian age, that core of Europe consisted of two parts only: the western which was Romance and the eastern which was Germanic, with a controversial frontier zone between. Now a third part was added which was predominantly Slavic and situated much farther to the east so that the eastern half of the limited Carolingian Europe from now on constituted the central part of the fully integrated Euorpe. The new eastern part was, however, so large and so ready for a further expansion toward the east, into the transition zone between Europe and Asia, that there were prospects of its future division into two halves: one of them, the original, so closely associated with the West, that it could be considered an East Central Europe next to the Germanic West Central Europe, the other more specifically East European, if not of a colonial, Eurasian character.[22]

Before studying in detail the constitution of the new part of Europe in the tenth century, it is indispensable to survey the simultaneous changes in both parts of the old one in order to realize that for them, too, whether central or western, that century was the beginning of a new historical period: the millennium of Europe as a whole.

CHAPTER VII

The Millennium of the Holy Roman Empire

I T HAS BEEN RIGHTLY SAID that nobody can understand Europe without understanding the Holy Roman Empire.[1] This should not be too difficult since there is hardly any other problem of European history on which more has been written by prominent scholars of many lands, especially in our time. There remain, however, numerous controversial issues and even fundamental differences of interpretation, and there are striking contrasts in the judgments of value regarding that empire, though favorable opinions seem to prevail, especially among those who are interested in European unity and historical continuity. In a study of the millennium of Europe a re-examination of the problem is all the more essential, since the millennium of the coronation of Otto I, in 962, is obviously an important part of any such commemoration.[2] And in connection with the different meanings of any millennium three different points have to be considered: the primary question as to what really happened in the memorable year, the role of the empire in the 844 years of its continuous existence, and the impact of its tradition up to the present.

First, however, the very name of that venerable body politic requires some preliminary comments. It was not before the fifteenth century that the full name of Holy Roman Empire of the German Nation was generally used. But even in the tenth a distinction had to be made between the Roman and the "non-Roman" imperial idea, the latter obviously German, and, strictly speaking, Saxon. Even before the greatest of the Saxon kings of Germany was crowned in Rome, he, Otto I, and even his predecessor, Henry I, were considered and even called emperors, not only because of their acclamation as such by their victorious armed forces but also because they were considered the rulers of other kings and peoples. For the contemporaneous Saxon chronicler Widukind of Corvey,[3] both Henry I and Otto I, especially after their spectacular victories over the Hungarians in 933 and 955 respectively, were the greatest among the European kings, the masters of almost all of Europe, since their imperial power *non solum Germania, Italia atque Gallia, sed tota fere Europa non sustinet*. Whatever we may think about the obvious exaggeration and wishful thinking contained in such interpretations and statements, they clearly indicate that in the mind of the people to whose king so much *potentiae maiestas* was attributed, the whole conception of the empire was based upon the idea of conquest leading to the domination over other peoples.

The role of an empire thus conceived could indeed be a contribution to the constitution of Europe as a united community and would recall the idea of the *pax Romana* and of the old pagan Romans who believed themselves to be destined to extend their rule over the known world. But such an idea was neither acceptable to the non-German Europeans nor reconcilable with the Christian principles upon which the empire was supposed to be based from the time of its conversion. Why, then, was a German king whose admirers and supporters had such views of his role in Europe, crowned by the pope, receiving the formal sanction of the Church and of Christian Rome?

It can be said, of course, that the situation of 800 repeated itself and that the popes of the tenth century, and John XII in particular, needed the protection of a powerful secular ruler much more than Leo III had needed it. Furthermore, the restoration of the Carolingian Empire, after an interruption of not much more than half a century, could seem to be something natural, a *translatio imperii* from the Franks to the Saxons, from one Germanic people to another.

There were, however, at least two important differences. First, the protection which the Papacy at this time needed and requested was to be a protection against the Italians, especially the Roman aristocracy, not against foreign invaders who had settled in Italy. Even more important was the fact that the non-Italian power which was to interfere with the Roman and, in general, the Italian situation, was, much more than the still undivided Frankish kingdom had been, a national state established on ethnic grounds. The ruler of the Franks—partly Latinized after being established for several centuries on the territory of old Celtic, Romanized Gaul—could be considered in later centuries a national hero of both France and Germany, *Charlemagne* being at the same time *Karl der Grosse*. The German king, a descendant of those Saxons whom the first restorer of the Western Roman Empire had to conquer so ruthlessly, could not possibly have any claims to supranational leadership. Such an approach to the problem of European organization in the tenth century, and even such a terminology, could seem anachronistic. But the empire entrusted to Otto I and his successors was supposed to be a permanent institution and, as a matter of fact, did last for a long time when the national differentiation within the European community was steadily growing.

It is true that the restoration of the Western Empire in the tenth century was considered a return not so much to the recent but disappointing experience of the ninth, but rather to the remote but unforgotten and much more inspiring tradition of the Roman Empire of the first centuries A.D. It was this empire in its Christian form and interpretation, an empire much more universal than the Carolingian had ever been, and which was expected to last forever as the ultimate in the succession of world empires,[4] that the representatives of the imperial idea in its Roman form wanted to restore. Such a *renovatio* at the time when the first Christian millennium was approaching its end, could seem, indeed, an appropriate transition to, or beginning of, the next millennium which was to be the millennium of Europe, of a European community organized under the leadership of a supreme secular authority as was the Christian Church under the spiritual authority of the Roman pope.

However, the idea to give such a political leadership to a ruler who was neither Roman nor chosen from among candidates of different origin, but was always to be identical with the king of one and the same individual nation, was a challenge to the other peoples of Europe who were constituting at the same time their own kingdoms. For them, such a constitution of Europe was the more dangerous, because the German kingdom with which the imperial dignity was to be formally connected had imperial ambitions even before any papal sanction. It occupied a central position in the very heart of Europe, and was already aiming at an expansion of its territory at the expense of its neighbors. That expansion was to be achieved not only through a consistent drive toward the East, but also through a penetration into the original territory of Gaul, controlled only in part by the last West Frankish Carolingians, and into

Italy where no local power proved able to oppose the German. The old empire that had really been Roman had failed to give to the Mediterranean world a lasting peace and a permanent organization. It could hardly be expected that a thousand years later the privileged place given to one of the European nations simply because it happened to be the strongest one would guarantee to the European community a "tranquillity of order" based upon the Christian principles of justice and charity.

Furthermore, the fact that the royal dignity in Germany was and remained legally elective—though in practice the succession within the same dynasty, at the given moment the Saxon, continued until its extinction—was to be a constant source of trouble. Since it was the German king who was *ex officio* designated to be Roman emperor and in later days was even called *rex Romanorum* before his imperial coronation, all succession-problems and rivalries among candidates to the German crown would necessarily affect the succession to the imperial throne and have their repercussions outside Germany. Whether the new German king would be at the same time an appropriate candidate for the imperial dignity depended on the qualifications of the given person over whose choice nobody but the German princes could exercise any serious influence. The original choice of Pope John XII, who, after having considered the possibility of turning towards Constantinople, created a precedent, decisive for more than eight centuries, by crowning Otto I, may well have been justified, and the first of the new Roman emperors could seem in many respects similar to Charlemagne. But it was doubtful from the outset whether the following German kings would be better qualified for their imperial mission than the Carolingians had been. As a matter of fact, no emperor after Otto I was called "the Great" even in Germany.

The precedent of 962 made it quite clear that the restored Roman Empire was to be based upon the close cooperation between emperors and popes, the latter being freely elected in Rome among candidates of various origin, most frequently Italian and very rarely German. But that same principle had failed to perpetuate the unity and continuity of the Carolingian Empire after Charlemagne and in 962 there was even less chance that it would work satisfactorily in view of the alarming decline of papal authority. There were indeed only two alternatives. As long as the popes would need imperial protection, their leadership in Christendom could not be expected to counterbalance the power of the emperors.

If, on the contrary, the crisis in papal Rome would prove only temporary —and so it was—there was to appear a serious danger of rivalry between Roman popes and Roman emperors who were primarily German kings.

That danger is not only obvious for the historian who looks back to the tenth century with the experience of the following ones, but it manifested itself immediately, in spite of the real greatness of Otto I and the shortcomings of John XII, which seem so scandalous that the question has been rightly asked[5] whether they have not been described with biased exaggeration by contemporary critics who were favorable to the emperor. In any case there must have been from the outset a deep misunderstanding between the two men which revealed the difficulty of cooperation between the two powers, each of them having even then a different interpretation of the constitution of Europe. Otto I at once raised two claims which were unacceptable to John XII: not only was the emperor to be the suzerain of the papal state, but the elections of the popes were to be controlled by the emperors. That meant that the German king, elected without any papal interference, was to be the real master of all Christendom.

In view of John's opposition, Otto considered it necessary to depose the pope immediately after his coronation, an arbitrary decision which resulted only in confusion and in the restoration of John XII. Only after his death, in 964, could the emperor's candidate, Leo VIII, exercise his authority for a short time. Thus the whole conflict between the *imperium* and the *sacerdotium,* which was to be the main obstacle to a sound constitution of the European community, could be anticipated at the very time of the renovation of the empire, and in the subsequent course of the tenth century there continued to be troubles in papal Rome, imperial interferences resented not only by the ecclesiastics but also by the Roman people, and even emergences of anti-popes.

The second restoration of the Western Empire did not achieve even the most immediate objective of assuring peace and order in Rome. There was, however, a chance that through their imperial role the Saxon kings of Germany, though coming from the north of that country and continuing even after 962 their program of German expansion in the eastern direction, would come under the influence of the original, southern part of the empire, the Latin and, strangely enough, also the Greek world. Two marriages are rightly considered significant in that respect:

that of Otto I himself in 951, soon after his first appearance in Italy when he was proclaimed king, and that of his son, the future Otto II, celebrated in Rome in 972, the year before his father's death.

It now seems well established that Adelaide of Burgundy,[6] the wife of Otto I, was not of Italian but of Germanic origin. However, it was she, who, at a time when the imperial crown was still refused to the Saxon conqueror by Pope Agapetus II, the saintly predecessor of John XII, gave to her husband his first claims to the Italian crown, through her first marriage to the son of King Hugh of Italy. As daughter and sister of kings of Burgundy, she also abetted the later claims of the empire to suzerainty over the southeastern part of ancient Gaul. Nothing could be more important for the supranational character of the new empire, not only from the political but also from the cultural viewpoint. The empress, who was soon canonized, represented indeed the culture of Latin Christendom at its best. She herself was under the influence of that famous monastery of Cluny, in her native Burgundy, where that culture was being so successfully revived in the midst of the spiritual crisis of the tenth century,[7] and she transmitted that influence to Otto I, to their son Otto II, and even to their grandson Otto III. It was chiefly through that remarkable woman that the Saxon dynasty was, to a certain extent, Romanized, more perhaps than through the frequently hostile relations with Rome. Through her the dynasty became interested not only in northeastern but also in southwestern Europe where the German core of the Ottonian Empire would find opportunities, not of conquests under the pretext of Christianization, but rather of consolidating its own Christian character and its ties with the Graeco-Roman cultural heritage.

From the viewpoint of a sound political constitution of Europe it was rather doubtful whether the extension of direct imperial control—practically inseparable from the control by the German kingdom—over a large part of French territory was advisable. In any case, the integration with the empire of the so-called kingdom of Arles, including both Burgundy proper and the Mediterranean Provence, was never fully completed and lasted only for about one century[8] while farther to the north, particularly in Lorraine, German and French claims proved very difficult to reconcile, even in the tenth century. The disappearance of what in the first division of the Carolingian Empire had been a separate *Lotharii regnum* between the West Frankish and East Frankish kingdoms, was to have momentous consequences for the Ottonian Empire and for French-German relations in the whole millennium of Europe.

Imperial attempts to interfere even with the problems of France proper certainly did not improve the situation, indicating from the outset how difficult, if not impossible, it would be to have the authority of the new Roman Empire recognized even in those western territories which had been an integral part of the old one, as well as of the Carolingian.

Much more complex, however, was the situation in the East, separated from the West in the Mediterranean age and never fully reconciled with the renovation of the Western Roman Empire by Charlemagne. When after that first renovation—which, as expected by the Greeks, did not succeed—a second one was achieved by Otto I, he could not obtain in Constantinople more than a recognition as "Frankish" emperor.[9] Furthermore, if even in the Latin world, especially in Italy, the Saxon conquerors were considered culturally inferior, the Greeks had an even stronger feeling of superiority in their relations with the West in general, and especially with its new German masters. The famous report of a highly cultivated Italian, Bishop Liudprand of Cremona, on his mission to Constantinople, where he was sent in 968 by Emperor Otto I and was so badly received by Emperor Nicephorus Phocas, is a truly classical testimony in that respect.[10]

It was, therefore, a great success for the emperor of the West when four years later the successor of Phocas, John Tzimisces, gave his consent to the marriage of Otto's son to a Byzantine princess, his niece Theophano, a project which Phocas had refused to consider. This did not mean, in any sense, that the Eastern Empire formally recognized the Western: its rulers continued to consider themselves the only Roman Emperors, and Phocas particularly resented that Pope John XIII, in his letter of recommendation for Liudprand, had addressed him as emperor of the Greeks. But Byzantium was absorbed by the struggle against the Arabs and also against Bulgarians and Varangians in Eastern Europe, and was therefore satisfied with preventing Otto I from seizing her last western possessions in southern Italy. Thus Byzantium was ready to settle her relations with the Ottonian Empire by a matrimonial alliance which indicated at least a temporary compromise.

The marriage of 972 was not at all a return to the extravagant idea of uniting the two empires, as had been the project of a marriage between Charlemagne and Empress Irene. It did not imply any recognition of the imperial claims of the Saxon kings though it was celebrated in Rome. It was not even a recognition of equality, since only a little later another Byzantine princess really "born in purple" was given in marriage to the prince of Kiev, who only on that occasion was converted to Christian-ity.[11] Far from opening Constantinople to any Latin influence, it pro-moted, just like that other marriage, the spread of Byzantine influence outside the Eastern Empire. But the acceptance of Greek influence by the court of the new emperors of the West, who were not even fully Latinized as yet, was not only the beginning of assimilation of the two imperial centers, but a contribution to both Christian and European unity. Although Theophano died only a few years after her husband, and her son Otto III was to grow up under the influence of his Burgun-dian grandmother rather than of his Greek mother, his Byzantine herit-age was to prove extremely important for the development of his truly universal interpretation of the imperial idea.

Long before these astonishing prospects appeared at the turn of the century, the dualism of that idea—a lasting result of the original dualism of Europe's ancient heritage—contributed to the rivalry of the two em-pires, the Ottonian and the Byzantine, in their efforts to extend both Christendom and the European community. That rivalry, similar to that of Carolingians and Greeks at the time of the Moravian state, mani-fested itself now in the main successor state to Greater Moravia, in Hun-gary. There, after Hungary's defeat by Otto I in 955, it had to be decided under which influence, western or eastern, her conversion and integra-tion with Europe would be accomplished. But a similar rivalry seemed to develop at the same time, even before Otto's imperial coronation, in the most distant part of the Slavic world: in the Kievan state. More than thirty years before its final conversion, a first project of Christianization under Olga included both her visit to Constantine Porphyrogenetes and her embassy to the Saxon king with a request for German missionaries.[12] However, independently of any other reasons for the failure of that mission, such contacts between Germany and Kievan Rus' could hardly lead to any concrete result, in spite of the restoration of the Western Empire only a few years later, because the two were separated by vast Slavic territories which, except for Bohemia, already in the German orbit, were still pagan.

These territories, which for the Greeks were even more difficult to reach than Kiev for the Germans, continued to be considered by the latter, in Ottonian times as previously in Carolingian times, an exclusive field for their expansion, their chances being increased by the growth of prestige resulting from the "transfer" of the imperial dignity to the German kings. In contrast to the imperial expansion in a southwestern direction, into the old Latin world which Otto's marriage to Adelaide had opened to him, that northeastern expansion was to be, as in the past, a German conquest facilitated by the creation of a whole belt of marches along the eastern frontier of both the German kingdom and the restored Roman Empire. At the same time these would provide for the defense of that frontier and for the gradual incorporation of new, originally Slavic lands.

The marches north of Bohemia, between the Sudeten mountains and the Baltic, were created by the Saxon kings on territories which never had been reached by Charlemagne and, of course, even less by the Romans. The fight which was going on there in the tenth century was particularly brutal, provoking violent pagan reactions which, however, could not save the Slavs between the Elbe and the Oder from final annihilation. But south of Bohemia where the Alpine valleys led into the Pannonian plain, another march had been already created by Charlemagne, in a region which once belonged to the Roman province of Noricum and where Roman rule had left lasting traces. This march was developing among Slavic settlements which, after replacing the Celtic, were now subject to German pressure and colonization, but at the same time were defended against the Avars in the ninth and the Magyars in the tenth century. This was the early origin of Austria.[13]

In that case, as in so many others, the first initiative of Charlemagne had only a preparatory character and his Austrian march, not yet so called, lasted no longer than his empire. But under Otto II, before his reverses in the Elbe region, an eastern march on the Danube, soon called *Ostarici*—the *Oesterreich* of the future—was reorganized under much more favorable conditions in view of the change to a peaceful attitude on the part of the Hungarians. It was separated from Bavaria and given, in 976, to the family of the Babenbergs who were to rule there for 270 years and to be replaced, after a first Austrian succession war, by the Habsburgs.

The millennium of Austria, coming soon after the millennium of the foundation of the Holy Roman Empire, is therefore, along with the latter, part of the millennium of Europe. In spite of Austria's much more modest beginnings, simply as one of the eastern outposts of that empire, her final foundation is of unusual significance, and the two millennia, the imperial and the Austrian, are inseparable from each other. Three hundred years later Austria's drive for leadership in the empire began; from the middle of Europe's millennium that leadership seemed to be an accomplished fact, and when the Roman Empire, which had ceased to be really Roman long ago, came to an end, its tradition and the most constructive part of its European destiny were continued almost to the end of the European age by Austria, herself proclaimed an empire only two years before.

In 976 these future developments were impossible to anticipate. But there were already indications of such possibilities which make the historian understand why the reorganization of the Austrian march was so much more important than the creation of the other marches at Germany's eastern border. In the tenth century these latter played a much greater role, but their very names were forgotten in a not too distant future. The only march in the Elbe basin whose destinies are comparable with those of the Austrian, the March of Brandenburg, did not come into existence before the twelfth century, and even this case did not show the unique features of Austria's development and place in European history.

That place was determined to a large extent by the geographical position of Austria at the crossroads of southwestern, southeastern, and northeastern influences, on a river which had its source in the very heart of Germany and its mouth in the Black Sea, leading into areas where Germany proper had no interests at all. Furthermore, Austria originated in a place where not only Teutons and Slavs met, but where both of them had to face the Hungarians, and where the Roman traditions which were completely lacking in the other eastern borderlands of Germany, were very strong. For old Noricum had been a northeastern border province of the real Roman Empire long before it was supposed to serve as a defense of the German one, and it was a direct neighbor both to Italy, the cradle of the western world, and Illyricum, the gate to southeastern Europe.

In that connection it must be pointed out that Vienna, the capital of Austria through the whole millennium of her history, was not only an old Roman settlement which can be traced back to Celtic origins and where in the second century of the preceding millennium the great Emperor Marcus Aurelius resided and died. Recent research has shown that Vienna was also in such close relations with the second Rome that it is possible to speak of Vienna's "Byzantine millennium."[14]

It is, therefore, understandable that the Austrian March, small as it originally was, looked for a specific destiny—a "mission" as it is frequently said—independent of that of Germany to which Alpine Austria remained attached, and even of that of the new Roman or rather German

Empire in which Austria's later extensions never were completely included.

That Austrian destiny was not, as it originally seemed, a watch at the German or imperial frontier, nor an extension of that frontier through conquest of adjacent territories. But it was on the one hand, a share in the defense of the whole community of Christian Europe whenever hostile forces advanced from the East, and on the other hand, peaceful cooperation and cultural exchanges with those eastern, non-German neighbors who were ready to be integrated with that community.

The awareness of such a mission was slow to develop, and its interpretation by Austria's rulers and her people was always to remain controversial. The question as to whether it was a task to be accomplished by Austria as such, as a member of the European community, closer to the Roman center than Germany ever was, or by Austria as part of Germany, tied to her by race and language—that question has never been unanimously answered by the Austrian makers and writers of history. It is inseparable from another question which has to be raised in connection with the millennium, not of Austria in particular but of the Holy Roman Empire as a whole: the question of the real meaning of the renovation of the Western Empire and of its place in European history.

That place was from its promising origin to its disappointing end a central one, not merely in the geographical sense. But was the organization of that empire a constructive contribution to the constitution of all Europe, or only to that of Central Europe, or even exclusively to that of the western, German part of Central Europe? Was the empire really "Holy," as it was to be called for so many centuries, and therefore the body politic representing and leading Christendom, a supranational conception based upon the Christian principles of government? Or was its German character so predominant that it became not only a threat to the other Christian nations but even the most dangerous opponent of papal Rome, without any possibility of cooperation with the other Christian Empire, the Eastern Roman?

The last of these controversial points is important only for the study of the first half of Europe's millennium: until the fall of Constantinople. The others will reappear time and again in the study of the whole course of that millennium. With the interpretation of Austria's millenary destiny these questions regarding the Holy Roman Empire of the German Nation have one thing in common: the answers will always have to take into consideration not only general theories but even more their practical application by the men who represented these political conceptions at the given moment.

While the most appropriate solution of the Austrian problem was not tried before the approaching end of both the Austrian Empire and Europe's millennium, when it was much too late, the clearest and loftiest vision of the role of the restored Roman Empire had appeared in the lifetime of the first generation after that momentous achievement, at the turn of the tenth century. It was never to reappear with similar chances for harmonious imperial as well as papal leadership and of equal opportunities for all European peoples.

Was it perhaps too early for such a program to be envisaged or was it simply the premature disappearance of its authors which made impossible its fulfillment? Before discussing that issue, which is decisive for the interpretation of the heritage of the tenth century, a clear distinction must be made between the situation in the two main parts of Europe which remained outside the Ottonian Empire. Western Europe already had a long historical tradition which through its association with the old Roman Empire had prepared its various lands for their decisive role in the European community of the new millennium. Even there, however, the developments of the tenth century determined the place of the individual nations in that community. Equally important was that eastern Europe was at last constituted in a form which definitely made it share both the Christian and the Graeco-Roman heritage of old Europe, ready to contribute to the progress of the subsequent centuries.

CHAPTER VIII

The Constitution of Western Europe

T HE SIGNIFICANCE OF THE TENTH CENTURY for the final constitution of western Europe[1] can be summed up in the general statement that the origin of practically all nations which were to shape the history of that region in the next ten centuries can be traced back to that remote, apparently confused period. In some cases, the kingdoms which developed into the leading western powers in the course of Europe's millennium were already established in what has been called their "pre-national" form. In other cases the situation in the tenth century explains the difficulties of national unification which continued through a large part, if not the whole of the subsequent millennium.

Typical of the first group of cases is that of France, the "very Christian" kingdom, the "eldest daughter" of the Church, the nation which in spite of its composite ethnic background, largely Celtic and Germanic, was so strongly Romanized that it occupied for a thousand years the leading position in the Latin world. Such a conclusion of the long process which through the preceding ten centuries led "from Gaul to France,"[2] had been prepared, like so many other developments of the tenth, in the Carolingian age. But the West Frankish kingdom which emerged out of the partitions of Charlemagne's empire, was far from including all of the France of the future, and amidst a growing feudal disintegration only part of that kingdom was effectively controlled by the youngest line of the Carolingians, who at the turn of the ninth century, to all practical purposes, lost all real authority. It was not before

987, after the death of the last of them, Louis V, that the election of Hugh Capet (whose ancestors had already been for more than one hundred years "Dukes between Seine and Loire" with Paris as center of their power) marked the beginning of a truly national kingdom,[3] so that the millennium of France might be celebrated on the occasion of the approaching anniversary of that event.

Then began that long line of kings who, in the opinion of the French royalists, "in a thousand years made France." For it was indeed the Capetingian dynasty which under different names ruled that country until Louis "Capet" was deposed in 1792, or rather, with a brief interruption, until 1848; which governed even longer, in consequence of the expansion of French power, in parts of Italy and in Spain; and which survives today in the persons of legal pretenders to the royal crown of France.

Most important for the constitution of Europe was the fact that the founder of that dynasty, after his earlier cooperation with Otto III against one of the last Carolingians, succeeded in obtaining the recognition of his royal title by that emperor. Though in compensation Hugh Capet had to give up his claims to Lorraine and though, in general, his power was still very limited, he avoided any submission to imperial suzerainty. When his dynasty replaced the Carolingians,[4] the tradition of a universal empire of which France would be a constituent part disappeared in that country. France was clearly separated from Germany as a distinct national unit, and was determined to remain outside the new Roman Empire that had been transferred to the German nation. Hugh assured the continuity of his kingship, having his son crowned as successor soon after his own coronation. He thus began the constitution of a hereditary monarchy which never was established in Germany nor in the empire. And later, in successful opposition to universal imperial authority, the Capetingian kings would claim that on French territory they exercised such an imperial authority themselves.

There would even be occasions when their Valois or Bourbon descendants were candidates for the crown of the Holy Roman Empire. But since such candidates had to be elected first as German kings, their choice, which would have given to the empire a truly supranational character, had no better chance than the election of any other truly non-German candidates. What really happened at the time of France's *grand siècle,* the seventeenth, was that France assumed so great a predominance over a divided Germany and a rather fictitious Holy Roman Empire that it seemed that France, though without any imperial title, had taken the place of a Christian Empire, succeeding the German one just as the latter had succeeded the Carolingian.[5]

In any case, the obvious fact that the territory of former Gaul and later France, which had been one of the three constituent parts of the empire of Charlemagne, never could be included in the empire of Otto the Great and his successors, constituted a basic difference between the two. Even with that territory the former had not been really European. Without it, the latter could lay even less claim to universality, were it only in the European sense, though it reached so much farther towards the east.

Next to France, which frequently felt strong enough to compete with the empire on the Continent, there was another western kingdom which remained outside the Holy Roman Empire after having remained outside the Carolingian also, in spite of the temporary conquest of its territory by the ancient Romans. It is clear that in the case of England her situation on the largest of the British Isles—which she would later control in their entirety—was an important geographical factor which helped her to escape a suzerainty which, as a matter of fact, the restored Western Empire never seriously tried to impose upon her. However, her rather isolated, insular history was, on the one hand, not free from temporary invasions by outside, non-imperial powers, which connected her with other parts of Europe but retarded the final constitution of a truly national kingdom. And on the other hand, the origin of that kingdom offers an interesting analogy with that of other European states and of the European community itself.

In the case of England there was, as in the general formation of Europe a preparatory phase of development which transformed the southern part of Britain, the only one where the Roman impact had been really strong, into the powerful England of the European millennium, a country much stronger than Scotland or Ireland, in spite of the particularly impressive tradition of the latter in earlier centuries. And in the English case, too, that preparation was accomplished in the ninth century, though only in its last generation did there appear a prominent ruler, Alfred the Great, who was for England what Charlemagne had been for the western part of the Continent.[6]

There is, however, a rather surprising difference. A ruler who could seem to be a Charlemagne of the whole North, reappeared in England in the first half of the eleventh century, but as a foreign conqueror connecting her with his Scandinavian country of origin. This was Canute the Great of Denmark, under whom the earlier Danish penetration of Britain would apparently turn into a lasting transformation of the island's history and national character. His rule proved, however, in contrast to the Norman conquest which in the second part of that century came from France, only a brief interlude in a development which in the tenth century had already reached such a stage that even the Norman invasion could not destroy England's identity.

For in that same century which proved so decisive for the making of Europe and of most of the European nations, England, too, was made, though no single date of any individual year, similar in importance to that of 987 in the history of France, could be pointed out to serve as basis for a millennium celebration. In any case, the sons and grandsons of Alfred the Great, from Edward at the very beginning to Edgar toward the end of the century, can be considered the first true kings of England.[7] In spite of the continued Viking raids, they succeeded in conquering and absorbing the so-called Danelaw, the Danish settlements among the Anglo-Saxon people, so that only the Celtic fringe in Scotland and Wales remained independent of their kingdom, except, of course, Ireland, which had to suffer particularly from the Norse attacks.

Such a situation was to persist into the following centuries, when the Scandinavian danger had vanished, but even in the tenth it was obvious that England, created through the union of the formerly quarreling small kingdoms in the southern part of Britain, would hold a leading position in the British Isles. Her closeness to the European Continent certainly contributed to that position. But while the cultural ties with the countries across the Channel, which had been established in the preceding millennium through Roman occupation and Christianization, and which reached an early climax at the time of Charlemagne and Alcuin, were never broken, there was no political connection whatever with the Ottonian Empire.[8] More secure in her independence even than France, England was to be, along with that country though frequently in opposition to her, one of the cornerstones of the West, fully integrated with Europe but never with any Continental empire.

Another such cornerstone could have been the Iberian peninsula, which as a whole had already been conquered by the Romans at the time of the Republic and which played an important part in the early centuries of Christendom. But by the eighth century the Muslim conquest had cut off the Spain and Portugal of the future from both Graeco-Roman Europe and the community of free Christian nations, and in spite of the high level of Arab culture,[9] that Asiatic domination was a catastrophe whose consequences can be compared to those of later conquests by Mongols and Turks in the eastern parts of Europe.

The victims never accepted that situation. The *reconquista* was, therefore, the main problem of Spanish and Portuguese history and remained such a problem through the whole first half of Europe's millennium. It was completed only in 1492, after leading to a trend in the preceding century to turn the wars of liberation into an overseas expansion outside Europe. In spite of such a difference of historical development, the history of the Iberian peninsula in what is usually called the Middle Ages had some significant features in common with the contemporaneous history of the rest of Europe.

The dedication of the peoples of that region to Christianity and Latin culture was particularly strong, precisely because of the natural reaction against the alien invaders who were for so long their masters. That special dedication was to continue after liberation when Spain and Portugal at last became free members of the European community. To this well-known fact, a few other considerations must be added, which lead to instructive comparisons with the beginning of Europe's millennium in the other countries.

Though for obvious reasons no Christian power could be constituted south of the Pyrenees either in the ninth or even in the tenth century, the *reconquista* paralleled the making of happier European nations.[10] In this case so different from the others there also was a preparatory phase initiated by Charlemagne and a definite start, followed in unbroken continuity through the tenth century, particularly at its turn, so that the millennium problem reappears even in Iberian history.

Christian resistance was, of course, easiest to organize in the northern borderlands of the peninsula. Even in the eighth century, a Christian kingdom of the Asturias was created in the northwestern corner out of what remained of Visigothic power. But before that petty state was extended under the name of Leon, Charlemagne crossed the Pyrenees well before his imperial coronation, and in spite of the legendary defeat of his rearguard at Roncesvalles in 778, immortalized by the *Song of Roland,* finally established his Spanish March, in the northeastern corner of the peninsula, in Catalonia. It survived after the emperor's death as the County of Barcelona.

In that same preparatory period there emerged between these two Christian strongholds, in the land of the Basques, the kingdom of Navarre, defending itself against Arabs and Franks alike, so that in the tenth century the whole northern belt of Spain was independent. But only at the end of that century, around the year 1000, did a trend begin towards unification of the territories held by the Christians, chiefly thanks to Sancho Garcia the Great of Navarre. The tide definitely turned two years later, when the famous Moslem leader Al-Mansur died, after exercising the real power under one of the last and weakest Omayad caliphs and temporarily checking the Christian advance. Under their new dynasties, the Arabs were no longer able to resist the pressure of the Christian kingdoms, and though disunion retarded the final liberation, the heroic struggles of the founders of future Portugal and Spain were to be a valuable contribution to the rise of Europe in the first centuries of her millennium.

The achievements of Sancho the Great, which deserve to be commemorated after a thousand years, encouraged him to assume the title of *imperator Iberorum*. Though premature, that title suggests another analogy between these early beginnings of Spanish power and the attitude of the other west European kingdoms. It appears clear that even the smallest and youngest of those kingdoms desperately fighting against the Asiatic Mohammedan conquerors wanted at the same time to be fully independent from, and even equal to, the restored Roman Empire. That empire was so far away from the Iberian battlefields that it could not possibly bring any assistance to the Christians who tried so hard to regain the control of southwestern Europe. Therefore the German emperors could not pretend to exercise there any kind of suzerainty. On the contrary, the imperial title was to reappear in the eleventh and twelfth centuries in the kingdom of Castile, then the leader of the peninsula and anxious to gain equality not only with the declining caliphate of the Almoravids but with any Christian empire as well.[11]

That imperial claim proved impossible to maintain, but it left behind a tradition which perhaps explains why in the century following the ultimate reconquest and unification of Spain, a Spanish king, though of German origin, was elected Roman emperor and came nearer than any of his predecessors and successors to creating a universal empire. In the tenth century such ambitious dreams of a distant future could not possibly be anticipated, but even then, when the Spanish rise to power was only starting, it contributed to the awareness that the constitution of western Europe was to be achieved through the establishment of national kingdoms, all of which remained outside the restored Western Empire and survived after its final fall.

There arises, however, the question whether Italy, the central of the three south European peninsulas, the very cradle of western Latin culture and consequently inseparable from France and Spain, was not a glaring exception, since a united, national kingdom of Italy was established only in the last century of Europe's millennium. In the tenth century, when that millennium started, conditions in Italy were, on the contrary, more confused and chaotic than in any other part of Europe, and it could seem paradoxical to speak of any Italian millennium, comparable to those of so many other European nations.

Yet, even in Italy the tenth century was, no less than elsewhere, a decisive period of transition; and its study—in which Italian historiography is now particularly interested[12]—helps to understand the political destinies of that country up to the present. What happened there a thousand years ago explains, first, why in spite of the geographical unity of the peninsula and in spite of a political unification achieved by the Roman Republic in the first phase of its Mediterranean expansion, no similar unification on national grounds succeeded before the nineteenth century; why, in particular, there developed such a contrast between northern and southern Italy, significant even today; and why internal divisions opened the door to foreign invasions which proved hardly less disastrous in modern times than during the barbarian migrations.

Furthermore, what happened in Italy immediately before and after the renovation of the empire in 962, helps the historian understand why even that country, which to a large extent, though never as a whole, was included in that empire, was never fully integrated with its transalpine part. Although it would seem that the Holy Roman Empire of the German Nation was a union of Italy with Germany,[13] the Italian resistance against German interference and supremacy, starting immediately, always remained so strong that it diverted the attention of the emperors from their objectives as German kings, particularly in the East, and proved more than anything else that even in the West the universal, supranational character of the empire was merely a fiction.

The Carolingian antecedents of the events of the tenth century are instructive also in the Italian case. Charlemagne himself never gained control of the whole peninsula, and its southern part, where the cultural tradition of ancient *Magna Graecia* was so persistent, continued to belong to the Eastern Empire. Even the northern part was so clearly distinct from the rest of the Frankish Empire, that its founder had to create separate kings of Italy, chosen from among his descendants. Later in the ninth century it seemed indeed as if a united Italian kingdom, at least north of the Papal State, would emerge out of the divisions of Charlemagne's heritage. The strange connection of Italy with the belt between the West Frankish and East Frankish kingdoms, so striking in the division of 843, could not possibly last, and that of 870 clearly recognized Italy as a separate unit which, however, proved impossible to consolidate.

As a matter of fact, all that followed soon afterwards and continued into the tenth century was, unfortunately, something entirely different, and made that crucial century typical of what was to be Italy's tragic destiny throughout almost the whole millennium of Europe. On the one hand, there were repeated attempts in line with the Carolingian tradition, to connect parts, at least, of what was time and again called the Italian kingdom, with either the West Frankish or the East Frankish successor-states of Charlemagne's empire, attempts which merely contributed to the troubles and divisions in the peninsula. On the other hand, the rather exceptional local initiatives to create a kingdom of Italy as a nucleus of national unification, similar to what was beginning to materialize in France, England, and Spain, were completely unsuccessful.

While Rome was suffering from the quarrels among her aristocracy, and Sicily from the Arab invasion which threatened Byzantine rule in southern Italy, there appeared in the north an ephemeral Italian kingdom, though under Burgundian influence. Its last ruler, Berengar of Ivrea, was crowned king at Pavia right at mid-century, in 950, but by the following year his place was taken by Otto I, who united the Italian with his German kingdom. That artificial union which created the basis for the association of Italy and Germany in a restored Roman Empire under German leadership, was both far from being a satisfactory solution of the Italian problem and far from achieving Italian unity. In spite of the three Italian expeditions of Otto I, whose example was followed by Otto II, neither the emperors themselves, who made only temporary appearances south of the Alps, nor the *patricii* who were supposed to exercise supreme authority on their behalf, were able to control Rome, and even less to liberate southern Italy from the Arab danger, handicapped as they were by their troubles with the Papacy and their rivalry with the Eastern Empire.

It was, therefore, a truly problematic heritage which was left to Otto III, who was ready to grant Italy a position within the Western Empire equal to that of Germany. But even the title of the Italian kingdom had practically vanished before the appearance of that truly exceptional ruler, and never was his imperial power solidly established nor extended over the whole peninsula. The difficulties which Otto III encountered in Italy were one of the main obstacles to the carrying out of his constructive European program. If that program had materialized, there could have started "a new chapter, perhaps the first chapter of Italian history."[14] Since it failed, it seemed at the turn of the tenth century—a century no less decisive for the Italians than for the other peoples of Europe —that Italy was just a "geographical expression," as she was called at the beginning of the nineteenth. That this was not changed before the second part of the latter century was indeed a great misfortune not only for the Italian people but for Europe as a whole, whose normal development was to suffer for almost a thousand years from the abnormal political situation in one of Europe's most important constituent parts.

In that same tenth century it became apparent that notwithstanding some obvious responsibilities of the Italians themselves, the tragedy was not primarily the fault of the great nation which amidst all political crises never ceased to make outstanding contributions to European culture. On the contrary, the main responsibility rests with those foreign powers which continuously interfered with Italian problems. These interferences came chiefly from Germany, as in the past centuries of the great migrations, before and after the *translatio imperii,* which in the middle of the tenth century gave such an impressive sanction to her claims. However, early traces can be uncovered of interferences in Italian affairs by other Romance peoples, who in the later part of Europe's millennium would compete with the Germans in these affairs. Especially after the consolidation and unification of France and Spain, both of these nations would contribute, along with the empire, toward making Italy a quasi-permanent battlefield and preventing her unification.

Another obstacle to that unification, indeed, was the development of small Italian states with their own policies, sometimes leading the defense against foreign invaders, but never strong enough to make such invasions impossible and even less to unite a free Italy under the leadership of one of these local powers. Two of those whose role was to be particularly significant in the course of the following centuries were consolidated by the end of the tenth, which once more appears as a decisive turn in Italian history. These two powers, exceptionally important for European history as a whole, were the Papal States and the Republic of Venice. Very different from each other in many respects, they shared a historical continuity which was lacking in the case of the other, much younger Italian states. In the case of the Papal States it was to last until 1870,[15] reappearing in a modified form toward the end of the millennium of Europe; in the case of Venice, until 1797, leaving behind a proud tradition.

As a sovereign power with its own territory and administration, the Papacy has to be clearly distinguished from the See of Peter, the center of the Catholic Church. The latter was and is by definition universal and supranational, a power of purely spiritual character, while the *patrimonium sancti Petri,* as the Papal States were formerly known, was not only a guarantor of the pope's independence, but especially at the time of its largest extension was similar to other states. Being of purely Italian character, that state was necessarily involved in the policies of the peninsula which it practically cut in two.

The secular power of the popes, established in the very center of Italy, in her traditional capital, had manifested itself from time to time in earlier centuries, before the popes claimed any territory outside that city which they frequently defended against foreign conquerors. The emergence of the Papal State in Carolingian times, based on imaginary legal grounds like the *donatio Constantini* and on the recognition by Pepin the Brief and his successors, did not immediately contribute to the real political power and independence of the Papacy and did not prevent the decline of papal prestige in the tenth century. But in spite of that crisis, which affected both the religious life of the Church and the possibilities of papal influence in secular matters—even in local and Italian affairs— Pope John XIII (965-972) could reassert papal authority in all these matters.[16] And at the end of the century, with the pontificate of Sylvester II starting in 997, came a decisive turn which proved of lasting importance for the whole of Europe and is intimately connected with her millennium. Independently of the success or failure of any specific political initiative like that of Sylvester himself, the state of which Rome was the capital, which at the same time was the spiritual capital of all Christendom, was to remain, small as it was, a real power whose policy was to affect in particular the destinies of all Italy in the midst of her apparently hopeless division.

The same may be said of Venice and again it was at the end of the tenth century that her future role could be anticipated after a rather long preparatory phase. As a body politic, Venice was indeed older than the Papal State, but even more than the other it was a city-state only, slowly emerging on a few tiny islands far from Italy's center, at the distant northeastern corner of the peninsula. If the Papal State was originally dependent on the foreign dynasties which in two steps restored the Western Empire, Venice, before she was definitely constituted as the independent Republic of Saint Marc, was under the authority of the Eastern Empire, being the most distant of its Italian outposts. With no spiritual authority behind her, the economically rising city, with its strange patrician constitution, was throughout the first centuries of its development in such a precarious position that it would have been difficult to foresee that it would serve, along with Rome but in a different way, the cause of Italian freedom, and more than Rome, form a link between western and eastern Europe. However, in the course of the tenth century, Venice, thanks to a series of prominent doges,[17] succeeded without any spectacular change in her situation in consolidating her power to such an extent that it attained the eastern shore of the Adriatic Sea, the sea which the republic would later consider its unquestionable sphere of interest, long before Italy as a whole had such ambitions. At the same time the rivalry began between the Venetians and any other powers—then the kingdom of Croatia—which would challenge these claims, especially as far as the Dalmatian coast was concerned. That rivalry was to be a permanent feature of the history of one of Europe's important areas of transition, an obstacle to that otherwise desirable cooperation of the Italians with the southern Slavs and Hungarians. The tension between Venice and Byzantium, from whose control the republic wanted to liberate itself without any formal break that would be harmful to its economic interests, lasted much longer than what seemed decisive in the tenth century. That same rivalry with the immediate eastern neighbors was to be combined with a permanent Venetian distrust of the Western Empire and its German rulers.

This was and remained one more reason why even a divided Italy could never be fully controlled by, nor really integrated with that empire. And yet that country was the only one in the whole western part of Europe where such claims of the imperial power—established and recognized by Rome in 962—had any chance of success. Otherwise the constitution of western Europe, as it emerged from the crisis of the later Carolingian period and as it was shaped in the tenth century, was creating an entirely different basis for the further evolution of the European community. It was decided by that time that throughout Christian Europe's millennium there would remain western kingdoms of rising power, overcoming the feudal divisions of their territories, integrating these territories into fully sovereign nation-states, and frequently strong enough to oppose or even to replace the imperial authority in parts of Italy.

All this was not too surprising since the non-German peoples of western Europe represented older traditions, both culturally and politically, and in both respects had better claims to the Roman heritage than the German tribes, which were even less united as a real nation than their western neighbors. Also the Christian heritage of Europe, the most important one, was much older and better developed in the western and southern countries than in Germany. However, thanks to her geographical situation, Germany could claim the mission not only to defend the eastern border of Christian Europe, as the southwestern countries defended the border against the Arabs, and as the Byzantine Empire was doing both, but also to integrate with Christendom and western culture the vast areas of northeastern Europe which had just been opened to Christian and western influence.

There appeared, therefore, in the tenth century the decisive question whether the young peoples of these areas, entering at last the common course of European history, would be able to achieve what had been so much easier and natural for those of western Europe: to build up a constitution of the whole region east of Germany and north of the Byzantine Empire, which would give them an opportunity for free development. The answer which was given to that question a thousand years ago is another evidence of the basic importance of the tenth century, since it determined the forthcoming evolution of Europe's millennium in a region which proved to be the real line of defense for the whole Continent and for Christendom.

CHAPTER IX

The Constitution of Eastern Europe

IN THE HISTORICAL TRADITION of the East European nations, the millennium idea, evoking their origin in the tenth century, occupies a much more important place than in the western tradition, in which even dates like 962 or 987 do not always receive similar attention. That difference is, of course, quite understandable. In the history of western Europe earlier traditions, leading back to the first millennium of the Christian era, prior to the final constitution of the European community, preserved their vital meaning, so that even the most significant events of the tenth century are considered only turning points and not really beginnings of national history. And as far as the peoples of northern Europe are concerned, their integration with Christian Europe, though certainly not achieved earlier than that of eastern Europe, was such a gradual process that in spite of the decisive progress accomplished in the tenth century, hardly any specific dates of that century could be commemorated. For all these reasons it is instructive to point out the lasting significance of the dates which have been or will be recalled in the millennium celebrations of the three leading nations which emerged east of Germany and of the restored Western Empire: Poland, Hungary, and Russia—or rather Kievan Rus'.[1]

In the case of Poland the unique importance of what happened in 966 has never been questioned before the present Marxist impact on Polish historiography. Until recently, all that happened before the Christianization of that year was considered legendary prehistory, and only the amazing discoveries of archeological research permits us to trace the origin of the Polish state far back into earlier centuries. The Hungarians have celebrated the millennium of 896, considering the settlement of their ancestors in the Danubian plain the beginning of their national history, after the long migrations of the Hungarian tribes from their Asiatic homeland to the center of Europe. In imperial Russia, 862, the date of the calling of Rurik's Norsemen by the Slavs of the Novgorod region, according to the Primary Russian Chronicle, was interpreted after a thousand years as the beginning of the Russian state and nation, whose uninterrupted continuity through the Kievan and Muscovite to the Petersburg period was the basic conception of modern Great Russian nationalism. Without discussing here that controversial conception, it can be admitted that the years around that date were, in the history of the eastern Slavs, a turn from tribal existence to a nascent political organization.

However, in both the Hungarian and the Russian cases, different in that respect from the Polish, another date, leading into the middle of the tenth century and coming soon after 966, is rightly considered a much more important turning point, since it made the early pagan creations of Árpád or Rurik a Christian state with a culture which favored the national development of their peoples. Though the exact date of Hungary's Christianization can hardly be determined, that great event which so rapidly changed Asiatic invaders into defenders of the Latin West occurred somewhere in the 970's. Therefore, it took place between the two dates which can be given for the Christianization of Kievan Rus': the first one, 956, though it has been commemorated in due course a thousand years later, is only the approximate date of a first attempt which did not materialize; 988, the year of the final conversion of both the ruling dynasty and the peoples, was celebrated at the nine hundred and fifty-year mark, and certainly will receive attention at the millennium date even in the present situation which makes it so difficult to emphasize the old Christian tradition of the eastern Slavs.

In any case, these considerations clearly confirm that in the light of the individual national histories the inclusion of northeastern Europe in the European community was, in its final and lasting form, the result of the expansion of Christianity and of its culture far into that whole new area. This becomes even more evident if before studying in greater detail the significance of the Polish, the Hungarian, and the Kievan millennium, we examine the role of a Slavic people who were already Christian at the beginning of the tenth century, and played a particularly significant role as a link between western Europe, specifically its German section, and predominantly Slavic eastern Europe. This is the problem of Bohemia, which also deserves attention as the only Slavic successor-state of Greater Moravia, and therefore a link between the preparatory developments of the ninth century and the achievements of the tenth.

Even at the time of the Moravian state the Czechs felt obliged to enter into close relations with the East Frankish Kingdom, and their Christianization was largely a result of German missions and pressures. After the fall of Greater Moravia, such a policy proved even more necessary for a small people which was seemingly protected by its surrounding mountain ranges, but was being politically divided by the rivalry between the Přemyslid and Slavnik dynasties. The consequence was not only an ecclesiastical dependence on Germany which was to last until the middle of the fourteenth century and certainly contributed to the gradual disappearance of the Slavic liturgy, but also the recognition of German political supremacy. And most important was the fact that such an overlordship was established even before the German kings were made Roman Emperors.

Nevertheless, in addition to the consolidation of Christianity in Bohemia, it proved possible to develop her political power also. The first of these achievements was particularly spectacular under Duke Václav I, who became the patron saint of the Czechs and whose crown, though not yet a royal one, remained a symbol of Bohemian statehood for the next ten centuries. This tradition survived, therefore, until the present, although in the very middle of that period another national tradition, very different from the first, originated in connection with the Hussite revolution. After Václav's assassination in 929, a date so memorable that it approaches most closely the significance of a Czech millennium,[2] his brother and successor Boleslav I, while continuing Václav's cautious attitude toward Germany, achieved an extraordinary extension of Bohemia, reaching through southern Poland (where even Cracow came temporarily under Czech rule) to the border of Kievan Rus'. Such a territorial expansion did not last, but relations between the Czechs, the most western of all Slavs, with the eastern Slavs who never were a danger to them, continued through all the changes in the political structure of the Slavic world and were to be another permanent feature of Czech history during practically all of Europe's millennium.[3]

Hardly less surprising were two other aspects of Bohemia's history in the tenth century. In spite of the territorial controversies with Poland which were not setttled before the end of that century and even then did not disappear at least as far as Silesia was concerned, Czech-Polish relations were quite frequently so friendly that Bohemia contributed greatly to the Christianization of the Slavic neighbor country[4] which indeed preferred such an intermediary to that of the Germans. Furthermore, there was also a Czech contribution to the Christianization of Hungary, although in general the relations between the two countries were rather poor and remained so through most of the following centuries. In both cases the rapprochement was mainly achieved thanks to one man, probably the greatest Slav of his age. He was one of the few remaining Slavniks, an opponent of the Přemyslid leaders of the Czechs, and eventually an exile from Bohemia: Saint Adalbert, whose role in history was truly universal in the Christian and European sense, and whose memory was to inspire the vision of the year 1000.

But before the turn of the century there appeared both analogies and contrasts in Polish and Czech policies with regard to the all-important German problem, the different antecedents leading to different results. In view of the special difficulties of the Czech situation, it was remarkable anyway that Bohemia became a privileged part of the western, practically German Empire, that she preserved in that connection her Slavic character, and thus introduced into that empire a comparatively strong non-German element. However, the attitude towards the Germans who settled in larger numbers on Bohemian territory was to remain the main problem in the internal history of the Czechs,[5] much more so than in that of the Poles. The cooperation of the two Slavic peoples in these vital matters never succeeded completely, and even less successful were the various atttempts at creating a common Czech-Polish state. And neither of the two succeeded in cooperating with the Slavic tribes between the Elbe and Oder rivers, their closest kin and neighbors, whose long struggle against the German conquerors was hopeless because they definitely rejected Christianization. Only a small group of Lusatians is surviving after a thousand years.

Taking advantage of their experience as well as that of the Czechs, Poland worked out her own more satisfactory solution of the common problem, achieving full integration with Christian Europe without any integration with Germany.[6] In the case of the Poles, too, the task was not an easy one, and it is hardly an exaggeration to stress that in their history, too, there was a struggle of a thousand years against various forms of German aggression, penetration, and influence.[7] The first clash in Polish-German relations which has been recorded by contemporary sources occurred as early as 963, a date very near to that of the Christianization in 966. Both events are intimately connected. The defeat suffered at the hands of an isolated German adventurer was a serious warning that it was dangerous to delay giving up their paganism, which in all similar cases served as pretext for German conquest. But there was an even more important reason for taking that decision in these very years. More than by the frontier incident of 963, the Christianization of 966 was influenced by the restoration of the Western Empire in 962. Since the Poles, who despite their open frontiers had a better position in the very center of the Slavic world than the Czechs, had not recognized any German overlordship before, they could now take advantage of Otto I's new dignity by continuing to reject the authority of the German king and trying instead to determine their relations with the Roman emperor.

It was fortunate for them that at the time of Otto the Great they, too, had a ruler of real greatness, Mieszko I, the first member of the native Piast dynasty to escape the status of a legendary figure and whose heritage, developed by his even greater son and successor, was to be the solid foundation of Poland's destiny during the whole millennium of her historical evolution. Contrary to present misinterpretations,[8] the most valuable part of that heritage was and is the Christian faith. He accepted it spontaneously for himself and for his people, not in order to strengthen the feudal structure of state and society, which, as a matter of fact, never appeared in Poland in the real meaning of that term, nor for the sake of his personal authority, which in 966 was already so strong that a foreign traveler who visited Poland in that very year described Mieszko's state as the greatest power among the Slavs. As in all similar cases, the purely religious motives of his conversion, probably under the influence of his Catholic Czech wife, should not be underestimated. But even if the political reasons, so much easier to study, are stressed, they cannot be limited to the expediency which was dictated by the German danger. Mieszko must have been fully aware that without being Christianized, his state, powerful as it was, could not enter as a rightful member the community of Christian nations which was being formed in Europe, and this in turn was connected with the cultural advantages which the new faith was bringing to the Poles.

The question can be asked why Catholicism was not introduced in its Slavic liturgical form, which, according to recent research,[9] had been

spreading quite successfully in Poland, and which certainly had prepared the country for the decision of its ruler. But Mieszko had good
reasons for favoring the Latin rite: the official recognition of the Slavic
rite would hardly have removed the religious difficulties in dealing with
the Germans, but would have created troubles similar to those experienced before by the Moravian state; it would not have completely ended
Poland's isolation from which she had suffered in pagan days; and furthermore, the Czech experience proved that a culture that was simultaneously Slavic in its essence and Latin in its expression could develop very
well. In the Polish case this was to prove even more true, and throughout
the next ten centuries Latin Catholicism was to be the most essential
component of a national tradition based upon Mieszko's great decision.

His other achievements were to be no less typical of the whole Polish
millennium, and foreshadowed the permanent problems of Christian
Poland's future. One of them, inseparable from the German problem
which had appeared in pagan days, was the Baltic question which in
that connection seems to have received much of Mieszko's attention.
Trying to join the closely related Pomeranians with the Polish tribes
which were already under his rule, and thus to gain an access to the sea,
he had to face the opposition not only of the Germans advancing in the
same direction, but also of the Danes who had established their stronghold at the mouth of the Oder.[10] In general, the relations with Scandinavia, which were to be so important in many phases of Poland's history,
started under her first Christian ruler. There is no serious argument in
favor of the hypothesis of his own Norman origin,[11] but he established
matrimonial ties between the Scandinavian dynasties and the Polish
Piasts, and took advantage of lively trade relations with the northern
countries. To the Germans or rather to the empire he made the concession of paying a tribute from his new acquisitions north of Poland's original nucleus in the basin of the Warta. However, the whole area along
the Baltic coast from Szczecin to Gdańsk was included in the realm
which he kept independent from Germany, acting as "friend of the Emperor" and even trying to interfere with the succession troubles after
Otto I and II. Therefore, while avoiding a challenge of his much
stronger western neighbor, he established a tradition in Polish relations
with the Germans and the empire which would be a lasting element of
Polish policies in the centuries to come.[12]

Mieszko I was less successful in the East, being the first of Poland's
rulers to experience the difficulty of dealing at the same time with dan-

gers from two sides. The endless discussions regarding the statement of the Primary Chronicle that in 981 Vladimir of Kiev marched against the Poles and took their castles on the upper San and Bug, have failed to determine whether that border region of the Polish homeland belonged to Mieszko's state. In any case, he did not prevent its conquest by the eastern neighbors of the Poles, and there started a serious territorial dispute between the two peoples which was to affect their relations up to the present. The issue is connected with the question whether the Cracow region, the "little Poland" of the future, was retaken from the Czechs before or after Mieszko's death, in 992. The document which describes the frontiers of his realm towards the end of his reign merely says that they reached as far as Cracow, but it seems probable that they included the city and its area.[13]

That document whose summary, made by the papal chancery in the eleventh century, starts with the enigmatic words *Dagome iudex*—obviously a distortion of *ego Mesco dux*—has raised even more controversial questions[14] which never will be fully decided, since the correct original text is lost. There is, however, no doubt that the charter was a donation of Mieszko's Poland to the see of Peter and therefore was studied in Rome when under Gregory VII all claims of the Papacy were reviewed. The concrete importance of that donation has been questioned on the assumption that it was soon forgotten in Poland and was of no use to her in view of the weakness of the Papacy at the time of John XV to whom the document was addressed. However, as to the first of these doubts, it must be pointed out that the tradition of Mieszko's step must have inspired a similar donation made by another Polish duke early in the thirteenth century, at the time of Innocent III, and that even later the payment of Saint Peter's pence in all Polish lands—an argument used whenever the possession of one of these lands was in danger—must be explained by the relations established with the Holy See in the tenth century. The belief even survived that such a payment was the price for the papal decision which made the duke of Poland a king.[15] This was not so, but a royal crown was certainly the goal of Mieszko, who, turning to Rome, anticipated that in the future the Papacy could be the strongest support of Poland's integrity and independence whenever it was threatened by the empire, the leading secular power in Christendom, against which only the leading spiritual power could offer efficient assistance. After a brief interlude around the year 1000, when another solution of that problem seemed possible, it very soon became clear and remained clear for many centuries that what Mieszko had foreseen was, thanks to the rapid rise of papal might, the only sound basis for the policy of the Polish kingdom in the future.

In that respect, as in many others, a comparative study of the Polish and the Hungarian situations is highly instructive for the understanding of East European and even general European history.[16] First, however, the obvious differences in the respective situations must be considered. For the Hungarians the integration with the Latin West was much more difficult than for the Poles, yet it was achieved almost simultaneously. While the Poles had lived in their homeland from time immemorial, the Hungarians had first to consolidate the possession of the foreign land which they occupied around 896, pushing back the original Slavic population, a process which resulted in a lasting tension. Definitely hostile were the relations of the newcomers with their western neighbors, who had to suffer from their incursions until the hard lesson of the defeats inflicted upon the Hungarians by the Germans shortly before the re-establishment of the Western Empire made them aware of the necessity to change their policy completely and to adapt their way of life to that of their former enemies. That wise decision carried out in the second half of the tenth century gave to the Hungarian millennium its real and lasting meaning, making it part of the millennium of Europe.

Just like the Poles, the Hungarians were quick to realize the paramount importance of their conversion to Christianity, the only difference being that they hesitated for quite a time, not simply between two liturgies of which the Slavic could not possibly appeal to them, but between Western and Eastern Christendom, Latin and Greek. While for Poland Byzantium was a hardly known, faraway power, for Hungary the Eastern Empire was another neighbor whose influence seemed as it had seemed earlier to the Moravian state, less dangerous than that of the Western. It was Géza, whose place in Hungarian history is similar to that of Mieszko in the Polish, who in contrast to other leaders who had turned toward Constantinople, took the opposite decision which eventually made Hungary a strongly Latinized country.[17] One of the reasons might have been the struggle which Byzantium, at the turn of the tenth century, had to conduct with the Bulgarians and could not conclude victoriously before the second decade of the eleventh. At the very time when direct contacts with Constantinople were therefore rather difficult, Hungary, following the Polish example, succeeded in appeasing the Germans by spontaneously accepting Latin Christianity and in avoiding any recognition of imperial and even less of German suzerainty. This happened precisely in the years when the eastern march, the Austria of the future, was definitely established, mainly as an outpost against the Hungarians. However, unlike the aggressive marches north of Bohemia, that defensive creation under the Babenberg was not intended as a base for advances by the Germans, who were perhaps considering the possibility of playing off the Hungarians against the Slavic populations of the Danubian region. Also, the Germans seemed more interested in extending the eastern march in the southern direction, into Slovene territory.

Furthermore, it was obvious that the Pannonian plain could hardly be brought under German control as long as Croatia in the south and Poland in the north were independent. The relations with these two countries were, therefore, of great importance for Hungary's future. Croatia, which in the ninth century had been seriously threatened by the East Frankish Kingdom, was now, in the tenth, a well-established Catholic kingdom herself, which under Tomislav had received from the Holy See a royal crown in the year 925, the date of the Croat millennium.[18] Situated in the old transition region, the Illyricum, long an object of controversy between the Western and the Eastern Empire, Croatia, with her access to the Adriatic Sea, had a good chance of remaining free from either of them, though under strong Latin influence in contrast to landlocked and less developed Serbia, and in spite of a survival of Slavic liturgy which among the Croats lasted much longer than among the Poles or even the Czechs. Croatia had this Latin impact in common with Hungary, so that by the tenth century the conditions were established for the future connection between the two countries, united a hundred years later, the more so because Croatia's relations with her Latin neighbor in the West, the Republic of Venice, rapidly deteriorated after the turn of the century.

No less natural was the rapprochement between Hungary and Poland which was achieved even earlier, though except for short periods in much later centuries it did not take the form of a union. Separated by the Carpathian mountains or rather, in those early days, by the wilderness of that forest belt, the two countries had no controversial boundary problems, though Poland temporarily penetrated into Slovakia, which soon was to be absorbed by Hungary for almost a thousand years. At the time of Mieszko and Géza there was most probably a matrimonial alliance between the two dynasties.[19] And in addition to a similar attitude in relations with Germany and the empire, the two countries in the center of East Central Europe, converted almost simultaneously, had the same desire to gain the protection of the Holy See through a donation to Saint Peter—which however in Hungary came somewhat later with less conspicuous consequences[20]—and to obtain in that connection a royal crown, like Croatia. All three of them had a similar situation at the border of the Latin West, in spite of their ethnic differences, and therefore were to play in the future an important part in its defense and the spread of its influence. Nobody understood this better than Géza's greater son Vajk, baptized under the name of Stephen soon after his father. Stephen succeeded Géza a few years before Mieszko's place in Poland was taken by Bolesław I. Hungary's future patron saint, who realized his nation had to be a multinational state, was well prepared to contribute along with his Polish contemporary to the final constitution of an eastern Europe fully integrated with Western Christendom.

Such an integration did not necessarily imply any hostility against Eastern Christendom at a time when there was not yet any open break between Rome and Constantinople. Croats and Serbs, those close kin who later were so deeply separated by their religious orientations, were still far from being opposed to each other, and Hungary and Poland both found it in their own interests that pagan peoples in their eastern neighborhood be converted to their own new faith, were it even by the Greek patriarchate and not the Latin. This was particularly true for the Poles, who, after having been quite recently attacked by Vladimir of Kiev when he was still a heathen, later had peaceful relations with him and the East Slavic tribes under his rule, not too different after all from the Polish tribes. It was rather to Poland's advantage that such a conversion was not achieved through cooperation with Germany, as at a given moment, before the Poles were converted themselves, Vladimir's grandmother had planned it. For such a cooperation could easily have led to that encirclement of Poland by her western and eastern neighbors which would so often threaten her in later centuries.

We may very well doubt the Primary Chronicle story that Vladimir himself, when the Christianization of his large but rather isolated state appeared urgent, considered the possibility of accepting the faith and liturgy of the Latins or even to introduce Mohammedanism, the greatest danger for his western neighbors. It is, on the contrary, well established today[21] that in spite of contacts between Kiev and Rome even after 988, Rus' received Christianity from Byzantium, the participation of the Bulgarian Church, competing with Constantinople in connection with the political struggle, being quite uncertain. Not only some details of Vladimir's relations with Emperor Basil II at the time of his conversion remain controversial, but basic questions regarding the lasting impact of Byzantium on the history of the eastern Slavs can be disputed. And most of these problems are of vital importance for the formation of Europe and for the interpretation of her millennium.

Among the various reasons for disagreement between Kiev and Constantinople (which delayed Vladimir's baptism wherever it took place, as well as his marriage to a Greek princess), the dispute over the possession of Kherson on the coast of the Black Sea was of the deepest significance. It was indeed part of the problem whether that coast would be permanently reached and controlled by the rising power of East Central Europe.[22] The fact that neither the Kievan state nor its Lithuanian and Polish successors ever fully succeeded in that respect influenced the whole situation until the advance of the Russian Empire in the last two centuries. The problem was crucial for the whole of Europe all the time, because it was never exclusively—and soon ceased to be entirely—a question whether Byzantium would keep the outposts of ancient Greek colonization north of the Black Sea. The main question was whether and when, and for which European power, it would be possible to close the gateway which along that sea was leading one Asiatic invader after the other far into European territory. All those who, beginning with Kievan Rus', tried to oppose the invaders rendered valuable services to the West where thanks to them the common enemy could not penetrate. But it was a serious handicap for their own normal development, and in the case of the Kievan state was the decisive cause of its fall after the first quarter of the millennium following its conversion.

More than the initial territorial rivalries, the great distance between Kiev—to say nothing of Novgorod—and Constantinople, as well as the great difficulty of communicating through any land route, made impossible any closer political association between the two powers, which otherwise could have led to some kind of political control of the comparatively new and much less developed state by the old and glorious empire.[23] However, a lasting influence of Byzantium on the future development of northeastern Europe in the institutional and cultural, and particularly the religious field, was not only possible but fully materialized, the only controversial note being the degree of that influence in the various periods of East European history and in the various parts of an extremely vast region, still expanding through a continuous process of eastern colonization.

Thus, for example, the influence of Byzantine autocracy cannot completely nor exclusively explain the despotism which in Moscow and in the modern Russian Empire reached such a climax, thanks to various other factors appearing at the time of the decline and fall of Byzantium. But already in Kievan Rus' the impact of the Eastern Roman Empire decisively contributed to the consolidation of the power of the Grand Princes, who for two centuries remained in contact with the Macedonian dynasty and that of the Comneni. Yet the authority of Kiev and the unity of what has been significantly called the Kievan federation[24] would probably not have lasted even this long, if the influence of the Byzantine Church had not been added to that of the empire. Much more than in the case of Poland or Hungary, Christianization contributed to the consolidation and unification of the Kievan state, where indeed such a contribution was needed more than anywhere else. For that state, by far the largest in Europe and with a past of over a century, was more heterogeneous than any other in Europe, held together only by a dynasty of foreign origin whose members were continuously quarreling with each other.

That statement leads to two particularly controversial questions.[25] That the descendants of Rurik were of Norse ancestry cannot be denied, but the so-called anti-Normanist school in past and present historiography considers them, along with their Varangian followers, practically Slavicized by the end of the tenth century, and tries to show that long before that a native tradition of political organization existed among the East Slavic tribes. However, even if some of these tribes formed some kind of federation in earlier centuries, it was only under Norman leadership that a durable state was created which gradually included all the tribes enumerated by the Primary Russian Chronicle and gave to the area thus united the name of "the land of Rus'."

Controversial, too, is the origin of the name "Rus' " which originally, contrary to the various hypotheses of the anti-Normanists, seems to have designated the Norse Varangians only, and then the territories and peoples controlled by them, first the region of Novgorod and later that around Kiev. To translate it as "Russia" is misleading, although that name appeared in the Latin sources, because in modern times Russia became the designation of the empire created by the Great Russian people, a nation formed in the course of long centuries by the descendants of some of the northeastern tribes of old Rus' and by the originally Finnish population of the vast area colonized by these tribes. There were already tribes of Finnish, Baltic, Turkish and even—as pointed out by the chronicler—Polish origin among those which in the tenth century were included in Rus', but most of them belonged to the two groups of eastern Slavs, distinct from the Great Russian, which for a long time were jointly called Ruthenians, and now Ukrainians and Byelorussians or White Ruthenians.

To clarify these confusing questions of terminology is basic for the understanding of the whole course of East European history up to the present, as well as for the conditions at the time of Vladimir's conversion. It is impossible to accept the view that then all the peoples of Kievan Rus' were one "Russian" nation, differentiated only much later into three groups. But the conversion of all of them in one Church under one metropolitan residing in Kiev, though that see was probably established only fifty years later, gave to the Kievan state an element of unity which was to survive amidst all the dynastic divisions, and to the very name Rus' a lasting extension, including even the territories which the rulers of Kiev no longer directly controlled.

The political and cultural unification—the former only temporary, the latter permanent—of such a Rus' has introduced into eastern Europe, now almost completely converted to Christianity and therefore ready for integration with the whole of the Continent, that same element of dualism which was typical already of the old, much smaller Europe in the first millennium of the Christian era. To the part of eastern Europe which accepted the Christian heritage along with the Roman or Latin— a process completed with the conversions of Poland and Hungary—another part was added with the conversion of Kievan Rus', where the same Christian heritage was combined with the Greek.

Even before the final schism which less than seventy years later divided Christendom, this was extremely important for the political constitution of the enlarged Europe of the late tenth century. The restoration of a Western Roman Empire, besides the Eastern, soon after the middle of that century, had emphasized a political dualism which after the conversions in northeastern Europe likewise extended into that new area. Under such conditions the organization of the European community was made even more difficult than it would have been anyway, since the rivalry between the two Christian empires and between the two Christian churches was now reaching far into the new Europe where both Rome and Constantinople had so successfully extended their respective spheres of influence.

However, an amazing attempt to organize at least that part of Europe in which, on both sides of the Western Empire, national states with royal ambitions were being constituted under the authority of the Papacy, was made by a joint effort of the two universal powers of the West precisely at the turn of the century. If that exceptional project had succeeded, it would have affected also the part of the Continent which was under Byzantine influence; and a millennium of Europe, even more memorable than the one which is connected with the notable events of the tenth century, would have originated precisely in the year 1000.

CHAPTER X

The Vision of the Year 1000

W HEN THE LAST YEAR of the first Christian millennium was approaching, many Europeans were troubled by the feeling that a spectacular, perhaps even catastrophic event would occur: a turning point in the history of mankind, the beginning of a new era—if not the end of the world.[1] These vague fears or mystical expectations did not come true. What did happen in the year 1000 was significant enough and can be considered the promising climax of an unusual effort to realize a noble dream of reforming the world in a genuine Christian spirit which was to have penetrated not only the private but also the public life of the European community.

The most surprising event of that year was the visit of the young Emperor Otto III to Gniezno, then the capital of Poland, where in a remote, hitherto almost unknown corner of Europe an international congress was held and momentous decisions were undertaken.[2] Nothing like it was ever known until 1364, when another such congress with imperial participation gathered in Poland's new capital, Cracow. But when in 1157, during the long interval between these dates, another emperor, Frederick Barbarossa, penetrated far into Poland and met her ruler, it was as a hostile invader.

Otto III came as a friend, not so much of Bolesław Chrobry with whom he was to get better acquainted only at the congress itself, but of a man whom they both had greatly admired when he had been alive and whose dead body they now wanted to venerate in common. What happened in 1000 was, as a matter of fact, a consequence of the tragedy of 997: the Czech Adalbert, formerly bishop of Prague, who had contributed to the consolidation of Christianity in Poland and Hungary, went with Bolesław's support from Gdańsk as missionary to the Prussians in order to convert that Baltic tribe on the other side of the lower Vistula; but he suffered a martyr's death which gained him the crown of a saint. The death of the future patron saint of Poland, who prepared the way for the conversion of the Baltic peoples, the last pagans of Europe—a conversion which was to be achieved only much later and with far-reaching consequences for Poland—was duly commemorated there in spite of unfavorable conditions on the occasion of its 950th anniversary, in anticipation of the approaching millennium celebration.[3]

The connection with the Polish and also with the European millennium is indeed obvious, because it was remarkable that Poland, quite recently converted herself, would at such an early date promote missionary activities which were to make the Christianization of Europe entirely complete. It was also remarkable because the congress on Polish soil which resulted from Saint Adalbert's martyrdom completed the organization of her own Church as well as her integration with Latin Europe, and was designed to contribute decisively to the constitution of the enlarged European community.

Only the first point of that ambitious program was fully carried out through a decision whose interpretation is no longer controversial. The foundation of an archbishopric in Gniezno with both imperial and papal approval, a new metropolitan see for Poland where before only one bishropric had existed in nearby Poznań, directly under Rome, made the Polish church independent from any claims of the German hierarchy, an ecclesiastical province equal to those in the western countries. This was also an important step in the direction of a similar recognition of Poland's political independence and unity. Thanks to the simultaneous creation of three new episcopal sees under the archbishop of Gniezno —a see first occupied by a brother of Saint Adalbert—the ecclesiastical organization was at the same time a recognition of Poland's western boundaries. For these three bishroprics were established in Cracow, Wrocław, and Kołobrzeg: the first two in Little Poland and Silesia recently regained from the Czechs; the third in Pomerania on the Baltic shores, acquired by Mieszko and defended by him against German and Danish claims—a territory where Christianity was far from being definitely established and which now was formally united with Catholic Poland. Her ecclesiastical structure was also harmonized internally with the political, since the new dioceses corresponded to the constituent territorial units of the state in the part of the country where this was most urgently needed. The question of a similar organization for its large eastern sector was left open by the Gniezno congress, making possible the foundation of a second metropolitan see which, though probably established soon after 1000, must have existed for only a short time.[4]

All these ecclesiastical questions were, of course, discussed and agreed upon prior to the Gniezno congress with Sylvester II, the first pope of French origin. As Gerbert of Aurillac, he had already distinguished himself not only in the religious but also in the cultural field[5] and had been elevated to the see of Peter only a few years earlier with the support of his friend and admirer, the emperor. Remaining in close cooperation with Otto III even in political matters, he certainly must have been associated also with those aspects of the negotiations which took place in Gniezno. And the same is true of the posthumous impact of Saint Adalbert. His legacy was indeed primarily of a purely religious nature, and the emperor's visit was a pilgrimage to the place where the body of the martyr, redeemed by Bolesław from the Prussians, was now venerated. But the memory of the great Slav, which showed so clearly that Christian culture on its highest level was not limited to the Romance and Teutonic peoples only, without doubt also influenced the political decisions which were made at his grave. However, in what way his legacy influenced them and, most important, what these decisions really were—these are controversial questions which even today are far from being solved.

The recent hypothesis that Otto III was disappointed when he was not permitted to carry away with him the body of the saint as a priceless relic, and therefore, that he in turn disappointed Bolesław's far-reaching expectation,[6] has no foundation in the sources which agree that the emperor was most favorably impressed by the reception he received from the Polish duke and wanted to show him his genuine friendship. But the two accounts which remain the principal sources, the chronicle of the German bishop Thietmar of Merseburg, contemporary but strongly biased, and that of the anonymous foreigner, probably of French origin and therefore called Gallus, who wrote in Poland one hundred years later, give quite different pictures which lead to different interpretations. The two most extreme interpretations of Thietmar's reluctant admission that the emperor *tributarium fecit dominum,* and of the Polish tradition recorded by Gallus that Otto crowned Bolesław as king of Poland, are now even farther apart than ever before.[7]

For according to one of these interpretations, besides a rather informal recognition of the sovereignty of the Polish duke, nothing occurred except a flattering but practically meaningless gesture of the emperor who placed his own crown on the head of his host. This would mean that no political decisions at all were made in Gniezno. According to the opposite interpretation, Otto III, while he did not make Bolesław king of Poland—he was crowned as such only after a quarter of a century—did much more: he crowned him as *caesar,* which in the ancient Roman terminology that was revived, would mean co-regent and designated successor of the *imperator* himself. Astonishing as it may seem, the hypothesis is supported by sources which independently of the problem of Gniezno and of the relations with Poland tell us that the young emperor was seriously planning to abdicate, to enter a monastery, and to look for a successor not easy to find. But would he really have chosen the Polish duke whose record was then, after only eight years of rule, not yet so brilliant as it would appear a score of years later, and could he believe that the hostile Germans or even the Italians, who looked down upon all the peoples from the other side of the Alps, would ever recognize that Slav as their emperor?

All such questions would be almost insolvable, except that there is fortunately another source, strictly even more contemporary than Thietmar's narrative and without his or any other chronicler's personal bias. It shows the Polish or rather Slavic problem as part of the general European situation, as viewed by the emperor and his admirers. It is one of the priceless iconographical testimonies of the period, a beautiful picture in an illuminated manuscript, produced in the famous monastery of Reichenau in southern Germany around the year 1000, and illustrating eloquently Otto's conception of his role. That well-known picture has been reproduced and described time and again,[8] with the emperor on his throne and four symbolic ladies paying him their tribute. However, the names of these ladies: *Roma, Gallia, Germania,* and *Sclavinia,* which the artist has carefully noted next to each of them, still require further comments.

As to the first person, the name *Roma* given to her cannot possibly mean the universal, recently renovated Roman Empire, since she simply appears as *prima inter pares* and since the empire is obviously represented by Otto III himself. And she can hardly be the personification of the city of Rome only, since the three others represent whole countries, and since papal Rome could not be subordinated to the imperial power. The most acceptable interpretation would seem, therefore, that Rome stands for Italy, as the glorious center of the country which was not then a united body politic, but certainly deserved a place showing her as senior member of the Christian and European community.

That the next place was given to *Gallia* is, on the one hand, understandable, since Gaul, indeed, followed right after Italy as far as ancienty in that community was concerned. On the other hand, it may surprise us that she appears at all in the picture, since the France which had taken her place as an independent kingdom was not under Otto's authority, except for the Burgundian southeast.[9] This seems to indicate that the entire arrangement did not correspond to the real political situation at the given moment, but rather visualized the claims of the empire to universality, and in particular to some kind of supremacy over the recently established Capetingian kingdom.

Germania, the actual basis and core of the empire which was entrusted to her king, comes only third; this is again in disagreement with the concrete facts and the practical role of the individual countries and nations. But it is clear evidence that in the conception of Otto III the Roman Empire was not to be at all the rather artificial and arbitrary extension of the German kingdom, which it became, if not from the very date of the imperial renovation, at least in the near future. In the mind of the present ruler, that empire was truly universal and supranational.

Such an approach is best evidenced by the person called *Sclavinia,* who comes last but obviously is no more subordinated to the preceding one than Germany was to France or France to Italy; on the contrary, *Sclavinia* is placed on an equal footing with the other three, and directly, as they all were, under the universal imperial authority. This is the more significant in a picture made in Germany, because that fourth body represents nothing else but the Slavic world. Originally *Sclavinia* was the name given by ancient authors to only one of the three branches of the Slavs: besides the *Sclavini* there were the *Venedi* and the *Antes.*[10] While, however, the last two names soon became obsolete, the other one, probably first limited to the southern Slavs—the first who appeared on imperial territory—was eventually extended to all of them, being similar to the name they used themselves and surviving in not unsimilar forms in all European languages. Even in the German the name *Wen-*

den, sometimes given to their eastern neighbors, never acquired a general meaning like *Slaven.*

The addition of their area to those of Italy, France and Germany constituted full recognition of the historical fact that, in the course of the century which came to its end, the community to which only those three had belonged at the time of the Carolingian empire had been extended in the northeastern direction to include peoples different in origin from the Romance and Teutonic ones. To Charlemagne's Europe they added a new section of the Continent.

But that section, the vast area occupied by the Slavs, was certainly not a single unit comparable to those already constituted by the three older members of the European community. Even if politically divided, as was Italy, and far from any centralized unity, as were even France and Germany, these countries were slowly developing in the direction of unification and had achieved at least cultural unity to such an extent that it would hardly be anachronistic to call them nations. As for the Slavs, their prehistoric unity is very doubtful and out of their early differentiation there never emerged any Slavic nation nor body politic. Out of their great number—which can be compared only with that of the Romance or Teutonic peoples taken as a whole, and not with that of any individual nation formed within the two other racial and linguistic groups—there emerged on the contrary, and quite naturally, similar national units with their specific names. These names were, however, slow to replace the rather confusing tribal designations and not sufficiently known in the West to appear on a picture which was to symbolize in the simplest possible way the structure of the European community.

Some Slavic tribes had already been forcibly included in that community, coming under German rule or, at least, domination. In particular, we might mention the Slovenes and the Czechs; and even those between the Elbe and the Oder rivers, who still resisted German conquest and only recently had rebelled quite successfully, were hardly expected to be part of a *Sclavinia,* free from Germany and equal to her. On the other hand, it was rather improbable for that name to apply to those Slavs who had settled on formerly Byzantine territories or were in the sphere of influence of Constantinople, considerably extended through the recent Christianization of the Kievan state. In any case, the question of their position with respect to the community envisaged by Otto III depended on the solution of the general problem of his relations with the

Eastern Roman Empire, and must be considered separately in connection with that most delicate issue. Therefore, only the Polish tribes remained who were already united in the state of the Piasts, besides those Slavs who had come under Hungarian rule or formed the kingdom of Croatia, placed between Hungary and Venice. This situation of the latter was connected with the relations between the Western Empire and those two non-Slavic states. Therefore, it is likely that in the picture of the four ladies, the last one symbolized Poland more particularly, and that her position was mainly, if not exclusively, discussed when the political situation east of Germany was to be settled by the congress held in the Polish capital.

Impressed by Bolesław Chrobry's personality and realizing that he was the only qualified ruler in that whole area, Otto III wanted to include *Sclavinia* in his political system. Giving Poland due recognition in both the political and ecclesiastical sphere, Otto most probably made her duke his representative in the Slavic world. In order to bestow upon him the necessary authority, he gave him at once the position of a *patricius,* following the pattern used in Italy,[11] and promised him a royal crown. Such elevation of the Polish state to the rank of a Catholic kingdom—probably Mieszko's goal in his relations with the Holy See—required, of course, the approval of the pope and therefore was only symbolically anticipated by the emperor at Gniezno. Whether after the settlement of that question Otto III would have gone even farther, is indeed impossible to ascertain. If he really took Bolesław with him when he visited and opened the grave of Charlemagne immediately after the congress in Poland, and if the title which he had started using before, *servus apostolorum* instead of *imperator,* really indicated his determination to abdicate, it is quite possible that he had determined upon an exceptional position in the Christian and European community for his new friend and common admirer of Saint Adalbert. Before, however, any such plans could materialize, two unexpected events changed the situation altogether: In 1001 Pope Sylvester II, with whom the emperor continued to cooperate closely, granted a royal crown, not to the Polish duke but to another East European ruler, Stephen of Hungary; and in 1002 the young Otto died prematurely without having decided anything in the matter of the imperial succession. Both of these facts require a careful examination with a view to explaining why the whole vision of the year 1000 ended in failure and disappointment and never reappeared.

The reasons why Hungary was made a kingdom before Poland, and that with an "apostolic" character, are difficult to discover. Her ruler was later canonized, after a reign which was as brilliant as Bolesław's and as significant in the Hungarian tradition as was the latter's in the Polish one. But his achievements in the thirty-odd years following were even more difficult to foresee than those of his Polish contemporary. Hungary's conversion to Catholicism was even more recent than Poland's and Stephen himself, born as a pagan, had been baptized only shortly before. Did the position of his state in the immediate neighborhood of the Eastern Empire seem more important from the standpoint of both the Western Empire and the Papacy? Did those Germans, who like Thietmar were opposed to the rise of Poland—which they blamed on Otto III—prefer that the new royal crown be granted to Hungary, influencing the pope in that matter? Or did the envoy sent to Rome by Bolesław simply become disloyal to him and shift his allegiance to the other side? These questions will probably never be fully answered[12] and anyway it is more important to study the consequences of such a turn of events.

For the young Hungarian state these consequences were obviously very advantageous. Her place in the community of European nations was now secure and so was her independent position with regard to Germany, especially since, despite all the vicissitudes of Hungarian history, the royal dignity was never given up, not even after the Trianon treaty more than nine hundred years later. On the contrary, the crown of Saint Stephen remained until our day, when it had to be removed from the communist-controlled country, the venerated symbol of an uninterrupted and unchallenged national tradition, as well as of the territorial integrity of the kingdom. That royal crown was to play an even greater role in the destinies of Hungary than the ducal crown of Saint Václav in those of Bohemia; and if the Hungarian millennium has as its start the reign of Stephen rather than that of Árpád, the date of his coronation is perhaps even more significant than that of his baptism, which is not even precisely remembered.

For Poland and for Bolesław Chrobry personally, the decision made in 1001 was, of course, a serious disappointment. However, at the given moment it did not necessarily mean that a similar decision regarding a royal crown for the Polish ruler would be delayed for the twenty-four years it turned out to be. As long as Otto III was alive and his policy continued, there was no basic obstacle to the creation of not one but two

Catholic kingdoms east of Germany, and in his vision of the constitution of Europe there remained a place for *Sclavinia*, although a *Hungaria* was introduced into the picture before the promises made to Poland at Gniezno came true. Since the importance of the Slavic world had been recognized there, Poland could not simply be replaced by Hungary, which was no Slavic country at all. But in any case the crown granted to Stephen, whose relations with Poland do not seem to have suffered from that earlier elevation, must have contributed to the prestige of his country in the whole Danubian region, particularly in the relations with Croatia, and also in those with Venice.

Hungary's relations with Venice, which only became hostile later, after the union with Croatia, were of special importance at the time of Otto III, who wanted to include the Republic of Saint Marc in his political system and her Doge Orseolo in the planned "family of Kings."[13] How Stephen's matrimonial ties with the Orseoli contributed to a rapprochement of both powers is best evidenced by the fact that his nephew Pietro Orseolo could claim the Hungarian crown in the period of trouble which followed his glorious reign. That solution of the succession problem had no more chance than the pagan reaction—the other extreme. And in the entirely changed situation of the eleventh century a union with Venice could not any longer hold that interest for Hungary which perhaps it would have held around the year 1000. But if almost exactly one hundred years later the union with Croatia materialized,[14] under Hungarian leadership, such a success was possible only because of Saint Stephen's royal heritage, revived shortly before by another saintly king, Ladislas. The consequences of that union, which was to last more than eight centuries, included indeed the controversies with Venice over Dalmatia, which Hungary took over from Croatia; but at the same time the formerly landlocked country became, with its partner, an Adriatic power and gained for half a millennium a position which deeply affected European history.

It affected, among other things, the relations between the Latin West and the Greek East, and this leads back, from prospects of the future, to the policies of Otto III. For that one ruler of the restored Western Empire, half Byzantine himself through his mother and influenced by Byzantine culture, who could have achieved a lasting rapprochement with the Eastern, certainly did not limit his vision of the future of Europe and of Christendom to their Latin halves only. It seems equally certain that a better opportunity for such an achievement could scarcely have been found in history than at the turn of the tenth century.[15] In the course of that century there had been indeed the usual tensions between Rome and Constantinople, but not a single break similar to those which long before Photius had time and again separated the two centers of Christendom. As far as the political relations between the two empires were concerned, the Eastern then had an unusually ambitious, uncompromising ruler in the person of Basil II, who was much older and more experienced than Otto III. But the so-called killer of the Bulgarians was still absorbed by the exhausting war against them, which was far from being ended. And even after the total victory of the Greeks the war was to leave behind a deep split in the unity of Eastern Christendom.[16] Under such conditions a re-establishment of some kind of unity with the Latin West could seem more desirable than ever. Last but not least, in addition to the two separate fronts, one in Spain and the other in the Near East, where Latins and Greeks had to fight against the Muslim danger, a third and common front had been added in southern Italy, where their cooperation was indispensable.

It is very difficult to interpret the legation which Otto III sent to Basil II in 998[17] and the latter's agreement, three years later, to a marriage of his niece Zoe to Otto, whom he apparently was ready to recognize as another Roman emperor. But before that marriage could be concluded and the negotiations brought to a successful end, Otto III died and the unique opportunity which had appeared toward the end of his reign was never to repeat itself.

There was, however, another East European problem which must have attracted the attention of Otto III as soon as he had decided to include Slavdom in his great scheme, a problem which concerned not the old southeast of Europe, but her historically new northeast, and not those Slavs who had turned toward Rome but those who had definitely entered the Byzantine sphere of influence. It would have been only natural to approach them, not through the intermediary of faraway Constantinople, especially as long as the relations between the two empires were still unsettled, but either directly as had already been tried in the time of Otto I, or through Poland, now not merely converted but supposed to represent *Sclavinia* in the new structure of Europe. For this, too, little time was left between the congress of Gniezno and the death of Otto III, and the reference of much later sources to contacts between Rome and Kiev around 1000 is difficult to verify. It is, however, significant that Bolesław Chrobry's encouragement of missionary activities in the East, which had started three years before when Saint Adalbert tried to convert the Prussians, was continued a few years after the congress of Gniezno thanks to another friend of the Polish ruler, this time a German, Saint Bruno of Querfurt.[18] Before he was killed in 1009 at the border of Lithuania, while visiting another Baltic tribe, famous in the future, that missionary went to Kiev vainly trying to work among the Pechenegs. This was in the obvious interest of the Kievan state, plagued by these Asiatic invaders, and could be planned only in cooperation with the Grand Prince Vladimir himself, whose relations with Poland were quite peaceful at that time. And Otto III, whose interest in Bolesław had first been raised in connection with Saint Adalbert's mission, could only welcome the new initiative of his Polish *patricius*. At stake would be not only the conversion of the Baltic peoples but also a mission at the border between Europe and Asia which would have Kiev as a basis and the friendly relations with the eastern Slavs of Rus' as both a prerequisite condition and a natural consequence.

Considering all this against the background of the Gniezno congress and in the light of the contemporary picture of Otto III on his throne, it is perhaps easier to interpret his intentions regarding not only eastern Europe but the whole community which he hoped to organize under his own and the pope's leadership. There is no evidence that he identified that community with Europe, a name which still appears very rarely in the sources,[19] more rarely than at the time of Charlemagne whose work he wanted to complete. In one of Otto's charters a distinction is made between the Christian and the barbarian areas which he controlled, giving the impression that non-Christian peoples were also included. There is, however, no doubt that he expected the conversion of such areas, as, for example, the pagan Slavic tribes between Germany and Poland, and that he had in mind a united and politically integrated Christendom. Christianity expanded only gradually to the northern and eastern limits of Europe. Yet, on the other hand, it still survived outside Europe, especially in the Asiatic possessions of the Byzantine Empire. But the Roman Empire which Otto III wanted to renew in a truly universal sense would have been in any case basically European though it obviously was to be in some way associated with the "new Rome" on the Bosphorus, and though a contemporary poet pretended that along with Greece even Babylonia and the old churches of Antioch and Alexandria were ready to serve him.[20] This empire was unable to recover the Asiatic and African areas lost to the Arabs, and had as its main constituent parts

Italy, France, Germany, and a *Sclavinia* which was not yet precisely defined.

To a *Sclavinia* more or less identified with Bolesław's Poland, other Slavic and East European countries, especially Hungary, were soon to be added; and in addition to the three sections of Charlemagne's Europe, the other kingdoms emerging in the West and in the North were certainly considered prospective members of the Ottonian Empire, although they were not symbolized in the picture. Only in the case of France did it go beyond the countries really united around 1000 under Otto III. Inseparable, however, from the expected extensions of his *renovatio imperii,* is the question of the very character which that empire was to have according to his conception. The case of Poland, specifically discussed in the decisive year at the turn of the century, clearly shows that he was not thinking of any imperial or even less of a German conquest, but of a free association with the other equal members of the planned community, even with regard to a country which at the time of the ancient Roman Empire had been in the "barbarian" part of Europe, and which the empire that had been "transferred" to the German nation wanted to conquer on so many occasions before and after Otto III.

What, then, was that community to be? Was the *renovatio* as seen by that truly exceptional emperor really a return to that imperial idea which Saint Augustine had, from the Christian viewpoint, so severely blamed, although in his days the Roman Empire was already officially Christian? It cannot be merely accidental that on Otto's documents the imperial title began to disappear at the time when in the symbolic picture of his realm the name of Rome was given only to one of its equal members. Though the terms might seem anachronistic, it is perhaps not inappropriate to call that realm a federation or a commonwealth rather than an empire. In any case, that European and, above all, Christian body politic, would have been an ecclesiastical empire under the leadership of both emperor and pope.[21]

These are, of course, speculations only, and unfortunately, nothing else is possible in view of the decisive event of 1002: the untimely death of Otto III. Much more important than the change of 1001 when the crown promised to Bolesław went to Stephen, that sudden catastrophe was again most detrimental to the Poles; whatever succession plans the deceased emperor might have had, the German and consequently the imperial succession went to Henry II, personally a saintly man and soon canonized, who started his reign with a war against Poland which lasted sixteen years. The contrast between the friendship of the year 1000 and that first major Polish-German conflict is best evidenced by two facts: Bruno of Querfurt had to blame the new emperor for using the help of pagan Slavic tribes against Bolesław, and instead of acting as an intermediary between the empire and Kievan Rus', the Polish ruler had to face, toward the end of Vladimir's reign, an encirclement and simultaneous attack by his western and eastern neighbors, ominous for the future.

But relations with Poland had only been part of the program of Otto III, equally important for western and eastern Europe, the Polish case being a test of the turn which he wanted to give to the general policies of the empire. Therefore, the return to the anti-Polish policies of the past was, to a large extent, evidence that the whole political conception of the late emperor, which so many Germans had considered unrealistic, would be given up under his successor. Whether Otto's vision, which had never been clearer than around the year 1000, would have materialized had he not passed away two years later, is again a matter of speculation only. He had to realize that even in the relations with Italy, which were basic for any conception of the restored Western Empire, he had not been too successful, and the memory of the ruthless repressions which shortly before 1000 he felt obliged to use against his opponents in Rome troubled his conscience and was the main reason why he was thinking of abdication. However, had more time been granted to him, there would have been a chance that, more balanced in his mature age, he would have made the noble dream of his youth come true. Such a chance for Europe and Christendom was unfortunately never to return.

This does not mean that the vision of 1000 was completely lost. As far as the northeastern extensions of both Europe and Christendom were concerned, it could seem that Bolesław Chrobry would carry out in the new area of *Sclavinia* some ideas similar to those of his imperial friend, though in opposition to Germany. Trying to replace German control with his own in Bohemia, an attempt which was the initial reason for his conflict with Henry II, and interfering with the internal situation in the Kievan state after Vladimir's death and the end of the war with Germany, Bolesław could not possibly think of annexing these countries, as he did in the case of Lusatia. He rather thought of some kind of confederation, as we would say today, uniting all northern Slavs under his leadership, in peaceful relations with, but independent of any empire, whether western or eastern.[22] That this was beyond the strength of the young Polish state became apparent soon after Bolesław's death, though at the end of his reign he obtained the royal crown at last, against German opposition but probably with papal consent.

That last success, so important for the Polish tradition, leads again from the Slavic world to the general problem of the future of Christian Europe. More important for the survival of Otto's ideas than any regional developments was the continuity of papal policies in contrast to the imperial ones. The late emperor's friend and collaborator, Pope Sylvester II, died soon after him, and though his immediate successors were not equally prominent, and the harmonious cooperation of the two leading powers of Christendom did not last, the Rome of Peter was more and more determined to give to Europe what the heirs of Caesar's Rome had failed to promote after Otto III: a constitution based upon diversity in unity, and a just peace based upon the equality of all nations which were being formed within the European community.

After those memorable events of a thousand years ago, which, through the spread of Christianity and Graeco-Roman culture, brought these nations closer together, the millennium of their community started with a bold project conceived at the turn of the century and aimed at the lasting integration of Europe through the application of Christian principles in international relations. That perhaps premature project, born in the minds of a few precursors, was doomed to failure, but it has not lost its actuality. It has been rightly said[23] that the problems which Otto III so passionately wanted to solve are the same ones which even in our own time exercise their impact upon the destinies of the countries and peoples of Central Europe, and even of Europe as a whole. In the interval between the beginning and the end of Europe's millennium, the vision of the year 1000 continued to be, consciously or not, a guide for the subsequent generations. And it even seemed as if the next three centuries would come near to seeing that inspiring goal achieved.

PART II

The Christian Commonwealth

CHAPTER XI

Europe and Christendom

THE STUDY OF EUROPE'S MILLENNIUM in its first meaning, i.e. the survey of the events which in the second part of the tenth century brought almost all countries and peoples of Europe into regular relations with each other, helps one to understand the basic problems of the millennium of Europe in its second sense, the problems of the continuous development of the European community until our own times, times of momentous change for Europe's position in the world.

By the end of the tenth century it had become evident that the most important problem was the durable internal organization of the European community as it had been finally constituted through its expansion toward the northern and eastern limits of the Continent. Such an organization had appeared by that time, almost a thousand years ago, that was indispensable for the establishment of peace among the Christian nations of Europe and for the defense of their common culture, their freedom, and independence against aggressions from the outside. It also was a prerequisite condition for any further progress of culture combining Christianity and the pre-Christian heritage of the Graeco-Roman world. To the extent that the progress thus conceived was really made in a truly Christian and humanistic spirit, this is the most objective and penetrating criterion for subdividing the thousand years of what might be called the European age into shorter periods.

The first of these periods corresponds to what is usually called the Middle Ages, but not in the conventional interpretation which misleadingly includes the so-called Dark Ages which followed the great migrations as well as the so-called waning of the Middle Ages which belongs to quite another period. The truly "mediaeval" one, viz., the time which is dominated by the most typical features which the historians have in mind when using that term, is limited to the eleventh, twelfth, and thirteenth centuries, the preceding and the following ones being of a transitional character.[1]

In order to understand the character of those three centuries themselves, the meaningless or rather, ambiguous, term which is still used for their designation ought to be at last replaced by a more appropriate name. Considered from the viewpoint of Europe's millennium, these centuries certainly do not constitute any "middle ages," since they stand not in the middle but at the beginning of the European Age and since they are dominated by the first constructive attempt to organize the European community immediately after the failure of the projects of Otto III. Among all the aspects of the period, this attempt and its partial realization are definitely the most striking and memorable, and therefore should suggest a name replacing the old one. In Latin it would be the well-known expression, *respublica Christiana*.

Before justifying its use as name of the European community in the first part of its millennium, the most adequate translation must be discovered. This is no less important than the best translation of the term *civitas Dei*, which had already appeared far back in the preceding millennium but remained familiar to all those who in the following centuries spoke of the *respublica Christiana*. To translate in that context the word *respublica* into "republic," as is usually done, is no more correct than to translate St. Augustine's *civitas* into "city." In both cases the English word, as it is used today, has quite a different meaning, and this is also true of the corresponding words in other modern languages. In English, fortunately, there is a word which comes nearest to the real meaning of the Latin *respublica* as it was used in bygone ages,[2] not exclusively in the so-called Middle Ages; that word is "Commonwealth" or "commonweal." It is not a mere adaptation of a word borrowed from another language, as is "republic," but an accurate translation which safeguards the rather broad meaning of the Latin term.[3] If the English includes, as it does today, the idea of federation or confederation, it comes particularly near to the idea of the *respublica Christiana,* which never was supposed to be a unitarian, centralized body politic. Such an interpretation corresponded to the ideas of Otto III, and is even less anachronistic with regard to the three following centuries.

Strangely enough, the term *respublica Christiana* appears more frequently in the following period, in the age of the Renaissance when it corresponded much less to the real structure of Europe than before, and it even survived, not infrequently in the French translation *république chrétienne* throughout the seventeenth century, when the idea of Christian solidarity was definitely vanishing.[4] That solidarity was strongest from the eleventh to the thirteenth century, so that it is fully justified to speak of a Christian Commonwealth at that time. But it is difficult to discover to what extent that conception, then unquestionably basic for the constitution of Europe, was identified with Europe in the minds and in the consciousness of the contemporaries, at least of those under whose leadership and responsibility the Christian community developed.

These leaders were then, in contrast to the formative years before and around 1000, in particular to the reign of Otto III, almost exclusively the Roman popes, more frequently than not in latent or open conflict with the Roman emperors. Before examining the causes and consequences of that conflict which formed the main obstacle to Europe's real unity, it is, therefore, instructive to study how the relationship between Europe and Christendom was interpreted in the pronouncements of the Holy See. One of them has already rightly received special attention in that respect,[5] viz., the famous address of Urban II in 1095 at the Council of Clermont, where he made his appeal for a crusade against the enemies of Christendom. Even the term *Christianitas* is very rarely used in the accounts of that speech, the exact text of which has not been preserved, and it has been correctly pointed out that far from identifying the area controlled by *Christiani* or *Christicolae* with Europe, the pope insisted upon the fact that it was reduced to a very small part, a *portiuncula,* of the world and of Europe. Starting from the idea of Christian universalism and therefore equally interested in all three parts of the world which were then known and distinguished, Urban II first complained that both Asia and Africa, once so important and glorious in Christian history from the time of the Apostles, were now occupied by "the enemies of God," so that if there were any Christians left, they had lost their freedom and could survive only in the most precarious condition. And then he added that even in Europe, where the Saracens had conquered Spain three hundred years before, only a limited part was

Christian, since it was impossible so to call the barbarians in distant islands on the frozen ocean.

It is, however, important to note, first, that the pope, rightly minimizing what remained of Christian populations outside Europe, was obviously exaggerating when answering the question *quantulam partem* of Europe Christians inhabited. This was certainly much more than a *portiuncula,* since speaking about Europe's non-Christian part, he could only refer to a few remote islands in the north. Even of these islands the really important ones, as far as Iceland, were definitely Christianized, and even if the areas of the Continent east of the Baltic sea, which continued to be pagan, were considered, it could hardly be denied that by far the largest part of Europe was not only inhabited by Christians but ruled by them, recognizing papal authority or in any case so near to each other that Urban II did not mention at all the recent Eastern Schism.

That omission, as well as the over-pessimistic picture of Christianity's position in Europe, can be easily explained by the purpose of the papal address. Trying to convince the faithful of the necessity and urgency of undertaking the crusade, Urban II, who wanted to combine both the liberation of the Holy Land and the reunion with the Eastern Church,[6] exactly as Gregory VII before him and so many great popes after him wanted, gave a picture of the situation which would serve this twofold purpose. His statement can rightly be quoted as a particularly pertinent proof that the Papacy was not at all inclined to identify Europe with Christendom as far as principles and doctrine were concerned, but on the contrary, since it was faithful to the idea of the Church's universality, wanted to see all parts of the world become Christian. However, that same statement of 1095 clearly shows that at that time Asia and Africa were considered practically lost, as were even some parts of Europe. And it was only in the remaining part of Europe that Christendom was really ruling, with a good chance of reconquering the southwestern areas occupied by the Muslims and of penetrating gradually into the northeastern regions where the missionary efforts of the past had not yet achieved their goal.

In order to understand such a *de facto* identity of Europe and Christendom, which became more and more obvious in the next centuries, while the inclusion of the Holy Land in the Christian Commonwealth lasted for only a short time, the very character of that community has to be clarified before its limits are studied in detail. Not all lands where Christians survived in larger or smaller numbers—most of them separated from Rome and even from Constantinople in ecclesiastical matters, and all of them politically under non-Christian domination—could be considered members of the Christian Commonwealth as conceived by the Papacy. Christian unity, the typical feature of the first three or four centuries of Europe's millennium, was only achieved where the Christian faith had not only gained individual souls but had penetrated the whole cultural life of the community and was recognized as the unquestionable basis of the whole political structure as well.

That Europe's culture was then Christian, in contrast to the cultures of other parts of the world including areas where scattered Christians were living under non-Christian rule, and that there was no other culture in Europe except where it had been temporarily imposed upon its population by non-Christian conquerors—these are matters of general knowledge. It is equally well established that this Christian culture, which in the course of the preceding millennium had absorbed all the constructive elements of the Graeco-Roman heritage, was the main element of European unity in the first period of the next.[7] But that unity would not have been so complete, more complete than in the following periods, if politics had not at that time been included in the sphere where Christian principles of morality were to be respected. It is that intimate association of ethics and politics that makes for the exceptional greatness of the period, a greatness which in retrospect is being praised today, not only in papal encyclicals but also by leading historians who, far from sharing all the beliefs of orthodox Christianity, are looking for principles of human unity more efficient than those which any universal empire or the evocation of its ghost can possibly offer.[8]

It is, of course, hardly necessary to recognize the obvious fact that the practice of European life was never, not even at the time of the Christian Commonwealth, in full agreement with Christian ethics, and that the political actions of all European nations and of their exclusively Christian rulers violated, perhaps as frequently as in other periods, the Christian principles which were so solemnly proclaimed. But the equally obvious fact that they were proclaimed so consistently, never openly challenged by anybody, and generally accepted as the only admissible rules of human behavior, resulted in a common European way of life which was basically Christian. Violations of these principles were universally condemned, even if committed in political matters and by the most powerful monarchs who, just like any private individual, were subject to excommunication by the ecclesiastical authorities. This spiritual weapon

—then a truly threatening sanction—was misused on various occasions, but the very fact that it existed and was, in general, quite efficient, served on much more frequent occasions as a guarantee of respect for both divine commandments and human rights.

As far as the European order and what today would be called international relations were concerned, two points deserve special attention. The first, of general significance, was the concern of the Church with the preservation of peace.[9] The well-known institution of the *treuga Dei* was a check against any kind of warfare, including that most frequent and troublesome kind which resulted from internal divisions in the individual countries. Such divisions permitted any feudal lord, exercising local power, to disturb the "tranquillity of order" which Saint Augustine recognized as the prerequisite condition of real peace. Without the strict limitation of such semi-private warfare through elaborate rules issued by the Church, the normal life of civil society would have been seriously handicapped in spite of all general Christian principles. These principles were, of course, much more difficult to enforce in the relations between fully sovereign states. Therefore the most prominent theologians of the period, including Saint Thomas Aquinas, were anxious to work out a Christian doctrine in matters of war and peace, more precise than the Augustinian had been. Among the conditions for a just war was one which might seem self-evident but still was badly needed in the confused stage of political organization: the rule that such a war could only be declared by the legitimate authority. Furthermore, in order to be just, i.e. morally permissible, any war had to have, first, a just cause, and secondly, a right intention. And the Church, in particular the Holy See, was always ready to determine through its mediation or arbitration, whether in a given case these conditions had been observed.

The international law, which, without being so called, came into existence in that early period of European history, was derived from natural law and from the foremost law of Christ: the love of our neighbor including even the enemy. This was an outstanding contribution to a sound constitution of the European community, making it, more than anything else, a real Christian Commonwealth. And while it is easy to point out rulers who, calling themselves Christian, did not respect that law even at the time of the fullest development of the commonwealth, it is also less difficult in that period than in any other to find shining examples of the opposite, the truly Christian attitude in international relations. The classic example is indeed the glorious rule of King Louis IX of France,[10] who became the patron saint not only of his own dynasty and country, but of all those who wanted to exercise the difficult and responsible royal profession in a Christian sense and in full loyalty to the *respublica Christiana* as a whole. Such rulers remained exceptions, unfortunately, but the unanimous admiration of contemporaries is convincing evidence that in spite of all the deviations in the practice of life, there was a *communis consensus* as to the fundamentals of a sound political philosophy. And this is the second point which must be well remembered.

Those contemporaries who molded such a universal public opinion were at first almost exclusively members of the clergy, who continued the prominent role in Europe's cultural development which they had played in the course of the first Christian millennium and the threshold of the second, when the Cluny movement proved of more lasting importance than the Carolingian renaissance.[11] At the time of the Christian Commonwealth, whose cultural unity and achievements had been so prepared, decisive progress resulted from the development of an institution which was perhaps the greatest contribution then made to the growth of European civilization. That institution was the *studium generale,* the University as it was called until our day. Typical of the Latin West, with only very few antecedents in Eastern Christendom and in the world of Islam, these centers of higher education and learning remained until the end of the period limited to the Romance countries where they originated, and to England. But even so they attracted scholars and students from all parts of Christendom, including the Teutonic and Slavic peoples, the Parisian Sorbonne being particularly outstanding in that respect.[12] An intellectual cooperation on the highest level was thus started which was to spread in the following periods of the European millennium to all parts of the Continent and eventually to all parts of the world, where universities on the European model, representing the most constructive and uncontroversial element of European influence, were created.

In spite of its later secularization, the ecclesiastical origin of the University has to be remembered, as well as the leading role of the Papacy in the multiplication and earliest development of the *studium*. However, with a rapidly growing lay participation in its organization and activities, the *studium* became a third universal power in the Christian Commonwealth alongside the *sacerdotium* and the *imperium,* sometimes exercising a not insignificant political influence. Long before the universities were affected by the rise of modern nationalism, they were instrumental in promoting a supranational Christian culture which independently of all political troubles was the main pillar of European unity. And long before the Renaissance in its specific sense, which developed mainly outside the universities, revived all the traditions of Graeco-Roman humanism, the *studia generalia,* while giving the first place to Catholic theology, made their own contribution to the continuity of Europe's ancient humanistic heritage. They made possible earlier "renaissances" like that of the twelfth century, which is generally recognized,[13] and that of the thirteenth, when the place of Aristotle in Thomistic philosophy gave evidence of the impact of ancient pagan thought on Christian learning.

That thanks to the impact of Arab and Jewish learning, Aristotle became better known than ever before, is instructive to recall for two different reasons. It shows, first, that the Christian culture of Europe was even in that early period not at all isolated nor closed to the influence of other neighboring cultures. But this non-Christian cultural influence did not affect—any more even than the consequences of trade relations with the Far East—the spiritual unity of Europe, which remained based upon the universally accepted Christian doctrine, harmoniously combined with the well adopted heritage of ancient Greece and Rome. And this leads to the second reason why the destiny of Aristotle is so significant. A contribution of non-Christian thought which was nothing but a revival of Hellenic philosophy could be readily accepted and integrated by the most orthodox theologians of Christendom, because it was in agreement with their respect for the tradition of classical antiquity and with their desire to take advantage of its lasting values. Otherwise, even in those parts of Europe which were for centuries under Muslim rule,[14] the undisputably high but basically alien culture of the conquerors left significant traces only in the mathematical and natural sciences and, to a certain extent, in architecture, and met with opposition not only in the political but also in the spiritual field.

Arab control, which, in the ancient *Magna Graecia*—especially in Sicily—lasted only for a very short time at the beginning of Europe's millennium, had to be removed by long, heroic efforts where the Iberian peninsula was concerned. Its reconquest by nascent Christian powers which had hardly begun their history in the crucial tenth century was not completed before the fall of Granada in 1492. But the protracted existence of that last Muslim stronghold in the southern corner of Spain had only a limited, almost symbolic importance, since by the end of the thirteenth century all the rest of the peninsula had been liberated. The result of that *reconquista* was the definite inclusion in the Christian Commonwealth of three nations: the Spanish in the strictest, Castilian sense in the center; the Catalonian, whose Aragonian kingdom in the northeastern corner had been the first to be free; and the Portuguese in the southwest, which in 1940 celebrated the eight hundredth anniversary of its independent existence. Soon after liberation all three were to exercise an influence far beyond the geographical boundaries of the peninsula, an influence which long before the Spanish and Portuguese expansion outside Europe made Aragon a great Mediterranean power extending as far as Sicily and through the famous Catalonian companies even as far as Greece.[15]

This was toward the end of the first period of Europe's millennium, but in its earlier course it had already become apparent that the long domination by a non-European and non-Christian power, far from changing the character of the Iberian peoples, had made them, in reaction against the traditional enemy, even more determined, truly militant Christians. It also demonstrated that the loss which Europe, as a spiritual and political community, had suffered for so many centuries, had been fully repaired and regained. This was indeed a great contribution to the practical identity of Christendom with geographical Europe, an identity which therefore remained questionable only in the opposite, northeastern part of the Continent.

There, two different areas have to be distinguished, of which the Baltic continued to receive the attention of the Latin West in spite, or rather because of the failure of the first missionary efforts around the year 1000. In that year it seemed as if at least the Slavic part of the Baltic lands, Pomerania united with Catholic Poland, was largely Christianized and ready for integration with the Christian Commonwealth. Yet, one hundred years later the resistance of the Pomeranians against both Christianity and Polish rule was still so strong that military expeditions as well as missionary activities had to be resumed. German participation in these activities, more often than not in political rivalry with Poland, resulted toward the end of the twelfth century in a division of Pomerania:[16] in the western section Pomerania's native Slavic princes recognized the overlordship of the empire, while those of the eastern, with Gdańsk (Danzig), remained so close to Poland, in spite of occasional troubles, that after another hundred years the last of them bequeathed his duchy to a Polish Piast who was restoring the unity of the kingdom.

By that time all of Pomerania, from the mouth of the Oder to that of the Vistula, was unquestionably part of Christendom, but on the eastern bank of the lower Vistula were the still pagan lands of the specifically Baltic tribes—Indo-European but neither Slavic nor Teutonic—from Prussia to Livonia at the mouth of the Dvina, with Lithuania in the center, hardly reaching the coast. The conversion of these peoples· was of considerable importance for the unity of Europe, if only because of their crucial geographical location, and of serious interest for their Christian neighbors who frequently suffered from their incursions. As far as the old Prussians were concerned, there arose, as in the case of Pomerania, the question of cooperation or rivalry between Poles and Germans. It was a Polish duke of Mazovia, who, hoping for the former, assisted the Teutonic order, the so-called Knights of the Cross, in the creation of a strong ecclesiastical state in Prussia whose very name was to be taken over by the German conquerors. This was in any case an extension of the Christian Commonwealth, but to the advantage not of Poland but of the German·knighthood, which in spite of its monastic organization was more loyal to the empire than to the Papacy. Another ecclesiastical state under German leadership originated in Livonia even earlier, at the beginning of the thirteenth century, and was soon united to the Prussian state with a view to jointly conquering Lithuania; and though in that rather distant region imperial suzerainty was even more nominal than in Prussia, it was not, by that token, any easier for the Holy See to establish its control over a scarcely converted territory where not only the natives but also the young hierarchy had to be protected against the ambitious Order, here called Knights of the Sword.

The well-known facts about the establishment of these German colonies in Prussia and Livonia confirm once more that conversion by force and imposition of foreign rule were not appropriate forms for extending the Christian Commonwealth. These territories were indeed opened to western culture, but the native peoples either disappeared completely—as happened in Prussia, and in the Slavic lands between the Elbe and the Oder—or remained subject to alien masters almost to the end of Europe's millennium, a fate which the Baltic Latvians of Livonia shared with the Finnish tribes of that region. One of them, the Livs, left their name to the whole country, while another, the Ests north of them, after whom Estonia was called, had to be conquered with Danish participation. Denmark's rule in Estonia, which lasted for more than a century

until that country too came under German control, was part of the expansion of the Scandinavian kingdoms. These kingdoms, after a rather
difficult start in the tenth century, were now an integral part of Christendom, and tried to extend their rule east of the Baltic. The Swedish
conquest of Finland, which started in the twelfth century, was by far
the most important part of that process, with lasting consequences
throughout the millennium of Europe, because in that case it became
particularly striking what notable contributions to western culture the
submerged peoples of the whole area were able to make, when at last
an opportunity was given them.

What had become clear in the thirteenth century was, on the one
hand, the impossibility of conquering the strongest of the Baltic peoples,
the Lithuanians, and on the other hand, the obvious fact that any aggression by Latin powers delayed the integration of the eastern Slavs[17]
with the Christian Commonwealth, including the area of their own
colonial expansion, in a direction where even the geographical limits of
Europe were far from being determined. When the great Pope Innocent IV, in the middle of that century, tried to encourage both the earliest project of a spontaneous conversion of Lithuania to Roman Catholicism and a contemporaneous plan of religious union with at least the
nearest part of the Ruthenians, granting in both cases royal crowns to
the native rulers, his initiative—which would have meant an extension
of the European community in a truly Christian spirit—unfortunately
failed. In the case of the Lithuanians, the aggressive policy of the German Knights discouraged then, and for more than a century, the attempts to make their rapidly growing state a Catholic power. As far as
the old Kievan state was concerned, its gradual disintegration had been
punctuated—just before the pontificate of Innocent IV—by a catastrophe
which was to effect the destinies of the whole eastern part of Europe,
cutting most of it off from the West. This was the Mongol invasion, another Asiatic aggression against Europe and Christendom, second in
importance only to the Ottoman one in the next century.

It is true that Kievan Rus', from the time of her Christianization, had
been under a strong Byzantine influence which after the Cerulanian
schism became definitely anti-Latin. But, as it must be stressed on so
many occasions, this was an opposition, regrettable indeed but still
within Europe and Christendom, connected with the original dualism
of the European heritage. Furthermore, the repercussions of the Greek
schism were slow to reach Constantinople's distant sphere of influence

in northeastern Europe, so that it is hardly possible to determine the time, and even less an exact date, when the eastern Slavs were really separated from Rome.

A distinction must be made, however, between those who remained in their original homeland, in continuous though not always friendly relations with their Latin neighbors, and those who colonized the origially Finnish Volga region where Christianity had no traditions going back to the time of unity with Rome and where, on the contrary, a strange dualism of recently introduced Christian beliefs and the old pagan way of life was to last for centuries. Even so, a gradual integration with Christian Europe might have been possible if the invasion of 1238-1240 had not resulted in a long-lasting Tartar domination.[18] Its consequences were much deeper than those of the Mongol raids of 1241 into Poland and Hungary, which later were so frequently repeated with respect to the first of these countries. For Poland the Tartar neighborhood was an occasional danger and a permanent nuisance that made her even more conscious of belonging to the Christian Commonwealth. For the eastern Slavs the Tartar period during its tenure made impossible their integration with the European community, separating them from their Christian neighbors by a kind of "iron curtain."[19]

Again, however, a distinction is necessary: not for all eastern Slavs was the Tartar period equally long nor the Tartar yoke equally oppressive. For the new colonial Russia "beyond the forests" and, as a matter of fact, beyond the frontiers of Europe as the ancient tradition saw them, inclusion in a Tartar realm with its capital on the lower Volga—the semi-European successor state of the Eurasian Mongol Empire—was the determining factor of her destinies until the middle, if not the end of the fifteenth century. For the core of the old Kievan state, liberation from Tartar domination, which in the western part of Rus' had never been too well established, came, strangely enough, through the amazing expansion of Lithuania in the later thirteenth and the first part of the fourteenth century.[20]

Since that Lithuanian state. which was second in area only to the Holy Roman Empire and included most of what is called today Byelorussia and Ukraine—definitely within Europe's boundaries but still under pagan leadership—could hardly survive without accepting Christianity, the question as to the methods and influence that should accompany that Christianization was of utmost significance for the whole Christian Commonwealth. Before the integration of the Lithuanian Grand Duchy, the eastern boundaries of that commonwealth coincided with those of the Scandinavian and German colonies in the Baltic region, of the Kingdom of Poland, restored at the turn of the thirteenth century after long internal divisions, and of Hungary, which merely changed its dynasty and under a branch of the Anjous was closer than ever to the Latin West. A conquest of Lithuania proper, which was planned all the time by the Teutonic Knights, and which would leave her Ruthenian dominions exposed to eastern influence, would have been of doubtful advantage from the European point of view. Only a free association of the Grand Duchy with a Catholic power, respecting the Orthodox faith of her East Slavic populations with possible prospects of religious reunion, could extend the Christian Commonwealth far into the Dvina and Dnieper region, making it truly identical with a united Europe, with only the Tartar-controlled transition area between Europe and Asia being left outside.

That whole vital issue was quite insufficiently realized in western Europe, not only in view of geographical remoteness of a little-known area whose fate was to be decided, but also because the Christian Commonwealth continued to face three even greater problems of more direct interest to its original members. One of them, typical of the whole period, was the relationship between the two universal powers which were supposed to lead Christendom: the Papacy and the empire, a problem inseparable from the relationship between the empire and the rapidly-developing national states, all ready to recognize papal, but never imperial authority. While this twofold problem of European unity or diversity was strictly western, another concerned the agelong dualism of Europe and Christendom, which after the final schism between the Western and the Eastern Church had become particularly dangerous and was inseparable from the rival claims to Roman universality raised by each of the two Christian empires, one of them practically German, the other Greek. Last but not least, both Western and Eastern Christendom had to face the problem of defense against Asia, now once more particularly aggressive under Muslim leadership. While the reconquest of the Iberian peninsula from the Arabs was an exclusively western concern, and the Tartar threat exclusively eastern, the crusade for the freedom of the cradle of Christianity and its defense against the Seldshuk, and then the Ottoman Turks, should have united Latin and Greek Christendom. Unfortunately, after initial triumphs outside Europe, the crusading movement, so highly inspired but so frequently misused, left the whole Christian Commonwealth exposed to dangers which were steadily growing in the next period of European history.

CHAPTER XII

The Quest for European Unity

NO PROBLEM OF what is usually called mediaeval history seems to be better known than that of the relations between Papacy and empire. As the main issue of Europe's destiny throughout those centuries which are considered the Middle Ages in the strictest sense—and which saw the fullest development of the Christian Commonwealth—that problem was of special interest both to contemporaries, as evidenced in the historiography and the political philosophy of the period, and to the scholars of later ages even to our time. It is, therefore, not surprising that all the related facts are comparatively well known to historians and even to those who have at least some general information on the so-called mediaeval mind.

The importance of the problem is particularly evident to anybody who is concerned with the idea of European unity. If it is true that such a unity was best achieved in the period of the flowering of the Christian Commonwealth, the reason seems to be that there were in that Commonwealth two universal powers responsible for its harmonious development and supposed to supplement one another in close cooperation. It is, however, no less evident that this was merely an impressive theory, even as such highly controversial in its specific interpretation and never fully realized in practice. If in spite of the cultural unity of the European community, which was almost identical with Christendom, its political unity always remained precarious and its history rich in internal troubles, it was mainly because the two universal powers of the Christian

Commonwealth rarely cooperated in full reciprocal understanding and more often than not were in rivalry with each other. The tension in their relations led time and again to violent conflicts and to a division of Europe into two hostile camps.

It is easy to say in advance that, as is usual in such situations, both sides must share the responsibility for the shortcomings of an apparently very remarkable conception. And it is easy to point out mistakes made by individual popes and emperors who by uncompromising attitudes, even because of personal ambitions, contributed to that basic weakness of the Christian Commonwealth. After the promising start made by men like Sylvester II and Otto III, who had a common vision of that Commonwealth and jointly did their best to make it come true, the high hopes which inaugurated Europe's millennium never fully materialized because of the opposition between its leaders. The judgment of the historian regarding that disconcerting tragedy will always depend upon which of the two competing powers he sympathized with.

What is surprising, however, is the fact that Catholic historiography, which was practically the only one at the time of the great struggles between Papacy and empire, and which always took a leading part in the study of the period, while regretting that there was such a conflict, was nevertheless inclined to glorify the empire and to consider it indispensable for the normal development of the Christian Commonwealth. The idea of imperial authority in the secular field seemed to many of these historians to be as important and uncontroversial as the idea of papal authority in the spiritual field.[1] In their opinion, the source of all the trouble was the difficulty of delimiting both spheres clearly and the only too human inclination of prominent representatives of either power to encroach upon the sphere of the other or even to claim a general superiority.

In such an approach to the problem there is a serious danger of oversimplification and of missing the point which is at the root of the whole difficulty and which leads once more to the basic dualism of the European heritage. The institution of a universal Church was an essential part of Europe's Christian heritage. The institution of a universal empire was, on the contrary, part of the pre-Christian heritage of the ancient world. Two questions remain open: first, whether the imperial idea was an essential part of the Graeco-Roman tradition, and secondly, whether it could be successfully and permanently combined with the Christian conception of the world. Neither of these questions was new, and in the course of the first Christian millennium there had been serious attempts to answer them positively as soon as the Roman Empire had been officially Christianized. The idea of the succession of empires of which the Roman was supposed to be the last one, an idea appearing in the writings of some of the earliest Fathers of the Church, had reappeared time and again in the chronicles of the period of the Christian Commonwealth.[2] However, of all the empires whose names were given on the usual lists before the Roman, only the Macedonian Empire of Alexander the Great could be considered at least partly European and of Hellenic origin: the earlier ones were all non-European and had nothing in common with the heritage of ancient Greece and of the Roman Republic. And in spite of the early Christianization of the Roman Empire, its very idea remained more difficult to reconcile with the Christian idea than any other part of the Graeco-Roman tradition, simply because that part was originally neither Greek nor Roman but taken over from Asia in the last phase of the Mediterranean world.

The very term *imperium* clearly indicates the character of the institution: an autocratic power which had nothing in common with the Greek ideal of freedom nor with the Roman ideal of law, since the emperor, the *princeps,* was supposed to be above the law, *legibus solutus.* Such a power was even more in opposition to the Christian conception of the inalienable dignity of the human person, created to the likeness of God, endowed by Him with a free will under His divine law and the law of nature. Christ recommended recognition of the authority of Caesar, but only as long as it was not in conflict with the supreme authority of God who had to be obeyed more than any man. Therefore all depended on the personality of the ruler, who could be just and human, as was the pagan Augustus under whom Christ was born. But his tyrannic successors had to be opposed by Christ's followers until martyrdom, and even their conversion was no guarantee that they never would overstep the limits of the legitimate authority of a Caesar nor place before their subjects the alternative of obeying either God or man.

All this is obviously true of any political, secular authority, even a non-imperial one; and coming back to the problem of the relations of the Papacy with such authorities, exercising their power within the Christian Commonwealth, it is only fair to recall that in no conflict with any emperor did the Vicar of Christ suffer a greater humiliation than in the struggle with a king of France. This was, however, a rather exceptional case in which that king claimed an authority equal to the imperial one within his particular realm. In general, the danger of such conflicts, so harmful to European unity and to the very concept of the Christian Commonwealth, was naturally greatest in the relations with a power which was stronger than any other and universal like the Papacy itself. And the only such power was the empire, which aimed by definition, if not at world domination, at least at predominance in the world.[3]

The Holy Roman Emperors of the Germanic nation never called themselves officially "autocrats" as did the Eastern Roman Emperors in Byzantium. Even their power as German kings was limited by tradition, by feudal disintegration, and especially by the regional power of the various German dukes. While, however, the Byzantine emperors never claimed any authority over territory outside their realm, the western ones considered themselves the supreme authority of all Christendom, at least of its Latin part which recognized the primacy of the Roman pope in religious matters and was supposed to recognize a similar primacy or suzerainty of the Roman emperor in matters of politics. The character of that imperial overlordship was never clearly defined, but in any case it was much more difficult to accept for the non-German parts of Western Christendom than was the spiritual authority of the pope, since it was the German king who by the mere fact of his imperial coronation became Roman emperor and even before that ceremony was "King of the Romans" also. For that same reason, the Germans were more than any other peoples opposed to any kind of interference of papal Rome, except in cases when local opponents of a German king were playing off papal against imperial authority.

A special source of trouble was the equivocal situation of Italy whose own royal tradition had vanished through the personal union of the Italian with the German kingdom. Italy's central part, including the city of Rome, was under the secular rule of the pope, and separated the southern part, where various alien influences—Greek, Arab, Norman, later also French and Aragonian—were clashing with each other, from the northern part, the only one where the control of the emperor and German king could be exercised more or less efficiently. It was in Italy, and particularly in Rome, where even an emperor like Otto III, facing so much confusion, would occasionally act as a real "autocrat," in spite of his high conception of his imperial mission.

His cooperation with Pope Sylvester II which, in general, worked so well, and which had been preceded through most of the tenth century by the supremacy of strong emperors over rather weak popes who needed their protection, gave way from the middle of the eleventh century onward, to a reversed situation: a pope as prominent and powerful as was Gregory VII could oppose, and temporarily even depose and humiliate an emperor as ambitious as Henry IV when they disagreed about the limits of their respective authorities. The struggle over the investiture of ecclesiastical dignitaries would seem a comparatively minor issue, one of those legal and administrative questions where it was difficult to determine what belonged to either of the two powers: the spiritual or the secular, whether the latter was represented by the emperor or by any other ruler. But in the eyes of the contemporaries, this was a test case which was to decide whether or not the Papacy could challenge the empire when matters of principles and of human freedom from abusive state control were involved. Therefore it is quite justified to look today upon that conflict of a distant past as upon a first "European revolution,"[4] if we mean by revolution a struggle for rights and liberties.

The specific question of lay investiture was settled after the death of both original protagonists by a compromise, by one of those concordats which the Papacy would conclude through the following centuries with any secular power, not only the imperial. But in that same twelfth century, the relations between the Papacy and the empire entered into a particularly critical phase which best reveals the essence of the conflict. The main reason for the deterioration of these relations was the emergence of a German dynasty, the Hohenstaufen, whose members were elected almost regularly to the royal dignity, whose imperial ambitions went especially far, and whose methods came nearest to an arbitrary, despotic government. It is significant that precisely those two who occupy an outstanding place in the German tradition were the most violent opponents of the Papacy: Frederick Barbarossa and Frederick II.

The first of these two was to live in national tradition as the ideal German emperor, and in the legend as the immortal leader who would reappear when most needed. As far as the relations with the non-German peoples of the Christian Commonwealth were concerned, Barbarossa was almost equally interested in both programs of imperial expansion which so frequently represented conflicting alternatives of German policy: the advance toward the East at the expense of the freedom and independence of the Slavs, particularly the Poles, and the consolidation of German rule over the Italians. It was there, in the south, that he clashed with Pope Alexander III in a conflict which was no longer limited to the rivalry between ecclesiastical and secular authority, but touched the

problem of the liberty of the various peoples of the Christian Commonwealth and therefore the basic structure of Europe.

Even more instructive from that point of view is the story of Frederick II. At the beginning of the thirteenth century, after the premature
death of one of the Hohenstaufen, Henry VI—another emperor with
universal ambitions—and the controversy of his heir-apparent Philip of
Swabia with the rival Germany dynasty of the Welfs, it seemed that the
unity of Europe would be achieved under an exclusively papal leadership. Innocent III, one of the greatest popes of all times, was indeed eminently successful not only in his reform of the Church but also in exercising a strong political influence in all European countries at a moment
when the imperial power was vanishing and one ruler after the other entered in some kind of feudal relationship with the Holy See.[5] Yet, toward the end of his pontificate, that same pope who almost made the
Christian Commonwealth dependent on one universal power only, the
spiritual, supported the candidature to the imperial throne of the young
Hohenstaufen, who was to work for the exactly opposite solution in violent opposition against the next three popes: a European community
under the exclusive direction of the secular power of the emperor.

In the European tradition Frederick II is much more than a German
imperialist. Starting his political career in southern Italy, and open even
to Arab influence, he built up in Sicily the prototype of a totalitarian
state which, contrary to the persistent policy of the Holy See, he wanted
to unite not only with the Italian north but also with his German kingdom, where he had restored the supremacy of the Hohenstaufen. He
even wanted to monopolize under imperial guidance that joint concern
of Christendom which was from the outset a papal initiative: the Crusade. His "pilgrimage without faith"[6]—he had been excommunicated by Pope Gregory IX—succeeded in liberating Jerusalem for a second time, and he used the German Order of Knighthood, no longer interested in the Holy Land, for extending German and imperial influence
in the Baltic region.

Admired by many historians even to our time,[7] who like many contemporaries consider him a real *stupor mundi,* he, the "least mediaeval
of all mediaeval men,"[8] did indeed inaugurate an amazing trend in the
European tradition which though it appeared only after the first quarter of the European millennium, was to influence very deeply all the rest
of it. But it was a trend which, under the appearance of Christian principles—still impossible to reject openly in his days—and of one more re-

vival of the Mediterranean heritage, was in opposition to the soundest elements of both, and nothing but a revival of the imperial idea in its original pagan form. He was certainly one of those who, if successful to the end, could have achieved a kind of European unity, but at the price of transforming the Christian Commonwealth into a quasi-universal state under his absolute government. It is typical of Frederick II's methods that he who so strongly opposed the authority of the Church and was himself of rather doubtful orthodoxy was responsible for the establishment of an inquisition which was to be used against dissenters considered dangerous to either state or church.[9] The cultural syncretism at his court, brilliant as it was, certainly did not contribute to the strengthening of a common Christian civilization, a prerequisite condition of Europe's spiritual unity.

Therefore the popes who opposed Frederick II, especially Innocent IV, who during his whole pontificate was absorbed by that violent conflict between Papacy and empire which threatened the unity and peaceful development of the Christian Commonwealth, were defending not merely the interests and claims of the Church, but the very existence of that commonwealth. Not only the crushed Hohenstaufen dynasty, and not only the empire, but both universal powers which were supposed to cooperate suffered from a protracted tension which diverted them from all other objectives and left their authority seriously impaired. But it was precisely during the following interregnum, the years without any emperor which appear so dark in the German tradition,[10] that there was a chance of solving the problem by electing as German king a non-German with little power, of Dutch, Spanish, or English origin, who would have been a truly supranational emperor, ready for cooperation with the Papacy. None of these rather insignificant candidates prevailed, and the only non-German—though one of the princes of the empire—Bohemia's King Přemysl Otakar II, who came near to his ambitious goal of gaining not only the Austrian succession but also the German and Roman crowns, lost both to his rival, Rudolf of Habsburg.

Nor did the latter wield a power comparable to that of the earlier German dynasties, and it took more than a century and a half, almost to the middle of Europe's millennium, before his family, the House of Austria as it was later called, succeeded in making the imperial crown *de facto* its hereditary possession, at a time when the universality of the empire was already a mere fiction. The first Habsburgs were even less dangerous to papal authority than Otakar would have been, and it was during the reign of one of them that Boniface VIII could proclaim, in 1300, a first jubilee year which gathered in Rome pilgrims from all Christian countries in an imposing manifestation of their spiritual unity. But after the defeat of that same pope in his conflict with Philip the Fair of France, and the transfer of the papal curia to Avignon, the Holy See had to deal with emperors belonging to various new German dynasties and to face again the agelong problem as to which universal power would be supreme in the Christian Commonwealth.

One of these emperors, Henry VII, deserves attention despite his premature death, because it was from him that the greatest citizen of that commonwealth,[11] the Italian Dante, expected the salvation not only of Christian Europe but of the whole world,[12] through the establishment of a universal monarchy. Likewise, Henry's dynasty, the Luxemburgs, was, much later, to make a last attempt to save imperial universalism. How utopian it was to hope that the empire rather than the Papacy could achieve the real unity of Christendom and world peace became apparent when the successor of the first Luxemburg emperor, Louis the Bavarian, entered into a conflict with Pope John XXII, which revived the whole controversial problem in spite of the minor issues which seemed to be at its root.

The so-called Babylonian exile of the Holy See was more a symptom than the basic reason for a crisis during which the Papacy emerged victorious from a last open struggle with the empire but did not recover its earlier authority. That authority had proved unable to guarantee peace and order in the Christian Commonwealth even at a time when it was exercised by the greatest popes residing in Rome and when it remained practically unchallenged at least in the spiritual sphere. Now at the time of the first Avignon popes, such a challenge, which not only questioned their political leadership but also undermined the doctrinal position of the Papacy, came from a prominent writer and political philosopher, Marsilius of Padua, who, while pretending to be a *defensor pacis,* can be considered a precursor of the religious revolutions of the following period.[13] Far from contributing to any real peace, the new trends which that sensational treatise represented endangered even the spiritual unity of Europe and made it clear that in order to establish the political unity of the Christian Commonwealth, the leading role of the Papacy had to be implemented and supported by a supranational secular organization, more reliable and acceptable to both the Church and the individual states than the empire had been at the height of its power.

Shortly before, there appeared another treatise,[14] which attempted to find the best ways of regaining the Holy Land by outlining a first project of such an organization based upon the idea of arbitration in all conflicts between the various sovereign states. This project respected the authority of the Papacy, but it had no better chances of being universally accepted than the imperial claims: coming from Pierre Dubois, an advisor of the king of France, it would have placed the Christian Commonwealth under the leadership of one individual country. The popes of the second part of the Avignon period, much less dependent on the French power which was declining in the Hundred Years War, had the advantage of finding the loyal cooperation of an outstanding emperor, Charles of Luxemburg, who though of German origin, was first of all king of Bohemia and strongly influenced by French and Italian culture.[15] Since he lacked any autocratic leanings and was even gradually reaching understandings with the empire's eastern neighbors, Charles IV could perhaps have prevented the western Schism if he had not died in that very year, 1378, when that disastrous division of Latin Christendom originated.

Much more dangerous and scandalous than the temporary residence of the popes at Avignon—though facilitated by the aftermath of that anomalous situation—the Great Schism, as it is rightly called, not only delayed promising prospects for ending the old schism between West and East,[16] but marked the end of the Christian Commonwealth: the first period of Europe's millennium. The idea and even the name of such a commonwealth did not, of course, suddenly disappear, but it ceased to correspond to a reality representing the unity of Europe. However, during the western Schism, under the impression of its disastrous consequences, serious efforts were made to save that unity and to give it better foundations, and though all that was saved was the unity of the Roman Church, these attempts are instructive to study from the point of view of general European history.

What is particularly striking in that respect are the political implications of the so-called conciliary movement, a trend which wanted to utilize the old institution of ecumenical councils for a pacification and reunion not only of the Church but of Europe as well. While during the first Christian millennium all these councils had met in the East, those of the second millennium, that of the European community, were convoked in the West, in or near Rome. At least one of them, the Fourth Lateran Council of 1215, the climax of the pontificate of Innocent III, was certainly of general European significance.[17] So was, to a certain extent, the next council at Lyons in 1245, the first to be held in France; however, on that occasion the struggle against Emperor Frederick II proved a great obstacle to the constructive initiatives of Innocent IV. Now, after two more councils of limited importance had gathered in France, and with an interruption of about one hundred years, the great councils of the early fifteenth century turned into international congresses with unusually ambitious agenda including the re-establishment of peace between the quarrelling European powers. However, that belated attempt to reorganize the Christian Commonwealth under the leadership of regular assemblies in which all the European nations were represented with a large participation of laymen was doomed to failure.

Even the purely ecclesiastic matters directly regarding the universal power of the Papacy were only partially settled. The urgent task of ending the schism by the election of a universally recognized pope was accomplished in 1417 after long negotiations, but barely two decades later another schism resulted from the conflict between papal and conciliar authority, the latter claiming to be superior. Alarmed by that experience, the Holy See hesitated for a long time to convoke any council, thus postponing indefinitely the badly needed reforms which the troublesome earlier councils had but started. Their treatment of a heresy more dangerous than any of the past, the revolutionary Hussite movement, was never coordinated with the attitude of the popes and turned from violent repressions which failed to a vague compromise which did not satisfy either side. The role of the new universal power, the universities, proved of little help because the leading institutions sided with the extreme doctrines of conciliarism. And as to the imperial power which once more, in the person of Sigismund of Luxemburg, tried to dominate if not supplant the papacy, it had been so weakened by a political schism between candidates to the crown, that its authority was even farther from being universally accepted than in past centuries.

These disappointing developments, which clearly indicated that the European community had entered an entirely new period of its history, and which were in sharp contrast with the general situation during the outgoing one, help us to understand why even then the constitution of the Christian Commonwealth had been far from perfect. It is rather surprising that for three centuries the Papacy had succeeded, through its own endeavors, to keep that Commonwealth alive. The empire, which all along had been an obstacle rather than the expected help, failed completely at a time when its part in the direction of the Christian Commonwealth was particularly responsible during the worst crisis of western unity. No other institution, neither the ecumenical councils nor the community of scholars, was ready to fill the gap and to create a link between the ecclesiastical and the secular elements of European unity.

Thus it seems even more surprising to note the constructive achievements of the period, when, under papal leadership, the Christian Commonwealth was not only a symbol of European unity but gave to that unity a real meaning. The dualism between the Christian and the ancient tradition seemed to be successfully overcome, because without rejecting or neglecting the uncontroversial values of the latter, Christian faith and morals were even more uncontroversial in all spheres of life, including the political. Particularly obvious was the progress of spiritual culture both in thought and in art: philosophy and historiography developed the European conscience while architecture and poetry enriched the daily life of the European peoples. The Latin language continued to serve as an intellectual bond among these peoples without hindering the growing use of the vernacular wherever and whenever it was ready to be an additional vehicle for various kinds of writing. Furthermore, the Christian inspiration which remained common to all these activities of the mind found its most eloquent expression in the lives of so many saints, among whom Saint Francis of Assisi, the most appealing of all, represents the best synthesis of the period.

His greatness has always been recognized even by non-Christians. And likewise, after exhaustive critical research, all now recognize the greatness of the civilization of a period which is no longer included with the preceding "dark ages" nor unfavorably contrasted with that flowering of European culture which occurred in the following centuries. This flowering would have been impossible without the preparation of the real "Middle Ages." If that term makes any sense at all, it is with specific reference to these first centuries of the European millennium, midway between the equally millenary process of Europe's making and the beginning of the world-wide influence of the European community.

It is in these same centuries of the Christian Commonwealth that the social and economic life of most of Europe was shaped by feudalism, a term which even more than mediaevalism suffers from a vague and generalized interpretation, or rather, misuse. Under Marxist influence,[18] it is employed to cover a much longer period of European and even universal history, at least to the French Revolution, with repercussions until our time. It also suffers from a prejudice, which is even stronger than the old one against everything "mediaeval": feudalism is frequently considered the opposite of our present conception of democratic equality and freedom for all. However, even without stressing the anachronism of such an approach, it must be recalled, again in the light of specialized research,[19] that the real feudalism, i.e. the structure of society in Romance and Teutonic Europe from about the tenth to the fourteenth century, led to processes of feudalization in the East European countries but that it never fully developed there.[20] The real feudalism established a system much less oppressive and arbitrary than the social and economic conditions of not only the earlier but also the subsequent centuries, controlled and mitigated as it was by the Christian principles of the period.

The fate of the peasants was certainly better then than in the following period of serfdom, which in some countries was a return to pre-feudal conditions of near-slavery. At the same time the cities of various parts of Europe, especially Italy and the Low Countries, which were endowed with that broad self-government that was typical of all "mediaeval" communities, enjoyed not only prosperity but a considerable amount of freedom. And if full freedom and political influence was largely limited to a privileged land-owning knighthood that eventually became the European nobility, such a limitation of the absolute power of the rulers in favor of a substantial, and in some cases, a quite large part of the population, was an unquestionable advance on the difficult road to liberty. It was truly in the spirit of the best traditions of the Graeco-Roman, pre-imperial world, and of the Christian ideas applied to public life.[21]

There was the possibility of a progressive evolution on that road, and it certainly was not the fault of the Christian Commonwealth nor of its heritage if in most European countries the normal development of the Estates was interrupted by the rise of modern absolutism. The most famous charters or bills of rights of the "mediaeval" period, like the English *Magna Carta* of 1215, followed seven years later by the Hungarian Golden Bull, both similar to the first privileges granted still later to the Polish knights, may today seem inadequate. But it must be remembered that they led to parliamentary forms of government which, therefore, like so many other achievements, have their roots in the early centuries of Europe's millennium. These examples lead from the problem of European unity in a Christian Commonwealth to that of diversity in its individual nations.

CHAPTER XIII

The Development of European Diversity

IN THE WHOLE COURSE of Europe's millennium no conception had a better chance to achieve European unity than that of the Christian Commonwealth. The conflict between Papacy and empire was certainly one of the reasons why this unity of Europe was never completely nor permanently established. Probably that conflict was the principal reason for such a failure because it opposed to each other the two universal powers on whose cooperation the Christian Commonwealth was to be based, and because both of them were seriously weakened by their repeated struggles. Yet, these struggles and rivalries were obviously not the only reason why at the end of the first period of its existence as an integrated community Europe remained far from being successfully united and organized. An almost equally important reason was the high degree of diversity within the European community: a diversity which had been typical of the original nucleus of Europe that was ancient Greece; which survived in the whole Mediterranean world in spite of its rather superficial unification by force under the pagan Roman Empire; which was respected, except in faith and morals, by Christianity; and which was steadily growing with the expansion of Christian Europe toward the extreme limits of the Continent and with the inclusion of more and more diverse peoples in the community of Christendom.

These two obstacles to European unity, though entirely different from each other, were not unconnected. The claim to leadership and supremacy, raised by the restored empire, made the idea of European unity particularly difficult to accept by the various peoples, except by the Germans to whom the Roman Empire was transferred. This was so even in times of mutual understanding between the empire and the Papacy, when the latter sanctioned, at least in theory, the political claims of the former. The opposition to these claims was, of course, still stronger and had better chances of success whenever the two universal powers were in disagreement. At such times, the spiritual power was ready to protect against the secular all the nations which resented the privileged position of one of them.

The repeated use of the word "nation" in a discussion of European diversity of these remote centuries immediately raises the doubt whether such a terminology is not anachronistic, projecting into bygone periods the issues which appeared in the latest one, and particularly in our own time, as consequences of the development of nationalism. But even if it is accepted that the nationalism which is called "integral" and even considered a kind of modern "religion" is a product of the last two hundred years—strictly speaking, of the period following the French Revolution[1]—this does not necessarily mean that other forms of nationalism did not exist before and that the idea of nationalism cannot be traced back to the earliest origins, Hebrew and Greek, of our civilization.[2] And even less does it mean that the idea of nation cannot have existed and exercised an important influence before the idea of nationalism— that of a primary if not exclusive dedication to the nation—was fully developed.

The trouble is, however, that there is not, and never had been, any universally accepted definition of the term "nation," no more than of the term "nationalism" which distinguishes it clearly from other "isms." Therefore, when the word *natio* appears, as it frequently does, in the sources of different ages including the so-called Middle Ages, the historian is not sure of its real meaning, which may possibly be very different from any present one. In each case he has to make an effort at specific interpretation; and how difficult that is can be illustrated by two examples, taken from the transition period when the universalism of the Christian Commonwealth was already in retreat.

One at least of the great councils of the Church—that of Constance, which tried so hard to promote a truly Christian universalism—decided to divide itself into nations, deliberating and voting separately, simply because it wanted to prevent the supremacy of one of them, the Italian. But while the latter, as well as the French, English, and the Spanish (the last-named was eventually added to the original group), corresponded more or less to the peoples which would be so called today, the German nation at that council included a great variety of peoples, indeed, practically all the others, even the Poles who at Constance were in open conflict with the Germans.[3] In ecclesiastical councils such a formal division was rather exceptional and, since it did not help much in Constance, was abandoned at the next council in Basle. On the contrary, the distinction of separate nations was then a rule in the organization of most universities,[4] in spite or perhaps because of the cosmopolitan character of their teaching staff and student bodies. There, however, the difference between these academic nations and those of modern times is even more striking. Thus, for instance, a crisis at the University of Prague, only a few years before the Council of Constance, was caused by the repartition of the German students in three nations out of four, all three corresponding to regions or provinces only, an artificial measure which gave to the Germans a strong majority over the Czechs.

If the terminology in that matter was confusing even in the early fifteenth century, it is not surprising to find it even more so three hundred years earlier. A recent study on the problem of the "nations" in the first crusade[5] has shown that the contemporary chronicles were even then well aware of the great diversity among the *Christi membra*—the citizens of the Christian Commonwealth—participating in that common enterprise of Christendom, at least of all western Europe. It was pointed out that these *membra* were *linguis, tribubus et nationibus differentia,* but since three terms were used to describe that difference, the interpretation of any of them is very difficult, especially that of the last one. That it must have had a much less precise meaning than language or tribe is best evidenced by the fact that the name of the people which even then seemed to come nearest to the modern concept of a nation, *Franci* or *Francigenae,* was used in the sources in three different senses. Rarely does it correspond to the inhabitants of what was called France in later centuries and what then was split into at least three parts like ancient Gaul. Usually the *Francia* of these *Francigenae* designated only the area controlled directly, or through immediate vassals, by the king of France. However, at the same time, the name *Franci* was very frequently used not in a smaller but in a much larger sense than in modern history, since all the crusaders were called *Franci,* especially in the Christian as well as the Mohammedan East: the French predominance among them made it natural to extend their name to *universos occidentales populos.*

Before trying to determine whether, or to what extent, it is legitimate to call these *populi*—which must be distinguished in western Christendom from the very outset of Europe's millennium—by the ambiguous term "nation," it seems advisable, as in so many similar cases, to give some thought to the strictly philological sense and origin of the Latin *natio* from which that word is derived in modern languages. That noun is indeed derived in turn from the verb *nasci,* i.e. "to be born." A *natio,* therefore, must be in any case a group of men and women whose community is primarily based on their common origin by birth. And that reminds us immediately of the origin of the closely associated word, *patria,*[6] which literally means the land of our *patres* and therefore of all those who are of the same ancestry. However, such a community, the *natio* to which a certain group of peoples belongs, as well as the *patria,* to which they owe their "patriotism" or loyalty, can be conceived in very different ways as far as its smaller or larger extension is concerned. Between the family, the smallest human group of common birth which certainly is not a nation, and the population of a whole continent, which even if of common racial origin, is hardly a nation either, there were throughout the evolution of mankind intermediary communities of different sizes. In the period under consideration, the enlarged family, including all those who shared the tradition of a common ancestor, still played an important part in the history of some regions of Europe, whether it was called a clan as in Ireland and Scotland, or a *gens* v. *genus* as in the Latin terminology of Poland and Hungary.[7] Almost everywhere the much broader tribal tradition was very much alive, and especially in Germany it influenced the creation and delimitation of the various duchies very strongly. And almost everywhere the first loyalty of the people would go to the individual region, usually called *terra* in a sense which reappears in the vernacular of the various European tongues, the loyalty to an individual city being a comparable phenomenon.

While such local subdivisions were favored and perpetuated by the feudal structure of society, there was, on the other hand, a parallel development leading to the integration of such comparatively minor territories under the same political authority. While the ramifications of a ruling house would multiply regional units and take advantage of their local traditions, ambitious members of the same dynasty would represent an opposite trend, one toward centralization in a larger state unified under their individual control. Such a process was facilitated when the larger area was united by its ecclesiastical organization and inhabited by a population speaking the same language, and when the ruler succeeded in obtaining a royal crown which had an almost mystical significance.[8] There remained only one further stage: the unification of such states, including even kingdoms, in an empire.

On each of these successive stages, a community which would deserve the name of a nation in the modern sense could come into existence. Various factors contributed to such a result: the tradition of a common origin, the geographical conditions, the use of the same or of similar languages, the creation of ecclesiastical provinces at the top of the parochial and diocesan organization, and last but not least—perhaps even more decisive in many cases—the inclusion in one and the same body politic. To what extent the state can be or should be identified with the nation, and which communities have the right to claim self-determination—these problems which seem so typical of our time have their roots in the earliest centuries of the European millennium. And among the various individual cases which have to be studied in that connection, that of the restored Roman Empire, typical of these centuries, is particularly instructive.

Though that empire was supposed to be universal or, as we would say today, supranational, it was called, at least from the middle of the fifteenth century,[9] the Roman Empire of the German Nation. That *contradictio in adiecto* can only be explained by the fact that contrary to the original, theoretical conception, that largest European state was practically identical with the nation whose king was its head. For that very reason, in the study of that early period, it is hardly anachronistic to speak of a German nationalism, promoted by the *translatio imperii*. On the other hand, in spite of the fact that peoples of Teutonic origin, speaking the same German language though in various dialects, constituted not only the leadership but the great majority of the empire's population, there was an extreme diversity within the imperial boundaries. That diversity resulted from the existence of various communities which occupied an intermediary position between the empire and the individual families. Out of these communities, by far the largest and most important was, of course, the German kingdom, older than the restored empire itself, but neither before nor after 962 a homogeneous unity, since it was divided into the even older tribal territories, now constituted into duchies under their hereditary dynasties. New duchies were gradually created out of some of the marches along the frontiers, the case of Austria, which broke away from the duchy of Bavaria in the twelfth century, being the most significant.[10] Division was a source of trouble, as evidenced by the long and hard struggle between the emperors of the house of Hohenstaufen and the dukes of Saxony of the Welf dynasty, but obviously none of these duchies was ever considered a separate nation. Their regionalism and rivalries simply retarded the merger of all these territories and their peoples into one German nation, though only in the marches like Austria did non-German, Slavic populations survive as submerged minorities.

There was, however, one exception: the duchy of Bohemia,[11] with a predominantly Slavic, Czech population and until 1306 under the native dynasty of the Přemyslides. The emperors tried in vain to separate from Bohemia proper the margravate of Moravia and in both lands it was the German settlers who constituted a minority. That there was between the two ethnic groups a growing antagonism is expressed in sources of the twelfth century, to mention only the chronicle of Cosmas and the decree of Duke Soběslav, guaranteeing the rights of the separate German group. Since the linguistic difference contributed to that opposition, it can be considered an early example of nationalism as a dividing issue. Furthermore, in the year 1158 of that same century, the dukes of Bohemia, one of whom had personally received the royal title in 1085, were made hereditary kings by the emperor whom they supported against the Papacy, and the exceptional, foremost position of Bohemia within the empire became even more conspicuous. It was finally recognized in 1212, by the so-called Golden Bull of Sicily, and there is a strange coincidence in the fact that the much more famous Golden Bull of 1356, which settled the problem of the emperor's election by establishing seven electors including the king of Bohemia, was issued by an emperor, Charles IV, who was himself king of Bohemia, and though of German origin, the heir of the Přemyslide tradition. The problem of the rights of that Slavic kingdom within the practically German Empire, which were symbolized by the crown of Saint Václav, was mainly a constitutional issue but naturally was not without national implications. This constituted another early factor contributing to the rise of a Czech nationalism opposed to a German one.

Originally there had been within the Ottonian Empire but outside the German kingdom two other kingdoms, older than the Bohemian, which were completely non-German but of an ephemeral character. The kingdom of Arles or Burgundy,[12] which never was fully integrated with the empire, was composed of territories which in agreement with their French character soon came under French political influence, contributing to the difficulty of establishing a definite frontier between the empire and the Capetingian kingdom of France. The Kingdom of Italy, now practically reduced to Lombardy, left behind strong Italian populations in opposition to the German emperors who claimed at least the northern part of the peninsula, and that opposition was another case of nationalistic tension within the empire. It is true that these populations constituted no nation in the modern sense, but some basic elements of a different national consciousness undoubtedly appeared even then on both sides. Each of them spoke its own language and, proud of a distinct tradition, claimed some kind of superiority, political on the German side and cultural on the Italian.

The extreme diversity of political structure within the boundaries of the empire was indeed favorable to the protection and development of local and regional liberties. But at the same time it resulted in dangerous tensions even in the purely German part and was combined with even more dangerous national rivalries where these internal differences were of an ethnic character. It is thus readily understandable that the much greater differences between the imperial territory and the countries outside of it made any extension of that territory very difficult and the claims of any kind of imperial overlordship practically impossible to enforce, especially since all these other countries were non-German.

Therefore the only territorial expansion of the empire in the period of its greatest power and authority was the final conquest of the Slavic territories between Germany and Poland, where the old marches were enlarged and integrated with the empire and the native population Germanized.[13] The areas of German colonial expansion in the Baltic region were also under the empire and required a similar form of armed conquest, though the connection with the State of the Teutonic order, which was separated from Germany geographically, always remained rather loose. The case of the Kingdom of Sicily and Naples, which had been gained by the Hohenstaufen, was different but it was only in personal union with the empire and was lost to it as soon as that German dynasty was replaced by French or Aragonian rulers.

All the other states of Europe succeeded in defending their complete independence from the empire, including those which at the time of Otto III had seemed prepared to enter into some kind of association and cooperation with it, like Poland and possibly also Hungary and Venice.[14]

Later attempts by Otto's successors, who did not share his vision of a truly supranational community, to take advantage of internal troubles in Poland and Hungary in order to obtain some recognition of their suzerainty, merely provoked an even stronger opposition and resistance against this German penetration. The Republic of Venice, rapidly growing in power, not only preserved its own liberty but began defending that of Italy as a whole.[15]

Corresponding to that situation along the empire's northeastern and southeastern frontiers were the attitude of its immediate western neighbor, the Kingdom of France, which considered itself equal to Germany in spite of the latter's imperial title, and the political position of the various kingdoms in northwestern, southwestern, and northern Europe. Except for Denmark, these did not have a common frontier either with Germany or the empire. Not even in the Danish case, where a comparatively small state attained a leading position in the Scandinavian world, could German territorial claims nor those of imperial authority materialize.[16] Faraway England, whose independence could not really be threatened because of the geographical situation, and whose own ambitions aimed at a leading position in the British Isles including Ireland, and at the preservation of the French heritage of her dynasty after the Norman conquest, did not fail to raise her voice in opposition to the idea that the emperor could have supremacy over that non-German kingdom.[17] Last but not least, the kingdoms which expanded in the equally distant Iberian peninsula, though involved in a continuous hard struggle with the Moors, were not interested in gaining assistance from a foreign imperial power and would rather try to strengthen their own authority by using an imperial title themselves.[18]

All these states fully recognized the universal authority of the Papacy, which, though basically a spiritual one, would sometimes interfere with their internal problems and try to mediate in their rivalries whenever moral issues were involved. But none of these independent countries, large or small, was prepared to admit any universal authority of the empire which would have been purely political.

In that connection there reappears, of course, the question whether such a diversity within the Christian Commonwealth, especially in the European community outside the empire, had a national character comparable to the divisions of Europe in the later periods of her millennium. All these divisions were, to a certain degree, the consequence of the great geographical diversity typical of the European part of the world, and even more, determined by the historical process of the formation of the European states, whose origin can be traced back, in many cases, farther than the origin of the European community. The rivalries among these states, as well as their reluctance to submit to the leadership of one of them, were primarily motivated by dynastic or even simply personal ambitions of their rulers. But nevertheless, living together in a region with its own special interests and under a rule to which its inhabitants were becoming accustomed could not but create among the given people a feeling of community which made them conscious of their difference from other peoples, in spite of the bonds of common religion which united them all. And though the general aspects of culture and way of life were similar in all countries which had been Christianized by Rome, cultural differences rooted in their pagan past, their racial background, and particularly in their language, all developed.

The linguistic factor which was to prove so strong and sometimes decisive in the growth of European nationalism, was of lesser importance at a time when those actively participating in political life and cultural production were all using the Latin language. But with the cultural progress of the common people and the growing use of the vernacular even in literature and administration, the linguistic differences among the Europeans, especially between those who were unable to understand each other because they belonged to different linguistic groups, were more and more contributing to their divisions and to their consciousness of separateness. This factor has much in common with the national consciousness of modern times.

These elements of diversity were strengthened by two other factors, one of them positive, the other one negative but particularly influential. Not only the leaders but also their collaborators and subjects were becoming proud of their achievements, of their traditions and prospects of further advancement, which they were not prepared to share with other people living beyond their frontiers. And when, from the other side, there appeared any kind of pressure dictated by the desire of conquest and by a feeling, justified or not, of superiority, it created in reaction a determination of self-defense and even a feeling of hostility which easily made dynastic rivalries truly national struggles.

The fear of foreign rule and of the loss of freedom, that negative but well understandable feature of rising nationalism, is, as a matter of fact, as old as human history. At the time of the Christian Commonwealth this fear appeared wherever one of the European countries, in disregard of Christian principles, wanted to conquer another one—the relations between Ireland and England being a striking example—and especially when in the name of the universal authority of the empire, German expansion threatened neighboring peoples. In Poland, for instance, a clearly national antagonism against the Germans and their influence was expressed as early as the thirteenth century, and when the defense against the Teutonic Order and the territorial losses suffered in that struggle increased the tension, the national consciousness became so strong that in an exceptionally interesting document of 1339[19] it is expressed in almost modern form. When representatives of all classes of society were requested to testify as to Poland's rights to occupied frontier regions, they said in their answers to a detailed inquiry that Poland meant not only the territory under her king or Polish dukes, but all lands which were originally Polish and where the Polish language was spoken, the language which the Teutonic invaders pretended not to understand.

The statements of these Poles are of general interest, because they were submitted to the papal delegates who were to arbitrate in the conflict between the kingdom of Poland and the Teutonic Knights. The whole story is therefore an example not only of strong national feelings at an early period but also of the mediating role which the Papacy tried to play among the members of the Christian Commonwealth even at the time of its residence in Avignon. On that occasion, as on so many others in better days, the whole effort was made in vain: the Order, in spite of its ecclesiastical character, did not even care to be represented before the papal judges. This shows clearly the weakness of an international structure in which the only truly supranational power was a spiritual one with a merely moral authority. The crisis of that authority in the fourteenth century definitely put an end to the high hopes of the first period of the European millennium.

This does not mean, however, that the diversity within the European community was only an evil with destructive consequences. The development of individual nations unquestionably enriched European and Christian culture and could lead to the *diversitas in unitate* which always remained a distinctive feature of that culture and a source of its greatness. What was needed in such conditions was peaceful cooperation among all members of the community, and this was precisely the ideal which both the Papacy and the empire were supposed to promote. Since the cooperation between the two did not materialize and the empire became nothing more than one of several rival secular powers, strong enough to raise apprehensions among the others and yet too weak to enforce its control, there appeared the necessity of finding new ways and means for reconciling the ideas of unity and diversity. Such a reconciliation would stabilize the European order which, after all, had survived for almost four centuries. And here again the historian meets a problem which, like that of nationalism, is a permanent feature of Europe's millenary evolution in spite of the changing forms: the problem of federalism.

At least one example of federalism is to be found in the ancient Mediterranean world, where so many issues of Europe's later destiny have their antecedents. But the Achaean League,[20] which did not even include all of Greece, was so limited in scope and so incapable of assuring the freedom of its members—all absorbed later by the Roman Empire—that it is hardly an encouraging example. In its restored, Christian form, the empire itself can be considered some kind of federation, and it is perhaps because of that federal constitution that it lasted so long, notwithstanding so many imperfections. It is true that the lack of unity within the empire was a source of weakness, but only because federalism was not well enough organized in that early and unusually difficult case, and contained no guarantees of equality among the component members. This was precisely the reason why within the empire local federations were formed, which come much nearer to our present conception of federalism than the general structure. The two most striking examples are the League of the Lombard cities in the twelfth century and the Swiss Confederation in the thirteenth.

In the first case, the federation was directed against the empire, originating in the part of it where the internal diversity had a national character. But the Lombard League, which included only a few city-states and not the whole Italian area opposed to German domination, though strong enough to create serious troubles to Barbarossa, proved too weak to liberate itself from imperial rule or even to create within the empire an autonomous member-state. Thus, it was doomed to disappear as soon as Frederick I succeeded in coming to an agreement with the Papacy, the only possible protector of that abortive and ephemeral federation which could have been an early nucleus of Italian unity.

The Swiss case is entirely different and much more instructive.[21] In that case, too, the area included in the federal system was originally very small, just a few mountain valleys with a rather scarce population. Furthermore, the population of the primitive cantons was purely German and had no intention of seceding from the empire nor of opposing it. It looked, on the contrary, for imperial protection against oppressive feudal lords. Nevertheless, if that covenant, which was finally signed on August 1, 1291, after a process of maturing that lasted almost the whole century, is celebrated even today as the national holiday of Switzerland, and rightly considered the start of the most perfect federation in Europe, it is because the Confederation, enlarged in a slow, organic development, gradually including peoples of different ethnic origin, and separated from the empire as soon as it had become a real nation, gave to the other, more homogeneous and much larger nations of the Continent, a perfect example of a peace-loving state based on freedom for all which combined diversity and unity in a truly Christian spirit.

In the century following the foundation of that extraordinary body politic, there also appeared a trend toward uniting kingdoms with much older traditions through dynastic ties. These could turn into real federations.[22] First, the idea of uniting Bohemia and Poland reappeared, this time under the leadership of Bohemia, whose dynasty also tried to succeed the Arpadians in Hungary. But the Přemyslids themselves died out immediately after apparently attaining that double objective. Furthermore, there was a basic obstacle to their projects: Bohemia remained part of the empire, and therefore any union with her would endanger the full independence of nations which were inclined to remain outside of it.[23] Soon, however, dynastic unions between just such nations were to be prepared, the first examples in the Scandinavian region being followed by similar developments in the large area east of the empire, where in spite of a particularly great diversity, or perhaps because of it and all the inherent dangers, such a trend toward federalism was particularly strong.

The first of these unions was concluded between Poland, where the royal branch of the native Piast dynasty was coming to an end, and Hungary, where a branch of the French dynasty also ruling in southern Italy contributed to cultural ties with the Romance West that were closer than ever before. That combination, well prepared and corresponding to an already traditional cooperation between the two nations, proved less successful than expected and had to be revised anyway when the Anjous of Hungary soon died out. This happened at a time when the first period of Europe's millennium was definitely ending, a few years after the western Schism which shook the very foundations of the Christian Commonwealth. The entirely new, quite unexpected federal system which emerged instead and which changed the destinies of the whole

region is already typical of the next period of European history, though
the outstanding personality who made possible such a turn of events is
one of the noblest incarnations of the spirit of the preceding centuries.

This brief reference to Hedvige, the Hungarian princess of French
descent, who as Queen of Poland married the pagan Grand Duke of
Lithuania in order to convert him with his whole nation,[24] naturally
leads to the two remaining problems which make the history of the
Christian Commonwealth so difficult to understand fully: the unfortunate division and rivalry between western and eastern Christendom and
their respective spheres of influence, and the defense of both of them
against the dangers which in changing forms were threatening the
European community from the non-Christian and non-European East.
Both of them explain why the Christian Commonwealth, as a lasting
organization of Europe, in spite of the greatness of that conception,
could not fully succeed and remained only an inspiring tradition.

CHAPTER XIV

The Eastern Schism

A MONG THE MANY PROMISING PERSPECTIVES which seemed to open around the year 1000, there was one which only recently[1] received due attention in the study of history. There was, indeed, a unique chance of understanding being reached between the two Christian empires, western and eastern, at a time when there was not any schism between the Latin and the Greek Church. After a legation in 998 from Otto III to Basil II, which may have convinced the latter that the views of the two regarding the imperial authority and its relations with the Papacy were not irreconcilable, the Byzantine Emperor, when he himself was in a rather critical situation three years later, was ready to give his niece Zoe, the daughter of Constantine VIII, in marriage to the son of Theophano, the half-Greek Emperor of the West. This could have meant recognition of Otto III as another Roman Emperor by associating him with the imperial family of the East, just as Otto himself was creating a family of Christian rulers by matrimonial or at least spiritual ties with many of them. However, in the following year the death of the young Western Emperor put an end to that project, as to so many others which were part of his inspiring vision, and no similar opportunity for establishing a Christian Commonwealth embracing all Christian Europe was ever to reappear.

On the contrary, the interlude between Photius and Cerularius, between the first serious threat of a break that would set Rome and Constantinople at odds in the late ninth century, and the final schism in the middle of the eleventh, was approaching that truly tragic end. The tensions, which in spite of the apparently preserved unity of Christendom had manifested themselves time and again in the course of the tenth century, resulted in an estrangement between West and East which was deeper than ever before when Basil II died soon after his triumph over the Bulgarians. The unsettled relations between the two competing empires were less of a decisive factor than on earlier or later occasions, if only because of their common opposition to the Normans in southern Italy. Neither the successors of Otto III, who were not particularly interested in Constantinople and who were frequently in conflict with the Papacy, nor those of Basil II, the last, weak representatives of the outgoing Macedonian dynasty, were responsible for the deterioration of the relations between the western and the eastern churches. But the most recent research regarding the origin of that break has made it quite clear that in addition to the political factors—not always equally important— and to the purely ecclesiastical factors, at first concerning problems of administration rather than of faith, cultural factors, deeply rooted in the traditions of either side, were leading to the events of 1054.

These cultural differences between Latins and Greeks, which in view of the difference of language found their expression in daily life and intercourse, gave an exaggerated importance to questions of rite and liturgy. Furthermore, the different theological methods made any doctrinal discussions extremely difficult. All these obstacles lead back to the dualism of Europe's ancient, Graeco-Roman heritage, which survived through the first Christian millennium and in the second made the constitution of the European community an almost impossible task if all of Europe was really to be united. But those deeper reasons which so decisively contributed to the final schism should not make the historian overlook that on that occasion, as on so many others, there was no predetermined, unescapable necessity of a tragic outcome. This outcome resulted, instead, from fateful mistakes made by individual human beings, unprepared to meet their responsibilities and hardly conscious of them. This, too, has been clearly shown by modern research, most recently on the occasion of the nine-hundredth anniversary of the schism,[2] and deserves the attention of those who are interested in the impact of that event on the millennium of Europe.

By no means is it an overemphasis on the role of leading personalities in history to present the conflict of 1054 as the clash between the characters and ambitions of two men, representing the Latin West and the

Greek East. The Greek was not the emperor: on the contrary Constantine IX Monomachus did his best to avoid the break—one more piece of evidence, not the only one in the story of schism and reunion, that one has to be careful in speaking about caesaropapism in Byzantium. The Latin was not the pope: Leo IX was already dead and the see of Rome vacant when his legate placed the document of excommunication on the altar of Saint Sophia's. Therefore it was not the "hybris" of one of the successors of Peter which made an understanding impossible, nor could the question of papal infallibility be raised in connection with the condemnation of the Patriarch of Constantinople and of his adherents on July 16, 1054.

Rome was indeed responsible for the choice of her principal representative, Cardinal Humbert, a prominent, scholarly man who unfortunately was not at all qualified to negotiate with the Greeks, having no understanding either for their position or for Patriarch Cerularius in particular, a man as proud and impassionate as his opponent. That the patriarch was in addition ignorant and devious, even more concerned with minor, formal questions than the other Greeks had been, made things even worse and practically hopeless as far as an agreement between the two protagonists was concerned, who represented the extreme viewpoints in the matter of papal primacy.

All this now seems well established, as well as the reason why the emperor's last-minute attempts to reconcile the two were doomed to failure. More difficult to explain are the lasting consequences of the break which were to affect the destinies of Europe and Christendom until our day, though just now, at the close of Europe's millennium, the prospects of reconciliation seem better than ever before. From the outset it was a question not only of the direct relations between Rome and Constantinople—which were important enough—but also of whether the schism would have its repercussions in the whole area controlled by the Greek Church. We know today that the papal delegation did not return to Rome via faraway Kiev,[3] where there was at the same time a tension in the relations with Constantinople and no awareness of what had happened there. The slowness of the repercussions of the Greek schism in northeastern Europe explains, among other things, how twenty-one years later one of the grand princes of Kiev could have placed his realm under the protection of Pope Gregory VII, as if nothing had happened since the conversion of Rus' in the days when Christendom was still undivided.[4] On the other hand, such contacts between Kiev and Rome are easier to understand in view of the fact that the same great pope made attempts to heal the break of 1054 by negotiating with the Byzantine Empire, as if even there the break with the Papacy had not been final.

The history of attempts toward reunion started almost immediately after the Cerularian schism and would continue until the fall of the Eastern Roman Empire, an event which made an ecumenical union between western and eastern Christendom impossible. During these four centuries, until the very middle of Europe's millennium, there were time and again situations when such a union seemed to be close at hand, having been twice proclaimed. And during the same period parallel negotiations were started repeatedly, which aimed at a regional reunion of Rome with parts of the Orthodox Church—especially in Kievan Rus' —which were expected to prepare for the universal reunion.

It is not easy to determine exactly when, among the eastern Slavs, the separation from Rome, which was never officially proclaimed before Moscow did so in the middle of the fifteenth century, became an accomplished fact under Greek influence. The failure of the rather promising negotiations in 1112 between Pope Paschal II and Emperor Alexius I, the founder of the Comneni dynasty, was probably decisive.[5] This was at the time of Vladimir Monomachus, when the relations between Constantinople and Kiev were particularly close. There appeared, however, only sixty years later, under the third of the Comneni, the most pro-western of them, Manuel I, a surprising possibility of restoring not only the ecclesiastical but also the political unity of Christendom. At the height of the conflict between Pope Alexander III and the Hohenstaufen Emperor, Frederick I, the former seemed ready to recognize Manuel as legitimate ruler of "old Rome and all Italy," if in turn the Greeks would again recognize papal primacy.[6] This would have been nothing less than the transfer of the *imperium* from the Germans to the Greeks, making it again one empire for all Christendom in cooperation with a *sacerdotium* directing the whole reunited Church.

Such a bold vision of what would have been a real Christian Commonwealth in an integrated Europe, had, however, even less chance of success than the forgotten vision of the year 1000. While the latter, though certainly not shared by the emperor nor the patriarch of Constantinople, was not formally opposed by them, now there was not only a strong opposition on the part of that patriarch against religious reunion on papal conditions, but an even stronger, very understandable hostility of the powerful and ambitious German ruler who two hundred years after the coronation of Otto I was to lose the imperial dignity. Furthermore, the West was no more prepared to accept the supreme authority of the Greek βασιλεύς than that of the German king. The rather fantastic project was soon abandoned, and though the reconciliation of Alexander III with Barbarossa did not remove the quasi-permanent tension between the Papacy and the Western Empire, the old tension between western and eastern Christendom grew deeper, not only in the form of a conflict between the two imperial dynasties, but also as a consequence of the schism which continued to divide the Church.

However, independently of the political question as to whether there was a real danger of a conquest of the Byzantine Empire by the Hohenstaufen, it should not be overlooked that in spite of a growing prejudice separating Latins and Greeks which made them overrate even minor differences in rite and liturgy, there still remained a real Christian fraternity, at least as a "precarious survival of an ideal."[7] Both sides recognized fraternal obligations of Christians to Christians even amidst political rivalries, and a long time intervened before they would accuse each other of heresy even in isolated, exceptional cases.

Such a situation lasted until the fateful year of 1204. While the importance of earlier misunderstandings between the West and Byzantium in connection with the first three crusades should not be exaggerated, the diversion of what was supposed to be the fourth crusade affected the relations between Latins and Greeks even more profoundly than the Cerularian schism, creating, after a century and a half, a real hostility among Christians. Today, after exhaustive studies of that diversion,[8] which in its first phase was not directed against Orthodox Greeks but against Roman Catholic Hungary and which finally made the planned expedition to the Holy Land impossible, it is obvious that the whole action does not deserve at all the name of a crusade. Its only result, the establishment of a Latin Empire in Constantinople, failed to restore either the religious or the political unity of Christendom and of Europe. Besides the fact that the Greek Empire, before retaking Constantinople after little more than half a century, survived "in exile" on Asiatic soil,[9] it must be noted that nobody even considered the possibility of restoring any kind of imperial unity, at least in Europe. There continued to be two Christian, even Catholic, empires there, contrary to the basic conception of the Christian Commonwealth, the Latin Empire of Constantinople being, under a resounding title, just one more independent Catholic power outside the Roman Empire of the Germanic nation.

Although that full title of the latter empire was not yet used formally, it already had a national, rather than universal character. The new, artificially created empire of Constantinople was certainly not a national state, but definitely non-German, a sphere of influence of the Romance peoples, of the Italians, especially the Venetians, and even more of the French, then at the height of their power; along with the crusader states in Syria and Palestine, as well as Cyprus, that empire was considered part of the new France *d'outre mer*.[10] Its only contribution to European unity was a symbiosis of Latin and Greek culture in the empire itself and its feudal dependencies on the soil of ancient Greece and the adjacent islands. That in spite of this, or rather because of an enforced Latinization in the ecclesiastical field, the product of the so-called fourth crusade was no contribution to real religious unity, was soon recognized by the popes themselves, who well before the retaking of Constantinople, when the Greek emperors still resided in Nicaea, started negotiating with them on that matter.[11]

The situation which thus developed in the middle of the thirteenth century was entirely different from that at its beginning. It had happened that almost simultaneously with the conquest of Constantinople by misled crusaders, there occurred two other aggressive advances of the Latin West toward the East which alarmed the Orthodox. In the north, at the opposite end of the dividing line between them, German knights founded a semi-ecclesiastical state in Livonia and Estonia, subjugating the Baltic and Finnish tribes of that crucial area and threatening, along with the Swedes who conquered Finland proper, the Russians of the neighboring city-states of Pskov and Novgorod.[12] In the center, Polish-Hungarian intervention in the internal troubles of Halich and Volhynia had as its aim the establishment of a Catholic kingdom in that border region, which once had been at least partially Polish, but which for the last several centuries formed one of the principalities of Kievan Rus', now definitely Greek Orthodox like the others. These three actions were completely independent of each other, and though the great pope of the early thirteenth century, Innocent III, anxious to unite all Europe in the Christian Commonwealth under his leadership, welcomed the apparent progress of Catholicism in the East, he was by no means responsible for any of the initiatives[13] which necessarily contributed to the tension between the Catholic and the Orthodox part of Europe.

Furthermore, it so happened that only a few decades later the eastern Slavs had to face a much greater danger, coming once more from non-

Christian Asia, the great Mongol invasion, and therefore found themselves under pressure from two sides. It is however, hardly necessary to
point out that the two threats, the limited, merely temporary advances
of other Christians—not adhering to Byzantium but to Rome—and the
brutal annexation by an alien, Asiatic empire which from paganism was
turning to Islam, cutting off its victims from Christian Europe, cannot
even be compared.[14] Not only was there no connection between the two,
but no institution was more anxious to defend Christendom against the
Mongols, later called Tartars in eastern Europe, than the Papacy, which
soon realized that the idea of converting the invaders and using them
against Turks or Arabs in southwestern Asia was nothing but a dangerous illusion.

In spite of his simultaneous conflict with Emperor Frederick II, Pope
Innocent IV did his best to establish a solid line of defense in eastern
Europe. He was deeply interested in the conversion of the last heathens
of Europe, the Baltic peoples, not through that violence and conquest
which the German Orders of Knighthood were employing, not only in
Livonia but a little later in Prussia as well, but through the encouraging
of missionary activities and the peaceful integration of a still free and
rapidly growing Lithuania with the Latin West. And along with the
first outstanding Lithuanian ruler, Mindaugas, the Ruthenian prince,
Daniel, who after the decline and fall of Kiev was building up a new
center of old Rus' in Halich and Volhynia, received from Innocent IV
in 1253 a royal crown.

Unlike his formerly pagan Lithuanian neighbor, Daniel was the representative of an Orthodox dynasty which never ceased to conclude matrimonial alliances with Latin families.[15] He had become a Catholic and
after a few years of negotiations concluded a regional religious union
with Rome. These negotiations were parallel with those which the pope
conducted with the Greek Emperor John Ducas Vatatzes, and in both
cases a principle was adopted which was to be basic for all subsequent
attempts towards reunion of western and eastern Christendom until our
time: Rome, while requesting unity in doctrine (including the recognition of papal primacy), recognized in turn the traditional differences in
rite and liturgy, giving up the idea of Latinization which had always
proved an obstacle to reconciliation.

Dealing with the eastern Slavs, the Papacy did not make any distinction between the various parts of *Russia*—as the name of Rus' was formerly translated into Latin, the peoples themselves being called *Rutheni*.

In addition to the princes of the nearest, southwestern part of the former Kievan state, always in close relations with the Catholic world, Rome also approached the rulers of the remote northeastern colonial Russia in the Volga region with Suzdal as a center,[16] where there was no tradition of original religious unity with the West. But no union with Suzdal, similar to that with Halich, could be concluded, and the ruler of the future Great Russia where Moscow was slowly emerging as a new center, Alexander Nevsky, impressed by his struggles with Swedes and Germans, considered appeasement of the Tartars the lesser evil.[17]

Daniel's agreement with Rome did not last, since he did not receive the expected help from the Catholic West; and Tartar control, though less direct and complete than in the northeast, continued for the time being in Halich also. The simultaneous death of the Roman pope and the Greek emperor in 1254 was another reason why the end of the schism, which seemed so near in both main sections of Orthodox Europe, did not materialize. But exactly twenty years later, at the second ·Council of Lyons, a union was concluded which was supposed to be universal and to fulfill the highest hopes of those who for more than two centuries had tried to heal the great schism. The origins of that union and the reasons for its failure are equally instructive for an understanding of the rise and decline of the Christian Commonwealth.

In the religious controversies between the Latin West and the Greek East political issues unfortunately always played an important part. But never was that part so predominant as it appears in the history of the Union of 1274.[18] This is particularly obvious as far as the Greek side is concerned, where this time the role of the emperor was decisive. But even the saintly Pope Gregory X had to take the political aspects of the problem into serious consideration. In similar cases those aspects were usually connected with the assistance that the Greeks expected from the Catholic West against the non-Christian, Asiatic East and with the difficulty of loyal cooperation against the common enemy. If, on some other occasions, the policy of a western power proved dangerous to both the Eastern Empire and the Papacy, and thus contributed to a rapprochement between the two, it was the policy of the Western Roman Empire. This time there seemed to be no threat to Constantinople coming from the non-European, Mohammedan world. A threat from the Latin West was decisive, but it did not come from the empire, which had hardly recovered from the defeat of the Hohenstaufen and had not yet replaced them with another powerful dynasty. The enemy whom Michael

Palaeologus had to fear, after having reconquered Constantinople and put an end to the existence of the Latin Empire, was not the powerless pretender to that empire, but the Anjou king of Sicily, who under the pretext of supporting his claims, wanted to gain Constantinople for himself. The French dynasty which in the person of Saint Louis had represented the highest conception of Christian principles in politics— the only possible basis of a real *res publica Christiana*—now through the unscrupulous ambition of his brother Charles replaced these principles by mere power politics. The reunion of western and eastern Christendom depended therefore on issues which had nothing to do either with common defense or with the interpretation of the imperial idea. Instead, these issues anticipated the political game among individual states— wherein the interests of Europe's Christian community were disregarded —a game which was to be typical of the following periods of European history.

In the midst of concerns which had nothing to do with religion, no time was left for serious theological discussions that would pave the way for a union that was supposed to be ecumenical, embracing all the followers of the Eastern Church. In this respect, even the Greek representation, the only one that came to Lyons, was obviously inadequate. Against those in Constantinople who opposed such a union,[19] severe imperial pressure was applied which in one individual case, that of Patriarch John Beccus, resulted in a sincere conversion. As is usual in such cases, however, it only harmed the cause of reunion in general. Under such conditions the Union of Lyons could not endure and remained nothing but a useful experience warning how the schism could *not* be ended. The agreement proclaimed at the Council lost its last chance with the death of Gregory X who, however, did his best to save it; with the policies of his successors who were of French origin, under French influence, or both; and eventually with the unexpected, sudden end of Anjou rule in Sicily. The so-called Sicilian Vespers[20] made the union useless for Michael Palaeologus, blamed and distrusted by both sides, and even more for his successor Andronicus II, called "the emperor of the schism" because during almost all of his long reign there was an interruption of any attempts toward reunion.

But it was precisely during that reign and, through a strange coincidence, at the time when the Papacy, no longer challenged by any empire, met its deepest humiliation at the hands of Philip the Fair of France, that a problem appeared which made the unity of Christian Europe more necessary and urgent than ever before. It was the rise of the Ottoman Empire at the Asiatic border of the Greek Empire. While Spain was not yet fully liberated from Arab rule and almost all of eastern Slavdom was still under direct or indirect Tartar domination, the advance of a seemingly minor Turkish tribe in Asia Minor initiated the most serious external threat which the Christian Commonwealth ever had to face, a threat from which Europe had to suffer when that Commonwealth had already ceased to be a concrete reality. The idea of such a Commonwealth had its place in European history until the moment when after four hundred years—throughout the whole central part and totalling almost half of Europe's millennium—the Ottoman advance toward the heart of the Continent was definitely stopped. But the Balkans and a large part of the Danubian area were under the yoke of the Turks much longer than Russia under that of the Tartars. Whatever may be said in favor of Ottoman administration,[21] the invasion cut off the Balkans from Europe in a similar way to Russia under the Tartars. The Balkans suffered a painful interruption of their normal development as well as a total loss of their freedom.

All this was impossible to foresee at the beginning of the fourteenth century, when merely extra-European possessions were gradually taken away from a Byzantine Empire that was more than ever before alienated from the Latin West. But toward the end of his reign, even Andronicus II, to whom at first only the Catalonian companies had given a rather doubtful assistance, felt obliged to turn to Catholics for cooperation; and exactly one hundred years before the Union of Florence, there started a long series of negotiations between the Greek emperors and the Avignon Papacy.[22]

The popes of that period—certainly not a brilliant era in the history of the Church but not at all as dark as usually believed—never made reunion a prerequisite condition for calling upon the West to save eastern Christendom. But obviously, both sides realized how much easier it would be to cooperate after ending the schism, and an understanding seemed particularly near when in 1369, during a first, though only temporary, return of the papal curia to Rome, a Byzantine emperor arrived there in person for the first and last time in history and made his profession of faith as a Catholic.[23]

There were, however, two reasons why that spectacular conversion did not lead to any union between the Latin and the Greek churches. First, John V and a few of his followers became Catholics of the Latin rite, and in general the French popes of the period favored a Latinization which the Greeks were never prepared to accept. Secondly, their legitimate condition, put forward in 1339, that an ecumenical council be convoked to discuss reunion, was not fulfilled.

It is true that such an assembly of the Latin and the Greek hierarchy was difficult to organize as long as the popes resided in faraway Avignon; and they had scarcely returned to Rome for good, when the next year the Great Western Schism shattered the very foundations of the Christian Commonwealth and made the healing of the old eastern Schism more difficult than ever before. Even prior to that crisis which marks the end of the first great period of Europe's millennium, the appeals of the Papacy to join the Greeks, reunited or not, in the defense of Christendom against the Turks received little attention in the West, where the last great conflict between the Papacy and the empire was hardly over when the outbreak of the Hundred Years War set the two principal western powers outside the empire at odds to each other. Independently of these internal struggles in the Catholic world, there was a deeper reason why a general anti-Ottoman league was not easier to form then than in subsequent centuries. This can only be explained by turning from the problem of the eastern schism—that most striking challenge to the unity of Christian Europe—to another problem which through the centuries was always intimately connected with it. This is the problem of the crusade, which as we see it today, emerged in the history of Christendom long before the first Latin expedition to the Holy Land and had its long aftermath when the last western possessions in Palestine and Syria had been finally lost.

CHAPTER XV

The Idea of the Crusades

NOTHING IS MORE TYPICAL of the period of European history commonly called the Middle Ages than the crusades. Furthermore, it is significant that the seven expeditions to which that name is traditionally given all occurred in those three centuries, from the eleventh to the thirteenth, which are more specifically "mediaeval," because everything that usually is associated with that term was most fully developed in this period. The same centuries are precisely those when the Christian Commonwealth, a term, or rather a concept, much more meaningful than that of the Middle Ages, came nearest to its realization.

It can also be said without exaggeration that no problem of that period of history received more attention in past and present historiography than that of the crusades. These fascinating campaigns and all the events, in general, from the origin of the first crusade in 1095, to the apparent failure of the whole movement in 1291, have been described so many times that the facts are by now very well established and very few details could be added by further research. It seems, therefore, more important to discuss the idea of the crusades[1]—incidentally, one more piece of evidence to show that the understanding and interpretation of leading ideas is really basic for the study of history.

The old-fashioned overemphasis on the story of battles and diplomatic negotiations could easily lead to the conclusion that the crusades were, after all, a striking manifestation of aggressive imperialism. The modern, equally misleading overemphasis on the socioeconomic factor could equally well produce the impression that they were an early example of colonialism in its feudal form. Neither of these approaches would be fair to the crusaders and to the heritage of Christian Europe, though obviously frequent distortions of the crusading idea in the practice of life can justify, in individual cases, both critical charges.

Two aspects of the idea of the crusades are particularly important from the general European point of view. It has been rightly pointed out long ago[2] that they were the first common enterprise of almost all European nations, well before the great discoveries in the extra-European world. It was formerly stressed in that connection that the crusades were jointly undertaken mainly, if not exclusively by the Romance and Teutonic West, by those whom their opponents called the Franks, a designation which corresponds indeed to that group of European peoples. However, in order to realize how one-sided such a limitation of the universal, fully European and Christian character of the crusades would be, it might suffice to turn to the other leading aspect of the crusading idea.

More than any other achievement of the period, the crusades were planned and to a large extent also conducted under the inspiration and even the leadership of the Papacy. Their idea was, as indicated by their very name, a Christian idea and accordingly, an integral part of the larger idea of the Christian Commonwealth and its policy. This is so, not only because their main goal, especially of these crusades to which the name is most intimately attached, was the liberation of the Holy Land from non-Christian, Mohammedan rule, and the guarantee of a free and secure access for the Christians to the places where Christ had lived, taught, and suffered. In addition to that limited, almost symbolic objective, which had of course a particularly strong appeal, there were other reasons of a religious character which explain the papal initiative and enthusiastic interest in the crusading movement.

Most important among these reasons was the desire to oppose the onslaught of Islam and to defend Christian culture, already submerged not only in Palestine but in almost the whole Asiatic and African area of the original expansion of Christendom, and now seriously endangered in Europe also. That defensive character of the crusades and of their idea becomes even clearer, if the struggle for that idea before and after the period from 1095 to 1291 is included, as it ought to be, in the study of the problem.

This consideration reveals in turn another reason behind the papal policy in that matter and at the same time the wrongness of the belief that the crusades belong to the heritage of western Europe only. Truly revealing in that respect is the well-known fact that even the French knights fighting in the crusades of the thirteenth century, and the French chroniclers who glorified the *gesta Dei per Francos,* admitted that the first crusader, the precursor of all the others, was the Byzantine emperor Heraclius. He played his role far back in the seventh century when the Muslim advance was beginning.[3]

Parallel to the defensive struggle against the Arab invaders of western Europe, which began in the following century and continued in the *reconquista* of the Iberian peninsula, Byzantine crusades in the Near East, including time and again the defense of Constantinople, were going on long before the West was concerned with that eastern wing of the front against Arab or later Turkish aggression. This was at a time when no schism yet separated eastern and western Christendom, and it was only natural that after that schism the Papacy considered Latin participation in that more and more difficult struggle of the Greeks as the best way to achieve reunion. Recent research has made it highly probable that the objective of Pope Urban II in launching the so-called First Crusade was not only the reconquest of Jerusalem but also reunion with the Greeks.[4]

Before considering the question as to how and why that hope ended in failure, we must recall another East European side of the crusades, in the larger sense of the word. From the dawn of European history Asiatic aggression had penetrated not only through Asia Minor, south of the Black Sea and in the direction of the Straits, but also north of that sea and through the steppes which formed an open gate to the heart of Europe. When at last a state of European origin was consolidated in that crucial area and when that state, with Kiev as its center, was Christianized, its defense against the successive invasions following those of the period of the great migrations was a crusading effort no less than those on other fronts along the border of Europe. All those who tried to continue that defense when the Mongol invasions made it particularly difficult deserve to be called crusaders whether they were eastern Slavs, already separated from Rome as were the Greeks, or Catholic Poles and Hungarians. The Papacy was the first to recognize that in view of their defense of Christendom in northeastern Europe they could not be expected to participate, except in rare cases, in the expeditions toward Jerusalem.

It is true that the papal bulls encouraging these struggles on a remote and little known front and granting the usual indulgences to the defenders of the faith sometimes mentioned among their enemies not only pagans but also schismatics.[5] Such statements would seem to indicate that the latter too were not considered real Christians and that the crusades in this part of Europe were also directed against them. Dangerous as it was, such an approach can be at least partly explained by the fact that these Ruthenian Christians, separated from Rome, were on some occasions participating in the invasions of the Tartars against their Catholic neighbors. The popes could not always understand to what extent these Christians were simply forced to do so nor how frequently their attitude was influenced by political differences with the Latin West. Furthermore, the whole problem is connected with the failure of Rome's expectations that the crusades in the Near East would end the schism, and with the general impression that, contrary to any such hopes, the relations between Latins and Greeks were deteriorating instead.

It would be an exaggeration to say that the failure of the original hopes was complete and that the impact of the crusades on the relations between western and eastern Christendom was mainly negative.[6] The contacts between both sides, more frequent than ever before and never completely interrupted even amidst the growing tensions, contributed at least to a better reciprocal knowledge. But there was more than that: in spite of all the distrust and misunderstanding which started when the first western crusaders, much larger in number than expected, appeared in Constantinople on their way to Jerusalem, there were cases of cooperation between them and the Byzantine Empire during the following century. Therefore, the possibilities of an even closer cooperation, discussed just before the diversion of the Fourth Crusade, were not altogether illusionary. After all, in spite of the controversies regarding formerly Byzantine territories retaken by the crusaders from the Muslims, some of these earlier losses, to mention only Nicaea, were restored to the Greeks. Even in cases where Greek claims were disregarded, that of Antioch being the most troublesome, it was better for the Greeks to have in such areas Latin instead of non-Christian neighbors.

Nevertheless, no religious reunion materialized and occasional reappearances of such projects, for instance in the reign of Manuel I, originated in the intervals between the various crusades, not in connection with them but with the situation in the West. The same is true as far as the Union of Lyons is concerned, and when the Asiatic danger reappeared in a new form with the advance of the Ottoman Turks, the idea of the crusade in the specific form of the preceding three centuries seemed to have vanished: the second loss of reconquered Jerusalem left hardly any hope of achieving once more what was considered the main objective of the whole movement, and there were no longer any crusader-states in Syria which could have hindered the rise of Turkish power in Anatolia. How useful their continued existence would have been for the defense of Christendom in the new opening phase is best evidenced by the role of Cyprus, that last remnant of Christian gains in the eastern Mediterranean, in the next three centuries.[7]

Failure of the idea to use the crusades for promoting the reunion with the Greeks became final, therefore, only when the idea of making the Holy Land a Christian country had failed too, contrary to the high hopes of 1099. Its first loss, as early as 1187, proved irreparable because when Jerusalem was regained for a short time in 1229, through negotiations of Emperor Frederick II with the Muslims, it was under such precarious conditions that its final loss only fifteen years later came as no surprise. Worst of all, the Hohenstaufen, when he at last decided to undertake a crusade, did it in continued opposition to the Papacy and was even excommunicated by Gregory IX. And this leads to the consideration of what was perhaps the greatest failure of the crusading idea.

Among the various objectives of the popes who sponsored that idea, there was one which is frequently overlooked, but whose achievement would have been the greatest possible contribution to the unity and lasting constitution of the Christian Commonwealth, independently of the military success of the movement. Internal strifes among the Christian powers were indeed the main reason why that Commonwealth was always more of a noble dream than of a concrete, efficiently working political system, and why the European community, even in that early period full of hopes, was far from being perfectly organized. When other attempts of the Church to pacify the faithful had proved inadequate, it seemed to some of the greatest popes that peace in Christendom could be established by showing to all its members a common goal which would put an end to their petty and selfish rivalries, and divert the warlike inclinations of the European knighthood from fratricidal, useless fights to what could be considered a just war in defense of the faith and of Christian culture.

However, even during the First Crusade—consisting of knights without the official participation of any of the great powers of the period— a papal legate of the high qualifications of Adhémar de Puy could hardly appease the rivalries of the secular leaders which so seriously retarded the advance toward Jerusalem.[8] Such rivalries and jealousies continued throughout the existence of the kingdom of Jerusalem and its dependencies, where the worst features of western feudalism could develop, while none of the successors of Godefrey de Bouillon, except perhaps the tragic figure of the Lepper King,[9] had the same lofty conception of his role or his moral authority. In the meantime, the later crusades, which, because of the participation of the foremost monarchs of Europe, could brighten the hopes of maintaining the kingdom of Jerusalem, became on account of that participation a dangerous occasion for conflicts among practically all of them, including the Holy Roman emperors. Even the most deplorable conflict between the empire and the Papacy had its repercussions in the matter of the crusades, that of Frederick II being only the most striking example, and the final crusades of Louis IX, the exceptions in the sad story of big-power policies behind the scenes of what was supposed to be the *gesta Dei per Francos*.

If it was regrettable and disappointing that the crusades, far from establishing a lasting peace between Latins and Greeks, eventually made their opposition even deeper, it was even worse that the same must be said, to a large extent, of the international relations among the Latins themselves, including those between Christendom's two highest authorities, both of which were supposed to be universal. But worst of all was the constant danger that the very idea of the crusade would be misused for purposes which had nothing in common with it or were even opposed to it, serving merely the interests of individual powers. The example of the diversion of the Fourth Crusade, so disastrous as far as the relations with the Greeks were concerned, is not the only one. The role of the Italian republics, particularly Venice and her dominant concern for commercial advantages, was not much more disgraceful than that of other powers on various occasions. So it could happen that even in western eyes the moral standards of a Mohammedan enemy like Saladin would seem higher than those of the Christians whom he defeated.[10]

All this is part of a problem which lays bare the reason why the idea of the crusade was so difficult to put into practice, a reason similar to that which explains, in general, the shortcomings of the Christian Commonwealth. That Commonwealth, boldly conceived on the pattern of the City of God, could endure only if the divine laws that were supposed to govern it were not only proclaimed but applied by all members of the human community—specifically, the European one—which wanted to be identified with Christendom. In the same way, the crusades, which were planned not only as just wars, but wars in the name of Christ Himself with His cross as guiding symbol, could be worthy of their name and succeed only if all those who were bearing that holy cross and claiming religious privileges as reward for their struggles were conducting these struggles not only heroically, as so many of them did, but in a truly Christian spirit, respecting Christian principles even in the midst of the excitement and turmoil of military action.

Unfortunately, these far-reaching requirements were rarely met. Even the inspiring climax of the whole movement, when after so many courageous efforts and sacrifices Jerusalem was taken and the Holy Sepulchre liberated, was degraded by wanton cruelties of the conquerors. Not only was the treatment of enemies cruel, and therefore irreconcilable with the supreme commandment of charity, but the treatment inflicted by crusaders upon peoples whom they simply disliked or suspected—including sometimes, the Jews[11]—was equally cruel.

The dangers involved in such behavior became particularly apparent in connection with two uses of the idea of the crusade which could most easily lead to its abuse. The first use recalls the violent methods of Christianization which had been used in Europe long before the formal crusading movement. At the very time of the expeditions to the Holy Land such methods continued to be used against what remained of Slavic paganism between the Elbe and the Oder, and against Europe's last pagans in the Baltic area, in the latter case under the leadership of one of the orders of knighthood founded in Palestine for defense against the Muslims and under the invocation of the Blessed Lady. It was easy and tempting to call crusades bloody invasions directed against peoples who constituted no real danger to Christendom at all, as well as aggressive wars with political conquest as the main goal and the conversion of pagans merely a pretext.

The highly controversial idea which seemed to be expressed in the words *compelle intrare*[12] was thus practically identified with, and supported by the crusading idea, and that same idea was used in the struggle against heretical movements inside Christendom. That such a struggle was a necessity for the Church and for the consolidation of the Christian Commonwealth is obvious, the controversial question being whether in addition to predication, education, and persuasion, methods of compulsion and violence should be also used. It so happened that two extreme solutions were tried at the same time, during the reign of the same pope: Innocent III. One of them is personified by Saint Francis of Assisi, who hoped to convert even the Muslims by meekness in the spirit of the Sermon on the Mount. The other solution is exemplified by the crusade against the Albigensians.[13] These were indeed fanatic followers of a doctrine dangerous not only to the Church but to the whole social order. But no other crusade resulted in a more shocking example of an idea distorted for political and personal purposes, a distortion which had nothing in common with the intentions of the pope and which was pursued with a brutal cruelty in opposition to all Christian principles.

In the period of the crusades this was, fortunately, an exceptional case which, however, set a precedent followed two hundred years later in the struggle against the Hussites. Particularly dangerous was the influence which on such occasions the secular powers exercised on the Church and its institutions. That influence appeared simultaneously in the development of the inquisition, which, from a natural inquiry into the spread of wrong doctrines, turned then, contrary to the original tradition of the Church, into an instrument of violent repression through trials that lacked the necessary safeguards for the defendants and had death as a usual punishment.[14] But even before the Papacy decided to turn to the *bracchium saeculare* for the carrying out of such sentences, its foremost opponent, Emperor Frederick II, had made heresy a crime against the state and decreed, first for his Italian possessions and then for his whole realm, that heretics must be burned at the stake.[15] This was part of his general policy which introduced the principles of totalitarian government into the Christian Commonwealth, contrary to its basic conceptions. It also was a precedent, fully developed after more than two centuries in the Spanish Inquisition, which to the great harm of Christendom placed the control of orthodoxy in the hands of secular, national authorities and made it serve the interest of the state.

There is some analogy between these trends of the thirteenth century and the attempt made at the beginning of the next to use the idea of the crusade as a tool for the rise of an individual power, not at all friendly to the Papacy. At the turn of the century Philip the Fair, the French king who wanted to have imperial authority in his state, was supported against Boniface VIII by the famous jurist, Pierre Dubois. A few years later Dubois wrote a treatise, *De recuperatione terrae sanctae,* which is typical in that respect.[16] On the one hand, it was not only a return to the crusading idea in its strictest sense, but a project for a league which would establish permanent peace in Christendom. It is therefore considered the first plan for an elaborate international organization, an early precursor of the League of Nations idea. On the other hand, however, this belated effort to give to the Christian Commonwealth a regular constitution which would entrust the leadership of both the European community and the crusading movement to the kings of France represented an idea that was no more acceptable to the other nations than the supremacy of the Holy Roman Empire, which even the great Dante had vainly recommended to his contemporaries.

As a matter of fact, while regaining the Holy Land was already out of the question, the defensive aspect of the idea of the crusade was soon to gain a more urgent importance than ever before. In the days of Philip the Fair or Emperor Henry VII—the hero of Dante's *De monarchia*—the advance of the Ottoman Turks was still a remote issue, vital only for the schismatic Byzantine Empire. But by the next generation that same problem afforded the Papacy not only an opportunity for reopening negotiations with the Greeks in the matter of religious unity, but also represented an appealing means of reviving the idea of the crusade in the form of an anti-Ottoman league. In that sense it is correct to speak of the crusade of the fourteenth century continuing well into the next.[17]

The first of these anti-Ottoman leagues was organized, on a modest scale, as early as 1335 by Pope Benedict XII; and under his successor, Clement VI, the new, defensive crusading idea seemed to have definitely replaced the earlier one. The taking of Smyrna in 1344 from one of the Turkish states in Asia Minor gave the Christians a valuable outpost until the end of the century. But ten years later, almost exactly one hundred years before the fall of Constantinople, the conquest of Gallipoli by the Ottoman Turks—briefly lost to the Christians and then regained—placed the Turks on European soil and should have sounded an ominous warning.

Nevertheless, in the next decade there was a surprising return—the final one—to the idea of liberating the Holy Land from Muslim rule. Once more the idea was combined, as it had been on several previous occasions by earlier crusaders, with an attempt to reach that goal by first conquering Egypt. In spite of a trip taken by the king of Cyprus, Peter of Lusignan, to almost all western countries, he failed to find any assistance except for the moral support of Pope Urban V, so that his isolated expedition remained limited to a brief occupation of Alexandria.

Thus the last old-style crusade failed, but it is significant that the project was discussed in 1364 at an international congress held in the Catholic country of Poland in the eastern part of Europe. Poland's participation in the crusade was for the first time considered of serious importance. This was likewise true of Hungary, whose King, Louis the Great, was on that occasion one of the royal guests of Casimir the Great in Cracow, prepared to take over the Polish succession.[18] The role of East Central Europe in the Christian Commonwealth thus became more obvious than ever before, the presence at the Congress of Charles IV, Holy Roman Emperor and King of Bohemia, showing the intimate connection of that border region of Europe with its center and the West.

These were, however, only prospects for the future, while in the western countries the situation was then particularly unfavorable to any crusade, whether in the old or in the new sense, mainly because of the war between France and England which had broken out just at the time that the attempts to create an anti-Ottoman league were starting. And since the usual rivalry of the two most important naval powers, Venice and Genoa, continued through the whole century, the Papacy could rely only on the Knights Hospitalers, who, established in Rhodes,[19] perpetuated the crusading tradition, but could not give adequate support to the Greeks.

It is, therefore, not surprising that in Constantinople, at the very time when Emperor John V went to Rome, the majority of the Greeks was looking to the Orthodox peoples of the Balkans for help, since they were directly threatened like themselves. But the Serbs, who quite recently under Stephen Dushan (called emperor of both Serbs and Greeks) had been the leading power in the peninsula, now were unable to face the challenge alone. When no coalition with their neighbors materialized, the Serbs were defeated in 1371 by the Turks near Adrianople, the Ottoman capital already established in Europe, even before the decisive blow of Kossovo, in 1389.

A failure, too, was the amazing project in 1374 of the last Avignon pope, Gregory, to sponsor another international congress in eastern Europe, this time in the old Greek city of Thebes, then in the hands of the Catalonians, where all Christian powers were supposed to coordinate their action against the common enemy.[20] And when the Western Schism started, after the return of the papal curia to Rome, and following Gregory's death in 1378, the hopes not only for a crusade but for a survival of the Christian Commonwealth in its original form vanished after almost four centuries of attempts to make it the foundation of a united Europe.

It seems justified, therefore, to consider that the first period of

Europe's millennium which can be named after that Christian Commonwealth came to an end around 1378, after a gradual decline in the first three quarters of the century, the crisis over the idea of the crusade being one of the clearest manifestations of a great change. There did not even appear at the end of that period a vision comparable to that of the year 1000, which had marked its hopeful beginning.

Nevertheless, just as the crusades, in spite of so many distortions of their idea, left behind a tradition of glory, and just as crusaders who really wanted to fight for Christ did not die in vain, so the heritage of the Christian Commonwealth as a whole enriched the earlier heritage of Europe through an inspiring experience, with even the obvious failures being instructive for the future. The issue was now whether the subsequent periods of European history would benefit from that experience, make their own contributions to the development of the European community, and succeed in finding for its lasting organization better forms and methods without abandoning its basic values.

In that respect, it was encouraging that just as the period of the Christian Commonwealth had started with an extension of the European community in a northeastern direction, so it ended with a progress of that extension through peaceful Christianization. At the time of crisis for the real crusade, misuse of the idea by an order of knighthood—more fortunate than the Templars but less faithful to its original mission than the Hospitalers—continued in the form of almost regular invasions of Lithuania. Yet strangely enough, the project of converting that country, which had only been delayed and discouraged by these aggressions, ended at last in a spectacular success, announced in 1385 and completed two years later.[21]

Five years before, it seemed that a first victory of Orthodox Moscow over her Tartar overlords would be transformed into a genuine and successful crusading effort right at the border between northeastern Europe and Asia. But the victory on the Don was followed within two years by a setback which delayed the liberation of Muscovite Russia from Asiatic domination for about another century. Meanwhile, the vast, but heterogeneous realm into which the Lithuanian state (originally no larger than the Muscovite and even more alien to Europe because of its paganism) had developed in the preceding century through union with and conversion by Catholic Poland, became part of a federal system integrated with the European community.[22] Though not altogether Slavic, that federal union took the place of the *Sclavinia* of the premature conception of the year 1000, which now had chances for realization in an entirely different form.

Entirely different was the case of the empire, which, soon after the Papacy, entered into long years of troubles similar to the ecclesiastical schism and never regained the universal position as the Papacy did. Nor could it serve as the unifying center between Europe's East and West as it had in the mind of Otto III. In contrast to the first Luxemburgs on the imperial throne, the last one would soon complete its practical identification with *Germania*. How the various national or even multinational states of Europe would cooperate in a community without any unifying authority or organization in the sphere of politics was to be the decisive question in the next periods of the European millennium.

PART III

The Great Transition

CHAPTER XVI

The Continuity of Europe's Millennium

IT WOULD BE IMPOSSIBLE to speak of a millennium of Europe if the continuity of European history through the last ten centuries could be questioned. Unfortunately, this is being done, though without awareness of the far-reaching implications, by the continued use of an obsolete division of history into periods whose names are as misleading as their limits. In spite of all the objections which have been raised, it is still taken for granted that somewhere towards the middle of the last thousand years there was a break between what is called mediaeval and modern Europe. Those two periods are supposedly two entirely different fields of study and specialization, and while the Middle Ages are to include the first half of the last millennium as well as the second half of the preceding one, Modern history is being gradually extended by each generation in order to reach the beginning of what is called contemporary history.[1]

The universal acceptance of such a periodization is best illustrated by two surprising facts. First, though that division originated in Europe at a time when European history was practically identified with world history or at least considered its center, it was maintained when the wrongness of such an approach had become obvious. Not only the earliest period of history, called Ancient, which as a matter of fact could never be considered exclusively European, but also the following ones, conceived exclusively from the European point of view, were considered *a priori* the natural divisions of the histories of any part of the world and of all mankind.

What is even stranger is the attitude adopted in that matter by the new school of historical materialism. Marxist historiography seems to be revolutionary also with regard to the problem of periodization. According to the materialistic interpretation of history, the evolution of all peoples and cultures has followed the same pattern, the dialectical process leading from primitive society through slavery, feudalism, and capitalism to socialism. But the same historians who claim that only such a periodization, using the changes in the methods of production as absolute criterion, is truly scientific, hesitate to reject, especially as far as European history is concerned, the terminology of "bourgeois" historiography. Their new periods of feudalism and capitalism correspond more or less to the Middle Ages and to Modern history, though they admit that the choice of the date, separating the two periods, may be a matter of discussion.[2]

The difference of the two schools is indeed much more than a question of chronological details. It is significant that in the opinion of the Marxists the period which they call feudal in most European countries lasted much longer than the Middle Ages. Much more important is the fact that they all consider periodization a basic problem of philosophy of history, while so many non-Marxists, questioning its interest for the scholar, would dismiss it as a purely formal, practical question of organizing and presenting their material. In the light of the consequences of both attitudes, it appears that in this respect the school of historical materialism is right.

If it is true, as both sides want us to believe, that European history is cut in two by a break between two periods which have little in common with each other, the continuity of that history disappears and the heritage of the first period is of doubtful value for the present and even less for the future of Europe. Only the later part of the millennium of the European community—certainly not more than the second half, if not less—would be of lasting importance. The great conflict of our time could be reduced to the question of whether the heritage of these last centuries is to be rejected and replaced by something better, viz. socialism in the Marxist sense, or whether at least this limited part of the European tradition is worth defending and preserving. If that part is called modern, which it hardly is for our contemporary generation, such a relative designation cannot be a lasting inspiration. And since it is unquestionable that the development of capitalism occupies an important place in the history of these centuries, their more specific designation as "period of capitalism" can have a certain appeal, creating the impression that what the non-Marxists want to defend and to preserve is, after all, primarily that socioeconomic system which has little in common with the Christian and humanistic foundations of European civilization.

Such a misleading impression can be avoided only by considering as an indivisible whole that civilization in its historical evolution from the time when all European peoples participated in it, i.e. from the tenth century on. In the course of that evolution of a thousand years, there were changes, of course, not only of social and economic conditions but of political systems, literary and artistic styles, philosophical conceptions, and others. Such changes and varieties of expression are typical of a civilization which, like the European, is truly historical, that is dynamic and progressive, that is willing to admit diversity in unity. The turn from feudalism to capitalism was only one of many other changes, and none of any such changes interrupted the continuity of European history, since none of them destroyed what remained essential: the Christian and humanistic basis which is so much more important than the material superstructure.

In connection with all these changes, not merely the socioeconomic ones and even less those in the methods of production, the European millennium indeed went through various periods which, however, are simply phases of a continuous development. It is a development so continuous that no single date can be indicated as frontier between them, and the shorter or longer transitions from one period to the next are of special interest for the historian. This, too, has been already pointed out many times in theoretical studies of history but is frequently overlooked in practice.

The Christian Commonwealth is a good example to prove that an important period neither begins nor ends suddenly, even though that concept is much more precise and distinct than that of the Middle Ages or of feudalism. The Commonwealth emerged from the first Christian, not yet totally European, millennium after a preparatory transition period which included the whole tenth century and perhaps even the ninth: the post-Carolingian times. It vanished as a concrete reality in the course of the fourteenth century, yet even after the unusually important date of 1378—a date at least as important as the later dates usually given as the termination of the Middle Ages—no equally long, new period of a different character began at once. Even those who want to maintain the distinction between mediaeval and modern Europe are embarrassed by the difficulty, if not the impossibility, of finding in their rigid periodization a suitable place for one of the most significant phases of the development of European civilization: the Renaissance.[3]

So long as the whole thousand years which are covered by the name "Middle Ages," and not only its first centuries, were considered "dark ages," the Renaissance could not possibly be included, although its beginnings, especially in its Italian homeland, must be traced back far into the last centuries which are still called mediaeval. And since the later part of the Renaissance, its widest expansion in the sixteenth century, definitely belongs to what is called modern history no matter which of the conventional dates is chosen as the start of that new period, not only European history as a whole but the development of the Renaissance in particular is cut in two by an arbitrary chronological division.

On the other hand, as soon as it was realized that the contrast between the darkness of the Middle Ages and the splendors of a reborn humanism had been overemphasized, and when movements very similar to the Italian Renaissance were discovered in much earlier centuries of mediaeval culture, it became more and more artificial to oppose to that culture the modern one which originated in the Renaissance. Any such revision of the conventional approach is, of course, rejected by Marxist historiography,[4] because it leads necessarily to a rehabilitation of the age of "feudalism," more convincing than its idealization by Romanticism had been. The objective historian simply comes to the conclusion that something must be wrong with a periodization which makes it so hard to do justice to a problem as important as the role of the Renaissance.

The only solution seems to be to admit that the Renaissance era, shorter than the preceding and following periods of European history, was a long and momentous transition between the two, a link which makes us realize, better than any other consideration, the uninterrupted continuity of European history and its basic unity. It is perhaps not just an accident of chronology that such a critical transition period had its place in the very middle of the millennium of the European community, half way between its tenth-century origin and its present, unprecedented crisis. In contrast to the violent crisis of our time, that earlier one, between the end of the fourteenth and that of the sixteenth century, did not question the foundations of European civilization. For that reason the name which is given to it, though subject to different interpretations, is rather well chosen: it means that the Renaissance, far from being a revolutionary break with the past, was a revival of some elements of the

European heritage which seemed to have been neglected in the preceding centuries. Comparatively neglected, but by no means altogether rejected, because at the time of the Christian Commonwealth the dedication to the Christian basis and character of the European community never excluded a genuine interest in, and concern with, its ancient Graeco-Roman foundations.

It was, therefore, only natural, though it may seem confusing,[5] that the same name of Renaissance was given to earlier developments when that interest and concern manifested itself time and again. The Christian Commonwealth was prepared by two such renaissances: the Carolingian and the Ottonian, and reached its height in that of the twelfth century. Its flowering in the thirteenth was a reconciliation of the most exalted Christian faith with the reason expressed in Aristotle's philosophy. And while theology was supreme in the curricula of the universities, classical learning continued to be cultivated. Last but not least, the role of the Latin language, by no means a dead one, in both the ecclesiastical and secular life of western Europe, and similarly the role of the Greek in the southeast, in both cases strongly promoted by the Christian Church even among peoples of neither Roman nor Hellenic background, was the best evidence that all that was left for the Renaissance to do was to return to the ancient purity of the classical languages.

In addition to the rebirth of Graeco-Roman antiquity, there was indeed in Renaissance culture an emphasis on purely human values. But even that humanism in its new, all-embracing sense was not necessarily irreconcilable with the divine inspiration of traditional Christendom. It was the Christian doctrine, fully developed in the philosophy which is called mediaeval, which had best explained the dignity of the human person, and examples of the most extreme individualism can be pointed out in the history of the Christian Commonwealth.[6] In connection with these well-established facts, there even appeared a trend in recent scholarship to trace the origin of the Renaissance so far back that it would almost cease to be a distinct, specific period.

A question which received much less attention leads chronologically in the opposite direction, from the Renaissance center of Europe's millennium, which would deserve the name of a "middle" period much more than the preceding one, into the second half of that continued evolution through a thousand years. In other words, the question must be asked whether there were not phases and movements in the so-called modern period which could be called renaissances with no less justification than those appearing in the course of the first centuries of the millennium.

Some of these more recent renaissances, not yet designated by that name, were new returns to the Graeco-Roman roots of the European heritage. None of them was so far-reaching in that respect as that which had started in fourteenth-century Italy. But there was a strong classical element in the Baroque culture which originated in France's "great century," the seventeenth,[7] as well as in the culture of imperial France at the turn of the eighteenth century, with its classical style in art and literature. Thanks to the progress of historical, philological, and especially archaeological research, the whole world of classical antiquity was also reborn in the nineteenth century, though in a different sense. And the alarm of our generation about the decline of classical studies is part of a much larger problem: the quest for a new humanism.[8]

That humanism which in the eyes of many is supposed to save the European tradition in the present crisis at the end of its millennium, is frequently called, or at least expected to be, Christian. This leads to another aspect of the question concerning the appearance of renaissances in the later part of the European millennium. That part compared to the earlier one was obviously less inspired by, and less faithful to the Christian element of Europe's heritage. Therefore, a rebirth of the Christian tradition was repeatedly felt to be even more necessary than that of the Graeco-Roman. Not all attempts in that direction were unqualified successes, to mention only the trend which centered at Port-Royal at the time of Pascal. The defense of the *génie du christianisme* by the Romantics of the early nineteenth century had a larger appeal all over Europe. However, the turn of that century was decisive, thanks to an uninterrupted series of unusually prominent and universally respected popes, the adaptation of the Church to the social needs of the time, the rediscovery of the values of Thomist philosophy, and the movement towards Christian unity.

The conclusion is clear: the Renaissance to which that name is specifically attached and which developed so brilliantly in the middle of the millennium of Europe, was but one of many similar phenomena which through these thousand years recalled, whenever it was necessary, the two spiritual foundations of European civilization. They can be compared with early antecedents in the remote centuries, when the making of Europe began at the dawn of the Christian era, with the so-called Augustan and Theodosian renaissances, of which the former was of

Graeco-Roman, the latter already of primarily Christian character.[9] The dualism of the European heritage, which is reflected in the obvious difference between these two precursors of the renaissance movements, continued in later days when so much more had to be reborn and readapted. That dualism explains why some of these trends were returns to, and developments of, the lasting achievements of secular ancient culture, while others were more concerned with the religious tradition of Christendom. In spite of sometimes rather long intervals between them, they all represent the continuity of both traditions and of the attempts to reconcile and harmonize the two. All these renaissances are landmarks of the evolution of the European community and keys to a deeper understanding of European history.

All this is particularly true with respect to what might be called the "great" Renaissance. It was great not only because it lasted so much longer than any other and because it strongly affected all countries of western Europe, including the center of the Continent, and influenced even its East wherever and whenever this proved possible.[10] It was great also because it produced so many outstanding personalities who achieved prominence in all fields of human activity—at times the same individual in nearly all fields. And this again resulted from the fact that all these fields were touched by a movement which had the ambition to revitalize the whole world, reborn, rediscovered, and renewed at the same time.

There was, however, one decisive reason why that proud ambition did not fully achieve its objective and why the apparent universality of that exceptional Renaissance was neither complete nor harmonious. There is no doubt that of the two constituent elements of the European tradition one received much more attention than the other from Renaissance man. In general, he was interested in the Graeco-Roman much more than in the Christian heritage. It is with that attitude in mind that the Renaissance was for long interpreted as merely a rebirth of classical antiquity and its pure humanism contrasted with the theocentric conception of the world in the Middle Ages. Even in the limited field of art, especially of architecture, such an opposition seemed striking: the new style, influenced by ancient models, was indeed quite different from the mediaeval Gothic. Such an interpretation leads at the same time to today's prevailing opinion, that the Renaissance is the root of modern secularism and responsible for it.

There certainly is a certain amount of truth in such views,[11] but it is difficult to accept them without qualifications, especially if the Renaissance is considered something more than a style of art and of life. As a period which coincides with the great reform movements, whether moderate or revolutionary, in the history of the Church, it was an age of serious and even impassionate religious concerns, nearer in that respect to the preceding than to the subsequent period. Furthermore, the identification of Europe and Christendom went farther than in the time of the Christian Commonwealth:[12] the necessity of defending both was more obvious than in any other period, and the spread of Christianity in other parts of the world was inseparable from the beginnings of Europe's overseas expansion.

These considerations lead from the permanent, twofold basis of the European community to the problem of the changing forms of the organization, in other words to its political conceptions. Here the difference between the conception of the Christian Commonwealth and the relations among the Renaissance states is again a matter of common knowledge. In that field the new period was less constructive than in the others, and hardly was more than a transition to the purely empirical methods of the future. For this reason alone the otherwise so creative Renaissance age, with its rather negative skepticism in these matters, became largely responsible for the ultimate failure of Europe to organize political life on the basis of Christian principles. This was indeed a grave limitation of its achievements.[13]

In view of so much ambivalence, the idea of the Renaissance is unusually difficult to define. The endless discussions of the matter[14] continue to prove that in this case, as in so many others, the understanding of the idea is much more important than the mere description of the facts, interesting as they are in their colorful variety. A preliminary distinction must be made between the idea of renaissance in general and that which underlies the Renaissance of which both the historian and the cultivated non-specialist think first when hearing that name.

There is a renaissance idea of truly universal character which appears in the evolution of mankind and even in that of any form of life. For the human conscience in civilized societies it is a comforting idea that helps to meet the challenge of decay and death, and to grasp the vision of Eternity amidst the vicissitudes of Time. That idea underlies faith in real progress, in the lasting sense of human endeavors, and even in a future golden age. It is therefore inseparable from any millennium idea which is more than an anniversary celebration, from the idea of continuity through a long era of a thousand years, and from the millennium in a metaphysical interpretation—the most controversial but also the most fascinating one. In the case of the millennium of Europe, such a connection of the two ideas is particularly natural, since no other period of history of similar length was richer in strenuous drives towards inspiring goals. Such drives towards improvement or even perfection were part of both the Graeco-Roman and the Christian tradition of Europe. Especially in the latter, represented by the Fathers of the Church, the renaissance idea was essentially an idea of reform, beginning with that of individual life and developing into the collective reform movements in the history of the Church. Significantly enough, they reached a critical climax precisely at the time of the Great Renaissance.[15]

In the whole development of European civilization the renaissance idea never was a vain desire to recall to life cultures of the past which were definitely dead. This is particularly true of the men of the Italian Renaissance. For these the civilization of the ancient world, whether Greek or Roman, was by no means a dead one. They rightly felt that their own culture was its continuation, and that they were its legitimate heirs, responsible for its preservation and adaptation to new conditions. It was indeed a turn to the past, but to a past which never had ceased to be a living one and which was considered the foundation of a better future. Here again the idea of transition from one form of European civilization to another without any break between the two is clearly apparent.

It is equally true that Renaissance men in Italy and elsewhere were extremely anxious to add something new to the old heritage, to make their own contribution to cultural progress. Their humanism was therefore more than a mere revitalization of antiquity, as it is generally admitted today. And it needs no elaboration to show that they were eminently successful in that respect as far as culture in its strict sense, in arts, learning, and intellectual life is concerned. Considered from this point of view, Renaissance culture is a priceless link in the uninterrupted chain of Europe's achievements. But the life of a civilized society, as fully developed as the European had already been for centuries, requires more than that. And in fields other than the purely intellectual, the generations of that great transition period developed conceptions which are also part of the Renaissance idea of their time.

It is usually said that they wanted to be free from all the limitations which the so-called mediaeval mind had accepted for centuries in the religious sphere. This is not true of all those who created the culture of the Renaissance or participated in it. For very few of them, if any, the rebirth of Graeco-Roman antiquity was to include a return to its approach to religion or its pagan beliefs. On the contrary, just because such extreme views about faith and morals failed to gain genuine acceptance, these critical centuries proved that Europe could not cease to be Christian, even though the religious unity of even western Christendom suffered cruelly. We can only state that the Renaissance idea made ecclesiastical reform more radical than it had been earlier and that these reforms were a transition from the religious unity of the Christian Commonwealth, at least in the West, to the subsequent variety of religious thought in Europe which even included unprecedented anti-religious trends.

Furthermore, the reform of the Christian Commonwealth could not remain ecclesiastical only. Its structure included a political side as well where the need of an even more drastic reform was much greater. As a universal power the empire was in a much more serious crisis than the Papacy, a crisis which proved impossible to solve. Here again the main concern of the men of the Italian Renaissance was freedom, in particular the freedom of the Appenninian peninsula from foreign control and invasion. Their age was a transition from the period when national freedom was threatened by the Holy Roman Empire, still claiming and, in part, exercising supreme power in Christendom, and the period when in spite of the decline of the empire, a divided and partitioned Italy was helpless before various foreign powers and dynasties.

Why, at the time of the Renaissance, the much-desired unity of Italy was not established any more than the unity of Christian Europe has to be explained by the tragic deficiencies of the political ideas of the period, which are in sharp contrast to the flowering of its culture under Italian leadership.

The same deficiencies must be held responsible for the fact that neither the Europe of the Renaissance nor Italy herself were free from the danger of Ottoman conquest, from what has been called the anti-crusade of Islam.[16] Never was the common defense of Europe and of her Christian culture more urgent and at the same time more inadequate. It was a transition from the period of the crusades to the period when the eastern question in a new, much less inspiring form was at least partly solved by the gradual elimination of the Ottoman Empire from the considerable part of Europe which it had conquered.

The whole problem of Europe's defense was then, in the Renaissance period, common to western and eastern Europe, as it usually was. It was again the area between those two main parts of the Continent which was particularly threatened. Occasional examples of heroism and sacrifice, though mostly in vain, can be credited to the period where so few otherwise remarkable leaders, with the exception of the Papacy, were fully aware of the issues involved.

In view of this, it is surprising and needs explanation how in that same period the overseas expansion of some European powers could make progress and lead to the gradual discovery of the world in the spirit of the restlessly searching Renaissance mind. These first great discoveries and European conquests in other parts of the globe, which thus were opened to the propagation of Christianity, are a particularly impressive transition from the largely isolated position of the Christian Commonwealth of the past, when even the overseas crusades extended it only insignificantly and temporarily, to the following period of Europe's predominance in the world. They lead through the amazing successes of European colonialism to the unexpected decline of that predominance through an anti-colonial reaction which reversed the situation at the end of the millennium.

The very character of the great transition called the Renaissance has been obscured by the importance given to dates which were supposed to indicate a break of continuity in all respects. These have to be briefly considered before discussing the various aspects of Renaissance developments.

CHAPTER XVII

The First Crisis of the European Conscience

IN RECENT SCHOLARSHIP the crisis of the European conscience which occurred at the turn of the seventeenth century in connection with the so-called scientific revolution has been studied in detail[1] and sometimes is even considered the starting point of modern western culture. Its unquestionable importance should not, however, make the historian overlook that there was another crisis of the European conscience at a much earlier date, in connection with a religious revolution. That first crisis, which made the second possible or at least prepared for it in the European mind through its far-reaching consequences, is one of the dividing lines which have been established in historiography between the Middle Ages and the modern period, the date of 1517 being frequently chosen for that purpose.

That date has been rather overrated in retrospect, because when Martin Luther posted his famous theses at Wittenberg, he had not yet decided to break with the Catholic Church.[2] And what is more important, the spectacular event of 1517 and the whole Protestant Reformation that followed, decisive as they were for the religious development of the West, can be properly understood only as parts of a long process which started with the great Western Schism and lasted in its critical phase until the conclusion of the Council of Trent and the Catholic Counter-Reformation or Restoration. In other words, it lasted through the whole Renaissance period.

That Huss was the precursor of Luther and that the Hussite revolution prepared the Protestant one is now admitted by most historians,[3] even as it was by most contemporaries. In spite of all that was original in the approach of the Czech reformer and of the pre-Hussite heresies in Bohemia,[4] these trends in Central Europe were part of a movement which had found in England a leader in the person of Wycliff at the very time when the Western Schism originated. Without that schism and its implications for the whole Latin West, the heresies of the turn of the fourteenth century would not have proved so much more dangerous for the unity of the Church and even of Europe than earlier revolts against ecclesiastical authority had been. And though that unity seemed to be successfully restored by the great councils of the first half of the fifteenth century, the religious crisis of that century leads from that of the preceding to that of the following one. The conflict between the Council of Basle with Pope Eugene IV resulted on the one hand in another, though briefer schism and on the other hand was well remembered by Luther and his followers. It has even been said about the Council of Florence, where the Pope triumphed, that it made the Protestant Reformation inevitable.[5] It is in any case unquestionable that the alarming experience of the Holy See with the conciliarism of the fifteenth century—that product of the scandal of the Great Schism—was responsible for the delays in holding other councils when in the sixteenth century this was particularly urgent. The Fifth Lateran Council ended its inconclusive debates no earlier than the year of 1517, and the Council of Trent achieved the reform of the Catholic Church when other Christian denominations had already established their own churches separated from Rome.

The connection between all these well-known facts, and therefore the unity of the whole process which deeply troubled the conscience of Europe for no less than two centuries, seems entirely obvious. It is equally clear that the great religious crisis, an integral part of the history of the Renaissance period of transition, was at the same time a consequence of the preceding period's concern with religious problems and a cause of the changed attitude in religious matters which was to be typical of the next. Well before scientific discoveries and hypotheses pretended to replace faith by reason traditional beliefs and loyalties were shaken by a whole series of troubles which continued with only short interruptions.

They had their roots in the Great Schism even though that first division was not of a doctrinal character at all. More than that, it was originally so difficult to discover which side was right, viz. which of the rivalling popes was the legitimate successor of Peter, that even future saints had different opinions in that matter.[6] The confusion was therefore much greater than on earlier occasions when in the conflicts between the Papacy and the empire an anti-pope was put forward by the secular authority. Now the spiritual leadership of the Christian Commonwealth was divided, a shocking division that had its repercussion in all Catholic countries. Even within the same country, for instance Germany, each of the two popes had convinced partisans and followers who for reasons of expediency would shift their allegiance from one to the other.[7]

Today there can be no doubt that the popes residing in Rome were legitimate. Those who returned to Avignon and who, in contrast to the Avignon popes before the schism, are not counted in the lists of supreme pontiffs, were not legitimate. But how misleading the election of a third pope by the Council of Pisa must have been is best evidenced by the fact, that this pope, Alexander V, is still counted in these lists; and only quite recently, when after many centuries a pope took again the name of John which the second Pisan pope had chosen, and called himself John XXIII like that of the fifteenth century, instead of John XXIV, the claims of the third series of popes were tacitly but clearly invalidated.

That detail is important because it is connected not only with personal problems of bygone days but with the question of conciliarism. Conciliarism was the lasting by-product of the schism and introduced into the whole dispute a doctrinal element. How dangerous that was became obvious when the same Council of Constance which deposed the fifteenth-century John XXIII, and after the resignation of the legitimate Roman pope ended the schism, proclaimed before the unanimous choice of his successor the doctrine that an ecumenical council was supreme over the pope himself. Never sanctioned by the Holy See, that doctrine was, as a matter of fact, a heresy undermining the structure of the Church and questioning the dogma of papal primacy. It was an additional tragedy that the same men who, obviously in good faith, issued that wrong statement, condemned as heretic John Huss at a time when shortly after the resignation of Gregory XII and before the election of Martin V there was no legitimate pope at all. Tragic, too, was the fact that Huss, shortly before the Council of Constance, attacked the practice of indulgences, starting his opposition to Rome exactly as Luther would do one hundred years later. Huss acted because of indulgences which John XXIII—no real pope as we know today—had granted to those who were "crusading" against the supporters of the legitimate Gregory XII.[8]

In view of so much confusion, it is not surprising that the issue raised by the claim of conciliary supremacy reappeared during the long Council of Basle. It led to another schism, which in spite of the clearly illegitimate election of another anti-pope made many Catholic rulers and members of the hierarchy adopt a neutral attitude. On the contrary, it is surprising that at that very time Eugene IV succeeded in concluding a union with the whole eastern Church at the Council of Florence—an achievement which continues to be strangely underestimated. In the light of the source material which has been carefully collected and published in connection with the five-hundredth anniversary of the great event of 1439,[9] it is unquestionable that this time, in contrast to the Union of Lyons, the agreement had been well prepared by thorough discussions and that all eastern Christendom was duly represented. The emperor and patriarch of Constantinople appeared in person and the patriarchs who were under Mohammedan control appointed substitutes. The formula in which papal primacy was recognized was important even for the position of the Holy See in the West where Rome's supreme authority was being questioned. No more precise definition was given in that crucial matter before the First Vatican Council of 1870.[10]

It is true that in the East the Union of Florence met with no less opposition and lasted only a little longer than the Union of Lyons. But the role of the Greek opponents, which requires further study, seems to have been rather overrated. At the same time, sincere supporters of reunion remained faithful to that idea even if they had to go into exile. Its chances in Constantinople ended only with the Turkish conquest which the West failed to prevent. The Florentine tradition continued to be invoked whenever in later times at least regional unions were considered. This is particularly true in the Ruthenian lands of Poland and Lithuania where the decisions of 1439 were accepted almost at once, revived after twenty years, and never formally rejected, as they were in Moscow.[11]

The negotiations at Ferrara and Florence, conducted in the atmosphere of the Italian Renaissance, contributed to a cultural rapprochement between Latins and Greeks[12] which continued to influence even those among the latter who did not favor religious reunion on the conditions of 1439. In any case, a precedent of promising contacts had been created at a time when the common interest in the heritage of classical antiquity made them easier and when the common danger to all Christendom was a serious warning to save the Christian character of European culture in all its forms.

For the Slavs for whom the religious, cultural, and political consequences of the Eastern Schism proved particularly deplorable, it was fateful that the movement towards reconciliation between Rome and Constantinople at the time of the great councils of the fifteenth century coincided with a conflict between Rome and a western Slavic nation. This nation, one of the first to be Christianized, was the Czechs. When the Council of Basle had not yet broken with Eugene IV and was still presided over by the same Cardinal Cesarini[13] who later followed the pope to Ferrara and Florence, an agreement was concluded between Basle and Prague which seemed similarly successful. Cesarini, who was to sacrifice his life ten years later in a real crusade against the Turks —an attempt to save Constantinople and the Union of Florence—had also conducted the military expedition against the Hussites. Though these were considered crusades, he realized that they were not appropriate means to re-establish peace among Christians. He tried, therefore, to replace them by an agreement with the moderate wing of the Czech movement, which after a victory over the extremists restored peace in Bohemia. Unfortunately, the much discussed *Compactata,* subject to diverse interpretations, did not fully satisfy either side; and the Hussite revolution, which was religious, national, and social at the same time, left behind a tradition which was in conflict with that of Saint Václav.[14]

In the second half of their millennium the Czechs therefore had two national traditions which their last native king, George of Poděbrady, was unable to reconcile. And though the renewed conflict with Rome which troubled his reign was appeased under his Polish-born successor, both trends of the Hussite movement survived until the time of Luther, when a new phase of the religious crisis affected all Europe, this time not for a few decades like the Western Schism, but for the whole future. The Protestant revolt like the Hussite included moderate claims similar to those which had been satisfied when the Greeks concluded their union with Rome, especially as far as the form of Holy Communion, the celibacy of the clergy, and the use of a non-Latin language in the liturgy were concerned. But in the sixteenth-century crisis, even more than one hundred years before in Bohemia, those acceptable claims were everywhere so intimately associated with a challenge to the whole doctrine of the Church that a break in its unity could not be avoided.

That break went much deeper than the Eastern Schism which the Union of Florence had not ended. This time it was a division within the Latin West which threatened to result, as the Western Schism had, temporarily, in divisions even within individual countries, a threat which in the case of Germany was to come true. Such a continuation and aggravation of the religious crisis of the late fourteenth and the early fifteenth centuries made the whole Renaissance period a time of trouble for the European conscience. If in the interval between the Hussite and the Protestant revolts that conscience, with a few individual exceptions like that of Savonarola, was not fully aware of the growing danger, it was to a large extent the consequence of the worldly concerns of Renaissance culture at its height, which influenced even the Roman curia. That consequence alarmed even such outstanding humanists as Erasmus of Rotterdam, but it was then too late.

The greatness of the danger to not only the ecclesiastical but also the entire spiritual unity of Christendom became evident even in his time and in that of the last Renaissance popes. Then, movements even more radical than that of the most extreme Hussites shocked the followers of Luther no less than faithful Catholics. Even the Bohemian Brethren, proud of their Hussite heritage, were nearer to the German Lutherans and later to the Reformed Church of Switzerland[15] than to Moravian Anabaptists or to the Antitrinitarian movement. This latter spread from the south of Europe towards its center. The Protestants, anxious to preserve what they considered the orthodox Christian doctrine, were in basic matters much further from Roman Catholicism than were the Greeks. But the small groups which revived the Christological heresies of the early part of the first Christian millennium made the crisis in the middle of the second millennium an unprecedented threat of disintegration.

Disintegration threatened Christendom not only in the religious field. The new radical sects, opposed to Catholicism and Protestantism in the essentials of the Christian doctrine concerning Christ himself and the Holy Trinity, disagreed among themselves in these same matters, and went to the extreme limit in individual interpretation of the Scriptures, a principle which the Protestant reformers had introduced without going to the last consequences. But the same rapidly multiplying sects, and even more, their individual leaders, disagreed with one another, as well as with the established churches, in questions of political philosophy and social order as well. What they had in common was a revolutionary approach to these questions, inspired by generous humanitarian ideas. Independently of all the doctrinal issues, they tried to apply the moral principles of Christianity as they saw it to questions like the proper attitude toward the secular power, war and peace, social justice with respect to serfdom, and other issues.

These progressive, though sometimes utopian, ideas and the high intellectual level of many of their writings explain the sympathetic interest which that extreme wing of the religious reformers of the sixteenth century has raised in modern historiography.[16] The persecutions which these men, sometimes considered precursors not only of Unitarianism in its present form but also of socialism and even communism, had to suffer on many occasions from their contemporaries contribute to such a sympathy. All this leads to a question which has always troubled the European conscience, but has gained supreme importance in connection with the religious crisis of the Renaissance period and with its consequences for the European community.

For the historian it is, first of all, a question of scholarly objectivity, always difficult in the historical and social sciences, but especially when his personal religious convictions are involved. That difficulty does not disappear when he does not have such convictions, because in that case he cannot have a genuine understanding for the deepest concerns of any religious group and can easily adopt an attitude not only of indifference but even of anti-religious prejudice. He can also be inclined to reduce what basically was an involved religious conflict among equally convinced protagonists, sometimes ready for martyrdom, to socioeconomic struggles. These did indeed appear simultaneously and affected the religious situation, as for instance the Peasant War in Germany at the time of Luther,[17] but they cannot be compared in importance with the great spiritual crisis.

It seems, however, that all historians can agree on two points. First, it certainly was an obstacle to Europe's normal development and a source not only of trouble but of endless suffering that such a crisis developed at all. And since the European community was still primarily a religious one, the religious character of that crisis made it particularly alarming. Secondly, it certainly would have been the only satisfactory and truly Christian solution to find a way out of that tragic situation by exclusively peaceful means: by proceeding without delay with the constructive reforms which were indispensable in order to end all the real abuses which in the Renaissance period more than in any other had disturbed ecclesiastical life and organization; by clarifying which claims of those who were dissatisfied with the existing situation could be met without compromise in the essentials, that is in matters of dogmatic truth; by defending faith and morals, and the principles where no compromise was admissible, through preaching, writing, and education; and last but not least, by treating even those who were breaking away from the Church with the greatest possible charity, not as heretics but as separated brethren, as they are called today.

Today, with four centuries and their experience of painful separation behind us, it is easy to outline such a program. There were also among the most religious minds of the sixteenth century many who favored it and made serious efforts to put it in practice, inspired as they were by the noblest traditions of Christianity. Unfortunately, the whole atmosphere of the period made such practice extremely difficult, and the same dissenters who complained about Catholic intolerance did no better in their relations with those faithful to Rome or in the reciprocal relations between the new denominations.[18]

The worst of it was that religious division was then leading, as it had on a smaller scale at the time of the Hussite movement, to political and military conflicts in the form of both civil and foreign wars.[19] Though the alignment in international relations never fully corresponded to the religious grouping, only too frequently religious arguments were used at least as a pretext for open warfare. While the most persistent rivalry and almost uninterrupted struggle was between the two leading Catholic dynasties, Habsburg and Valois, the religious factor in the hostility between Spain and England was indeed inseparable from the political.[20] So it was in certain revolts against foreign rule, the situation in the Netherlands being typical in that respect. But most disastrous were the civil wars on religious grounds, like the Schmalkaldian War in the empire and particularly the internal struggles in France, although even in such cases factional and personal rivalries contributed to these bloody troubles.

Such a spectacle was a strong argument in favor of religious freedom. This principle was frequently invoked in Poland where at the time of the strongest religious tension in the western countries peace among all who differed in religion was solemnly proclaimed.[21] Freedom of worship and of religious discussion was claimed by the Polish nobles, the class which was most involved in the Reformation, as integral parts of all their other liberties. But such a tolerance was also the natural result of two other factors typical of the religious situation in the Polish-Lithuanian Commonwealth. With the exception of small Transylvania, also a haven of religious freedom, that Commonwealth was the only body politic in Europe where peoples of different religion, Catholic and Orthodox, and even minor groups of Armenian Christians, Jews and Muslims, had lived together in almost undisturbed peace even before the Reformation. Furthermore, the religious reform movements of the sixteenth century penetrated there in all their variety. There were Lutherans, Calvinists, Czech Brethren reviving the tradition of Hussite penetration in the preceding century; and in addition to these Protestants in the strict sense, who themselves had great difficulties in coming to some kind of agreement, there were all the Anabaptist and Antitrinitarian radicals, sometimes called Polish Brethren. Most of their leaders, however, were of Italian origin and they never formed a fully unified Church after breaking away from the Calvinists.

The role of Poland as *asylum haereticorum* seemed to offer an excellent opportunity to achieve there a religious union among all denominations in a national church which could be opposed to the traditional one. What really happened was just the contrary. The failure to create a truly ecumenical movement on non-Catholic ground,[22] and the contrast between a confusing variety of doctrines in the camp of the dissenters and the clear definition of the Catholic faith by the Council of Trent, made the tolerant king, the last Jagellonian, accept before any other monarch the decrees of that Council. It also determined the overwhelming majority of the Poles, to whom a free choice was left, to decide in favor of Rome, whence their forefathers had received Christianity six hundred years before.

The Catholic restoration which was achieved by peaceful means in Poland had a significance for Europe which can be compared with that of her decision of 966, at the beginning of Europe's millennium. Now, in one of the largest countries of the Continent, situated between the part of Germany where Protestantism triumphed, and a Russia where the very limited repercussions of the spiritual crisis in the West[23] hardly affected the strong position of the Orthodox Church—when the crisis at the middle of Europe's millennium endangered the religious continuity of its life—Catholicism emerged even stronger than before and continued to be an outpost of western Christendom. It was then that in the limits of the Polish-Lithuanian Commonwealth the attempts toward reunion with the eastern Church could be resumed and could succeed to a large extent in the Union of Brest in 1596.[24] But it was then, too, that Catholic Poland found herself exposed to the onslaught of all her non-Catholic neighbors: to the old danger from Islam represènted by both the Ottoman Empire and the Crimean Tartars, to the intensified hostility of Moscow, and to the new tension in the relations with Protestant Brandenburg and Sweden. An identification of Catholic and national consciousness in Poland, similar to that in Ireland at the opposite corner of Europe, was the natural result of such a situation.

With the exception of those two countries of which the Celtic was no longer free, Catholicism fully triumphed only among the Romance nations of the European community, including even France, where its victory was achieved only at the price of long civil wars, with the Huguenots being reduced to the position of a tolerated minority. Similar triumph of the old faith seemed obvious in the vast domains of the Austrian line of the Habsburgs. But in their non-German kingdoms, Bohemia and Hungary, Catholicism, identified with the rule of a German dynasty, found its place in the national tradition seriously questioned: the independènce movement appeared there either under a revived Hussite or a new Calvinist influence. And in Germany only the Wittelsbach dynasty followed the example of the Habsburgs, while most of the other states utilized the new principle *cuius regio illius et religio* as a policy opposed to that of the House of Austria.

In view of such an outcome of the great religious crisis, it is a surprising, but also a decisive, proof of the historical continuity of Christian Europe that its spiritual unity still survived to a large extent in its western part. True, there was henceforth also in that part a dangerous dualism in religious beliefs and ecclesiastical organization which was added to the agelong dualism of Christian and ancient traditions. But some of the essential Christian doctrines remained common, besides the principles of Christian ethics which had never been questioned, even if disregarded in practice in the conflicts between Christians. A basically Christian way of life continued, therefore, in spite of a dividing line which frequently cut in two not only individual countries but even smaller communities and families.

It was still more surprising that this division within the western world which followed the Renaissance period was never so deep as the old division between western and eastern Christendom, although the new differences in the religious field were so much greater than those which caused the Eastern Schism. Both Catholics and Protestants[25] tried to arrive at a rapprochement with Constantinople or Moscow or both, as soon as they realized after the Council of Trent that their division was final. All such attempts remained vain; in Constantinople because the patriarchate was under the control of the Sultans; in Moscow, now the main center of Orthodoxy, because of a persistent prejudice against the West. Strangely enough, the old prejudice against the Papacy remained the greatest one, so that on many occasions Orthodox and Protestant would join in their opposition to Rome, especially when common political interests overshadowed the doctrinal differences.

However, the European community which survived the shock of the Eastern Schism hardly one century after its constitution, survived also the consequences of the Protestant Reformation. And though the influence of the Roman center of that community was now seriously limited, the Catholic Restoration was so successful within reduced territorial limits that the Papacy, in spite of the most violent attacks, continued to occupy its unique place as the only supranational authority in Christendom, in spite of, or perhaps mainly just because of, the drastic limitations of its political power.

The first great crisis of the European conscience found different solutions in the various parts of Europe, but everywhere it found a solution which was no definite break with the past. How much the religious reformers, including the most radical ones, wanted to avoid such a break, is best evidenced by the claim of all of them that their reforms were not really a revolution but a return to the original purity of Christianity. Nevertheless the doubts which had been raised concerning almost all dogmas of the Church and the preservation of the Gospel teachings by ecclesiastical authorities opened the door to a secularism which was to be much deeper than that of the Renaissance. Therefore, new crises of the European conscience were to follow whether that conscience was Catholic or not. Additional proof of Catholicism's vitality through the whole millennium of Europe was reflected when Catholicism remained in a better position to meet such crises, did not suffer any more losses on the map of Europe, and occupied a leading position in some of the cultural trends which followed the Renaissance.[26] Europe's religious division remained, however, a serious handicap for her political integration, for her defense and, to a certain extent, also for her expansion.

CHAPTER XVIII

The Struggles for Freedom and Peace

THOSE WHO ARE PRIMARILY INTERESTED in political history, in problems of war and peace and international relations, hesitate between 1494 and 1519 when trying to find a date which would neatly separate the Middle Ages from the modern period. Both years were indeed turning-points in Europe's military and diplomatic history, but in very different senses.

The first was the beginning of the Italian Wars which were to last more than sixty years,[1] depriving a great European nation of her freedom without establishing lasting peace and order in the war-torn region. Involving quite a few of the other nations and chiefly motivated by the ambitions and rivalries of their dynasties, the Italian Wars were indeed an international issue, but like a long series of dynastic conflicts which were to follow in the next centuries, they were not fought in the name of any principle and merely perpetuated the political divisions of the European community, contrary to the tradition of the Christian Commonwealth.

In 1519, in the midst of the Italian Wars, the election of Emperor Charles V started a reign which was a last attempt to return to that tradition by establishing a universal empire under the leadership of the House of Austria with a bold vision of world-wide peace.[2] That belated attempt proved, however, even less acceptable to the various national powers outside the empire than its original conception had been, and far from leading to peace in Europe, contributed to new wars which were supposed to defend the freedom and independence of the individual nations.[3]

The significant turns of 1494 and 1519 were not without precedents in the earlier part of the Renaissance period, and therefore, instead of being chronological divisions, they rather confirm, just like the climax of the long religious crisis in the year 1517, the unity and continuity of that period of transition.

In western Europe, the Hundred Years War, especially in its second phase after 1415, was a dynastic conflict with far-reaching international repercussions which turned into a war in defense of the freedom of an invaded country. In this earlier case the defense of national freedom and unity was successful. But this protracted war proved very harmful to the idea of European unity, leaving behind a tension between France and England which time and again troubled the peace of Europe. One can speak of another Hundred Years War between the two countries three centuries later[4] and their entente became possible only at the end of Europe's millennium.

In eastern Europe, the long series of wars which Moscow started against Lithuania and Poland, only two years before the beginning of the Italian Wars and with comparable consequences, also had antecedents leading back to the turn of the fourteenth century.[5] And in this case, too, what had originally been a rivalry of two ambitious dynasties, turned into a lasting tension between two nations, each of them looking for allies in the West.

Equally instructive is the study of the preceding century's antecedents for the imperial scheme based upon the election of 1519. When the Habsburgs were preparing for their future role, the last of the Luxemburgs tried to revive the Holy Roman Empire's leadership in Europe, particularly during the Council of Constance whose convocation he had urged and which he wanted to control. But the role of the King of the Romans (not yet crowned as emperor) as universal peacemaker was doomed to failure, a failure even more complete than the last effort of the ecclesiastical authority to settle not only religious matters but international relations as well. Sigismund's mediations or arbitrations, instead of appeasing the Hundred Years War in the West or the conflict between Poland and the Teutonic Order in the East, were considered too partial by the French and the Poles, who refused to recognize any imperial authority.[6] And instead of leading a crusade against the Turks in defense of his Hungarian kingdom, Sigismund failed to establish peace in the

Bohemian one, where not only his role in the crusades against the Hussites but also his promotion of German influence made him even more unpopular.

It was in opposition to the influence of a German-controlled empire as well as to papal authority that a Bohemian project of international organization made its appearance in the next generation.[7] To a certain extent that Renaissance project might be compared with that of Pierre Dubois in the last phase of the Christian Commonwealth. But the approach of George of Poděbrady, suspected of being a Hussite, was even more secularistic, though it included the idea of opposing the Ottoman advance. Only his negotiations with individual national powers outside the empire, with Venice, France, and Poland, led at least in the cases of the last two to bilateral alliances. France under Louis XI, in sharp contrast to the France of Louis IX two hundred years earlier, was thinking only of her national interest, while the Jagellonians of Poland and Lithuania were building a political system which was to serve peace and cooperation, but only in the area of East Central Europe.

At the same time the Habsburgs, who, after Sigismund of Luxemburg had gained the imperial crown which was to remain in the House of Austria until the end of the Holy Roman Empire—except for one brief interruption in the eighteenth century—showed a similar interest in that same region, particularly in the Bohemian and Hungarian succession with the view toward strengthening the domestic power of the Austrian dynasty. Even under the weak Emperor Frederick III the drive towards leadership in a vast region of Europe was part of a dream of world domination, expressed in both the Latin and German interpretation of the initials A.E.I.O.U.[8] And a happy matrimonial policy of Austria enlarged the realm of her dynasty from the center of Europe far to the West, including part of the Burgundian heritage and all of that of the recently united Spain, and prepared in the East the gain of the Hungaro-Bohemian heritage of the Jagellonians.

At the same time the election of 1519 placed—instead of the king of France—another non-German ruler, the King of Spain, on the German and imperial throne. But in spite of his birth on Belgian soil and of his first crown, the Spanish, Charles V was, after all, a German Habsburg. Four years before, a first Congress of Vienna,[9] a meeting of typical Renaissance rulers and statesmen from West and East, had given to his brother Ferdinand a good chance to succeed to the Jagellonians in both

Danubian kingdoms. And in 1526, the year after the victory at Pavia of Charles V over his rival, Francis I of France, the death of Louis of Hungary and Bohemia in the battle of Mohács left those two crowns to the younger Habsburg.

Cooperation of the two brothers began: the emperor who a few years later put another crown, the iron crown of Lombardy, on his head, and the king of Hungary and Bohemia, soon elected King of the Romans, or heir-presumptive of the empire. That cooperation was indeed a step in the direction of uniting most of the former Christian Commonwealth in a supranational body politic much larger than the Holy Roman Empire itself had ever been. Furthermore, even after the abdication of Charles V and the division of the Habsburg possessions into those of the Austrian and the Spanish branch, there were prospects of an extension of the former in eastern Europe[10] and of a worldwide expansion of the latter, especially when in 1580 Portugal was united with Spain for sixty years.

Nevertheless, the melancholy of the founder of that universal power, when he meditated upon his achievements, was fully justified. No Habsburg candidate succeeded in gaining the Polish crown in any of the three elections held in the latter part of the century following the extinction of the Jagellonians. Therefore, the ambitious goal of uniting the whole heritage of that once rivaling dynasty with the Austrian lands was never attained, in spite of repeated attempts to secure the support of Moscow. And the *pax Austriaca*[11] supposed to unite the whole world which was being discovered toward the middle of the millennium of Europe, was an even greater illusion than the *pax Romana* which at the beginning of the first millennium of the Christian era was established for some time in what was then the *occumene*.

The imperial dream of the House of Austria in the age of its greatest representative, Charles V, seemed to have better chances of realization than that of Augustus, fifteen centuries earlier. During these centuries Christianity, only nascent in the days of the pagan Roman emperors, had become a unifying spiritual force which had never existed before. The Habsburgs were proud of what they considered to be their historic mission as Christian emperors and as defenders of that faith which the King of England, honored by the pope with such a title, had abandoned. But for that very reason it was particularly shocking that Charles V himself came in conflict with Pope Clement VII and was at least indirectly responsible for the *sacco di Roma,* a tragedy without precedent even during the old struggles between the empire and the Papacy. The Habsburgs' defense of Catholicism against German Protestants did not succeed in saving for Rome the whole empire, but occupied their attention at the very time when all their forces were badly needed for the defense of Christianity against the Turks.[12]

They were absorbed also by their dynastic struggle against the other leading Catholic power, France, and by their involvement in all the Italian Wars. In that connection, the darkest side of the otherwise brilliant Renaissance diplomacy[13] became fully apparent. In Italy the desperate struggle against all foreign invaders amidst the endless rivalries among the native, much weaker powers, led to the conviction that politics, in order to be fully efficient, had to be completely divorced from ethics. That principle, a negation of all Christian ones so far as public life and international relations were concerned, was most clearly formulated by the great Florentine Machiavelli.[14] But in practice the policy of Venice, which more than any of the states of the peninsula claimed to be the defender of Italian liberty, was not at all different from that of Florence and others. And similar methods were used without much scruples when France, endangered by the rise of Habsburg power, felt obliged not only to support German Protestants but also to ally herself with the Turks.

On the other hand, Philip II of Spain, the Habsburg who would seem the most devout Catholic, while sincerely considering his efforts to conquer England a service to the Church of Rome,[15] created on various occasions serious troubles for the Church when his own state interests were concerned. The use, or rather misuse, which he made of the Inquisition brought no credit to the cause of the faith. In his days, as in those of his much greater father, Habsburg policies were identified with what would be called imperialism today. Even Catholic rulers became convinced that these policies had to be resisted, because they aimed at the control of Europe and of the world by mere force under appearances of universalism inspired by religion.

The rulers opposed to, or at least suspicious of the dynasty which was building up the strongest power on the Continent, were supported by the majority of their peoples because of the rapid growth of the new forces of nationalism in the Renaissance period. Although the roots of nationalism can be traced back far into the preceding period, at least in some of the European countries, the great transition of the Renaissance contributed to these trends for two different reasons.

One of them was the reaction against pressures from the outside, sometimes combined with internal tensions between different ethnic groups in the same countries. The rise of the French people under Jeanne d'Arc against the English and the Hussite movement in Bohemia are simultaneous examples in both respects. In the first half of the period the climax of the struggle against the Teutonic Order hastened the development of Polish nationalism[16] and so did the long series of foreign interventions and invasions through the whole Renaissance age as far as Italian nationalism was concerned. Since Habsburg rule was generally identified not only with Catholic but also with German predominance, the opposition against it had everywhere national implications which were an obstacle to the creation of a supranational empire under Habsburg leadership. However, the second reason for a rapid progress of nationalism in Renaissance Europe was even deeper, independent of the current political contingencies, and therefore of a more lasting significance.

In its larger, not necessarily aggressive or defensive sense, nationalism, far from having always a negative character, is intimately connected with cultural development. In this sense, "national consciousness" is perhaps a more appropriate term. Renaissance culture, no less than that of the Christian Commonwealth, was of a supranational character, and, like the former, influenced all European peoples and promoted their intellectual intercourse. But diversity in unity, typical of all forms and phases of Christian and European civilization, was to become particularly conspicuous in the Renaissance. The movement started in Italy and contributed to the spread of her cultural influence in all other European countries, the more so because Italian culture was the most immediate heir of that culture of Roman antiquity which was being revived. Yet, in addition to a certain spirit of national competition in the process of that revival, there was also an entirely different side to the problem: the growth of individualism in the humanistic trends of the Renaissance.

Inseparable from the individualism of each human being which, of course, came first was also the individualism of each nation within the European community, especially in political life. While Latin remained, as in the past, the international language of that community, with a special interest in the perfection and purity of the tongue of the ancient Romans and their greatest writers, there also appeared a growing interest in the vernacular, in which each nation hoped to find its individual expression. The use of the vernacular in literature as well as in administration came earliest in Italy where it was closest to the Latin. The situation was different in countries of Latin culture which, remote from that culture's cradle and center, constituted its outposts: these countries were the last to use the vernacular in place of the language which symbolized their integration with the western world. In Hungary the use of Latin was to prevail until the nineteenth century,[17] without, however, preventing the development of a strong nationalism among a people who were ethnically isolated and endangered from various sides. In Poland, equally proud of her part in the *Latinitas,* it was in the middle of the sixteenth century, when Renaissance trends and Italian influence were at their height, that Polish took the place of Latin both as official language and in most literary production.[18]

In the same country, and even more in Germany, the Protestant Reformation's anti-Roman attitude and its claim for the use of the vernacular in liturgy contributed to that process. Where a national or state church was established, its role in the development of nationalism was considerable. Those like Cardinal Stanislaus Hosius who were familiar with the German situation and feared a similar religious separation from Rome in Poland criticized Catholic bishops even for using their native tongue in private correspondence. On the other hand, the Latin alphabet, which was used in Polish as in other West Slavic languages, emphasized the difference between that language and the otherwise rather similar Ruthenian, used in the eastern part of the Commonwealth and recognized as official not only in the Grand Duchy of Lithuania but also in some provinces of the Kingdom of Poland.[19]

In that connection a problem must be touched upon which in central and eastern Europe became important for the evolution of nationalism in these early days. In the West this problem is not fully understood even today, because until recently no distinction was made there between state and nation, and between the loyalties to either of them, both being lumped together as nationalism. In the eastern part of Europe the political boundaries of the various states also influenced the development of national consciousness. Thus, for instance, in spite of the differentiation among the eastern Slavs which can be traced back to the dawn of history, the clear distinction between those of them who formed the Muscovite state and modern Russia, and those who were included in the Jagellonian federation, the Commonwealth formally proclaimed in 1569, resulted to a large extent from their different citizenship.[20] The Ruthenians of Poland and Lithuania, whose differentiation into Byelorussians—then called White Ruthenians—and Ukrainians—then mostly called Ruthenians in the stricter sense—was influenced by the internal boundary of 1569 between the two parts of the Commonwealth, were all conscious of their difference from the Muscovite Great Russians. Yet, while they wanted to be free from the latter and were, in the great majority, loyal citizens of the Commonwealth, they also wanted to preserve not only their provincial regionalism, but also their Ruthenian nationality even when their upper classes were gradually and spontaneously Polonized under the influence of Poland's Renaissance culture. The Latin terminology used in those days is, however, rather confusing from the modern point of view, so that the famous expression used by one of their leaders: *gente Ruthenus, natione Polonus,* really means that he considered himself of Ruthenian nationality and Polish citizenship.

The correct interpretation of such situations is made difficult also by the social and constitutional implications of the problem. In the Commonwealth, whose constitution was supposed to follow the pattern of the old Roman Republic, the *szlachta*—about one tenth of the population enjoying equal civic rights—was gradually identified with the nation and made homogeneous through the spread of Polish culture. A similar identification of a numerous nobility and gentry of diverse ethnic origin with the nation, which through all the political crises of the period preserved the continuity of the state idea, took place in Hungary.[21] At the same time the imperial policy of the House of Austria was supported by a cosmopolitan aristocracy and bureaucracy, not without the participation of Czech and Hungarian elements. These elements, however, in their great majority defended their constitutional rights against Habsburg absolutism.

Absolutism and their German origin were the main reason why the Habsburgs failed to gain the crown of Poland. In the course of the Renaissance period the idea of civic freedom with a parliamentary form of government and far-reaching limitations on royal power was making steady progress there. In that respect it was assimilating the Grand Duchy of Lithuania. That development, which remained unchanged until the fall of the Commonwealth, contrasted sharply with almost all other European countries. In those countries the centralized state under absolute rulers triumphed in the same period. They continued to control national life throughout the next two centuries with consequences which were felt until the end of the millennium of Europe, especially in the policies of her great powers. The Holy Roman Empire turned into a loose community of larger and smaller absolute states. In France the Estates General had lost their significance by the end of the period,[22] and even in England, after the crisis of feudalism in the fifteenth century, Tudor absolutism severely restricted the role of Parliament in the sixteenth. In general, Renaissance humanism, which seemed so favorable to the freedom of the individual, failed to protect civic liberties. Instead of being developed on the basis of earlier traditions, these liberties were sacrificed to the power of the state. The reception of Roman law with all its rigidity, as it developed in the remote days of the old Roman Empire, certainly contributed to that process.

Those European states which had not lost their freedom and independence through foreign conquest or the supremacy of foreign dynasties, fully developed the idea of unlimited sovereignty. A policy inspired by such a philosophy must be called nationalistic, even if the state was hardly directed by the nation at large. Such a transformation of the Christian Commonwealth was a permanent danger to European unity, though the conception of Europe as a community to which all these states belonged was generally accepted and even more frequently expressed than in the preceding period. In view of the separation of politics from ethics, that conception was, however, no longer based on Christian principles and therefore no guarantee of European peace, in spite of an ever growing cultural community of at least western Europe.

Even the outstanding minds of the Renaissance, though certainly favorable to peace made scarcely any contribution to international organization within the European community, not even by working out schemes similar to that of George of Poděbrady. All that remained of the imperial dream of Charles V was a European state system based upon national or rather state individualism, empirically trying to find ways and means to settle the problems of their territorial disputes and political and economic rivalries, which only too frequently resulted in long wars. There appeared, however, two ideas which could contribute to a better European order, or at least, were supposed to do so: one of them was inherited from the past, while the other one, a new Renaissance product, was to influence the history of Europe to the end of her millennium and to our time.

The idea of federalism, which had played a growing part in the last phase of the Christian Commonwealth, was further developed during the Renaissance in only two cases. Particularly important was the gradual transformation of the Polish-Lithuanian union from the dynastic agreement of 1385 into a real federation concluded by the representatives of the two nations in 1569.[23] That long evolution, though once interrupted by a civil war in the 1430's, was achieved by negotiations and discussions. It established a lasting peace between the united peoples, though it would have been preferable to establish their Commonwealth on a trialistic rather than a dualistic basis with an equal position for the Ruthenian part. Even so, the principles of freedom and cooperation which inspired the so-called Jagellonian idea, attracted larger and smaller neighbor countries through the whole Renaissance period: earlier projects of unions with Bohemia and Hungary resulted in the middle of that period in at least a dynastic connection with those two kingdoms, fully respecting their national independence. Most of what had been ecclesiastical German states in Prussia and Livonia sooner or later joined the Jagellonian domains, at least as feudal dependencies like East Prussia and Curland, and, for a while, the principality of Moldavia. What remained of that political system after the loss of Bohemia and Hungary to the Habsburgs still was one of the great powers of Europe, different from the others through its federal structure and lack of aggressive imperialism. Projects for further extending that system through unions with Sweden and possibly even with Moscow, which appeared at the turn of the sixteenth century, were, however, destined to be total failures.

That the path from regional unions to a European federation was a difficult and, given the situation, a hopeless one, was experienced by the Holy Roman Empire. To a certain extent it continued to be a federation in the very heart of Europe, but in spite of the reform projects under Maximilian I, it never succeeded in giving itself a lasting, workable constitution. Through the conflicting policies of the different German dynasties, it was involved in power politics outside the imperial boundaries in addition to all the internal tensions, aggravated by the new religious divisions.

It is instructive to observe that these same divisions of the sixteenth century did not disrupt the unity of the comparatively small Swiss Confederation, though the original union of a few German-speaking cantons included French- and Italian-speaking areas in the fifteenth. Practically separated from the empire at the turn of that century, Switzerland, after an ominous defeat in 1515,[24] gave up her own ambition in power politics and forceful aggrandizement and adopted a restrained policy of neutrality which helped her to preserve freedom and peace within her frontiers and with her stronger neighbors. The structure of that federation which eventually became an unsurpassed example of democratic union and a model for all Europe, was still rather involved, with some territories dependent on others, or only in loose alliance with each other. But the very slowness and difficulty of arriving at a perfect solution in a region—even though limited in size—with old traditions of self-government and cooperation, explains the impossibility of finding a similar, federal solution for Renaissance Europe as a whole.

Federalism was chosen as a form of government in another area of the empire, which toward the end of the period achieved independence: the United Provinces of the Netherlands. In Italy, however, whose northern part continued to be considered part of the empire, there developed a new political conception which later was called the "balance-of-power system." That idea which in Italy can be traced back to the fifteenth if not the late fourteenth century,[25] that is, to the origin of the Renaissance period, was accepted by the end of the period as the basis for international relations in all of Europe. It remained so until the end of her millennium and, in spite of a growing criticism, is today an almost worldwide practice.

The experience of Renaissance Italy should have shown that such a purely mechanical conception, void of any moral principles, was leading neither to freedom nor to peace, though it was supposed to protect the independence of weaker nations against the supremacy of any individual power and to act as a deterrent against war among those whose power was apparently equal. As a matter of fact, as Erasmus of Rotterdam rightly observed,[26] the new approach to politics could justify, without any other reason, a war against any country which seemed to be stronger than the others. Furthermore, it resulted in a continuous change in the grouping of individual states into temporary coalitions, since after breaking the feared supremacy of one power, the victors would soon be faced by the rise of another one. Last but not least, it proved in any case impossible to determine exactly who was the strongest among rivaling powers or when the forces of two competitors ceased to be equal.

As far as Italy was concerned, such an unscrupulous political game, arbitrary in the interpretation of a given situation, prevented any power in the peninsula from becoming a center of national unity and made impossible any cooperation in the defense against foreign invaders. On the contrary, it gave to those non-Italian powers continuous opportunities to interfere with Italian problems and to attack individual Italian states which occasionally would also attack each other.

Instead of serving as a warning, that Italian example was followed by the non-Italian powers in their mutual relations during that same sixteenth century which saw the lamentable results of the Italian wars for both the freedom of a great nation and for European peace. It is true that Habsburg plans to dominate Europe could serve as an excuse for coalitions against them which themselves were motivated by power politics. But even when these plans had obviously failed, the game was going on, while England was carefully watching that no power on the Continent should emerge as definite victor.

Only isolated voices were recalling the Christian principles whose application to international relations would have been the only guarantee of a just peace with freedom for all. Even the two great Jesuit writers, Vittoria and Suarez, who in the sixteenth century laid the foundations for international law which were developed but hardly applied in the seventeenth, did not include in their general considerations any practical suggestions for the establishment of a European order. Yet, the disorganized European community, no less than divided Italy, needed a supranational organization and cooperation inspired by the idea of the Christian Commonwealth. This was especially true since Christian Europe was continuously threatened by the advance of a non-Christian and non-European power toward the heart of the Continent throughout the age of the Renaissance.

CHAPTER XIX

The Defense of Europe[1]

A MONG THE VARIOUS DATES which are proposed to divide the Middle Ages from modern times, 1453 certainly is the most justified.[2] If there was any event which seemed to interrupt the continuity of Europe's millennium, it was indeed the total and final disappearance of Europe's oldest power, the Eastern Roman Empire. This empire, as such, had a history of more than a thousand years, and with much better reason than the western could claim to continue the uninterrupted tradition of the ancient one.[3] In spite of the opposition and rivalry between the two empires of Christendom, the eastern had been a link between the European community, as constituted in the tenth century, and the first millennium of the Christian era, a link now broken and never to be replaced. It was a strange coincidence that at the same time, squarely in the middle of the millennium of Europe, an invention was made which more than any other caused a revolutionary change in the development of European civilization: this was the printing press. Without affecting the essence of that civilization but immensely facilitating its rapid and universal spread, that invention, in sharp contrast to the not much earlier one of gunpowder, was to serve exclusively peaceful objectives: the progress of education, literature, and learning.

This happened in the midst of the flowering of Renaissance culture, but also in the midst of a transition period, which besides the great crisis of the European conscience experienced an equally great external danger to Europe's peace and security and to her Christian culture. The conquest of Constantinople by the Turks was symbolic for the rise of that danger, but this exceptionally dramatic event was only part of the long process of a rise which lasted through the whole Renaissance period and is one more factor in its unity. The alarming growth of Ottoman power had started threatening Europe almost exactly one hundred years earlier when the Turks first succeeded in establishing themselves on European soil. After their great victory of 1453 that growth was to continue for more than one hundred years, until the death of Suleyman the Magnificent—easily comparable to Mohammed the Conqueror[4]—ended the uninterrupted line of Osman's outstanding successors in 1566.

Long before 1453 the collective defense of the disintegrating Christian Commonwealth became practically impossible when the Great Western Schism reached its climax in the first decade of the fifteenth century. This was the main reason why a unique opportunity to check the Turkish advance was missed, when their power was crumbling in the ten years following the defeat of Angora inflicted upon the Turks by Tamerlane. The appearance of a Mongol conqueror second only to Genghis Khan was another warning that the defense of Europe had to be organized not only on the southeastern but also on the northeastern front where Tamerlane, before turning against the Turks in Asia Minor, had been attacking the Christians of Rus' and Lithuania. However, the connection between these two distant fronts was not yet sufficiently realized except by the Venetians,[5] whose trade was threatened both in the Mediterranean and in the Black Sea region, and by the Polish-Lithuanian Union, the only land power which had to fear the Turkish and the Tartar advance alike.

What was particularly needed for an efficient defense of Christendom was the cooperation of these two powers with Hungary. That country, the first to be exposed to the onslaught of the Turks after the latter's conquest of the Balkans, was under the rule of Sigismund of Luxemburg from 1387 to 1437. His bad relations with both Venice and Poland were, in addition to the Hussite wars, a major obstacle to his crusading projects and typified the lack of unity among the European powers. That situation was evident even before Tamerlane's appearance, contributed to the failure of the crusade of Nicopolis,[6] and continued after the decade of troubles in the Ottoman Empire, when a joint action against the reappearing Turkish danger was so urgent. Such an action had to wait until the authority of the Holy See, which realized its necessity even during the Western Schism, was strengthened by the success of the

Council of Florence, and until Hungary was united with Poland under a Jagellonian king who had no difficulty in cooperating with Venice. The possibility of success was therefore very great when that king, the young Vladislav, encouraged by Pope Eugene IV, marched against the Turks in 1443 and 1444.

It was the last time that a Catholic coalition had a chance of cooperating with a Greek Empire, which in spite of its desperate situation was still ready to fight against the common enemy. The defeat of Varna, due to unforeseen circumstances, sealed the doom of that empire.[7] After the fall of Constantinople and the Turkish conquest of Morea a few years later, there was no longer at the enemy's rear a free Christian territory whose very existence had been an inspiring goal and a strategic advantage for the western forces. There was instead a triumphant Mohammedan power which extended on both sides of the Straits, like the Byzantine Empire in the days of its greatness, and which pretended to be its successor-state.

Between the two there was indeed a geographical continuity, but nothing more. The Eastern Roman Empire, in spite of four centuries of ecclesiastical schism, had always been an integral part of Christian Europe, and never, in spite of all political rivalries with Latin powers, a real threat to the West. The Ottoman Empire, though it moved its capital to Constantinople, remained a non-Christian and non-European conqueror and a growing danger to what remained of Christian Europe. Furthermore, that reunion of western and eastern Christendom which had seemed so near in the fourteen years before the fall of Constantinople was now out of the question as far as the Greek Orthodox populations of the Balkans were concerned. Under Turkish rule they were granted religious tolerance with the Patriarch of Constantinople as their spiritual head. But no relations with the Papacy were tolerated and the patriarchs were entirely dependent on the sultans.[8]

In addition to Moldavia, which defended her independence for at least half of a century, there remained a large country of Orthodox faith free from the Turks and, were it only for obvious geographical reasons, not even threatened by them, a power which soon would also pretend to be the successor-state of the Byzantine Empire. That power was Muscovy, which at the very time of the fall of Constantinople consolidated her position in all respects. The civil war which for two decades had troubled the reign of Basil II ended with his complete victory, and the Muscovite Church which had contributed to that success

was made autocephalous in 1448. This momentous decision, then motivated by the fear that the Patriarchate of Constantinople would come
under Roman influence by accepting the Union of Florence, proved
even more important when five years later the Greek Church lost her
freedom of action because of Turkish control. After two hundred years,
at almost the exact time when Turkish rule was established in Constantinople, Tartar control over Moscow was coming to an end. In the long
process of liberation which had started in 1380 and was completed with
the fall of the Golden Horde in 1502, the decisive turning point was not
so much the Tartar withdrawal in the conflict of 1480, but rather the surprising fact that in 1452, shortly after repeated Tartar interferences with
the civil war in Moscow, her overlordship was recognized by one of the
Tartar princes in a reversal of the mutual relationship.[9]

In view of all these events, it was a vital question for Europe's future
what attitude Moscow would take in the conflict between the European
West and the Asiatic East, which entered into a new phase with the disappearance of the Eastern Roman Empire. It even seemed that Muscovite
Russia—a Christian power who through the Byzantine intermediary
shared in the heritage of ancient Greece and had suffered so much from
Asiatic invaders—would join the European community in the middle of
Europe's millennium as Kievan Russia had done at its beginning, would
compensate that community for the temporary loss of southeastern
Europe, facilitate the defense against Islam especially on the northeastern
front, and perhaps even participate in the cultural progress of the
Renaissance period. Time and again the Papacy also would share such
hopes which were the more justified at the critical moment in 1453,
because only four years before Basil II had concluded a peace treaty with
his Catholic western neighbor, Casimir the Jagellonian. This treaty
with Casimir, the Grand Duke of Lithuania who after the death of his
brother in the battle of Varna was also elected King of Poland, seemed
to replace the rivalry between the two powers by a division of eastern
Europe into their spheres of influence. The failure of all those expectations requires careful investigation.[10]

The religious opposition between Moscow and the Latin West proved
deeper than Rome had expected, deeper than the one between Rome and
Constantinople had ever been. Nowhere in eastern Christendom was
the Union of Florence so immediately and definitely rejected as it was in
Moscow, where there was no tradition of original religious unity with
western Christendom, since the Christianization of the vast area of East

Slavic colonization from which Moscow emerged had been achieved only after the Greek schism and its repercussions in northeastern Europe. Moscow had never participated in these earlier attempts toward reunion, which, though unsuccessful, had maintained an almost uninterrupted contact between Latins and Greeks. In general, there had been scarcely any contacts of the remote Volga region with western Europe, similar to those of old Kievan Rus', while even those with Byzantium were rather scarce, until eventually the Tartar domination completed the cutting-off from Europe as a whole.

Among the many deplorable consequences of this domination[11] one particularly contributed to the alienation of Moscow from Europe. Much more than the impact of Byzantine autocracy,[12] and more than the hard conditions of life in the new area of colonial expansion, it was the Asiatic form of government in the Mongol Empire which influenced the subject princes. Especially those of Moscow used the unavoidable cooperation with the Khans for consolidating their own power until it became as despotic as that of their overlords. This process, hardly comparable to the rise of absolutism in many western countries, was in sharp contrast with the constitutional development of Moscow's immediate neighbor, the Polish-Lithuanian Union, and therefore repulsed even those populations of the federation which, like the Muscovite Russians, were of East Slavic origin and Orthodox faith.

The lack of freedom under Moscow's rule made even the Great Russian Republic of Novgorod resist as long as possible when Basil II and later his son and successor, Ivan III, made the conquest of that state the first goal of a policy of expansion. This was another decisive reason why any cooperation with Moscow was so difficult to establish. Such cooperation was expected when, simultaneously with the preparations for the final conquest of Novgorod, Ivan III entered into diplomatic relations with the Holy See in order to marry the niece of the last Byzantine Emperor, who was educated in Rome as a Catholic. But the strange story of that marriage ended in a twofold disappointment for the West: far from leading to a religious union, it ended in the conversion of the bride to Orthodoxy, and became one of the foundations of the conception that Moscow was the Third Rome, its ruler being considered the rightful heir of the second one and the defender of the faith which Constantinople had betrayed at Florence only to be punished by the Turkish conquest. Far from turning against the Turks who a few years later became Moscow's neighbors by bringing the Crimean Khanate under their control, Ivan III tried to appease them and to use their Tartar vassals against Lithuania. It was against his western neighbors that he directed Moscow's expansion as soon as the conquest of Novgorod was completed. It was merely with a view to encircling these neighbors that he established relations with other Catholic powers: with the Habsburgs as western rivals of the Jagellonians, with Mathias Corvinus, the Hungarian rival of both dynasties, and with Denmark, anxious to control Sweden.

The new power that was rising in the transition region between Europe and Asia thus entered at the turn of the fifteenth century into the game of power politics in Renaissance Europe and through occasional contacts with Italy was even touched superficially by Renaissance culture. But this did not mean any real integration, whether political or cultural, with the European community and even less a participation in its defense. On the contrary, that community was unable to concentrate on the defense against Turks and Tartars, because those of its members who were most directly affected by that old danger now had to face the additional threat coming from Moscow. And since the Turks, after cutting off Moldavia from the Black Sea, came into contact with the Tartars, whose raids practically cut off the Polish-Lithuanian federation from that same sea, there was now one long, uninterrupted front on which Europe had to be defended. That line reached from the entrance to the Adriatic Sea—which the Turks crossed at the end of the reign of Mohammed the Conqueror, even occupying Otranto for a short time— along the frontiers of Croatia, Hungary, Moldavia, and Poland, to the steppes north of the Black Sea; from there along the frontiers of Lithuania and Livonia to the Gulf of Finland, and along the Swedish border in Finland to the Arctic Ocean.

It so happened that on the very day—July 14, 1500—when in a treaty concluded at Buda the Jagellonians tried to strengthen their position by an alliance with France and Venice, Moscow defeated the Lithuanians in one of her most sweeping invasions. The alliance with the Habsburgs which the Jagellonians made at the first Congress of Vienna in 1515, brought them neither an efficient mediation in their conflict with Moscow nor any assistance against the Turks. After the battle of Mohács in 1526 in which Louis the Jagellonian lost his life, and as a result of the civil war in Hungary which followed, the line of defense against the Ottoman Empire was pushed back far into Croatia and Hungary; Transylvania and Moldavia came under Turkish suzerainty, while farther to the northeast the wars which Lithuania, supported by

Poland, had to conduct against Moscow, were interrupted only by precarious truces.[13]

During all those years from the middle of the fifteenth to the end of the sixteenth century the Renaissance popes, though absorbed in their policies by the critical situation in Italy, continued their efforts to organize an anti-Ottoman league in order to defend Europe, the common fatherland and home, as Pius II called it.[14] The popes sought to turn the forces of a war-torn Christendom against the common enemy. In view of the rivalries among the western powers, and deeply troubled by the Protestant revolt, the Papacy of the sixteenth century tried not only to mediate in these conflicts but also to attract the new power in eastern Europe to participate in the planned league, in spite of the poor prospects for religious reunion.

The climax of these efforts came, strangely enough, at the time of Ivan the Terrible. The reign of the first Tsar, whose ambiguous personality raised a great deal of interest and illusionary hopes even in far-away Italy, began with victories over the Tartars and the annexation of Kazan and Astrakhan, victories which could seem to be an extension of the boundaries not only of Muscovy but also of Christian Europe. If Ivan had continued in that direction and turned against the Crimea, cooperation with Lithuania and Poland and the establishment of a common front against Islam would even have been possible. He turned, however, in the opposite direction, against the disintegrating ecclesiastical state in Livonia, encircling Lithuania from the north. There followed the first Northern War, a war for the *dominium maris Baltici* which once more involved Moscow in the policies of the European powers,[15] but again diverted the attention and the forces of all of them from the problem of a common defense of Europe.

Ivan himself should have been interested in this problem when toward the end of the first phase of the Livonian war his own country was unexpectedly invaded by the Turks. That first and only invasion of Russia by the forces of the Ottoman Empire, with the exception of the Crimean War three hundred years later, has only recently received due attention in the historiography of various countries.[16] We realize now that the course of history would have been changed if the almost fantastic Turkish project of reaching the Volga by constructing a Don-Volga canal had succeeded, if they had retaken Astrakhan from the Russians, established contact with the Muslim states of central Asia and western Siberia, thus encircling Persia, and if they had blocked Moscow's eastern expansion.

But we also know that in view of the insufficient support by the Crimean Tartars such success of the Turks would have been possible only if they had received the requested permission to pass through the Polish Ukraine. Sigismund Augustus, the last Jagellonian, who had just consolidated the Polish-Lithuanian Union, refused this for reasons of Christian solidarity, as he declared to the Sultan. The latter soon made peace with Ivan the Terrible and turned against Venice.

The hope of the Venetians, shared by Pope Pius V, that Moscow would join the anti-Ottoman league which needed the participation of the Christian land powers, after the naval victory of Lepanto, was an illusion, as the king of Poland knew only too well. Ivan the Terrible was more interested in the olish-Lithuanian succession and in resuming the Livonian War. When he was hard pressed in that war by the successor of the Jagellonians, the Transylvanian prince Stephan Báthory, he asked for papal mediation. The famous Possevino mission to Moscow was once more inspired by expectations that there would be a religious reunion and a common struggle against the Turks.[17] Having been disappointed by Ivan in both respects, the Holy See, convinced that the defense against the Ottoman Empire demanded a union of all Christian forces of eastern Europe, first welcomed the bold plan of Báthory to seize the control of Moscow after the death of Ivan; and then, when the king of Poland also died, it favored once more an Austrian candidate to the Polish crown, hoping thus to achieve the cooperation of the empire, the Commonwealth, and Moscow.

The century ended indeed with another project of such a league,[18] but in a rather unexpected situation. When the Ottoman Empire, in spite of its apparent weakness under the insignificant successors of Suleyman the Magnificent, initiated an aggression along the artificial frontier in Croatia and Hungary, even the weak Emperor Rudolf II felt obliged to react. There followed a war of thirteen years which Pope Clement VIII considered an excellent opportunity to liberate the whole of southeastern Europe from Turkish rule. There was indeed an independence movement and an expectation of western assistance among the Balkan populations as well as an unusual cooperation between semi-independent Transylvania and the Habsburgs. Never was papal diplomacy more active in its attempts to promote an Austro-Polish alliance and to gain the cooperation of Moscow without stipulating any conditions for religious reunion.

But once more that cooperation proved impossible to achieve. The

Poles, not without good reason suspicious of Austro-Russian "practices" against them, were facing two equally dangerous alternatives: remaining outside the planned league, Moscow would threaten the eastern frontier of the Commonwealth; or, while joining the struggle against the Turks, she would move her forces through Polish territory. The hesitation of Poland—which caused a similar attitude to prevail in Venice, equally suspicious of the House of Austria—as well as the confused situation in the Danubian principalities where the interests of all Christian powers clashed, confirmed both the Turkish sultans and the subservient Greek patriarchs in Constantinople that no joint action of these powers would materialize, and the long war remained inconclusive. It was, however, the first war with the Turks without any further Ottoman advance and was concluded by a peace treaty in which they recognized the Christian Empire as their equal. Even in the most critical phase there was no siege of Vienna, similar to that of 1529, and occasional Turkish successes could not compare with that of Sziget at the time of Suleyman's death.

Thus the defense of Europe in the Renaissance period ended in a stalemate, not only in the Mediterranean region—where Charles V had failed to take Algier or Tunis but, on the other hand, Suleyman had failed to take Malta—but also in Hungary and Croatia, whose partition was to last for one more century. With even Buda in Turkish hands, the whole southeast of Europe remained separated from the free community of Christendom at a time when the reconquest of the Iberian peninsula was a long accomplished fact and the last Tartar Khanate in north-eastern Europe, that of the Crimea, was merely a nuisance to both Poland and Russia.

If that vassal state of the Ottoman Empire north of the Black Sea— which remained a Turkish lake—continued to exercise a troublesome influence at the border of Europe through the next century, it was for two reasons. First, one of the neighboring Christian powers, the Muscovite Tsardom, had not been really integrated with Europe in the Renaissance period and was for Poland an even greater threat than the Tartars. Second, a new problem arose, that of the Cossacks,[19] which at the end of that period acquired international significance, at least as far as the Ukrainian Cossacks of Poland were concerned. They had their own aggressive Turkish policy which was not at all coordinated with that of the Commonwealth. They were approached in that matter by the imperial court and even by the Holy See, but they were to be a growing source of trouble at a crucial spot of Europe's eastern borderlands.

Moscow too had difficulties in controlling her Don Cossacks, which were to contribute to the "time of troubles" at the beginning of the seventeenth century. The approaching internal crisis of the Muscovite state seemed to make it a much less dangerous neighbor than before, especially since the personal union of Poland and Sweden under Sigismund III was supposed to strengthen their common defense. What really happened was just the contrary: at the turn of the century the break between the Polish Wasa and his uncle, who took away from him the Swedish crown, led to a most harmful conflict between the two countries and they were involved in a long series of wars with each other. When they also were involved, quite unnecessarily, in the Russian troubles, it was on different sides, a development which for many years upset the international situation in the Baltic region.

The years immediately after 1600 were therefore a turning point in the history of eastern Europe, which closed the "Golden Age" of the Polish-Lithuanian Commonwealth in the Renaissance period. The rising power of Sweden became a new threat to the peace of Europe and hopelessly confused all problems of her defense, while Ottoman power was unexpectedly rising again and Moscow, after an abortive project of union with Poland, became more than ever opposed to the West.

Western Europe in the strict sense—the nations west of Germany— was well aware of the internal crisis which was approaching in the empire, but hardly realized the implications of the events which inaugurated the new century at the eastern border of the continent. Feeling safe from any Turkish, Tartar, or Muscovite danger and therefore not interested in the defense of Europe against it, these nations observed the situation in Constantinople from the point of view of their conflicts with the House of Austria. Also, Elizabethan England wanted to develop her trade relations with Russia in spite of Polish misgivings and warnings.[20]

Under such conditions, the defense of Europe at the end of the Renaissance period was less than ever before a problem which would contribute to European unity. The decline of the Papal authority in international affairs, an unavoidable consequence of Europe's religious division, restricted the influence of the only power which had tried to make that problem of defense a common concern of all Christendom through the whole period. However, there seemed to be a compensation for all the losses and troubles of Christian Europe in the East thanks to a policy of the western powers which was not a policy of defense but one of expansion. It involved them in overseas expeditions, much more distant, adventurous, and rich in consequences than the crusades of the past had been.

The great transition period in the middle of Europe's millennium raised therefore entirely new questions: Would Europe, which continued to be a victim of aggressions from the East, so that even her crusades, old and new, had a defensive aspect, likewise emerge as an aggressor in other parts of the world? Must the roots of what today is called European imperialism and colonialism, typical of the modern age, not be traced back to the early days of the Renaissance?

CHAPTER XX

The Expansion of Europe

THE YEAR 1492 is certainly the most popular among all the dates which have been chosen for dividing the Middle Ages from modern times. And it must be admitted that if such a division has to have meaning not only for European but for world history, no other date has a similar importance. Furthermore, though difficult for contemporaries to realize immediately, that importance has been steadily growing as its far-reaching consequences emerged. The great event of 1492 is easily interpreted today in its historical perspective.

Once more, however, it must be pointed out that what happened on October 12 of that memorable year was only a link, though a decisive one indeed, in a long chain of events. These represent a significant new development in the history of the European community and of its relations with the outside world only when considered together and as a whole. Once more that development was a great transition from the preceding to the following period, a transition which chronologically coincides with the age of the Renaissance.

In the case of the great overseas discoveries which are such an outstanding part of what has been called the discovery of the world and of man by the Renaissance generations, two additional, more specific points must be made in order to understand better the millennium of Europe. The year 1492 is, as a matter of fact, the date not of one but of two significant events. What because of European initiative, happened in that year at the border of the New World beyond the Atlantic, was closely connected with an almost simultaneous event which occurred near the Atlantic border of old Europe: the fall of Granada. A Spain, at last united and under the same two "Catholic Kings" to whom Columbus submitted the project of his expedition, completed the *reconquista* of the whole Iberian peninsula by eliminating the last Arab stronghold on European soil.

Though a Moorish state survived for a long time in the southern corner of the peninsula, Spain's liberation from Muslim domination and from the danger of African invasions had been practically achieved by 1340, mainly because of the decisive victory of the allied Castilian and Portuguese forces in the battle at Rio Salado.[1] The conclusion of a struggle which had started at the very beginning of Europe's millennium not only made possible the outstanding participation of the Iberian nations in all the splendors of the new Renaissance age, but completely reversed the situation: the Christian nations of southwestern Europe which had had to defend Europe for so many centuries now passed over to an offensive against their former conquerors, crossing the narrow Strait separating Europe from Africa and soon navigating along Africa's shores and towards the islands of the Atlantic Ocean.[2]

The Portuguese, who at the end of Europe's millennium were to be the last to give up the remainder of their colonial empire, were the first to start the process of overseas expansion. They reached the Canary Islands immediately after the victory of 1340 and led the new crusading movement, combined with carefully prepared discoveries, under Prince Henry the Navigator, in the first half of the fifteenth century. However, before those spectacular successes at the end of that century which were to lead them around Africa as far as India, the nation of Bartolomeo Dias and Vasco da Gama had to face not only occasional reverses threatening their first conquests on Africa's northern shores but also the rivalry of their Castilian neighbors. They had to defend the independence of their homeland against them and to arrive at a compromise with the Spanish peoples regarding the delimitation of their respective discoveries and conquests. This problem led to the establishment of a demarcation line between Spanish and Portuguese rights and possessions by Pope Alexander VI in the year of the second voyage of Columbus.

This leads the historian to the second point regarding the place of the great discoveries in the process of the formation and consolidation of European unity.[3] Those discoveries and the overseas expansion of Europe which followed were indeed an achievement of various European nations, at least the western ones: the Iberian and Italian explorers were followed in the sixteenth century by the French and the English, and at the end of the Renaissance period by the Dutch and even by the Scandinavians, whose remote ancestors had been the first to reach the coast of the future America at the beginning of Europe's millennium.[4] But like the crusades of the past in which even more European nations had participated, the whole movement, instead of strengthening the solidarity of Christian Europe, increased the tensions among the colonial powers, reflecting the struggles between their respective homelands. While the main source of trouble in the relations among the old crusaders had been the schism opposing western and eastern Christendom, this time the trouble started when all colonial powers were Catholic. Toward the end of the period, when Protestant nations entered the race, the situation became even more critical: the religious conflicts in Europe had their repercussions overseas, and treasures coming from non-European possessions were used for waging religious wars in the old world.

Yet these were not the only dark pages in the history of the great discoveries. Something else, a rather new phenomenon in European destinies was even worse. The Christian Commonwealth had to a large extent been isolated in the world or exposed to invasions from the east and south. Even its crusades, if not purely defensive, had been struggles for the liberation of Christendom's holy places which had fallen into Mohammedan hands. Renaissance Europe, though it had to continue earnest efforts to defend its changing frontiers with Asia, was penetrating into vast areas on other continents, particularly in Africa and in the western hemisphere, reaching as far as eastern Asia, over newly discovered sea roads around the globe. And everywhere, without limiting themselves to explorations which were to extend their knowledge, the Europeans tried to occupy the discovered lands with a view to dominating and exploiting them. The descendants of the heroes of the *reconquista,* who had been the liberators of their homelands from foreign rule, were the first to turn into *conquistadores,*[5] forcefully establishing their rule over distant regions whose hitherto free populations had never done them any harm and could not be dangerous to Europe at all.

This was certainly a break with the Christian tradition and the moral principles on which the European community was based. But it might to a certain extent be considered a strange return to some elements which in Europe's dualistic heritage recalled the ancient, pre-Christian Graeco-Roman world: the Hellenic, though rather Macedonian than truly Greek, imperialism of Alexander the Great, and even more the lust of power and world-wide conquest which turned the Roman Republic into an empire on the pattern of the Asiatic ones which had preceded the Roman.

Strangely enough, it was precisely at the time when the imperial idea was already discredited in Europe, where it met with the determined opposition of the individual nations which wanted to be free, that some of those nations started creating empires out of their extra-European conquests, much larger in area than the homeland. The early case of Portugal is typical in that respect, while Spain showed a similar trend in connection with her drive to predominance in Europe. These precedents of the Renaissance period inspired, towards its end, imperial dreams on the part of other European countries, including Spain's rivals and opponents, which were to come true in the following period. Only the case of Italy is different. The Republic of Venice, which at the time of the Christian Commonwealth came nearest to the realization of a colonial, though hardly imperial expansion beyond the seas, was now in retreat, and at the end of the Renaissance age had lost its outpost of Cyprus, gained a century before. Individual Italians, to mention only Columbus himself, were indeed leading in the great discoveries, but to the advantage of other nations. Divided Italy, herself partly under foreign rule, could not possibly have imperial ambitions, though she was, after all, old Rome's most legitimate heir.

In many cases European conquest was limited at first to the coastal areas of other continents, to ports whose hinterland was difficult even to explore and impossible to control. It was only in such small areas and places that European colonists would settle, creating bases for merely economic exploitation. The case of the western hemisphere, soon called America, was a special one with a truly overwhelming significance for Europe's expansion. The voyages of Columbus, similar to those which opened African or East Asiatic shores, those which the "Admiral of the Ocean Sea"[6] originally wanted to reach, were soon followed by the systematic, total, and final conquest of large American countries, where old, indigenous cultures flourished in apparently well organized states though in almost complete isolation. Whatever might be said about the cruelties of the Aztec regime in Mexico and about the totalitarian form of government in Peru under the Incas, the equally cruel and ruthless destruction of these states and cultures by European conquerors cannot be justified. Nor can the subjugation, and in some cases, near-extermination of less developed, but harmless populations in the various Americas be vindicated, since the Spanish or Portuguese example was followed with even greater success by the subsequent waves of other European invaders in the northern part of the hemisphere.

As a consequence the Americas, even before their emancipation several centuries later, were almost from the outset something more than European colonies resembling many others of the same kind. The basic difference was that the European explorers and conquerors, soon followed by settlers in greater numbers than elsewhere, gradually created in what they called the New World a real extension of the Old, rapidly enlarging their hold deep into the mainland. The vast territories which they organized politically on the European model, with a large amount of self-government included, could develop in the next period into new states and nations which perpetuated their European heritage on new grounds, including the religion, language, and political ideas of their distant mother-countries.[7] Conditions varied, indeed, in the different parts of the western hemisphere and depended to a large extent on the percentage of Europeans among the population, on the degree in which intermarriage with the natives was practiced, and also on the original differences among the European nations which participated in the immigration movement. It is equally obvious that no dates could be given which would indicate even approximately when a given part of America became part of what might be called a New Europe beyond the Atlantic. Nowhere was that process accomplished in the period which for Europe was that of the Renaissance and for America that of discovery and occupation. But there was a beginning of such a process which turned colonization into Europeanization, a process which started only after several more centuries in other overseas territories then discovered by Europeans, particularly Australia and New Zealand.

More than anywhere else, the expansion of Europe in the Americas was also an expansion of Christendom. This very important point leads from the dark aspects of colonialism in its largest sense to its brighter ones, which ought not to be overlooked at a time when there is a general inclination to condemn severely the whole movement. It must be admitted in advance that the two aspects cannot be completely separated, as appears already in the discussion of the religious issue. Very frequently the Christianization of the natives was achieved by ways and means contrary to the spirit of the Gospel, recalling some of the most regrettable practices in the conversion of European peoples many centuries earlier, and in the case of the American Indians shocking those contemporaries who took the missionary ideal most seriously. But there remains the fact that the great discoveries made possible large-scale missionary activities outside Europe, where they were no longer needed. The preaching of Christian doctrines and morals which accompanied the other, highly questionable colonizing activities, introduced into the whole process of European expansion a purely spiritual element, in addition to its political and economic ones. This spiritual element, if compared with the old paganism, represented most constructive, positive progress.[8]

For the Europeans themselves it was a badly needed warning that historical circumstances alone had made Europe and Christendom *seem* identical, and that this could not be considered a permanent privilege, but rather a heavy responsibility, a real mission to spread Christianity all over the world. Unfortunately it also was a dangerous temptation to misuse that mission for worldly advantages, one more misleading justification of an un-Christian feeling of superiority. In any case, however, the possibilities of missionary activity on a much larger scale than at the time of the specifically European Christian Commonwealth and in areas of the world hitherto unknown was part of another most fortunate consequence of the great discoveries: the awareness that what was discovered was not merely this or that obscure place, but a part of the world at large, a world much larger than the three parts of Europe, Asia, and Africa which had formerly been distinguished.

However, this awareness, combined with the basic Christian belief that all men, whatever their race, were children of the same Father, redeemed by the same Savior, did not mean that the Europeans were prepared to give up their claim to an exceptional, leading position in the world. On the contrary: the unquestionable fact that contacts were being established at last among all the peoples of the globe, because of their initiative, could only confirm them in the proud conviction that their destiny was a providential, universal mission. Providential because Europe had been for such a long time the depository of Christianity and continued to be its unquestionable center; universal, because in that network of relations among the various countries and cultures, they, the Europeans, created the link between all of them, and they alone had established relations with each of the other peoples. That these relations had hardly been desired by the others and frequently were to their disadvantage, is, of course, another matter, but the situation would not have been better if the unescapable unification of the world had been achieved by somebody else, for example, by the conquests of an Asiatic despot.[9]

More convincing than any such speculations is another indisputable fact: that western Europe achieved such a result during a period in which her culture had reached a particularly high stage of development. While in the otherwise glorious days of the Christian Commonwealth there had been two closely related but nevertheless different cultures in Europe herself—the eastern for a long time on a higher level than the western—in Renaissance Europe, after the decline and fall of the Eastern Roman or rather Greek Empire, there remained only one, revitalized Latin culture happily combined with a variety of national expressions. Therefore such a Europe, rich in common cultural experiences of at least half a millennium, was in a position to contribute to the cultural progress of all mankind. It was, of course, regrettable that the great discoveries and their consequences, which raised the scholarly interest of Europe's leading humanists, were not and could not possibly be the work of that refined intellectual elite, but rather that of adventurers whose admirable courage was accompanied by unscrupulous ruthlessness and an interest in material rather than spiritual concerns. In the great transition period of the Renaissance, which was also a transition from a comparatively isolated Europe to one which wanted to be the center of the world, there were only very modest initiatives, besides the efforts of the missionaries, to share the highest values of European civilization with other peoples, and even less readiness to recognize the values of non-European cultures with a view to establishing a universal intellectual cooperation.

The real unification of the world was still a distant goal even in the spiritual field and absolutely impossible in another field, the political, in which Renaissance Europe herself was making little progress in comparison with the former Christian Commonwealth. When Renaissance scholars contemplated new maps or even globes showing recently discovered lands, they could dream of extending to the most distant corners of the earth the cultural ties which bound together the European nations. But no "utopia" could anticipate the political unification of the world at a time when such a solution was out of the question even within the limits of Europe. All that was possible was the inclusion of extra-European countries in the system of alliances and in the game of power politics, which, far from creating a peaceful European order, was at least developing diplomatic connections among the individual nations, even though these were unstable and changing.

There was, for example, through the whole Renaissance period a curious interest in the African Empire of Ethiopia which was supposed to be the country of the mysterious Priest John.[10] It was in any case an old Christian country, and though projects of its religious union with Rome ended in disappointment both at the time of the Council of Florence and at that of the Union of Brest, vague expectations continued that it could serve as an ally against the Mohammedans controlling Egypt. The same Pius II who tried so hard to unite Christian Europe in opposition to the Turks considered the entirely different alternative of extending Christendom by a voluntary conversion of Sultan Mohammed the Conqueror,[11] whose empire included a large part of Asia.

These were fantastic ideas, but in Renaissance diplomacy, particularly in that of the Holy See, there appeared time and again plans for an alliance with Persia against its Asiatic neighbor, the Ottoman Empire. Persia[12] was another Mohammedan country, but it was separated from the Turks not only by an old political antagonism but also by a religious schism which divided Islam no less than the old Greek schism and the new Protestant revolt divided Christianity. As a matter of fact, the Turks frequently had to consider the danger of an encirclement and simultaneous troubles on two fronts, a European and an Asiatic one, but in spite of exchanges of messages between popes and Shahs no real political or military cooperation materialized. Nevertheless, the persistence of such a bold conception, recalling hopes of earlier centuries that Mongol conquerors, whatever their religious beliefs, could be used as allies against Seldshuk or Ottoman Turks, was an indication that the chances of friendly relations with non-Christian, extra-European powers were making progress with the enlargement of the vision of the world.

In that connection a very special problem has to be considered which is usually overlooked in the history of the great discoveries and of colonial expansion. In spite of all that politically as well as culturally separated her from the European community, Muscovite Russia was a Christian power within the geographical limits of Europe. Though originally a colonial territory herself, with a considerable Finnish and Tartar element mixed in with the Slavic settlers, that Russia was a Slavicized if not purely Slavic nation, representing the white race in the Eurasian region of transition. While the other Slavic and East European peoples did not participate in extra-European explorations and conquests, were it only for geographical reasons, the Great Russians—the peoples of Novgorod even before those of Moscow—continued the process of colonization, typical of Russian history.[13] It went beyond those eastern frontiers of Europe which were never unequivocally determined and into territories which were unquestionably Asiatic.

At the end of the fourteenth century, before annexing Novgorod proper, Moscow penetrated into the colonial area of the Republic, which reached the Ural mountains through the extreme northeastern corner of geographical Europe. Two centuries later, at the end of the reign of Ivan the Terrible, the Muscovites, in cooperation with their Don Cossacks, crossed that chain which later was considered the rather inconspicuous dividing line between Europe and Asia. (According to the ancient tradition, still alive during the Renaissance period, that line was to be constituted by the much nearer Don river.) This advance into western Siberia inaugurated Russia's amazing expansion through the whole of northern Asia to the shores of the Pacific, a goal reached in less than half a century.[14]

All this was hardly noticed in Europe nor included in the conventional history of the great discoveries and of early colonialism. In addition to the remoteness of the Eurasian regions where the whole process of Europe's expansion at the expense of Asia developed in isolation from all the roads of western expansion, there was and is another reason for that neglect of an extremely important problem. Both the discoveries and the colonial conquests, as they started in the Renaissance period, were an overseas expansion of Europe in areas separated from her by large oceans, and this seemed to be a distinctive feature of the whole movement. Muscovite Russia, on the contrary, entered and annexed territories which were contiguous to her homeland and, in general, to the European Continent. Instead of crossing oceans, she had simply to advance through portages from one river basin to the next until her urge for the most distant seas was satisfied.[15]

It is true that the territories which Russia thus acquired could not compare in riches with the transoceanic conquests of the western sea powers. Scarcely populated by tribes which both politically and culturally were poorly developed, these territories were for that very reason comparatively easy to occupy. At the same time they were so large that added to the already large area of the Muscovite state, the largest in Europe, they made that state a truly gigantic land mass, larger than the rest of all Europe. A Eurasian empire was rising at Europe's border, and since its European and Asiatic parts were contiguous, it represented a power which no overseas colonization could give to any other body politic.

Since that gradual process started at a time when even the original *Moscovia* had to be "discovered" by Renaissance Europe, by diplomats like Herberstein and Possevino or by merchants from Venice and England, the far-reaching consequences were slow to be recognized even in the next century. The appearance of Russia's power under Peter the Great came as such a surprise because its earlier rise through Moscow's colonial expansion inside and outside Europe in the fifteenth, sixteenth and seventeenth centuries had not received sufficient attention.

This remark leads us back to the West and to a concluding comment regarding Renaissance Europe, proud indeed of her great discoveries in other parts of the world, but even prouder of her achievements at home. This pride extended to both her Christian heritage which had been reformed in the Catholic as well as in the Protestant sense, and to her Graeco-Roman heritage which had been reborn and humanized.

It has been rightly said that by discovering the world, Europe discovered herself.[16] By comparing herself to the newly discovered peoples beyond the seas, Europe became even more convinced that in a world so much larger than the Europeans had imagined before, they still were destined to occupy the first and central place. As an illustration of that proud conception, recent books on the European tradition have reproduced a picture which was published in late sixteenth and early seventeenth-century reprints of the *Cosmographia Universalis* by the Renaissance scholar Sebastian Münster. His "universal description of the world," which first appeared in 1544 after the most spectacular voyages and expeditions to the world's remotest parts, was adorned by a distorted map of Europe in the form of a queen, with only small sections of Africa and Asia appearing in the corner.[17] Such a symbolic presentation fully corresponded to the traditional conception which considered Europe the center and ruler of the globe, neglecting the new discoveries and even the changes in Europe's own structure in the course of the preceding century. The region around Constantinople was still called *Graecia* as if there had been no Turkish conquest, and *Moscovia* was still a small area beyond large forests, in the neighborhood of *Scythia* and *Tartaria*.

Many other details of that humanistic interpretation of Europe's place in the world give evidence of the persistence of ideas which were slow to be affected by what was new in the developments of the Renaissance period. It is equally significant that on that strange map, as well as on the other, truly geographic and less fantastic presentations of the same period, there are no frontiers separating the various European countries. Their names are simply indicated in more or less appropriate places. This would correspond to an equally persistent idea of European unity, inherited from the times of the Christian Commonwealth and surviving in spite of the clear division of Europe into individual states quarreling about their respective boundaries. *Hispania* appears to be the head of the queen wearing her crown, in recognition of Spain's predominance on the Continent, while the wide open *Oceanus* behind her, the gate to the New World, is the only recognition of the general situation toward the end of the Renaissance age of transition.

A transition from the Christian Commonwealth to what? Certainly not to anything entirely new, separated from the past by a revolutionary change. The next period inherited from the past the unsolved problem of establishing at last a European order which would correspond to the Christian principles on which the European community was supposed to have been based from its origin, and to the unquestionable heights which its humanistic culture had reached. The solution of that problem—decisive for Europe's millennium—had become even more urgent in view of the inadequate defense of Europe, and even more involved in view of her expansion in the Renaissance period.

PART IV

From the Christian Republic to the Great Republic

CHAPTER XXI

War or Peace

I<small>T IS NOT EASY</small> to find an appropriate name for the remaining part—more than one third—of Europe's millennium which followed the great transition of the Renaissance. In the conventional periodization of history, which is supposed to be universal but chiefly takes into account the European experience, that latest period is simply called "modern." Without discussing once more whether it is correct to include as its beginning the sixteenth century and to exclude, as a separate contemporary period, the most recent developments,[1] it must be stressed that the purely relative adjective "modern" cannot possibly give any clear idea of the real content of the final phase of European history. Furthermore, it seems to be generally admitted that there is a great difference between the centuries which preceded and those which followed the French Revolution and other revolutionary changes in Europe and even in the whole world. It could even be said that if the qualification "modern" still makes any sense, it is with reference to the historical evolution after the turn of the eighteenth century rather than to the times of the so-called *ancien régime*.

Remembering this well justified distinction, the historian of Europe ought to try, first, to find a designation—a short, descriptive definition rather than just a name—for the two hundred years from the end of the Renaissance to what has been called recently the age of democratic revolution.[2] As a matter of fact, contemporaries have discovered and frequently themselves used two significant expressions which give a good idea of what Europe was, or at least was expected to be, in these two centuries. The first of them—which inspired the leading minds of the early seventeenth century—*la république chrétienne,* seems to revive the old conception of the *respublica Christiana,* the Christian Commonwealth of the earliest part of Europe's millennium; while the second, coined in the later eighteenth century, *la grande république,* gives evidence of the victory of secularist trends which can be traced back to the Renaissance.[3] There is good reason for giving both designations in French, in the language used by the men who made them famous, because French predominance in the cultural and intellectual field was a characteristic feature of the European community of both centuries, even if it is admitted that French predominance in European politics was limited to the central part of the period, to the *grand siècle* of Louis XIV.

No more than the Latin word *respublica* should the French word *république,* as it was used at the time of the French kings, be translated by the English word "republic." "Republic," as it is used today, in contrast to "monarchy" corresponds to the sense acquired by the French word after the Great Revolution and the establishment of the First Republic in France. Whether its "Christian" or its "Great" character was emphasized, the *république* which Europe constituted in the seventeenth and eighteenth centuries, according to her intellectual leaders, was a Commonwealth in a sense similar to that held formerly by the *respublica* of the so-called Middle Ages—"dark ages" in the minds of many of these later leaders. How that sense was adapted to the conditions of their time can be clarified by examining the two most famous writings in which the two expressions appeared. But before doing so and at the same time stressing the shift of emphasis in the course of the period, it must be pointed out once more that there remained through Europe's accelerated evolution the same intrinsic continuity which made the Renaissance not a break but merely a transition between different phases of Europe's millennium. An eloquent proof of that continuity is the fact that even after the Renaissance the idea of the Christian Commonwealth had such an appeal that Europe was called by that name, even though in a different language. And no less interesting is the fact that in spite of their difference the two French expressions—after all, apparently similar ones—were sometimes used side by side.

However, the first difference between these two conceptions—a practical rather than a theoretical one—results from the different professions and positions in society which were held by the two outstanding Frenchmen who developed them most brilliantly: Sully and Voltaire.

It is well known that the *Grand Dessin,* the great design of organizing Europe attributed to Henry IV, was, as a matter of fact, the work of the Duc de Sully. It was not a formal diplomatic draft, but a series of suggestions made in his lengthy memoirs.[4] But though it was not *le roi très chrétien* himself but only his former collaborator who outlined the project of organizing Europe as a Christian community, the planned *république chrétienne* was recommended in the name of that king who had quite frequently tried to be a peacemaker and mediator between various European nations.[5] In any case, the author of the plan was an experienced statesman whose main interests and objectives were political, and who submitted to other political leaders specific proposals regarding the peaceful cooperation of the European states.

Sully's plan differed from similar projects of European organization, which were propagandized in the seventeenth and eighteenth century by a long series of private writers and thinkers lacking political authority and competence; one of them, Emeric Crucé, even preceded in his publication the minister of Henry IV. The "great design" differed even more from the whole approach of Voltaire who more than one hundred years later compared Europe, as it existed in his time, to a great republic divided into various states.[6] Rather sceptical with regard to the elaborate projects of legally organizing the cooperation of these states in order to secure permanent peace, Voltaire was convinced that Europe, in spite of all her imperfections due to a lack of political unity, to prejudice and intolerance, was still superior to the other parts of the world because of her cultural unity based on common principles unknown elsewhere. He was mainly interested in the development of a vast "republic of cultivated minds" on European soil, a republic formed by the outstanding men of the Enlightenment, a great republic, Christian in its foundations though divided into various sects, and maintaining orderly relations among all powers. He was satisfied with the cultural progress achieved in a period which he compared with the greatest ages of the past, when civilization flourished and made life worth living, as in ancient Greece at the time of Pericles, in the Rome of Augustus, or in the recent Renaissance period. He did not expect nor consider necessary any similar progress in politics that would go beyond the conception of a balance of power. This, in his opinion, would guarantee even the weakest against invasion by a stronger power.

This, of course, was not Voltaire's opinion alone. The balance-of-power idea, inherited from the Renaissance, had also been the starting point of Sully, who originally had considered the creation, not of a united Europe but of a league, both defensive and offensive, against papal and imperial predominance under Habsburg leadership. His final conception of a European confederation under a Council, in which all states, elective and hereditary monarchies as well as republics, would be represented, and which would decide all conflicts and settle all questions regarding the "Christian Republic" as a whole, would have represented real progress. Unfortunately, it had no chances of being accepted and perhaps was not taken too seriously even by the author himself. In any case, neither his own France nor any other European power took any steps in that direction, and the project of a leading statesman, associated with the name of a great king, had no more influence on the real development of European politics than the noble dreams of men like William Penn, who wanted to contribute to "the present and future peace of Europe," or the Abbé de Saint-Pierre, whose project for establishing a "perpetual peace" would replace the balance of power by a "European society" including all Christian rulers.[7]

Therefore, without enumerating once more all similar plans, one of them put forward by a philosopher as prominent as Leibniz[8] and another one by a king in exile, Stanislas Leszczyński,[9] it seems more important to consider how the problems of war and peace were really settled in the European community. This was during the time when that community evolved from the idea of a Christian Republic, which introduced Christian principles into its political life, to a Great Republic, which was great indeed from the cultural viewpoint, but hardly a firm believer in the possibility of political improvement.

The simultaneous secularization of a Europe, still called Christian and limited to Christian nations, but going once more through a deep crisis of her conscience, clearly appeared in the evolution of international relations.[10] It is true that even in the so-called religious wars of the sixteenth century religion was frequently a pretext covering political rivalries, and that the alignment of the various powers in their shifting alliances hardly followed the religious affiliation. In the seventeenth century, however, the issues which motivated the main conflicts were not religious at all. Even in the Thirty Years War, to the origin of which the opposition between Catholics and Protestants in Bohemia and in the empire as a whole had decisively contributed—and which led to the interference of Protestant Denmark and Sweden—the religious factor gradually lost its importance, and was replaced by the rivalry between the House of Austria and all its enemies, including above all Catholic France.

The old struggle between the Habsburgs and the French dynasty, once the Valois, now the Bourbons, continued to divide Catholic Europe and to affect the defense against the Ottoman Empire, which, along with Sweden and Poland, remained one of the eastern allies of France. Poland, the only Catholic power in the eastern part of Europe and as such exposed to the hostility of almost all her neighbors, was hesitating between cooperation with either France or Austria. These two, except for faraway Venice, were Poland's only possible allies.[11] In view of the attitude of Louis XIV, who seemed to be the greatest danger to European peace, it was not before the end of the century that a last "Holy League," uniting first Poland and Austria and later Venice against the Turks, put an end to their renewed aggressions. However, it was precisely when the Muslim danger was removed that the idea of Christian solidarity disappeared completely.[12] Instead the succession wars, typical of the eighteenth century began. The extinction of the male lines of the Habsburg dynasty, first the Spanish, then the Austrian, did not facilitate at all the establishment of a more acceptable European order. And the eastern question, now meaning the desire to liquidate the Ottoman Empire in Europe, was far from being motivated by a genuine sympathy with its Christian subjects, but turned into another source of endless rivalries among the powers of the Continent.

At the same time the Holy Roman Empire definitely ceased to be the leading center of these powers. It had lost the last appearances of unity first in the seventeenth century, after the Thirty Years War, and then in the eighteenth, after the Seven Years War. The survival of the empire was no less artificial than that of the Habsburgs in the House of Lorraine, which by taking their name, inherited their ambitions in central Europe and continued their method of using German culture as a link uniting heterogeneous possessions. This House thus also continued to raise the opposition of the non-German populations. A new wave of nationalism was added to the dynastic troubles even in the comparatively short periods between the various European wars.[13]

These intervals were short because none of the peace treaties after such wars represented any improvement of the European order. The only one which at least tried to do so was the famous Treaty of West-

258 FROM THE CHRISTIAN REPUBLIC TO THE GREAT REPUBLIC

phalia which, therefore, is considered a turning point in the political history of the Continent and in the evolution of the European state system. As a matter of fact, the *de facto* situation in Germany was merely recognized *de iure,* by a belated admission that the empire had failed to be a unifying and coordinating force in the heart of Europe and that its political and religious division into a growing number of fully sovereign states in rivalry with one another was final. The setbacks which the foremost of these states, the realm of the Habsburgs, had suffered in the later phases of the long war, did not reverse their initial success in Bohemia, which lost the last traces of independence. Ominous for the future of Germany, more than anything else, were the new possibilities opened before the rising power of Brandenburg toward the end of the war. As far as the non-German opponents of the Habsburgs were concerned, such possibilities were opened by the peace treaty for both France and Sweden. However, in that respect, too, the importance of the settlement of 1648 must not be overrated: it took eleven more years before peace was made between France and the Spanish branch of the Habsburgs,[14] while Sweden's gains came too late to serve her ambitious goals in Germany, which had vanished sixteen years earlier with the death of Gustavus Adolphus.

What is even more significant from a general European point of view is another aspect of the Treaty of Westphalia which is usually overlooked. In the same year in which a long and destructive war in western or rather West Central Europe came to an end, a whole series of almost equally long and bloody wars started in eastern, particularly in East Central, Europe, which had avoided involvement in the Thirty Years War. The peace of 1648 was, therefore, no truly European settlement at all, and it became obvious that what was called the Christian Republic was divided, in addition to its division into so many individual states, into a western and an eastern part, each with its different political destinies. Instead of contributing to European peace, the ties between the two resulted in the fact that in the very next decade the same western powers which had hardly recovered from their own troubles were involved in those of Poland: the Habsburgs soon after the Hohenzollern and Denmark soon after Sweden, though on different sides. As regards those truly eastern powers which were not considered part of the Christian Republic, Moscow could now take her revenge for Polish and Swedish interference in her "time of troubles" at the beginning of the century,[15] and the Ottoman Empire, which had gathered its forces during the Thirty Years War, could use them for a last threat to both central and eastern Europe.

While the peace settlement of 1699 was limited to the eastern part of the Continent, the next one, in 1713, was once more a purely western one and even as such limited to a division, not at all final, of the Spanish succession, a result which could have been achieved at least equally well by diplomatic negotiations. Absorbed by an unnecessary war, the western powers were not interested in the war which had broken out simultaneously in eastern Europe, until it was too late to stop the unexpected advance of Russia. That nation's so-called Westernization by Peter the Great had as its chief objective and result the rise of a new empire at the expense of Europe.

Muscovite Russia, which had only indirectly exercised influence on the Thirty Years War,[16] was to be, in its role as Russian Empire, a major factor in all wars of the eighteenth century, along with and usually in cooperation with the kingdom of Prussia, that other newcomer among the great powers of Europe. This made the task of making peace after these wars even more difficult and, since they hinged on the participation of Russia and Prussia, which as recently as the Seven Years War had been fighting each other, the peace settlements even more unstable.

The peace which after long negotiations ended a war which was called by the name but soon ceased actually to be a war for the Polish succession settled the minor problems of Lorraine and Tuscany, but none of the big European issues. The only concrete result of the protracted Austrian Succession War, which left the succession to the legitimate heir Maria Theresa, was the conquest of Silesia by Frederick the Great. This question, so painful for the empress, was soon reopened in the Seven Years War, which in spite of the so-called diplomatic revolution at its beginning and the temporary threat to Prussia's very existence, brought no change in the local or the general European situation. When at last peace was made again, the situation was connected for the first time with extra-European problems, because in one of the treaties of 1763 the colonial competition between France and Britain was decided in favor of the latter. This connection between European and world politics was one more reason which made the establishment of a sound European order more complicated than ever before.

It was, therefore, a Europe exhausted by so many useless wars, fought not for any principles but chiefly for dynastic reasons, a Europe which remained politically divided in spite of so many alliances and treaties,

that had to face the consequences of three political revolutions which in
the last quarter of the eighteenth century destroyed the whole balance-of-
power system—the great illusion which even the critical mind of Voltaire accepted as the political basis of his great Republic. He also accepted
the extension of that system to the Russian Empire, which originally,
similar in that respect to Sully, he did not want to include in the European community. Flattering Catherine II, he would even speak about
"the light now coming again to us from the East."

That travesty of the old Christian saying *Ex oriente lux* was just one
of the many indications that what mattered in the Great Republic of
the Enlightenment was no longer Europe's Christian character. The
original dualism of the European heritage, partly Christian and partly
Graeco-Roman, appeared once more with all its dangers, the Christian
tradition being more and more disregarded though occasionally lip-
service would still be paid to it, while the humanistic tradition of the
ancient world went through an evolution even deeper than in the
Renaissance period. The indisputable cultural predominance of France,
even stronger than the one-time Italian predominance, and the hopes
of the encyclopedists that Catherine's Russia, more European than Peter's
and inspired by ambitious "Greek projects," would contribute to a
rapprochement of West and East in an "enlightened" Europe, were
typical of the end of the period. Nor were they without political repercussions on the Great Republic, which after a long evolution eventually replaced the old Christian one.

That republic was truly great in spite of its obvious weaknesses of
organization and in spite of a growing spiritual crisis. It is remarkable
indeed that amidst almost continuous wars in which all European nations were engaged and which devastated large areas, cultural progress
continued all the time. This can be explained in part by the genuine
interest which the same despotic and warlike rulers—to mention only
Louis XIV who seemed to care only for personal splendor and territorial
aggrandizement—showed also for the letters and arts, similar in that
respect to their Renaissance predecessors. In most cases the absolutism
of the Enlightenment, so unscrupulous in both internal and external
politics, not only pretended to be but really was "enlightened."[17] More
important, however, was something else. Monarchical patronage would
not have been efficient were there not in all countries exceptionally
gifted minds which, apparently undisturbed by the political tensions
and troubles around them, were successfully working in all fields of

human knowledge and maintaining contacts with each other beyond the artificial and so frequently changing frontiers of these countries. While the Great Republic, which was supposed to unite the individual states, was, speaking politically, nothing but a fiction, there was a real, supranational community of outstanding Europeans who in close cooperation made lasting contributions to the European heritage.

One of these contributions reduced and mitigated the evils of the political chaos in the European community. Continuing the isolated efforts of Catholic theologians of the later Renaissance, the Dutch Protestant Hugo Grotius,[18] himself suffering from the consequences of the wars of the early seventeenth century, wrote *De iure belli ac pacis* in a treatise which is rightly considered the foundation of an international law, recognized, at least in principle, by all those who cared for European civilization. In the best European tradition, he looked for inspiration to both the ancient writers and the Bible, and in agreement with both, he avoided utopian dreams of establishing an eternal peace, particularly hopeless in his time. But he tried to make as clear as possible the conditions which would justify going to war and to humanize warfare according to natural law. Just because he did not ask too much from those responsible for war and peace, he exercised a salutary influence and opened the door to further improvements of the new *ius gentium*. Though not always respected, these were to influence the behavior of the nations of Europe in their mutual relations. Writing more than one hundred years after Grotius, even Voltaire, in spite of his sceptical irony, would emphasize that in his Great Republic certain principles of public law and policy had become common to all European nations, while remaining unknown in the other parts of the world. And he would enumerate some concrete improvements in international relations, regarding, for instance, the treatment of prisoners or the respect for ambassadors even in time of war.

These were modest beginnings of an international code which prepared an evolution continuing until our days. But they did not have the revolutionary character of the changes in other spheres of European life which originated in the seventeenth century in regard to science, and in the eighteenth, in regard to industry. These significant steps leading from the Christian to the Great Republic have to be considered separately as two successive aspects of the crisis of the European conscience, parallel to the crisis resulting from the interplay of the forces of war and peace. But in order to understand how both trends were leading to the political revolutions at the end of the eighteenth century, two more issues of a political character, which clearly appeared in that century as well as in the preceding one, must receive more attention than in the usual interpretations of European history.

Neither of these issues was entirely new, but precisely for that reason they are characteristic of Europe's millennium. In the millennium's course the same leading problems play their permanent part, with a different emphasis in various periods. From the point of view of both the humanistic and the Christian background of the European community, those problems which are related to the great idea of freedom in all its aspects, international and constitutional, deserve special consideration.

As soon as the various national states had freed themselves from any supranational universal authority, the consequences of such a development for the European community, whether favorable or unfavorable, depended on the question whether all of these individual states would enjoy the same degree of real independence and security. In other words, there appeared the decisive question, whether there would be an equality of rights among larger and smaller states or whether the latter would suffer from the dangerous predominance of one or more great powers as much as the various nations had earlier suffered from imperial supremacy.

The other big issue concerned the degree of internal freedom which the various national states would guarantee to their peoples. Would these peoples, or at least a substantial percentage of them, enjoy full civic rights and control those in power, or would they be subject to an absolute authority even more oppressive than before, because it would be more centralized and fully authorized to represent the nation with all its interests? In view of the great diversity within the European community, it is not surprising at all that no general answer, identical for all European countries, can be given to this question. On the contrary, there appear striking differences between the degrees of constitutional liberties and democratic progress in the various states. In view of the dualism within the European tradition, it is not surprising at all that distinctions must be made between the western and the eastern part of Europe when answering such questions, and that examples have to be taken from the histories of either.

CHAPTER XXII

Great Powers and Small Nations in Western Europe

IT HAS BEEN POINTED OUT TIME AND AGAIN that it is impossible to understand European history by simply summing up the histories of the individual European nations in some kind of mechanical juxtaposition. Furthermore, there is a growing awareness and recognition that not only the nations of western Europe but also those of eastern Europe must receive attention if Europe is to be studied as a whole. However, there remains another point of similar nature which still is neglected, one of great importance for a correct appraisal of the whole millennium of Europe and more particularly of its later part.

No less misleading than the emphasis on western Europe, which prevailed for so long a time, is the emphasis on the role of the so-called great powers of Europe, which still is an almost general rule. The conventional approach, which reduced the history of Europe to that of her individual nations, was not the sum total of all these histories, but added the histories of the great powers to each. For the same reason the extension of European history to the eastern part of the Continent continues to be inadequate, since what has been included is principally the history of Russia from the time when she became a great power.

This happened at the beginning of the eighteenth century and Russia's power has been rising ever since. But even in the seventeenth century, especially after the Thirty Years War had destroyed the central, if not the leading position of the Holy Roman Empire in the European state system, the decisive question of European history seemed to be which European powers were really great. Studies concentrated on whether they remained formally part of the empire, as were the principal domains of the Austrian Habsburgs or of the Hohenzollern, or had always been outside, as were the kingdoms of Spain, France, and England.

It seems appropriate to enumerate these three western powers in an order which is not that of their anciety but rather that of the predominance which they are supposed to have exercised, one after the other, in modern European history. Spain's predominance ended soon after the middle of the seventeenth century, to be followed by France under Louis XIV and then by Britain.[1] The latter, which is considered typical of the major part of the eighteenth century, was even then not a genuine predominance on the Continent but a consistent effort to prevent any such predominance by another power and to build up a new empire "beyond the seas" more successfully than Spain and France.

These well known facts, which in the case of Britain led to the last period of Europe's millennium, have to be recalled in order to arrive at a definition of what is called a great power. This is, of course, not a question of area nor even of population, but of political influence exercised beyond national boundaries. "Great," in the usual sense, refers to a power which is not only strong enough to defend its independence, integrity, and national interests, but willing and able to interfere with the problems of other countries—in the given case those of Europe; to extend its territory—even outside Europe if it is a sea power; and in general to dominate other peoples.

Such a definition applies, of course, not only to modern European history and to the structure of the European community as it emerged from the transition period of the Renaissance, but also to the great empires of the ancient world and to the empires which tried to continue the imperial tradition in the earlier history of Christendom.[2] It was certainly not the best part of either the Graeco-Roman or the Christian tradition which thus continued into modern times. This tradition was no longer represented by any quasi-universal, supranational empire, but by national or rather dynastic states. But whatever the form, the very essence of the idea was a threat to the so-called small nations, whose freedom was now endangered without even the benefit of an international organization to serve the common good of Europe.

These other nations were not necessarily small nor insignificant. It was not because of small area or population that any country was excluded from the privileged group of great powers. When, for instance, Sweden, a state of medium size and scarcely populated, started an aggressive and temporarily successful policy of expansion early in the seventeenth century she was considered a great power by contemporaries, although—or rather because—they were alarmed by her interference with so many other countries. It is only during this comparatively short period of Swedish imperialism that the Scandinavian problems receive a more or less adequate treatment in historiography.[3]

Italy is a different case. If in the whole course of Europe's millennium there was one nation deserving to be called great, it certainly was the Italian. To deny to the Italians the character of a nation because they were not unified politically and were to a large extent subject to foreign rule is a mistake which can be made only because state and nation are identified in the usual interpretation of western European history. Yet, since none of the political units into which Italy was divided in the seventeenth and eighteenth centuries could be considered great powers, her role in that period was indeed considerably reduced as far as the making of history is concerned. The decline of the political power of both the Papal State and the Republic of Venice, notable in the seventeenth century and complete by the eighteenth,[4] made them share in both respects the fate of the other small countries. Neither of them was in a position to defend the freedom of Italy as it existed in the sixteenth century, which now more than in any other period was a pawn in the game of the policies of the great powers.

To a large extent, that also happened to the nations of the Iberian peninsula, as evidenced by the Spanish Succession Wars: to Spain herself, which until recently had been a great and even predominant power, for sixty years controlling neighboring Portugal; and to the latter, which after her liberation had little to say in the general affairs of the peninsula. In their cases even the continued possession of a large colonial empire did not help to maintain their former political position in the European state system. However, in order to understand how important the problem of the small nations continued to be for that system, two other cases, one negative, the other positive, require special consideration.

The negative one, usually overlooked, is the case of Ireland. Almost from beginning to end, no other nation of western Europe suffered a more tragic fate in the history of Europe's millennium.[5] How outstanding the Irish contribution to Europe's Christian culture could be should have been proved beyond doubt by the record of a still free Ireland in the darkest centuries of the preceding millennium. Then, the European community had not been constituted, but it was prominently prepared for by Irish missionary activities all over the Continent.[6] Because the geographically isolated island did not care to exercise any political influence abroad and because it did not succeed in uniting in one strong body politic, its conquest by England began in the twelfth century. In 1495, this conquest led even to the loss of local self-government through the Statute of Drogheda. The tragedy which occurred there, when the rest of western Europe was recovering from the Thirty Years War, made possible Ireland's absorption by the so-called Commonwealth of Oliver Cromwell.

Even after Cromwell's death and the fall of his Commonwealth, the settlement of Ireland—or rather her complete subjugation—was reaffirmed by the restored English monarchy. At the turn of the eighteenth century, after the suppression of the last Irish insurrection, Ireland was finally forced into a merger with Britain in the United Kingdom. It is true that the kingdom included also the once independent kingdom of Scotland, another small nation with a great tradition. But here was a case of voluntary union,[7] which lacked that systematic oppression and exploitation which in Ireland was to continue until her liberation in our time. A whole nation was thus suppressed and submerged in a manner which makes its survival an eloquent proof that even without statehood a European people, conscious of its heritage, simply cannot be eliminated by a great power. At the same time the long tragedy of Ireland was an irreparable loss to the European community as a whole, which otherwise could have benefited from that country's continued contributions. For the Irish people themselves, the memory of their past contributions to the rise of a still undivided Christendom and their loyalty to the Catholic Church in opposition to their masters made Catholicism an integral part of their frequently assailed nationalism. As in other cases, the violence of that nationalism was a reaction against the dangers which threatened the national existence, especially since the normal bulwark of national culture, the native language, was almost completely lost.

No less instructive is another case, a twofold one, which shows that the emergence of new, small nations, far from being dangerous for the European community, can enrich the variety of European life and culture, as well as the European heritage as a whole. Among the dispositions of the Treaty of Westphalia, which sanctioned a *de facto* situation, was the recognition of the complete independence of two countries once included in the Holy Roman Empire: the Netherlands and Switzerland. In spite of some analogies, the formation of these two nations must be studied and interpreted separately, especially since the history of the first of them is part of the involved history of a whole region in a crucial area of Europe, a region which only in our days has at last found what seems to be the final solution of its problems.

At the same time, however, it must be remembered that the fate of that maritime region and that of the Alpine valleys of Switzerland, if considered from the perspective of Europe's millennium, are both parts of a complex problem which the European community, constituted in the tenth century, had inherited from its Carolingian antecedents of the ninth. In the process of dividing Charlemagne's empire, the *regnum Lotharii* included for a short time a large belt stretching from the Alps to the North Sea, in addition to its Italian part. An area of transition was thus created between the West Frankish and the East Frankish kingdoms, which could never in the future be fully absorbed by either France or Germany. Nowhere was the feudal structure of western Europe more involved nor the frontier between two great powers more difficult to establish, and the Burgundian attempt of the fifteenth century to unite that controversial belt of small territories in a new "Kingdom of the West"[8] ended in failure. While most of the Burgundian heritage was divided between Valois and Habsburgs, at the northern and at the southern end of the long belt the idea of buffer states separating France and Germany was making progress at the expense of the empire. The international recognition of two such states in the seventeenth century and the subsequent developments in both regions, as well as the endless controversies over Lorraine and Alsace between the two, constitute one more example of the continuity of European history through more than a thousand years.

As for the Low Countries, the creation of an independent state limited to the United Provinces of the Netherlands was only a partial solution, since only the provinces which by 1579 had liberated themselves from Spanish rule could be included in that federal state. It was only within these political limits that a part of the Low German population developed a distinct national consciousness and a separate language, the Dutch.[9] Their Flemish kin, speaking practically the same tongue, remained with the French-speaking Walloons in the Spanish, later Austrian, part of the Low Countries, the Belgium of the future.

It is hardly necessary to point out that at the very time that has been called "the autumn of the Middle Ages,"[10] and in the later Renaissance period, the whole of that region, independently of its political structure, had been one of the most vital centers of Europe's economy and even more importantly, of her culture. And that small group of peoples continued to make outstanding contributions to this culture. Political freedom and the accomplishment of statehood and nationhood at the same time created normal conditions for such a development. Though the Netherlands did not avoid dangerous involvements in great power politics, even creating a colonial empire, the very existence of that small but free country made it impossible for any of the leading European powers to gain the exclusive control of the strategically important area around the mouth of the Rhine.

Even more instructive for the understanding of Europe is the study of what happened simultaneously in the mountains where the Rhine has its sources next to those of the Rhone and of the main tributaries of the Danube and the Po. There, in the center of western Europe and, in a certain sense, of Europe as a whole, the independence movement of even very small groups—wise enough to federate in a body politic that, though small, was still strong enough to defend its freedom and integrity—had much older traditions than in the Low Countries and resulted in an exceptionally successful experience. Here again there is a continuity, if not from Carolingian days, at least from the origin of Swiss federalism in the thirteenth century to the final establishment of the Swiss constitution in the nineteenth.[11] But obviously the international recognition of the confederation's independence was a decisive turning point.

Accompanying the recognition of Dutch independence as it did, it was at the same time a recognition by the great powers that the existence of small countries was justified and in the interest of the European community. But it certainly did not mean for the Swiss that all their troubles had ended. It is true that they had a much longer tradition of freedom than the Dutch, having gained their freedom from the Habsburgs, defended it against Burgundy, and having been free, *de facto,* from imperial control long before this was formally recognized. At an equally early date they had given up their own expansionist ambitions and, landlocked as they were, could not be tempted by colonial adventures. Last but not least, their frontiers, instead of being wide open like those in the Low Countries, were to a large extent natural boundaries protected by mountains. Even so, however, the Swiss cantons, which were only loosely connected with each other and with the small republics not yet formally included in the Confederation, were not always in a position to defend their neutrality during the wars among their big neighbors.

This was particularly difficult in the seventeenth century and in areas where the boundaries were neither entirely natural nor uncontroversial. Thus, for example, during a substantial part of the Thirty Years War, in which the Swiss were not directly involved, long struggles between the Habsburgs and the French plus the partisans of both were going on in the Valteline valley at the border of the Grisons.[12] The opposition between Catholics and Protestants, which had troubled Switzerland's internal peace from the days of the Reformation, led to conflicts even after the Treaty of Westphalia; and since religious problems were taken rather more seriously by the Swiss than by the great powers, they suffered from these tensions not only in the eighteenth but also under entirely different conditions in the nineteenth century.[13] There also were clashes between strong cantons like Bern and territories which had not yet received a status of complete equality within the Confederation. But in view of Switzerland's independent position these troubles did not affect the general European situation, and, what is more important, had nothing to do with the heterogeneous ethnic and linguistic composition of the country. Populations of German, French, Italian, and Romanch origin were included and they developed a feeling of community which, in spite of all cultural differences, was leading to a truly Swiss national consciousness. Many Swiss continued to serve in French or imperial armies—not to mention the special situation of the Swiss guard of the popes—without identifying themselves with any foreign cause: all remained deeply attached to their own country.

It was, as it always had been and still is, a small country. Because so many problems of a general European character were reflected in its history, Switzerland could rightly be called not only the heart of Europe but a Europe *en miniature* and her experiences, whether successful or not for the time being, were always a lesson for the larger countries. The obvious fact that her most exciting experience in federalism proved difficult, in spite of the limited area in which such an involved political system had to work, explains the unavoidable failures of similar trends which were expected to develop on a larger scale. On the other hand, the ultimate success of the Swiss experiment, though slow to come, was and is an encouragement to try it elsewhere, eventually in Europe as a whole. Last but not least, the equally obvious fact that fragments of different European nations could live together on Swiss soil in peace and cooperation, realizing the great ideal of unity and diversity combined,[14] should serve as evidence that the same ideal, typical of the European community, can survive in spite of a national variety that is also typical.

Whether of Germanic or Romance origin, the Swiss who had made such outstanding contributions to European culture at the time of Renaissance and Reformation continued to do so in the ages of the Baroque and, in particular, of the Enlightenment. How far their intellectual influence was reaching beyond the narrow frontiers of their country is best exemplified by Jean Jacques Rousseau, whose name is so intimately associated with the trends leading to the French Revolution that the writer's Swiss origin and background is frequently disregarded.[15]

The cultural relations between Switzerland and France constituted one of the reasons why the Great Revolution had such a strong and rapid impact on the country at whose border a Frenchman as influential as Voltaire had lived in his old age. Neither Switzerland's social structure, which, except in the smallest original cantons, did not fully correspond to democratic principles, nor her constitution, which contemporary American federalists criticized[16] no less than the Dutch one for not sufficiently assuring the cohesion of the country, provided adequate protection when the invasion of revolutionary France made that peaceful country the scene of bitter battles among the great powers' forces, including even faraway Russia. However, it is at the same time the best proof of Switzerland's vitality as an independent nation that she survived the long years of turmoil at the turn of the century which concluded the whole period.

For the very reason that this small nation was completely independent and decided to stay so, she had a better chance than the numerous political units inside the declining empire to which the Treaty of Westphalia had granted such far-reaching rights. Many of them were really too small to save their position amidst a general upheaval. But some, even among the smallest, rightly receive attention as important cultural centers, and because of the truly enlightened patronage of their princely courts are comparable to the Italian city-states of earlier centuries. Weimar, which did survive the great crisis at the end of the eighteenth century, is truly typical of the intellectual advantages of the German *Kleinstaaterei,* which was far from being an obstacle to the progress of national culture in the framework of the European one. Even Potsdam, rightly opposed to Weimar as a symbol of aggressive Prussian militarism, to a certain extent contributed to the more attractive cultural aspect of the German enlightenment in close contact with the French. Among the other larger states inside Germany which were indeed an obstacle to national unity because of their individualistic dynastic politics, Saxony with her brilliant court in Dresden can serve as an example that political divisions were favorable to the development of numerous cultural centers.

Taking into consideration that even in France, which was truly homogeneous, the objectionable sides of centralization of national life in the capital of a large country were apparent even before the Revolution, it is well justified to ask whether the centralizing trends of another great power, the realm of the House of Austria, were not even more questionable from the cultural point of view. For that realm, indivisible according to the Pragmatic Sanction,[17] was composed not only of different provinces with traditional regionalism, but of different nations which had their own great cultural heritages and their own state rights deriving from the tenth-century origin of the European community. In particular, these nations were Bohemia and Hungary.

For Bohemia, the seventeenth and the eighteenth centuries were unquestionably the darkest in her history of more than a thousand years. It is true that almost from the outset her political independence had been limited by a connection, first, with the German kingdom and then with the Holy Roman Empire. But in the empire under German leadership Bohemia always occupied an exceptional, privileged position. This position had to be taken into consideration even when the Habsburgs, in 1526, acquired the Bohemian crown, soon recognized as hereditary in that German dynasty. It was not until the Thirty Years War—beginning with a revolt in Bohemia which was crushed two years later in the famous battle of the White Mountain—that the lands of the Crown of Saint Václav lost what remained of their independence. Even their local self-government was drastically curtailed by the regulations of 1627.[18] In the course of the eighteenth century, under Maria Theresa and Joseph II, there disappeared any difference between their position and that of the hereditary Austrian lands of the Habsburgs, since the center of their administration was gradually moved from Prague to Vienna.

Even the concessions of Leopold II and the "great" Bohemian Diet of 1790–1791—the last which had any significance—did not really change that situation.[19]

The revolt of 1618 had, like the Hussite uprising two hundred years before, its religious, anti-Catholic aspect. But in contrast to the former it had no nationalistic anti-German character. The consequences of defeat, however, affected not only Bohemia's state rights and religious freedom, but the national development of the Czech people as well. Another defection from the Habsburgs in the years 1741–1743, at the beginning of the Austrian succession war, had neither religious nor national motivations. Not only the Hussite tradition, which the Czech Brethren's great, internationally-recognized scholar, Jan Amos Komenský (Comenius), represented in exile,[20] but even the Czech national culture with its native Slavic language, which the Jesuit Bohuslav Balbín defended in vain, seemed to be doomed. In the transition region between western and eastern Europe the Czech people were threatened with a fate similar to the Irish in the extreme West: another small nation was disappearing in spite of its earlier, comparatively recent contributions to European culture. The Czech revival, which, preceding the Irish, started rather modestly at the end of the eighteenth century, came as a surprise and its full success in the following period was hardly anticipated.

For a better understanding of the problems of nationalities in the Habsburg empire of the nineteenth century, it is important to realize that the centralizing policies of the House of Austria, initiated in the seventeenth and eighteenth centuries, had nothing to do with any conscious German nationalism. Joseph II himself, who more than any other Habsburg tried to enforce the use of the German language in all his domains, pointed out that he would have promoted any other language which could have served equally well his basic objective: the unification of his lands in an empire which fourteen years after his death was to be formally proclaimed as such, under the name of Austria.

Even then, certain rather vague reservations, subject to controversial interpretations, were made in favor of the kingdom of Hungary.[21] Hungary's rights as a *regnum separatum,* so clear at the time of the proclamation of the Pragmatic Sanction, were recognized near the end of the eighteenth century by Leopold II after the inconsiderate measures taken even there by Joseph II. Nevertheless, it had not been without grave consequences that Hungary, whose national tragedy started immediately after Mohács, nearly a hundred years before that of Bohemia, was partitioned during a century and a half in a way which left the narrow "crescent" of her northern and western border regions completely under Habsburg control. Added to this is the fact that it was through Austrian armed forces that the main part of the country and its capital were liberated from Turkish domination. It was certainly to the advantage of the Hungarians that their Christian and Latin culture could survive the darkest days of the partition, not only in rather isolated Transylvania but also in a belt of territory contiguous to western lands. When Habsburg rule was definitely established in the whole, reunited country, it meant once more a close connection with the West and western influence replacing the Muslim. However, it was a foreign influence, and Hungary, which had always succeeded in remaining outside the Holy Roman Empire and completely free of its control, was now along with Bohemia included in a realm under German leadership, the apostolic kings of Hungary being also German emperors.

Throughout the seventeenth century there had been a national Hungarian independence movement directed from Transylvania which opposed the Habsburgs even more than the Turks. After liberation and unification this movement continued to oppose the German dynasty that was recognized as hereditary by the Hungarian Diet. The last insurrection under one of the Rákoczys, a family whose tradition survived as a symbol of freedom, did not end in complete defeat like that of Bohemia, but rather in one of those various compromises typical of Hungary's relations with Austria, the Szatmar Treaty of 1711. Thus, another of the smaller nations of Europe, which from the time of its conversion in the tenth century had occupied a prominent place among the free peoples of Christendom, had to face the same centralizing trends which submerged Bohemia. Here, the only difference was that the Hungarians, whose national consciousness continued unbroken in all classes of society, could offer a stronger resistance than the Czechs.

Bohemia's and Hungary's integration with Austria in what was to be soon a unified Danubian monarchy can be considered from two different viewpoints, which are at the same time two different interpretations of the European tradition. If the element of unity is put first in that tradition, such a development can be evaluated positively, but only if unification does not mean amalgamation, only if it favors a peaceful cooperation to replace the rivalries and troubles of the past. Considering, however, diversity as an essential feature of the European heritage, the elimination of small, but old, free nations at the eastern border of the empire was in alarming contrast to the establishment of new nations of this type at the western border. In any case the decisive question was whether the constructive conception of federalism which was making progress in limited areas of the West would be applied also in the reorganization of the Danubian area. Whether the extension of western power under an imperial dynasty would prove reconcilable with the preservation of internal freedom and that constitutional form of government which in both Bohemia and Hungary had deep historical roots would be an inseparable problem. The contrast between two forms of government can be studied even more successfully if the whole eastern part of Europe is included in the survey of her development in the seventeenth and eighteenth centuries.

CHAPTER XXIII

Freedom and Despotism in Eastern Europe

T
HE QUESTION of establishing a sound balance of authority and freedom was one of the permanent issues in European history, inherent
in both the Graeco-Roman and the Christian heritage of Europe. There
were, however, periods and regions in which the opposition between
the two ideas and the difficulty of reconciling them proved particularly
great. In the seventeenth and eighteenth centuries authority prevailed
almost everywhere on the Continent, taking the form of absolute government, while freedom was in retreat. One of the consequences of the
religious crisis of the preceding period was a strengthening of the power
of the state. The state could now even control the spiritual life, whether
it was Catholicism or one of the Protestant denominations that had
triumphed in the given country. Only in England did a "glorious"
revolution, though a restoration of royal power, bring new guarantees
of civic rights in its wake. But in the later part of the period, while the
Hanoverian dynasty did not enjoy the prestige of its predecessors, the
growing authority of the prime minister appeared as a check on the
influence of Parliament.[1]

Following the severe limitation of the role of the Bohemian and even
of the Hungarian Diet under Habsburg rule, there remained only one
country in Europe where the Diet was supreme and determined to
defend *libertas* against that *maiestas* which was always suspected of a
desire for an *absolutum dominium*. That country was Poland, a *respublica* even though it had a king at its head, situated in an East Central

Europe where all the other countries, including those which in earlier periods had been equally anxious to maintain both national and constitutional freedom, were now either under absolute governments of the western type or, what was worse, under despotic rulers whose methods of government were either definitely Asiatic or influenced by Asiatic models.

The first of these types was represented by the Ottoman Empire, which even after its losses in Hungary continued to control the unfortunate Balkan peoples and to cut them off from Europe with no chance whatever of free development.[2] The other type consolidated its autocracy in the Muscovite (and soon, imperial) Russia which emerged from the time of troubles at the beginning of the period. During these troubles it seemed momentarily that under the influence of Poland Muscovite autocracy, which reached its climax under Ivan the Terrible, would evolve in the direction already followed for centuries by the Slavic neighbor in the West. Poland's political interference, however, was hardly favorable to a peaceful reception of her institutions,[3] as had happened in the Grand Duchy of Lithuania. Most probably it was already too late for such an evolution in view of the entirely different background of the Muscovite state, consolidated for the first time during the centuries of Tartar domination. Now, after a short interlude when anarchy discredited freedom, the old order was restored in an even more durable form, which, as a matter of fact, was to last almost to the end of Europe's millennium and to influence strongly what followed after another time of trouble.

In Poland an order of completely different character, limited to the territory of the Commonwealth in its frontiers—which changed many times in the seventeenth century—lasted till the end of the eighteenth century. Then, a constructive reform movement, aiming at the appropriate balance of freedom and authority that would accord with the national tradition and with new western trends, was interrupted by the total destruction of the Commonwealth. Since the major part was annexed by Poland's eastern neighbor, the autocratic Russian Tsardom at the end of the period controlled a forcibly united eastern Europe, no free nations being left between the Russian and the Ottoman Empires and the two leading German powers. In the period preceding that revolutionary change, there was a sharp contrast between eastern Europe's two leading Slavic powers. In the matter of authority and freedom, they represented two extreme solutions that were inspired by basically different political philosophies.[4] A comparison between the two can, therefore, contribute to the clarification of an issue which created one more dualism in the millenary evolution of Europe.

The Poles of the pre-partition period proudly spoke about their "golden freedom." There were serious reasons for such pride, but the historian is obliged to make several equally serious reservations. To begin with one, the most essential, it was not only regrettable in principle but also inconsistent with the whole Polish approach to the problem that the constitutional liberties and civic rights which the Commonwealth enjoyed were limited to one privileged class, the *szlachta*. That name cannot be translated by the English term "nobility," even less by "aristocracy," and not even by "gentry." The Polish *ordo equestris,* as its members, always fond of Latin, liked to call themselves, included a group of aristocratic families. But that group, no larger than in other countries, constantly changed in composition and was not supposed to use hereditary titles. A much larger group of country squires was also included: some of them occupied an intermediary position between what in English would be called aristocracy and gentry, while others could scarcely be distinguished from free peasants cultivating their exiguous landed property. Altogether they constituted about 10 per cent of the population,[5] many times more than in any other country; all of them were legally equal and therefore were considered a democracy of nobles. The same coat of arms, a symbol of common origin, was used by many families of entirely different importance; and all of them, identifying themselves with the nation at large, looked down with shocking conceit upon the other classes of society: the townsmen whose professions could not be exercised by a nobleman, and the peasants.

If the exclusion of the burghers from political rights can be at least partly explained by the fact that the leading element in the cities was still German or Germanized when these rights were established,[6] there is unfortunately no excuse for the serfdom which the Polish peasants had to suffer, except the obvious fact that serfdom then existed in most European countries. However, even that excuse is of doubtful value in the case of a country which claimed to be a haven of liberty and therefore superior to the others. Voices in defense of the peasants were raised time and again, especially in the name of Christian principles, whether interpreted by Anti-Trinitarians or by Jesuits, and once, in the memorable year of 1656, a formal vow was made in public by the king to improve the conditions of the peasant population.

The question why nothing was done in that respect before the end of the eighteenth century, leads to another weakness in Poland's constitutional freedoms. Her constitution as a whole remained for two centuries as it had been established in the later part of the sixteenth, after the extinction of the Jagellonian dynasty. All reforms, not only those particularly urgent ones in the social field, but also those concerning the distribution of power, were postponed. If reforms were proposed, they were regarded with suspicion. Therefore, the progressive process of constitutional development, which had been so impressive in the truly "golden" Renaissance period, came to a standstill for two hundred years. The only significant change, far from being progress, was a most dangerous distortion of the unanimity rule of the Polish Diet: the acceptance of that most absurd practice, the *liberum veto,* in 1652.[7]

It is regrettable for the Poles, but quite understandable, that no other feature of their historical institutions receives more attention in the interpretation of their millenary past than the veto right. This is indeed a problem of unusual significance in the history of freedom, inseparable from the history of Europe as a whole. For the unanimity rule seemed to be always and everywhere the fullest guarantee of the freedom of the individual, of minority rights, and even, as it appeared in our time, of the sovereignty of the individual state in any international organization. And nowhere did the application of that principle in parliamentary government go so far as it did in Poland—with the most disastrous consequences. However, we must take into consideration, first, that for a long time unanimity was achieved in the Polish Diet through the moderating role of the Speaker; that an individual protest could end the Diet's whole activity only in the period from the middle of the seventeenth to the middle of the eighteenth centuries, and that even then, as can be seen in the *Volumina legum,*[8] many hundreds of bills were voted unanimously. But something else is particularly important from a general point of view. Strict majority rule would have been unacceptable in a Commonwealth where each region had its own tradition and various national and religious groups were represented in a common Parliament.

This was in itself a great achievement, the more remarkable because such an experiment was made in one of the largest countries of Europe and not, for example, in a land as small as Switzerland, where it proved difficult enough. If, to a large extent and for several centuries, it succeeded, it was precisely because the respect for freedom was typical of

Polish institutions and was guaranteed by them, if not to all, at least to a considerable percentage of the inhabitants. This guarantee of liberty attracted non-Polish lands where no similar freedoms had existed before. Moreover, these Polish institutions were jealously preserved at a time when those of neighboring countries were developing in an opposite direction. The extent of any such success depended on consistency in the practical application of these liberal principles. Thus the gradual limitation of religious freedom—once almost complete—understandable as it was in view of the struggles against non-Catholic powers throughout the seventeenth century, had disastrous consequences in the next, when the small Protestant and Orthodox minorities found external protectors in Prussia and Russia. But particularly instructive is the comparison of the Lithuanian and the Ruthenian problems and their treatment in the multinational Commonwealth.

The solution of the Union of Lublin, which in 1569 had recognized the full equality of the Lithuanian Grand Duchy in a dualistic structure, worked quite well.[9] It succeeded not only in days of common triumphs but also in those of common trials, so frequent from almost the beginning of the seventeenth century. The spontaneous cultural Polonization—at the same time a westernization—included the nobles not only of Lithuania but also those of the Ruthenian lands. Since, however, these provinces were not united and organized in a separate body politic within the federal system, dissatisfied elements were turning against the Commonwealth as a whole. A promising project for its trialistic reconstruction, in the Hadiach Union of 1658, came too late, following, as it did, ten years of civil war.[10] This war began in an insurrection of the Ukrainian Cossacks. While a continuous source of trouble, the Cossacks could justly complain that their liberties were severely restricted, and eventually they would appear as the representatives of the whole Ukrainian people. The Cossack problem became a real danger for the Commonwealth chiefly because of its international implications. For the Ukraine and her aspirations toward independence it proved to be a real tragedy. For, when the Cossacks placed themselves under Moscow's protection, their freedom was even more threatened than it had been under Polish rule, and their territory was finally partitioned between Poland and Russia.[11] Under such conditions even Cossack autonomy disappeared in the eighteenth century, and it was not before the end of that century that a national movement of at least cultural character started in the Russian-controlled Ukraine.

The general decline of Poland's power, to which the Cossack wars contributed in a decisive way, were also of international importance. But the question is frequently raised as to whether that decline was not an inescapable consequence, not so much of an inadequate application of liberal principles, but rather of the principles themselves. These principles, so the question goes, weakened the Commonwealth in comparison with the other European powers which were centralized under a strong absolute government. The limitation of royal authority and the free election of the kings of Poland are usually pointed out in that connection, not without a great deal of exaggeration. For the position of the king depended, as a matter of fact, on his personal qualifications. Even in the later seventeenth century a Sobieski could exercise an influence which was unquestionably constructive, while the equally strong but destructive influence of his successor, Augustus II, definitely destroyed for a long time any chance for those constitutional reforms which required the loyal cooperation of king and nation.

The main trouble was that the election of 1697, which placed the Elector of Saxony on Sobieski's throne, was the first election that was not really free but was decided by the pressure of Poland's neighbors. In the past, similar attempts or rather diplomatic intrigues had failed, and the royal elections in which each nobleman had the right to participate, their lists including each time many thousand names,[12] give the impression of a really democratic process, exceptional in Europe. On several such occasions the Polish electorate manifested the nation's desire to maintain the dynastic continuity as far as it was possible, through free consent. Strangely enough, for similar reasons even the Saxon dynasty, the worst in the history of the country, eventually gained some popularity in a nation which, exhausted by the wars of almost the whole seventeenth and the early eighteenth centuries, wanted more than anything else to be left alone and in peace.

Therefore, the contrast between Poland and her neighbors was no longer exclusively based upon the differences between liberal and authoritarian forms of government. It had turned into a contest between a country which in spite of its large area and population was tired of power politics, and great powers in the usual sense, especially the two at Poland's border which were rapidly rising to leading positions in the European state system. Of these two, the western neighbor, Prussia, did not achieve that goal until Frederick the Great. But in the case of Russia that evolution, decisive for eastern Europe, has to be studied not only, as is usually done, from the reign of Peter the Great but from Moscow's recovery after the time of troubles one hundred years before.

The achievements of Peter the Great would have been impossible without those of the first Romanovs. Two of them contributed decisively to the rise of Russian power and autocracy.[13] The case of Peter's great-grandfather Philaret deserves special attention, although he was not tsar but patriarch, acting as co-regent of his son, the less prominent Tsar Michael. The exceptional situation confirmed the intimate cooperation of Church and State in the government, which did not cease even after the abolition of the patriarchate by Peter. It was thanks to Philaret, too, that after the most serious troubles and setbacks Moscow could resume almost immediately a policy of revenge and aggrandizement similar to that of the sixteenth century. Under Michael that advance was already eminently successful in Asia where a colonial empire reaching the Pacific was created. Under his son Alexius the interference with what might be called the Polish time of trouble completely reversed the balance between the two powers. The same thing happened to the balance in the relations between tsar and patriarch, when the last really prominent head of the Russian Church had to yield to state authority.

These ominous developments, hardly noticed in the West because Alexius was less brutal than other tsars, were not fully appreciated even in Poland, since there seemed to be a chance of reconciliation between the two neighbors. The frontier of 1667, though very unfavorable for the Commonwealth, was to remain unchanged until its partition more than one hundred years later. In the interval between the reigns of Alexius and Peter there even was an attempt at cooperation against the Ottoman Empire, and it also seemed that the westernization of the Muscovite state would gradually develop through Polish intermediary. This, however, was at a time when there was no strong, despotic ruler on the throne of Russia,[14] so that it was not easy to realize the consequences of a basic change in the history of the eastern Slavs: a large part of the Ruthenians, both the Ukrainians and the Byelorussians, whose development had been for centuries entirely different from that of the Muscovite Great Russians, had now come under their rule. It was only a question of time until Moscow's old claim to control over them all would threaten the remaining eastern lands of the Commonwealth and, through a growing Russian penetration, the independent existence of the Polish-Lithuanian state.

That time was to come as soon as another aggressive despot would govern Russia and direct her destinies. Under Peter the Great his empire definitely entered the European state system. It seemed, as it still seems today to many historians (Russians of the school of "westerners" as well as non-Russians), that the whole gigantic area, from the Polish border which formerly limited Europe's "Christian Republic" to the extreme Russian conquests at the border of China, had become an integral part of the European, perhaps even of the western community.[15] This would have been indeed a turning point in the course of Europe's millennium. But such an interpretation can hardly be accepted, and it is contradicted by the Slavophile and the less important Eurasian school of Russian thought, both anti-western, if not openly anti-European.

The illusion that Russia's westernization under Peter, accomplished by direct contacts with even the most remote western powers, was a genuine integration with the European community, is mainly based on his famous reforms. They were unquestionably a stupendous achievement, the more so because they were introduced in times of war. But that very circumstance reveals the main purpose of these reforms and determined their character. They were to serve the military interests of Peter, to enable him to create a strong and well-equipped army supported by equally strong financial resources. They were to make not only Russia's neighbors but all of Europe feel that a great new power had arisen in a faraway region which had not even been considered part of the European community, a power which henceforth would affect the balance among all the others.

This was more important than Russia's superficial westernization which was enforced from above. But it was scarcely less important than the strengthening of her autocratic form of government by a despot who wanted to be enlightened on the western pattern, but who ruled in his new capital in a way which followed, adopted, and developed the methods of the first Muscovite Tsars. The new imperial title did not make the Russian Tsardom more European. But the continuity of Great Russian history and political conceptions, which contrary to external appearances was not interrupted at all by Peter, was not interrupted either by the six rather poor reigns—the reigns of three women, a young boy, a child, and a madman, as has been pointed out—which followed.[16] A confused order of succession, decided by palace revolutions, did not reduce the pressure of Russia's power upon all her neighbors and her impact on international relations in Europe, nor did it undermine her unshakable autocracy. An attempt of the Russian aristocracy to seize

the real power at the beginning of the reign of Empress Ann failed completely, and when after an interval of thirty-seven years and many
changes on the throne Catherine II started where Peter I had ended,
that daughter of a powerless German prince identified herself completely with the long tradition of Russian despotism. Her regime might
seem more enlightened, but she did not hesitate to interfere as brutally
as her predecessors when the influence of liberal western ideas went too
far.

Under Catherine, sometimes like Peter also called the Great, the
Russian nobility toward the end of the period received something like
a charter of rights, which assimilated the nobility based upon state service under strict bureaucratic control, to the nobles of the western
countries[17] but, in contrast to the Polish situation, without letting them
share the unlimited power of the ruler. The power which the nobles
exercised over the peasants remained unlimited, too. Serfdom, becoming
ever more oppressive through the preceding two centuries, reached a
climax at a time when it was being reduced everywhere in Europe. It
was of little comfort to the victims to know that in Russia nobody was
really free. Making her famous initial inquiry into local conditions early
in her reign, Catherine II did not fail to observe how badly reforms were
needed, particularly as far as the peasants were concerned. But she
noticed at the same time how strong the opposition would be in that
respect. The long discussions in her Great Commission were leading
nowhere. Any reform in the direction of liberty would have been a total
break with the Russian tradition, a break which the foreign-born empress was neither willing nor able to try.

That problem was closely connected with the fact that even before her
participation in Poland's dismemberment the Russian Empire was a
multinational one,[18] with an overwhelming predominance of the Great
Russians and a strong determination that the unitarian state should not
make any concessions to the national variety within its large borders.
The differences among the three East Slavic peoples which were to be
amalgamated under Great Russian leadership were simply ignored; the
Mongol tribes were really underdeveloped with the exception of the
Tartars whose conquest was completed with the annexation of the Crimean Khanate; and the situation in the Baltic provinces, that most important, completely non-Russian acquisition of Peter, proved rather
easy to handle: the native Latvians and Estonians continued to be
ignored as they had been under other rules, while the German upper

class, in particular the so-called Baltic barons, were ready to cooperate with the Tsarist regime, if only their social privileges were respected and opportunities in the state service offered to them. For them there was perhaps a little more freedom in Russia than for anybody else, but it was as a reward for their unrestricted political loyalty.

The inclusion of a small, but definitely western Baltic area was certainly the greatest change in Russia's structure, planned in the preceding centuries but not achieved before the eighteenth. Yet it was a minor change if compared with the continuity which, in spite of the shift of the capital, should be a warning against the usually emphasized distinction between the Moscow period and the Petersburg period of Russian history. On the contrary, there is no continuity between the Kievan and the Great Russian period. There was no all-Russian millennium beginning with the coming of Rurik in the ninth nor even with Vladimir's conversion in the tenth century. Both events, parallel to contemporaneous developments in the other European countries, started the recorded history of the eastern Slavs in their original, later Ukrainian and Byelorussian homeland, but not that of the Volga region, which was a product of early colonialism even before the Muscovite expansion into Asia. Nevertheless, what happened in the powerful state which originated in that region and reached such a strong position in the seventeenth and eighteenth centuries, has a very great significance for the interpretation of the millennium of Europe, and this for two entirely different reasons, one of them connected with the Kievan tradition, the other, with the prospects of St. Petersburg.

Kiev, which as capital of a large state had occupied a prominent place in the rising European community after its Christianization, was regaining such a place, after centuries of decline, in the seventeenth century. When still in the Commonwealth, the old city had become once more an important cultural center with an academy of Orthodox character but which was open to western influence that radiated through Kiev as far as Moscow.[19] However, when in violation of the treaty of 1667 the city was annexed by Moscow, it soon lost its importance, and the tradition of the original Kievan Rus' was claimed as part of the Great Russian heritage, distinct from the general European one.

The city founded by Peter on newly conquered soil, and called after him, was to be a gate to Europe for his empire,[20] replacing the earlier ties through Kiev. Situated between the Baltic provinces in the proper sense and the parts of Finland taken from Sweden in the eighteenth century, St. Petersburg, as a port on the "Mediterranean of the North," the Baltic Sea, was for Russia a challenge to integrate with Europe. Had this prospect come true, it would have meant an extension of the European community, comparable, if not to that in the tenth century, at least to that which resulted from the westernization of Lithuania at the end of the fourteenth. However, the question of whether these possibilities opened by Peter as part of his power politics would come true, in a sense which would change the cultural and constitutional evolution of Russia, was left as a big issue for the last period of Europe's millennium.

At the same time the question was raised how Poland would enter that new period. From the tenth to the eighteenth century there was no question that she was an integral, independent part of the European community. Her extension into a multinational Commonwealth under the Jagellonians was no break with the tradition of the ethnic Poland of the Piast dynasty,[21] whose last representative on the Polish throne, similar in that respect to the first king of Poland, had prepared for that eastern expansion, making it an advance of the European conception of freedom toward the East. Under the successors of Casimir the Great, who no longer belonged to the native hereditary dynasty and whose authority was therefore easier to limit, the political liberties of an unusually large part of the population continued to develop through Polish initiative in the whole Commonwealth. In the eighteenth century liberal trends from France and England reached Poland along with other aspects of the Enlightenment, and contributed to the awareness that it was high time to proceed with constitutional and social reforms which would adapt the old Polish ideas of freedom to the needs of a new age. No revolution was needed in a country which had remained free from the impact of modern absolutism and wanted only some decades of peace and security to concentrate on her internal problems.

Unfortunately, in addition to repeated foreign interventions with the elections of the kings of Poland, there was growing Russian pressure beginning under Peter and becoming particularly dangerous under Catherine. The latter cooperated in that matter with Frederick II of Prussia. The more or less enlightened despots in Poland's neighborhood, while opposed to any civic liberties in their own countries, pretended to protect and even to guarantee the most extreme freedoms of the Polish nobles with a view to keeping the Commonwealth weak, disarmed in the midst of militaristic powers, and unable to oppose their claims. Prussia, who herself had faced the danger of partition during the Seven

Years War, was secretly exploring the possibilities of a partition of Poland. Before becoming interested in such projects, Russia preferred to try to turn all of the Commonwealth into a Russian protectorate, cut off from the West and subject to Russian influence—a sharp contrast to the Polish tradition.

The solution to these problems which seemed to concern eastern Europe in particular, depended on the general situation, as the outcome was to prove. The solution hinged not only on the crisis in the balance of power, but even more on the new crisis of the European conscience, which from an intellectual revolution at the turn of the seventeenth century was to lead to the political revolutions at the end of the eighteenth.

CHAPTER XXIV

From the Scientific to the Industrial Revolution

I N THE POLITICAL FIELD the seventeenth and the eighteenth centuries, though frequently called "modern" in contrast to earlier periods of European history, produced scarcely anything new before the revolutions at the end of the eighteenth. The balance-of-power idea, inherited from the Renaissance age, was simply further developed and transmitted to the next century. Important elements of continuity can also be discovered in the cultural field: a reappraisal of the long underestimated Baroque culture has evidenced, on the one hand, that while it was less brilliant than the Renaissance, it constituted another phase of the traditional civilization inspired by both the Christian and the classical heritage; and on the other hand, that there are surprising links between the Baroque and the Romanticism of the future. All this is particularly evident as far as Catholic Europe is concerned, the French and the Austrian examples, different as they are, being the most instructive ones.[1]

However, the crisis of the European consciousness toward the middle of the period was much deeper everywhere in western Europe including France and led to a sharper break with the tradition of the past than the similar crisis of the Renaissance and Reformation. It has been pointed out that "neither the Renaissance nor the Reformation had liberated western minds from their mediaeval subservience to external authority," and that only the seventeenth-century intellectual revolution, which was much more "fundamental and radical," gave to "modern western civilization a vital spiritual force" that explains its predominance in the nineteenth and twentieth centuries. In a recent discussion,[2] a leading historian, suspected of lacking sympathy with the secular ideals of the Enlightenment, admitted that he had perhaps "underestimated the newness, the greatness, and the originality of the modern West" which originated in the seventeenth and eighteenth centuries.

In the revolutionary changes which occurred in the intellectual and cultural life of these two centuries, two stages ought to be distinguished in what was more a gradual evolution than a real revolution. The first one, sometimes called the scientific revolution, was a progress of scientific thought; the second, familiar under the name of the industrial revolution, was an application of scientific discoveries to mechanical inventions and technological progress. Furthermore, in each of these two cases, two different aspects of the problem must be considered: the importance of the achievement, which is, of course, uncontroversial and appears even greater if considered from the viewpoint of Europe's millennium; and the consequences of both revolutions, which can be fully appreciated only in the light of our present experiences, hopes, and fears.

To begin with the scientific revolution[3] which made possible the industrial one, a preliminary question which is usually underestimated must be examined first. It is, as happens so frequently on similar occasions, a question of terminology with far-reaching implications. The very term "science" urgently requires a clear definition, distinguishing between the original meaning and the current use, as well as between its significance in the various European languages. The word comes, of course, from the Latin noun *scientia,* which is derived from the verb *scire.* Since the latter means "to know," the former can only mean "knowledge." And this was indeed, and still is, the only correct meaning of the Latin term. It was also the original meaning of its transformations in all modern languages influenced by the Latin tradition, but unfortunately it no longer is so in all these languages. In many of them, especially in those which have inherited and only slightly changed the Latin form of the word, it does not mean any longer human knowledge as a whole nor even all branches and fields of learning, but only a specific part of them.

In present-day English the use of such words as science, scientific, or scientist is restricted to knowledge and learning in mathematics, physics, chemistry, biology, astronomy, and similar fields. These fields are sometimes qualified as exact or natural sciences, but in general such an adjective is not considered necessary, because there is a strong feeling that only this category deserves to be considered scientific in the strict sense. The same is true as far as the Romance languages are concerned, the French *science,* for example, meaning today exactly what is meant by the English word, identical in spelling and different only in pronunciation. The Italian *scienza,* too, though closest to the original Latin word, no longer has its universal sense.

It is not easy to determine when that sense began to be limited in the different languages. The Italian Gian Battista Vico[4] still called his philosophy of history a *scienza nuova* in 1725. And in some languages, such as the Germanic and Slavic, no limitation of the notion of science was ever introduced: the German *Wissenschaft* or the Polish *nauka* cover even today both the sciences so called in English or French and what in these languages is called arts, letters, or humanities. It is true that even in the latter languages some fields which are excluded from the sciences in the strict sense are designated as social, political, or historical sciences, the French term *sciences morales* being particularly significant. But without trying to explain such apparent inconsistencies or touching the involved problem of the classification of sciences, it remains a rather alarming fact that the opposition between their two main categories— out of which only one remained recognized as truly scientific, or at least more scientific than the other and therefore superior to it—continued to grow and to spread from the seventeenth century until our time.

This resulted from another striking fact, the phenomenon that the progress of knowledge which started in the seventeenth century was even then most amazing and truly revolutionary in the so-called exact and natural sciences, such a designation being in itself a judgment of value in their favor. If the scientific revolution of the period is sometimes called Newtonian, it is because it was and is taken for granted that the achievements of the foremost representative of these specific sciences were typical of, and decisive for, the whole progress of human knowledge in his age.

It could be said without exaggeration that such an interpretation introduced one more dualism into the structure of European civilization. Neither in its Graeco-Roman nor in its Christian heritage had there been such an opposition nor such a split between two categories of knowledge. Renaissance culture is considered particularly great because the same men would distinguish themselves in both fields and because the progress in both, including the creative arts and literature, was parallel and simultaneous. In the Italian Renaissance the case of Leonardo da Vinci is an illustration of the first of these facts, and in Poland's "golden age" the date of 1543 is very significant, because the publication of the famous astronomical treatise of Copernicus coincides with that of the first works of the greatest political scientists and writers of his time.[5]

Such examples deserve attention for another reason as well. They indicate that the intellectual achievements of the seventeenth and following centuries, great as they were, were not without precedent even in the strictly scientific field. Newton's discoveries, as well as those of Kepler and Galileo before him, were hardly thinkable without those of Copernicus. What was completely new in these centuries was the growing lack of balance in the progress of sciences and of letters, to use those convenient, though hardly exact terms. It is true that the age of Newton was at the same time the age of Milton, just like the French *grand siècle* produced not only Descartes but also Pascal. However, the belief had already originated that Reason, which more and more was becoming almost an idol, could best exercise itself in those mathematical and physical sciences which seemed to give to the human mind the only absolute certainty. Leibniz was perhaps the last great mind which in the midst of the spiritual crisis of his time, would aim at a sound balance in the pursuit of truly universal knowledge, and wanted to reconcile Reason and Faith in the best Christian tradition.[6] For it was too easily forgotten that even in the time of the Christian Commonwealth such a reconciliation had been attempted, with a great deal of success, by St. Thomas Aquinas.

If Reason was by no means disregarded when theology was considered the summit of human knowledge, it is equally true that Faith was not immediately nor totally rejected when a philosophy based upon the primacy of Reason took its place. Even in that respect the continuity of Europe's spiritual tradition was not definitely broken, nor does the heritage of which modern western man should be proud begin with the so-called scientific revolution. But secularization of life as well as of thought was now much deeper than at the time of the Renaissance, and the doubts regarding the essentials of Christian doctrine went much farther than at the time of the Reformation. To that uncertainty in the field of religious beliefs and even of moral convictions was opposed the apparent certainty of scientific discoveries, under the impression of their amazing progress.

The alarm of the Church in view of such trends is readily understandable, and while it is regrettable that even such well established theories as the Copernican system were temporarily condemned and the weapon of the Inquisition used against distinguished scientists like Galileo who defended it,[7] the subsequent history of science up to the present has justified the warnings that any new hypothesis should not be accepted at once as scientific truth of unquestionable certainty. No less dangerous was the idea that in view of the apparent contradictions between the facts discovered by scientists and the facts of Christian doctrine, two different kinds of truth had to be distinguished, one scientific, the other one religious.

Such a dissociation of science and religion reminds us of the dissociation of politics and ethics which had been one of the most harmful aspects of Renaissance thought; had continued through the following centuries; and at the time of the Enlightenment had influenced the political and social sciences, which, like the natural sciences, were turning away from the Christian tradition. In the writing and interpreting of history,[8] that tradition, represented in its old Augustinian form by Bossuet and in its adaption to new approaches by Vico, was replaced soon after them by Voltaire. It was he who first emphasized the history of civilization and used the term philosophy of history, but he oriented them both in a direction which was quite opposed to Christian ideas or at least to the teaching of the Church.

By no means were all these problems of a theoretical nature only, influencing scholarship and troubling individual consciences. The historical development of Europe was greatly affected by the practical applications of the new ideas. Here again the sciences in the new sense, those which used experimental methods and mathematical figures for formulating inescapable laws, could easily claim a striking superiority over the others. These others, along with literature and art, influenced man's thoughts and actions as in the past, but they did not change his daily conditions of life. Certain practical discoveries of the past, whether destructive like that of gunpowder or constructive like that of the printing press, had introduced such changes and therefore could also be called revolutionary. But the development of the natural sciences in the seventeenth century had consequences in the field of technology in the eighteenth. These gave to man the impression that he had achieved control of the forces of nature and could utilize them for his benefit through the invention of even more perfect and efficient machines.

That impression—almost a new creed, which stimulated human pride much more than the heliocentric system had been incorrectly accused of doing—was to grow and to find new arguments in its favor until the present. But only toward the end of the millennium of Europe did it become evident how dangerous it was that such material progress had been achieved in its last quarter. It had occurred prior to any progress in the moral and spiritual fields comparable to that of Europe's Christianization.[9] Even now, many Europeans, including the non-European representatives of western culture, share the belief of their eighteenth-century ancestors that the so-called industrial revolution which in that century implemented the scientific one was an unqualified blessing. They are even spreading that belief all over the world.

As a matter of fact, the new development of industry through the use of machines which applied technically the discoveries of the physical sciences, though revolutionary in its consequences first for Europe and eventually for the whole world, was not a real European revolution any more than the accelerated progress of science itself. It was a gradual change in the methods and tools of economic production, which started in England toward the middle of the eighteenth century—1765, the year when steam was first used for moving an engine, being the conventional date of the beginning—but in the further course of that century did not even spread over all of western Europe.[10] For the Marxist historian the industrial revolution, more than any other, without excepting even the French which soon followed, can serve as a convenient dividing line between the decline of feudalism and the rise of capitalism.[11] The economic problems, which are so greatly overrated by the school of historical materialism in its general interpretation of history, unquestionably gained more importance after the start of that revolution and with its further progress. But this is no reason for giving an importance to the last phase of European history so much greater than that of the earlier ones, nor for considering this or any earlier change in the forms of economic production the decisive criterion for the division of Europe's millennium into chronological periods.

There is even less reason for praising the process of industrialization from its early origin as a decisive, perhaps even *the* decisive, factor of progress which Europe is contributing to the full development of mankind after benefiting from it herself. In Marxist historiography, which is certainly not favorable to capitalism, that new period is considered progress if compared with feudalism, whenever it started in the individual countries, just as the latter was progress in comparison with the earlier slave society. The last point is easy to admit, but as far as the change from feudalism to capitalism is concerned, an obvious fact must be stressed independently from any progress of production. Much more important is the progress in relations between the various classes, in particular the question whether there was less exploitation of one class by another, more respect for the human person without distinction of origin or profession.

In studying this most serious question, it is easy to observe that at the precise time when there was almost everywhere in Europe a gratifying trend toward mitigating the evils of serfdom and eventually toward abolishing it altogether, a new class of industrial workers was brought into existence by the industrial revolution. This class was for a long time to be exploited at least as badly as the peasant had been earlier—an urban proletariat for which the conditions of life were even harder than those of the rural population as far as health and human dignity were concerned, and affecting the fate of women and children as well. It was to take more than one hundred years before industrial labor would receive protection. In that connection two additional questions must be raised, one of them concerning the place of both the scientific and the industrial revolution in the general evolution of European civilization, the other leading back to the specific situation in the age of Baroque and Enlightenment.

It is beyond any possible doubt that the progress made by the exact and natural sciences in that period was an outstanding contribution to the advancement of western culture. Like any other addition to human knowledge, it was a great victory of man's mind in its perennial search for truth and for a better understanding of the surrounding world. But that same progress, just because it was so unusually accelerated and rich in unexpected discoveries, created the dangerous illusion that absolute and complete Truth could be reached in that same way. As a matter of fact, the new hypotheses had still to be tested by further research, which frequently revealed their provisional and relative character, and even if confirmed, they could explain only the physical, material world, leaving open the old questions which continued to trouble man's conscience. Therefore, while making him better informed about many facts and figures, but leaving him in doubt about the essentials of life and the realm of the spirit, the scientific progress could not make the generations which it so deeply influenced, happier and better than the preceding ones.

What was decisive for the happiness and moral standards of the following generations was how the concrete results of all the scientific discoveries would be applied and what purposes they would serve. The industrial revolution which followed so soon after the first of these modern discoveries made that issue appear quite clearly. Again the achievement itself must be admired, particularly the practical improvements of material life through an unprecedented progress of technology. But even without these technical facilities offered by the applications of pure science, the earlier generations who had been unaware of such possibilities had been living quite happily, and those of the future, accustomed to their use, hardly became happier and certainly not better. On the contrary, they were to realize how much beauty, quietness, and harmony could be destroyed by a mechanical industrialization which was considered a goal in itself and a panacea for all the shortcomings afflicting humanity.

Furthermore, there was the danger that science would be used for purposes which, far from bringing man the material advantages of an industrialization kept within reasonable limits, would simply be destructive and harmful for him. Such considerations may seem inspired by mere hindsight, since it took a long time before such consequences became as evident as they are today. They were, however, the almost fatal result of the lack of balance in human progress, unprecedented in the scientific and technical field, but in all the other fields, no greater, if not actually slower than in the past.

The modern European, as he emerged from the intellectual crisis of the period, had to pay a heavy price for what seemed to be a liberation of the intellect from the fetters so long imposed by both the Christian faith and the ancient, Graeco-Roman heritage. He hoped, indeed, to find new and better solutions to all problems, including those which were beyond the reach of science and technology. In the eighteenth century a serious effort was made in that direction. In the midst of almost uninterrupted warfare and in spite of all the abuses of absolute power, which according to Lord Acton's well known saying, corrupted absolutely those who exercised it, there developed a truly humanitarian spirit along with efforts to correct many inveterate evils both through constitutional reforms and by educating public opinion.

One change to the better is frequently emphasized by those who are rightly critical of the mistakes made in earlier periods: the growing tolerance in religious matters, a sound reaction against the persecution of which both sides had been guilty at the time of Reformation and

Counter-Reformation and in the course of the religious wars, whether internal or international. Progress in that respect was slow to come. In France, for example, the Edict of Nantes had granted a large measure of religious freedom after the serious troubles at the end of the sixteenth century. But it was revoked at the end of the seventeenth century, when the Calvinist minority no longer constituted a danger. And even in the eighteenth century the same powers which protested against religious discrimination in once so tolerant Poland, were far from granting to their minorities the rights which they requested, out of political motives, for the dissidents in the Commonwealth.[12]

Something else, however, was more significant than any such obstacles on the difficult road to universal freedom of conscience and worship. Tolerance was supposed to be the logical consequence of the belief growing among the intellectual leaders that all religions were equally good, that traditional Christian doctrines could well be replaced by some vague deism, and that humanitarian principles did not require any moral code nor sanction. It was in their name, rather than in that of Christ's law of love for our neighbor, that the most shocking cruelties of the judiciary system were abolished and that those of serfdom at last received due attention. Yet, the very humanitarianism of minds proud of being at last enlightened was the product of those Christian principles which in the course of the preceding centuries had penetrated deep into the European conscience and succeeded in influencing even those who wanted to disregard them.

Once more the continuity of the European millennium manifested itself, including the heritage of the ten preparatory centuries from the coming of Christ to the constitution of the European community. And those who are proud today, at the millennium's end, of the so much nearer and more familiar heritage of modern centuries should be aware that it is only part of a much more comprehensive whole, just one phase in an uninterrupted development which cannot be separated from the earlier ones. Without them it would never have approached its lofty goal so successfully.

The Enlightenment approached but did not reach that goal, because, impressed by the dualism opposing science to religion and Reason to Faith, it questioned the Christian foundations of European civilization, and also because of a completely different and less controversial reason. Many centuries have been required to erect upon those almost forgotten foundations the modernized and liberalized—or rather secularized—

structure of a Great Republic, uniting Europe intellectually at least.[13] But in order to be completed, even if only as a purely secular and primarily intellectual creation, that structure needed much more time than was granted to the men of the Enlightenment. They were the first to realize the necessity of a rather long evolution before the constitutional and social changes which they planned and recommended could be implemented. And time was running short. Not because their own century was nearing its end nor because the European community, which in eight hundred years had failed to find its final form of organization, was approaching the end of a millennium. Nobody was less inclined than Voltaire's generation to attribute to a period of one hundred nor even of a thousand years any mystical significance. The rhythm of European history had simply been so accelerated and the hopes which had been raised by the leaders had made their whole generation so impatient that the revolutionary movements in the intellectual field, including their consequences for practical life, were leading to political revolutions which were supposed to make possible the immediate realization of a total reform.

The whole period ended, therefore, with a revolutionary crisis which interrupted more radically than ever before the process of Europe's evolution. Though that crisis at the turn of the eighteenth and the nineteenth centuries seemed to be interrupted in turn by the comparatively more peaceful course of the latter, it was to find in the twentieth a continuation or rather resumption, the magnitude of which our generation, the last of the European millennium, was to experience so painfully.[14]

The Great French Revolution is rightly so called because, as we see it now, it started more than just a new period of European history, similar to the earlier ones, though somewhat shorter. It started a transition— but not like that of the Renaissance—from one phase of normal European development to another: this time it was the much more momentous transition from the European community, which seemed to reach predominance in the world, to quite another age, in which not only that predominance but the continuity of the European heritage was questioned from the outset. It was the most appalling consequence of the scientific and the industrial revolution that this entirely new age was to be, independently of the change in Europe's position, the atomic age of the world.

In order to understand these implications, the French revolution which started in 1789, important as it was, cannot be considered in isolation. It was preceded, only a few years before, by the American Revolution, different in origin and character, and apparently non-European. But it was even more decisive for Europe and for the enlarged western community than was the French, and it was inseparable from the latter. When the two broke out, a third had already started that was so different from both that the connection that developed simultaneously among all three is not easy to grasp. And yet, only by comparing them and considering them as part of a process affecting the European community from its extreme western to its extreme eastern extensions, can the history of the outgoing millennium of Europe be properly explained.

CHAPTER XXV

Three Political Revolutions

Ｉｆ ｔｈｅ ｃｒｕｓａｄｅｓ are probably the best studied problem in the historiography of the Middle Ages, the French Revolution occupies a similar place in the study of modern European history. Since the source material is so much richer and the facts so much better known in all their details, the exciting story of that great revolution can be told almost day by day. Better knowledge and understanding, not only of the mere facts but also of the ideas behind them, can also be explained by the closeness to our own time of the events which started in 1789, at least in comparison with the remoteness of the Crusades. But this does not mean that the interpretation and evaluation of those facts and ideas is any less controversial. On the contrary, for the very reason that the tradition of the French Revolution is still so vivid and its impact on contemporary developments so strong, the events as well as the memories which they left behind continue to be an object of heated discussion in historical science and in current politics.[1] Since the revolutionaries of 1789 and the following years were animated by what might be called a truly crusading spirit, all that happened in France at that time had and still has repercussions everywhere in Europe and even in extra-European lands, just like the movement which started in that same country seven hundred years earlier.

It is only natural that the Revolution of 1789, a much more specifically French phenomenon than the Crusades despite the outstanding French participation in all of them, should deeply affect the national tradition of the French people. In that respect another comparison can be made, i.e. with the Hussite Revolution in fifteenth-century Bohemia which left behind a national tradition that was added to, or rather opposed to, an earlier one, and thus caused a split in the interpretation of the nation's past from which the Czech people have been suffering ever since. The same is true to an even higher degree of the Great French Revolution. The French people, who always had been rightly proud of their historical heritage, had an additional heritage after 1789, at least as different from the earlier one as was the tradition of Hus from that of Saint Václav. This division of the national tradition was deep and dangerous because both sides were convinced that the Great Revolution with all its consequences had to be either accepted or rejected as a whole, without distinction between principles and applications, or between the original character and the later phases.

In any synthesis of the millenary history of France, the Revolution of 1789 takes the center, as if all that happened in the much longer earlier part had been leading to that great crisis, and as if all that followed had been determined by it. Such a statement may seem an oversimplified exaggeration; but if general surveys of French history, written in recent days from the two opposed viewpoints regarding the Great Revolution,[2] are compared, they almost give the impression that they are histories of two different countries. And while the reconsideration of the whole pre-revolutionary period under the impression of the year 1789 and its aftermath could only lead to one-sided interpretations, it is true historically and it proved decisive politically that this aftermath has not yet ended.

The Great Revolution did not finally decide the big issues which it had raised. Even the Republic which it soon established was only the first of five, with long intervals and violent crises between each of them, including dictatorships of different styles, two empires, and a restoration of the kingdom in two different constitutional forms.[3] As far as France herself is concerned, it is unquestionable that the revolution which started in 1789 is still continuing because it turned into a quasi-permanent state of tension leading to repeated outbreaks. As not only the original movement but all the subsequent changes on the French scene had far-reaching European repercussions, it is difficult to question the conclusion that the whole European community entered into a revolutionary phase at the end of the eighteenth century, which in spite of apparent interruptions was to last until the end of its millennium.

Such an impression is confirmed by the fact that the example of the

Great French Revolution was invoked whenever after 1789 a revolution broke out in any European country, whether it was a liberal or a totalitarian revolution. In the first French Revolution there were both liberal, democratic, and progressive elements and methods, and others which created dangerous precedents for the totalitarian regimes of our own time.[4] The failure to make a clear distinction and a determined choice between the two explains not only the French tragedy that is inherent in the conflict between these extreme traditions, but also a confusion in Europe's political thinking from which the world is still suffering.

The original principles of the Great Revolution were in the best European tradition and could have been readily reconciled with that of royal France through a constitutional reform which did not even require the abolition of the monarchy. The truly inspiring formula, *Liberté, Egalité, Fraternité,* could easily find its place on the façades of France's Catholic churches, since the freedom of the human person, the equality of all children of God, and the idea of fraternity which is only another expression of the love of one's neighbor, correspond to the basic Christian principles. To replace them by another triad, *Travail, Famille, Patrie,* as was done by the so-called "National Revolution" after the catastrophe of 1940,[5] was unnecessary and misleading, because there is no real opposition between the two formulas, if only both are correctly interpreted and as long as neither is enforced through violence and terror.

As far as the first formula is concerned, the real trouble is caused by the endless controversy whether freedom or equality is more important. Freedom was rightly placed first in the historical text, because without freedom equality can easily be an equality of slaves, which is certainly contrary to the intentions of those who started the Revolution. Both ideas would be meaningless without the third, which reconciles them and indicates at the same time the only method and spirit through which the first two can be made into reality. To have proclaimed that truth in three brief words was certainly a real achievement of the French nation. Joan of Arc would have welcomed it, adding, however, her own favorite formula: *Dieu premier servi.*[6] Freedom, equality, and fraternity under God is indeed the only solution to the dilemma which the French Revolution has left behind, and the integration of its rather recent heritage with the whole millennary tradition of France and Europe.

It so happened that a revolution inspired by a similar ideal had broken out on non-European soil a dozen years before the French. And it exercised a considerable influence on the latter's origin. However, the American Revolution was of a different character. The principal difference was only partially a result of its colonial background. For it was not, like most of the colonial wars of the future and particularly of our time, a rebellion of natives against European domination, but a struggle of European colonists against their home country or rather against a government which was considered oppressive. The war for independence, fought between peoples of the same European origin, belongs along with the contemporaneous developments in the old world to the early history of the Age of the Democratic Revolution in both Europe and America.[7] However—and this is precisely what distinguishes the American from the French Revolution—the former, though at least equally democratic, was not so much motivated by the desire of revolutionary constitutional changes as by the determination to defend existing constitutional rights.

The violations of these rights by the King of England were listed in the memorable document of July 4, 1776, a date which occupies in the American tradition a place much more outstanding than that of July 14, 1789, in the French. First, it is an uncontroversial one; secondly, it is the date not of just one, diversely interpreted event in the course of an already long national history, but of the birth of a new nation. Besides the taking of the Bastille in the eventful year of 1789, something happened in Paris that can be well compared with what was declared in Philadelphia in 1776. Again, however, there is a significant difference. The principles employed in France as a Declaration of the Rights of Man and Citizen everywhere had been used in America to justify her Declaration of Independence.

Such a declaration had been the first exercise of the right of self-determination on a truly national scale. The only similar event during the French Revolution, the choice of French instead of papal rule by the people of Avignon, was of very limited importance and different character.[8] But was not the latter case, as it is sometimes said, the first self-determination in European history, while the Declaration of 1776 belongs to American history only? This apparently simple question raises another which has to be considered with greatest care if the American Revolution is to be included in a study of the millennium of Europe. It is the question of the relationship between European and American history.

Before its discovery by Columbus and his followers the history of the western hemisphere bore no relation at all to that of Europe and was even more distinct from the histories of Asia and Africa. For almost three hundred years after her discovery, if considered from the European point of view the history of America was nothing but the history of a colonial expansion of some European peoples on the other side of the Atlantic similar to that in other parts of the world. For that very reason 1492 cannot be considered a turning point in the history of Europe. Such a turning point came when the Europeans who had settled on the western shores of the Atlantic in comparatively large number, pushed back the natives and introduced to the new world European institutions, started to emancipate themselves politically from their home country, and founded outside geographical Europe an independent nation which was European in racial origin, language, religion, and general culture. This was no longer a colonial conquest by a European power, but a permanent extension of historical Europe, whose whole earlier tradition, based upon Christianity and humanism, had been brought by the settlers to the new world, whenever they arrived and from whatever European nation they came.

The whole European history before their emigration was their history and remained their cherished heritage. They had indeed a noble ambition to enrich that heritage, to make right what they considered wrong in the tradition of the past, to develop political and social ideas which, in their opinion, had never been fully respected at home, and to make their own original contributions to human progress. Within a comparatively short time they succeeded in creating in their new country a specifically American civilization[9] which, however, had nothing in common with any native culture. On the contrary, it had so much in common with the various European cultures that it scarcely differed more from them than those individual cultures, French or English, Italian or German, did from each other. Their colonial past left a particularly strong impact of English culture, not only linguistic but also institutional, the more so because the majority of those who founded the new republic were of English ancestry. Gradually, however, immigrants from other European countries, who had appeared even among the earliest colonists, contributed to what was first called a "melting pot" and later the pluralism of American civilization.[10]

Such pluralism was to be one more feature which the new civilization had in common with the old European, different in that respect from most if not all non-European cultures. The federal structure, which was given to the United States of America the year after the Declaration of Independence, corresponded to this feature in the political field, although the federal constitution was not finally adopted until ten years later. The discussions of that matter, summarized in the *Federalist,* especially the letters which survey and criticize all earlier experiences in federal government,[11] show that federalism was for the founders of the American Republic an old European heritage. They also show that in that crucial matter the Founding Fathers wanted to benefit from the rather inadequate experiments made in Europe in order to discover a more perfect form of federalism. They succeeded so well that the oldest European confederation, the Swiss, which in 1848 reached the final stage of its long evolution, to a large extent followed the comparatively recent American experience of 1787.[12]

This is just one example illustrating an interesting phenomenon. Many creative conceptions which originated in Europe before the trans-Atlantic expansion of western culture were developed and tested in America. America's achievements in this field would soon influence the old world to which the ideas returned with an even stronger appeal. This is true not only of the democratic ideals which the American and the French Revolutions of the eighteenth century shared, but also of many of the later consequences of the industrial revolution and of the technological development. But all this is at the same time the best evidence of how inseparable Europe and America are and how truly Europe's American extension is part of the story of her millennium.

This extension was a process which started in 1776 after a slow preparation in the colonial period and then occupied a considerable part of what still remained of Europe's millennium. Only at its very end was the process completed by the formation of the Atlantic community. This is true even if only the United States of America is considered. This country's expansion to the Pacific Ocean and Alaska, in the following century, made the addition to the original, European area of western civilization simply tremendous. Its policy, after at first trying to avoid involvements in purely European affairs, in the course of the last half century proved decisive for the destinies of Europe. But the creation of the United States as an independent nation of European origin and background in the northern part of the hemisphere served as an example for the establishment of no less than twenty states in its central and southern part. All were former colonies of European powers and emancipated themselves without breaking their cultural ties with their homelands.[13] In the northern part, out of another English, originally French colony, the new, bilingual nation of Canada emerged. It achieved the status of a

self-governing, practically independent dominion within a Commonwealth that today is no longer called British.[14]

The case of Latin America is different, because in the twenty republics
which came into existence there after the failure of imperial experiments, the natives were not reduced to insignificance as they were in the
north, and in some of the new nations they even constitute a majority of
the population. However, even the most highly developed of their cultures have not survived the European conquest: and everywhere the cultures of Latin Europe have been adapted to the new conditions. The
Latin-Americans are proud of their Spanish and Portuguese heritage
which peoples of different racial origin now share with the descendants
of their conquerors. Therefore it is also justified to speak here of an extension of Europe as a cultural community and of her historical tradition.

The case of Canada raises another problem, that of English colonies
in other parts of the world which reached a similar political status and
where other nations of European origin and culture were formed. In
these cases, the natives were scarce and culturally primitive. However,
such countries as Australia and New Zealand, though certainly parts of
the sphere of the so-called western culture, are so geographically isolated
from Europe that it would be really artificial to consider them extensions of Europe. This sense of "extension" must remain limited to the
parts of the world on both sides of the Atlantic. Nor can South Africa
be included for reasons which became particularly obvious in our time.

In any case the American extension of Europe in the last phase of her
millennium is even more spectacular than that expansion of Carolingian
and Byzantine Europe in a northeastern direction which inaugurated
that millennium in the tenth century. But did not this expansion, which
started at a time when the first European explorations of the North
American coast failed to achieve lasting results, continue in the further
course of the millennium? Did it not continue, by proceeding through
the Eurasian land mass, until it reached North America from the western side, and soon after the American Revolution contact there the Europeans who had advanced over the Atlantic and through the American
Continent?[15] In order to answer that surprising but pertinent question,
the third revolution, which at the very time of both the American and
the French transformed eastern Europe, must be examined.

That revolution was made in Poland but not by the Poles. The far-
reaching internal reforms which were accomplished there by the Four

Years Diet, in particular by the constitution of May 3rd, 1791, cannot rightly be called a revolution.[16] If Edmund Burke compared these reforms with the French Revolution, it was in order to point out the contrast between the two. The latter had indeed influenced the former, as had the American Revolution and the Constitution of the United States, as well as English political thought. But all this was only one more evidence of Poland's intellectual ties with the West. Western ideas were, however, adapted to Poland's specific conditions and needs, and applied without the radicalism which soon developed in France. The reforms of the Great Diet, far from being a break with the national tradition, perpetuated that tradition in a revised, modernized form as a lasting heritage of the Commonwealth. Representing distinct progress in the direction of full democracy to the advantage of burghers and peasants, these reforms abolished at the same time some misused liberties which had proved dangerous, like the free election of the kings and, above all the *liberum veto*. From the general European point of view, these achievements were an instructive example that it was possible to find a way from the old system of estates with exclusive privileges for the nobles to a constitutional monarchy with opportunities for all, without passing through the hard experiences of absolutism and revolution.

Unfortunately, what was fateful not only for Poland but for the whole European community was a truly revolutionary intervention of the three neighboring powers.[17] They prevented the Polish reforms from becoming effective by totally destroying the Commonwealth and dividing among themselves that old state, still one of the largest in Europe in spite of the territorial losses suffered in the later seventeenth century. The first of these partitions,[18] which occurred in 1772 and thus preceded the great reforms, had already created an ominous precedent; without even the formality of an ordinary war and without stirring any opposition in Europe, these stronger nations could dictate to a weaker one disastrous territorial cessions. By that time, as Burke quickly noted,[19] the balance of power that had long been considered the foundation of the European state system was seriously affected. The balance was actually destroyed, when in reaction against the Constitution of 1791, the second partition, in 1793, left Poland a doomed rump state. And after the Polish Independence War under Kosciuszko, who was inspired by his American experience,[20] the third partition, in 1795, eliminated the last island of freedom in East Central Europe.

Even in that eighteenth century, when international morality was at low ebb, it should have been realized that this was a dangerous precedent, not just for the future of one nation whose very name was to disappear forever according to the supplementary treaty of 1797, but for the European order as a whole. In this respect the partitions of Poland cannot be compared with Frederick the Great's earlier rape of Silesia[21] which, after all, was only a province. Nor can it even be compared with the partition of the Republic of Venice—strangely enough in the same year of 1797. That republic was in an irreparable decline and represented only a small part of the Italian people. In order to justify the destruction of Poland, it was and still is argued that her decline, too, was fatal and was caused by the Poles themselves. Poles themselves were to discuss endlessly the various causes of their national catastrophe. Such discussions have a general importance, because they concern the big issue of whether the decline and fall of states and societies is due, primarily, to internal or external reasons. But more important than any such theoretical speculations were and are the consequences of the revolutionary change in the structure of the European Continent. This change immediately alarmed public opinion even in faraway America,[22] but it was underestimated in western Europe. There the French Revolution and its international repercussions absorbed everybody's attention. And there the situation in eastern Europe was so badly misunderstood that the loss of Ochakov by the Ottoman Empire was considered more dangerous to the balance of power than the fall of Poland.[23]

Both of these otherwise incongruous cases had one thing in common: they were both Russian advances. However, while Russian plans to conquer as much as she possibly could of the earlier Turkish conquest in southeastern Europe continued to raise the strongest opposition of western powers, these same powers strangely underestimated the danger that the elimination of the Polish barrier to Russia's advance posed for themselves. Not even Russia's partners in Poland's dismemberment realized how much more Tsardom was gaining in the whole deal than they were. For Austria, the annexation of some Polish territories was a very doubtful gain because it made the composition of the Habsburg domains only more involved and heterogeneous. For Prussia, her acquisitions were valuable indeed from a geopolitical point of view, but they introduced into an essentially German state more Slavic elements than it could possibly digest. For both of them it was very dangerous that instead of Poland—which never had threatened their frontiers—

they now had a long common frontier with the Continent's most expansionist power.

It was a basic change for that Continent as a whole, that of its four long-existing centers of power—the French, the German, the Polish, and the Russian—one simply ceased to be. Even Britain, the nation most concerned with the balance of power, was to be affected by the new situation, which left only two alternatives: a domination of the Continent by the powers bound together through their cooperation in the partitions of Poland, or a tension between them now that they were immediate neighbors—hence a new danger to European peace. But even more troubling and truly revolutionary was something else, another alternative that raised once more the difficult question of how far the European community reached in the eastern direction. This question had received many different answers since the constitution of that community and was to remain controversial until the end of Europe's millennium.

The Christianization of Kievan Rus' had made the eastern Slavs an integral part of Europe. There was only doubt as to what extent their vast area of colonization would be included in that integration. The Mongol conquest cut off that area from Europe longer and more completely than the original homeland of the eastern Slavs. From the fourteenth century on that homeland was included in the Polish-Lithuanian Commonwealth, whose frontier was considered the border of Europe until the seventeenth century. When at the turn of that century Muscovite Russia, after conquering her former Tartar conquerors and extending her colonial empire as far as the Pacific, claimed a leading place in the European system and simultaneously tried to develop her cultural as well as economic relations with the West, it was not easy to interpret these prospects. Leibniz compared the initiatives of Tsar Peter of Russia "and almost the whole north" with similar trends which he noticed simultaneously in China and Abyssinia. A few years later, the Abbé de Saint-Pierre, in his project of establishing in Europe a "perpetual peace," gave to "Moscovie" one of the twenty-four places in the Senate of Europe.[24] And since her Asiatic possessions, in contrast to other colonies, were contiguous with the homeland, it seemed that the extension of the European community would include all of northern Asia. Would this really mean a shift of Europe's border from the eastern frontier of Poland to that of China? All depended on the progress of Russia's westernization and perhaps even more on her political attitude.

As for Russia, her interferences in the rivalries of the European powers and the appearances of her armed forces on the battlefields of central Europe were alarming even at the time when Peter's much less prominent successors had to disregard Poland's sovereignty and neutrality in order to penetrate farther West. On the other hand, Peter's rather limited territorial acquisitions in the Baltic area had already introduced into his empire new elements which were definitely western. In both respects Catherine's much larger annexations of formerly Polish territories were of decisive significance. On the one hand, they permitted Russia to exercise direct pressure on the very center of Europe, from which a substantial part had been cut off. On the other hand, more European elements than ever before were incorporated with Catherine's empire, since even the eastern half of the Commonwealth, Russia's share in the partitions, had by that time been integrated with the West. It was impossible, however, to foresee whether these elements would be able to exercise any influence or would rather be submerged, as were other non-Russian minorities, by a policy of Russification. In Siberia this policy was an advance of Europe, but in the new western provinces it could only result in a retreat of the West.

Important as this was for the Poles, it was even more so for their former partners in the Commonwealth, Lithuanians, Byelorussians, and Ukrainians, considerable numbers of whom had been absorbed by Muscovite Russia earlier. But this was also of general European significance, especially in the two decades of turmoil which followed the French Revolution. Before studying the consequences of the Napoleonic interlude for the next period of European history, it must be at once recalled that, though the Polish question was reopened because of that crisis almost immediately after the partitions, the outcome, as far as eastern Europe was concerned, was nothing but another partition of Poland. This time the Russian share, under the misleading appearance of a restoration of the Polish kingdom by the Tsar, was so considerably enlarged that all the problems which the disappearance of a free Poland had placed before Europe became even more alarming and obscure.

Therefore, at a time when the consequences of the French Revolution seemed to have been overcome and those of the American Revolution not yet fully realized, those of the East European Revolution of the later eighteenth century determined to a large extent the general European situation in the early nineteenth.

PART V

The Climax and the Collapse of Europe's Predominance in the World

CHAPTER XXVI

The European Concert

THE LAST PERIOD OF EUROPE's millennium was much briefer than the others, so that it might be considered merely a transition to another millennium. However, it was an age of great importance, and though it is near to us and therefore comparatively well known, it is subject to very different interpretations and evaluations. There cannot be any doubt that this period began immediately after the three political revolutions at the end of the eighteenth century, and we all remember the date when it ended, this time a very precise one: 1945.

It is equally obvious that the period was introduced by a series of European wars which with brief interruptions lasted for about two decades. It obviously was concluded by two great European wars which became world wars and, since they were separated by only twenty years, decisively influenced three decades, the lifetime of a whole generation. Between these two crises—of which the second was a hectic time of not only wars but also revolutions—lay a century, the nineteenth, which lasted, strictly speaking, from 1815 to 1914, and seemed to be a time of comparative peace for Europe, facilitating her position of predominance in the world.

In order to understand how on some occasions major wars have been avoided, and why nevertheless peace and order were troubled time and again, one has to ask whether any real progress in the matter of the political organization of the European community was made during the nineteenth century, as compared with earlier periods. Such a stable organization was then, as in any other phase of Europe's evolution, a prerequisite condition for normal progress in the non-political fields. Therefore, the positive and negative aspects of the political structure of Europe between 1815 and 1914 explain her achievements as well as her shortcomings in developing a civilization which began to influence the whole world.

The study of the peace settlement of 1815 is rightly considered the best starting point for examining that whole problem. Napoleon's experience had proved once more that it was vain to try to unify Europe by force under the leadership of one predominant power, even if that power had a leader who was a military genius of extraordinary appeal with constructive ideas in non-military matters as well. But, as is usual, to organize Europe by the decisions of a victorious coalition proved scarcely less difficult. The so-called reconstruction of Europe[1] by the Congress of Vienna, so highly praised in the historiography of our time,[2] did not include all of Europe and did not last more than fifteen years even in those parts of the Continent which received special attention. It is an even greater illusion to believe that there was "a world restored"[3] in 1815 thanks to one or two skillful diplomats. If in spite of the poor organization of the Congress, the immediate disagreements among the "Big Four" who wanted to decide everything, and the interlude of the Hundred Days—if despite all these, at least something was achieved in Vienna, it was for two rather paradoxical reasons.

First, it was easy to realize that after the elimination of their emperor, which Waterloo made final, the French were no longer a real danger to European peace. The fear of French imperialism, which was exaggerated even at the time of Louis XIV and even more after World War I, was overshadowed at the Congress of Vienna by another, more justified fear: that of Russia.[4] Out of fear of Russia, the "final act" of the Congress was based not on any principles, not even that of legitimacy, but on the peace aims which Alexander I had outlined in advance in his secret instruction to Nesselrode,[5] with only such modifications as he was prepared to accept.

In spite of Metternich's and Castlereagh's game, seconded by Talleyrand (who made a prospective ally out of defeated France), it was Russia which emerged as the only real victor after the Napoleonic wars—exactly as happened 130 years later after World War II. Though it would be unfair to compare Alexander I with Stalin, in both cases Russia was represented by a dictator, whether an autocratic, though enigmatic Tsar, or a less enigmatic but even more autocratic communist leader of Georgian origin. Both began by trying to share the control of Europe with the western dictator and only after being invaded by him contributed to his defeat. The comparison between Napoleon and Hitler, however, is again unfair to the former. Even more important is another difference between 1815 and 1945. While Soviet Russia was and is definitely an extra-European or rather anti-European power, imperial Russia of Alexander's time seemed to be more integrated with the European community than in any other period of her history. At the Congress of Vienna, the only Russian among the Tsar's advisers, Rasumovsky, was of Ukrainian origin and was called "the most Viennese among the Russians."[6] The others included a German, Freiherr von Stein, an anti-Bonapartist Corsican, Pozzo di Borgo, a Greek, Capo d'Istria, and most surprising, a Pole, Prince Adam Czartoryski.

Through all his life, the latter had been an outstanding promoter of the idea of European unity.[7] While in the last thirty years of his long life he tried to achieve that unity by opposing Russia, in the first thirty, including 1815, he did his best to reach his goal by loyally cooperating with Russia, especially as long as his friend Alexander was on the throne. Though deeply disappointed when the Tsar decided to cooperate with Prussia rather than with Britain, Czartoryski continued to hope that Alexander rather than Napoleon would restore Poland. It seemed that Alexander's solution of the Polish question, which with Czartoryski's support he forced upon the Congress of Vienna, was the best possible for the Poles and for Europe. Yet, the western statesmen, who, with the exception of Prussia's Hardenberg, accepted it so reluctantly and strove —without success—to reduce the area of that "Kingdom of Poland" which was to be permanently united with the Russian Empire, had good reasons to fear that such a solution was merely a disguised advance of Russia toward the heart of Europe. How real that danger was became apparent during the first international crisis which only fifteen years after the Congress of Vienna shook the whole political system so painstakingly established there.

By adding to the treaties of 1815 the declaration which was supposed to establish that so-called Holy Alliance, Alexander I made an unusual attempt to give to that system moral foundations in the best European tradition. It was, however, merely a pledge of the European monarchs to follow Christian principles both in their methods of government and in international relations. Even so it could have had considerable meaning if those who signed it had taken their obligations seriously and if a permanent organization had been established in order to promote the cooperation of all powers. The only substitute for such an organization —the lack of which constitutes the basic difference between the Holy Alliance and the League of Nations included in the peace settlement of 1919—was the quadruple alliance of the victorious big powers, to which defeated France was soon admitted. This was to work through a conference system that was expected to remove any threats to the European order of 1815. Alexander I himself, whose idealistic initiative had resulted from one of his occasional mystical moods, seemed to be quite satisfied with such a practical solution. For the first time in history the European community was placed under the regular control of a few self-appointed states.

However, even such a system worked only until 1822. Then, the last of the four minor congresses held in the aftermath of that of Vienna met in Verona without being able to respond to the first serious challenge, an insurrection in the Balkans which had broken out the preceding year. This was indeed the part of the Continent which the Congress of Vienna had completely disregarded, both because it did not feel qualified to interfere with the internal problems of the Ottoman Empire and because it strangely underestimated the growing trend of nationalism and self-determination.[8] Nobody seemed to have foreseen that among the Christian peoples of the Balkan peninsula, usually considered backward and troublesome, such a trend would be particularly strong and represent a permanent threat to European peace throughout the next century. It led indeed to the outbreak of the Great War of 1914, after a long series of minor ones.

Not only under Alexander I but even under his successor Nicholas I, who was otherwise so strongly opposed to any revolutionary movements, Russia wanted to play the role of protector and liberator of the submerged nationalities in the Balkans. They were all Orthodox and mostly Slavic, and, as they had frequently done before in the preceding centuries, looked for support to the leading Orthodox and Slavic power. Though the independence movement had started among the Serbs, the non-Slavic Greeks were the first to attain this goal, since they found more sympathy in the West. The Russo-Turkish war of 1828-1829, the first war in Europe after the Congress of Vienna, was, therefore, the beginning of Russia's advance toward the Straits, which was to be the main road of her European expansion and the main source of tension between her and the western powers. But that same war and the resulting international recognition of an independent Greek state, almost four hundred years after the fall of the old Greek Empire, was an encouragement for other nationalities, not only in the Balkans, but in the center of Europe, to rise against those decrees of the Congress of Vienna which had failed to satisfy their aspirations. It was in 1830 that a crisis in two distant, but equally crucial regions alarmed the defenders of the settlement of 1815 and Russia in particular, diverting her for several years from the Balkan problems and making her appear even more dangerous for the West. Thus, the apprehensions felt at Vienna were confirmed.

The first crisis of the Vienna system started, like the next, with another French revolution. Like the great one, it was of an internal, constitutional character, but it contributed again to the spread of liberal ideas all over Europe. These included the idea of freedom for nationalities which resented foreign rule and wanted independence in their own states. One asks why such a revolt succeeded in the case of Belgium, which was not homogeneous from the ethnic viewpoint and had no clear tradition of independent statehood, while it failed in the case of Poland, and why in both cases a war between the European powers was avoided.

The answer can be summed up in the statement that the cooperation of the great powers in the interest of justice and peace worked in the first case through patient efforts which after nine years resulted in a sound revision of the settlement of 1815. In the second case, cooperation that would lead to peaceful change was not even tried, and the revision, achieved through brutal force, was a change for the worse. In order to understand the dangerous precedent which was created, it must be remembered that the cooperation of great powers that was typical of the political philosophy of the nineteenth century, far from being based on any universal, truly European idea, was not even working any longer through a regular conference system. Under the vague name of a European "concert," based upon an equally vague balance-of-power idea—the poorest heritage of the past—nothing was created except the possibility of eventual consultation when the European order was threatened. Such a pragmatic method could lead to solutions of practical expediency only in cases when none of the powers belonging to the "concert" placed its own interests before those of European unity.

The power which after 1815 dominated the Continent much more than Metternich's Austria could possibly do it, the gigantic Russian Tsardom, wanted to interfere militarily even with the solution of the

Belgian problem, which like the events in Paris raised the issue of political liberty. But Nicholas I was prevented from sending his armed forces to the West not only by the distance, but even more by the Polish insurrection.[9] The desperate struggle for freedom should have made it quite clear that the Vienna settlement was even less satisfactory on the Vistula than in the Low Countries, but no "concert" of Europe could oppose in that matter its most powerful member. On the contrary, the West, including the countries whose free development had been made possible by the events in faraway Poland, had to recognize as a restoration of order a repression which justified the worst fears of 1815.

At that time Alexander I had promised, not only to the Poles but in a rather obscure statement of the Vienna Treaty itself,[10] that the new "kingdom of Poland" would receive an extension by getting back part, if not all, of the Russian annexations in the partitions of the eighteenth century. Such an extension would have established a kind of balance between the kingdom and the empire to which it was attached, and would have given to the Poles a chance that their constitution would be respected. Now this constitution, distinguishing the so-called Congress kingdom from autocratic Russia, was replaced by an "organic statute" which made it practically one more Russian province. The formerly Polish borderlands east of the "Kingdom" were subjected to violent Russification, and the settlement of 1815 that had been thus "revised" did not effect a penetration of western influence into Russia, but an extension of Russian influence and military power right to the frontier of a friendly Prussia. Meanwhile, Austria was bound to the partners in the dismemberment of Poland by a solidarity of doubtful values. When that solidarity, much stronger than that within the Concert of Europe, was reaffirmed in 1833, Russia could, in that same year, safely return to her imperialistic policy in the Eastern Question.

Just as at the end of the eighteenth century, the western powers, particularly England, continued to be much more interested in this question than in the problems of central Europe. In the next decade the European Concert succeeded in efforts to replace an exclusively Russian influence in Constantinople and the Near East by a joint action of the great powers. Then followed, however, another crisis on the Continent, this time a much more general one than that of 1830. It was again brought to a climax by a much more radical French revolution in 1848: in the years 1846 to 1851 all the questions which the Congress of Vienna had failed to solve to the satisfaction of the peoples concerned were reopened.

The fall of the Metternich system, which had attempted in vain to per-petuate the European order of 1815, was immediately followed by a whole series of wars and revolutions shattering the multinational Habs-burg Empire.

In that mid-century crisis, which could have resulted in a better organ-ization of Europe but instead left behind nothing but the memories of frustrated hopes for more freedom and justice, the pressure which Rus-sia could exercise at any time on the European heartland proved decisive. This time no rebellion inside his empire, the only country at whose fron-tiers the revolutionary movement was checked, prevented Nicholas I from interfering, directly or indirectly, through diplomatic or military action, wherever he wanted. In the excitement of the so-called Spring of the Nations, a trend to oppose Russian predominance by going to war with her if necessary[11] appeared even in traditionally pro-Russian Prus-sia. But even revolutionary, republican France considered this too great a risk for Europe, and a year later, Russian forces, after occupying the Danubian principalities, the gate to the Balkans, could invade the Dan-ubian plain in Hungary for the first time in history.

Taking advantage of one of the most fatal mistakes of Austrian policy, Nicholas I, under the appearance of rendering a service to a neighbor who needed it badly, emerged out of the confusion as the arbiter of Europe, without even claiming any territorial aggrandizement in the West. He did not fail, however, to claim new advantages in the relations with the Ottoman Empire as soon as the crisis and its aftermath was over, and he thus provoked at last the creation of an anti-Russian coali-tion which proved that the European Concert was a dangerous fiction. Why France and Britain went to war in support of Turkey, why Austria did not feel obliged to show gratitude for the crushing of the Hungarian revolt, why even Prussia was undecided and faraway Sardinia, though concerned with the unification of Italy, joined the Allies—all this can be understood only against the background of Russia's foreign policy in the years of trouble which preceded the immediate origin of the Crimean War.

This bloody and costly war, whose details have been much more ex-haustively studied than its earlier background,[12] has been called an un-necessary war. It can be considered unnecessary if only its direct causes in the Near East receive attention. And if the war remained practically useless, it was because it remained a war of containment. All ideas of making it a war of liberation were given up—the liberation of Poland

and the other non-Russian parts of the Tsardom, as well as the liberation of Europe from Russian predominance. In spite of the moderate terms of the peace treaty of 1856, the Congress of Paris, still insufficiently studied as compared to those of Vienna and Berlin, resulted in deep resentment on the part of Russia which was not accustomed to even minor setbacks and was determined to resume her drive in the direction of the Straits on the first favorable occasion.

Before such an occasion presented itself a score of years later, and before another well known congress, that of Berlin, had again to contain Russia, two more crises troubled the European situation. In neither of them did any joint action of the Concert of great powers help to save the peace which was broken no less than three times from 1864 to 1871. By 1863 another war against Russia seemed very near, though nobody really wanted it and only Napoleon III, after contributing to the unification of Rumania and Italy, was convinced that a general revision of the treaties of 1815 was urgently needed. After vainly trying to oppose Russian violations of these treaties through a joint interference of the other signatories in favor of the Polish insurrection of January 1863, the emperor of the French took the initiative of inviting all European states in November of that same year to an international congress. This would meet in Paris and settle not only the Polish question but all problems disturbing the peace of Europe, replacing exaggerated armaments by supreme arbitration.[13]

The bold project was favorably received by almost all the smaller powers, as well as by Pope Pius IX, who was ready to come to Paris in person. But with the exception of Italy and Turkey, both recently admitted to the European Concert at the Paris Congress of 1856, all the other great powers were skeptical and feared that the failure of Napoleon's initiative, unavoidable in their opinion, would lead to a general war. In spite of a second invitation issued by the emperor in December, the planned congress never met, the main opposition to the suggested reorganization of the Continent on French initiative coming from Britain.

It was not, however, the only one. Bismarck was also opposed, not only because he feared for the Polish provinces of Prussia, but because he already had in mind his own project of creating under Prussian leadership a strong, united Germany, predominant in central Europe. He did not hesitate to achieve this through three wars of which those against

Austria and against France had lasting consequences for the European state system: for various reasons they led to the catastrophe of 1914.

One of these reasons was the replacement of the German confedera-tion, as established in 1815 and still maintained after 1848, by the the so-called Second German Empire of the Hohenzollern. The Austrian Germans remained outside but were supposed to control the Empire of the Habsburgs, the real heir of the tradition of the Holy Roman Empire.[14] In the Danubian monarchy, of which no part belonged any longer to a German body politic, highly promising developments began in the direction of a federal reorganization with equal constitutional rights for all nationalities. Only one of them, though, the Hungarians, received almost complete satisfaction in the dualistic Compromise of 1867, which was disappointing for the most numerous Slavic peoples.[15] The main source of trouble was, however, the surprising turn in the foreign policy of the Habsburg monarchy. Under German-Hungarian leadership and forgetful of the humiliation of 1866, the monarchy decided on a rapprochement with the Prussian-controlled German Empire right after its establishment in 1871 following the defeat of France.

The resentment created by this defeat, particularly by the annexation of Alsace-Lorraine, was another source of permanent tension in Europe. Austria-Hungary became quite unnecessarily involved in that delicate issue when her rapprochment with victorious Germany developed into an alliance, first, between the Habsburg and the Hohenzollern emperors, and then also between them and the third emperor, that of Russia. Eventually the king of Italy, too, became associated with that political system, notwithstanding the controversies between the Danubian monarchy and the new kingdom which had joined Prussia against her in 1866.

This strange system, which had nothing in common with European unity but simply opposed the central and eastern parts of the Continent to the western powers, was consolidated during and after the Congress of Berlin, which apparently succeeded in containing Russia without another European war. The origin of the Russo-Turkish war which led to this critical situation can be traced back to the Prusso-French one which, among others, encouraged Russia to denounce one of the stipulations of 1856 and thus to reopen the troublesome Eastern Question. Russian successes, which threatened Constantinople and gave her a chance to create out of liberated Bulgaria a large satellite state that extended over most of the Balkan peninsula, seemed such a challenge to the balance of power that there followed one more recourse to not only the Concert of Europe but to the conference system.

This time, in contrast to the Congress of Vienna, the Balkan area was included in the plan of a lasting European order and was even the main topic of the discussion, with the general rivalry between the great powers for whom the peoples of southeastern Europe were only tools and pawns, pushed to the background. Revising the treaty which Russia had forced upon the Ottoman Empire after only three months, the Congress of Berlin was indeed a success, the last really important one of the system which had been inaugurated by the Congress of Vienna. The settlement of 1878 itself inaugurated a period of European peace in contrast with the preceding thirty years of recurrent crises, and this peace would last another thirty years.

The last period of European peace was, however, at the same time the period of the origin of the Great European War which by 1908 had become an alarming threat and which the Concert of Europe was unable to prevent six years later. As a matter of fact, that Concert was definitely replaced immediately after the Berlin Congress by a system of alliances which divided Europe into two hostile camps, both of which had an artificial character. The Triple Alliance which was first developed became a necessity for Austria-Hungary when she decided to occupy Bosnia-Herzegovina with the approval of the Congress. That fateful step made it impossible for the Dual Monarchy to remain neutral in the dangerous game of power politics in which the majority of the peoples of the multinational empire had no interest whatever. Instead of being a haven of peace and protection of these peoples against Germany's and Russia's growing imperialism, the Habsburg monarchy and its proud tradition were reduced to the role of a "brilliant second" in the close alliance with her former Hohenzollern rival. In spite of Bismarck's tortuous quest for Russian "reinsurance," the alliance did not improve at all the relations of either partner with the Tsardom. When after two years it was formally joined by Italy in another "wavering friendship,"[16] Austria-Hungary's position became even more precarious.

In spite of its inherent weaknesses the Triple Alliance alarmed the other three great powers of Europe and impelled them to join in another alliance system. Its original nucleus, the alliance between the French Republic and the Russian Empire, was particularly artificial, and only the next step, the *entente cordiale* of France and Britain in place of their traditional rivalry, was a constructive contribution to European peace. When, however, that agreement was developed into the Triple Entente including Russia, two groups of three nations with at least one militaristic and imperialistic power in each were facing one another in a growing distrust which found its expression in an unprecedented armaments race. Far from establishing a stable balance of power, such a split of the European Concert made impossible any real organization of Europe.

In the course of these fateful events, it was, strangely enough, Tsar Nicholas II who at the turn of the century took the initiative of a peace conference It was not supposed to end any specific war but to guarantee the precarious peace which still existed. Without invoking Christian principles as Alexander I had done when suggesting the Holy Alliance, his weak successor put forward practical ideas regarding disarmament and arbitration which were in agreement with the program of private movements in favor of international peace. Official diplomatic negotiations in that matter resulted only in the creation of a court of arbitration which was neither compulsory nor even "permanent," although so called, and which failed to create an atmosphere of security.

It is significant that the second Hague Peace Conference, no more successful than the first, can be traced back to a suggestion of President Theodore Roosevelt. Its actual convening was delayed by the Russian-Japanese war, which was ended through the mediation of the American president. Nothing could make it clearer that the problem of peace was no longer European but universal. There were now, besides the six great powers of Europe, two extra-European states which were recognized as belonging to the leading group of nations: one of them, the United States, being of European background and origin, an integral part of the western world, the other one, Japan, representing an entirely different, Far Eastern, Asiatic culture.[17]

Russia's war with that rising power was one of those colonial wars— the most important—which were ever more frequently absorbing the expeditionary forces of one or another of the European nations in the later nineteenth century when Europe was at peace. Fighting with native populations or with earlier European colonists as in South Africa, these metropolitan powers were in constant overseas rivalries with each other, and the crises which repeatedly troubled their relations in the early twentieth century were all connected with extra-European problems. They therefore seemed less dangerous than those of the past. Even the implications of the Balkan wars were underestimated, especially since the Concert of Europe and the conference system had a last success when the most violent of these wars was ended in London.

However, the very next year, 1914, was to show that the tensions within the European Concert had much deeper roots than their trade rivalries on distant oceans or their conflicting attitudes with regard to the independence movements in the Balkan mountains. The great powers of a divided Europe had to pay the price for their misuse of European predominance in the world and for the neglect of so many claims for self-determination inside Europe.

CHAPTER XXVII

The Climax of Colonialism

EUROPE'S MILLENNIUM WAS APPROACHING its end without having led to any real European unity and even less to a peaceful organization of the European community. At the same time Europe's predominance in the world, which had been growing from the age of the great discoveries, reached a spectacular climax. In order to explain this surprising phenomenon, it is usually pointed out that European colonialism reached a climax in the nineteenth century. The Europeans, whose earlier experiences with invasions by Asiatic peoples are easily forgotten, are severely blamed for the military conquest and economic exploitation of vast areas in Asia and elsewhere, for which the collapse of their predominance in our time seems to be a well-deserved punishment.

Considering, however, the story of Europe's millennium as a whole, a few questions must be raised in order to avoid the usual oversimplification of the problem. First, it is only fair to ask whether everything was really wrong with Europe's overseas expansion. Furthermore, it is frequently overlooked that European predominance was not exclusively the result of colonialism and that the understandable reaction against colonialism is not the unique reason for the collapse of that predominance. But before examining these important points, the basic facts, though very well known, must be briefly recalled, even if only to avoid unfair generalizations and to find out whether all Europeans, in particular all western nations, are equally responsible for the unquestionable evils of colonialism.

In that respect the nineteenth century, which saw the climax of the movement, is rather different from the preceding three which laid its foundations. In the western hemisphere, where the natives had suffered so much after discovery by the Europeans, it is hardly possible to speak of colonialism after most of the European possessions in the Americas had been emancipated. The aftermath of the tragic fate of the Indians, especially in North America, continued well into the nineteenth century, but Europe was no longer responsible for it. The European powers which had lost most of their American colonies were now anxious to at least preserve their overseas possessions in other parts of the world and to find there new compensations.

Substantial parts of the Spanish, Portuguese and Dutch empires survived in Asia and Africa where the colonial empires of France and Britain were also extended greatly. The former, after the losses of the eighteenth and early nineteenth century, had to be almost completely rebuilt on new grounds, the conquest of Algeria being the beginning, with total integration as the final goal, and that of Indochina the most astonishing achievement of the Third Republic. In no other cases were the consequences equally tragic for the present generation. It was, however, Britain which at the same time became the foremost colonial power, the only one to be formally called an empire, taking over the proud traditions of India. It was Britain which gained most from the latest discoveries in and around Australia—a fifth part of the world, with its galaxy of countless islands in the Pacific.

What was completely new in the colonialism of the later nineteenth century were the claims of two recently-established great powers and the initiative of one small European nation, which was only recently created as an independent state. That Belgium succeeded in carving out of central Africa—one of the last sections of the Continent to be explored—a state so much larger than herself and intimately connected with her under the name of Congo, was certainly an extraordinary achievement. Only today has it become apparent how artificial that creation was. It is no more artificial, however, than most of the other divisions of Black Africa into colonial units, since these rarely corresponded to the tribal areas of the past.

In the division of Africa, Italy wanted to participate in the north and Germany in the center and the south. Though the Hohenzollern Empire was the last to enter the race for colonial conquests, it was eminently successful, annexing important islands in the Pacific as well and obtaining its outpost on the Chinese coast. Penetration into the tottering Chinese Empire was another rather new feature of European colonialism which seriously contributed to the critical situation in the Far East at the turn of the nineteenth century and to the rivalries of the colonial powers, old and new.

The unexpected fact that the Japanese Empire succeeded in opposing such a European penetration and in winning victories not only over the Chinese and Koreans but also over Russia must not obscure the equally important fact that the Tsarist Empire, too, was all the time one of the colonial powers which placed large non-European areas under the rule of the white race. Having started by colonizing some of the most backward and underdeveloped Asiatic lands, the Russians extended their rule in the nineteenth century over Caucasian and central Asian countries which had their own old cultures and proud historical traditions, and therefore belonged to the category of conquered peoples which particularly resented European conquest. Strangely enough, the Asiatic part of the Russian Empire was soon to have a higher percentage of Great Russian population than the European part,[1] another significant fact which is connected with the exceptional situation of a colonial expansion contiguous with the home country, not separated from her, as in all other cases, by seas and oceans.

Russia's major responsibility for the partition of Asia into European colonies and spheres of influence of European powers clearly proves that colonialism was far from being an exclusively western movement. While the Russians had less racial prejudices than most of the western peoples, especially the Anglo-Saxon and German, their policy of Russification was as ruthless in Asia as in Europe. Furthermore, there were western countries, including some of the great powers past or present, like Sweden and Austria, which did not participate at all in the movement and even in the nineteenth century did not succumb to the temptations of colonial imperialism. That the Habsburg monarchy through its alliance with Germany became at least indirectly involved in the world-wide competition of the latter with the other colonial powers, is, of course, another question.

It is a separate question, too, which of these powers had harsher or milder methods in dealing with the native populations. In the case of the Negroes, whose treatment was in most cases particularly cruel,[2] the connection between modern colonial exploitation and the much older and even more inhuman slave trade would have to be taken into consideration. And it would be difficult to determine who suffered more from colonial rule: primitive tribes without political experience which were treated without any regard, or peoples with their own cultural traditions whose normal, historical evolution was interrupted. It would be superfluous to enlarge upon evils of colonialism which are now universally recognized. But simply because this is frequently done with one-sided exaggeration, historical objectivity requires some consideration of the other side of the picture also.

Such an approach would require a careful examination, in each individual case, of the conditions in which the populations of the European colonies had been living before the arrival of their new masters. If development of freedom and respect for human dignity are considered the decisive criteria as they ought to be, and if the Europeans are rightly blamed for having violated their own principles in these matters in dealing with the natives, the question arises whether the former masters of the given area had a better record and had made their subjects happier. It is certainly easier to accept injury from one's own kin than from foreign conquerors, but a comparison between European rule and the kind of government that rule replaced would rarely be to the unqualified advantage of the latter. It also must be remembered that in some cases the natives had been under foreign rule even before European interference and conquest. Returning to the particularly shocking case of the Negroes, it should not be overlooked that their troubles, including the horrors of slave trade, started not with European but with Arab invasions.

In that connection it is perhaps even more important to recall that the peoples of Asia suffered cruelly from the claim for world predominance made by one of them, the Mongols, long before any European colonialism could possibly reach them. This came at a time when Europeans had to defend themselves, not always successfully, against Mongol conquest. Similarly, in more recent times, parts of Asia and Africa suffered, along with parts of Europe, from Turkish imperialism. The empire of Genghis Khan and his successors, as well as the Ottoman Empire, had extensions which can be called colonies like the European conquests of later centuries.

Another comparison is equally instructive. It has been pointed out[3] that at the start of Europe's expansion at the beginning of the sixteenth century, there appeared in central Asia a conqueror, Babur, who one hundred years after his famous ancester Tamerlane, established with more lasting success such a vast empire that his initiative could have resulted in permanent contacts between parts of the world which had been living in isolation from each other. There is, of course, the great difference that in Babur's case such prospects were only a remote possibility which did not come true, while the European discoveries and their result, European colonialism, did achieve at its climax the lasting establishment of a network of relations among all continents and all cultures, whatever their stage of development was.

This was certainly no mean achievement. It did not mean that "one world" came into existence at once, but it opened the door to such prospects for the future. In spite of—or even because of—all the tensions among the parts of the world, which for the first time were in regular contact with each other, there could begin at last the making and the writing of a real, truly universal world history. From the point of view of Europe's millennium this means that a thousand years of development of the European community, which had been wrongly inclined to identify its history with that of the world at large, resulted in a European predominance in the world which even though temporary would lead to a world-wide community of all mankind at the threshold of the next millennium.

Such a development was in agreement with the genuine character of Christendom. Wrongly again, but for understandable reasons, this had been identified with Europe.[4] It also was in agreement with the ecumenical aspirations of the old Graeco-Roman world and with its humanistic ideas, both of which had been only noble dreams when Christ was born and now, at last, after two thousand years, found a chance of realization. It would, of course, be preposterous to say that the opening of such possibilities had been the conscious goal of European explorers or colonizers of the globe. But even as an unexpected by-product of the colonial process, such a result must be taken into consideration if the judgment of that process is to be objective.

That same objectivity makes the historian admit that the first steps toward world unity, made at a time when even European unity was far from being achieved, were not at all unqualified blessings either for the world as a whole or for Europe. For a world still torn by rivalries, hostilities and mutual distrust, the growing interdependence of all its constituent parts made it more difficult than ever before to localize any conflict. For Europe, which conducted its colonization not as a cooperative enterprise but in violent competition, it was a danger to expose the disagreement among Europeans to all the other races which were supposed to be controlled by one of them, pretending to be superior. But for that very reason there was scarcely any danger that the supremacy of a divided Europe would last in the disgraceful form of colonial imperialism. The question whether anything would be left of it depended on those positive features of colonialism which must not be obscured by the negative ones. These latter are, with good reason, held against the Europeans and trouble their conscience.

Which of these features prevailed is as difficult to determine in the study of European colonialism outside Europe as it is in the controversial interpretations of colonizations by individual nations within Europe. The German colonization in eastern European countries would be an example of the latter.[5] In both cases the spread of Christianity and the achievements of western culture were all too frequently used as mere pretexts to cover political and economic interests. Yet, in both cases high values of a religious and cultural character, spiritual and material, were brought to the colonized lands and peoples. The ambivalence of the whole process appears particularly confusing when the additional question is asked whether these peoples really wanted and needed those new values which to them did not seem superior to their own traditional beliefs and practices. The opinion of a convinced Christian and of a proud heir of Graeco-Roman civilization will always differ in that respect from that of an equally devoted follower of another religion and of an equally proud member of another civilized society, and even from the feelings of an underdeveloped group.

Nevertheless, when the case for and against colonialism is stated, it should not be overlooked that missionary activities, which were greatly facilitated by the colonial expansion of Europe, deserve unqualified praise, even if the problem is approached from an undogmatic viewpoint. In sharp contrast with the harsh treatment which the natives only too frequently received from those representing Europe's military and economic power, the missionaries of all the Christian denominations brought to them a message of love which the practice of charity in relations with them made particularly convincing. Just as the missionaries who came to the western hemisphere with the first European conquerors tried to mitigate their cruelties, and those who worked in China in the seventeenth century went as far as possible in respecting the local traditions,[6] so later, when colonialism reached its climax, the peaceful preachers of the Gospel who had nothing in common with national ambitions except the competition in fulfilling their spiritual task, brought to the whole world the most uncontroversial and attractive features of a civilization based upon Europe's Christian heritage.[7]

It is only fair to add that European laymen, who, without directly participating in the spread of the Christian doctrine, followed Christ's supreme commandment of love without any distinction of creed or race, made possible those constructive achievements in the field of health and welfare which ought to be stressed whenever and wherever the record of colonialism is evaluated. European doctors working unselfishly for the natives of foreign lands at the risk of their own lives[8] have no counterpart in non-Europeans who would do the same for the sick and the poor, who, after all, are not lacking in the western countries either. Thus European expansion was promoting not only world unity but also human solidarity.

Less general, indeed, were the gains which that same expansion brought in the field of education, with conditions varying greatly in different colonies. Everywhere, however, the cultural isolation which for centuries had prevented so many highly gifted peoples from participating in the intellectual progress typical for the European community was ended. And here again the private initatives of the Christian missions with their schools of all kinds and at all levels must receive special credit.

There were other colonial activities which were much less disinterested but no less advantageous for the native populations. It was, of course, in the interest of the colonial power itself that its administration in the overseas possessions have "as one of its principal aims the enforcement of order and peace." But in the numerous cases where no such order and peace had existed before the arrival of the Europeans they contributed to better conditions of life. When in our time they departed, there followed, in many cases, a period of chaos and sometimes of bloody struggles among hostile peoples which had been united under colonial rule. The accusation raised in such cases that the Europeans had not sufficiently prepared these peoples for full independence is at the same time an admission that such a preparation had been needed. On the other hand, when the natives were prepared to follow the European example in the field in which they could not possibly have a similar experience of their own, "colonialism invited its own doom."[9]

That statement requires, of course, some comment. It has nothing to do with the religious, social, and educational influences coming from

Europe, which did not involve any danger for either side and could continue to progress without any political control by European powers. But the political impact of European ideas, a natural consequence of the colonial system not always profitable to the natives, would eventually always turn against their conquerors. The idea of nationalism is typical in that respect, because suffering from European nationalism, the colonized peoples, just as had happened in the relations between various ethnic groups in Europe, developed their own nationalism. And this became even more radical and violent, directed not only against those responsible for the unquestionable evils of colonialism, but against Europeans in general.

Furthermore, the peoples under colonial rule became acquainted not only with European ideas in politics, but also with the ways and means of realizing them and reaching political goals. It can be said that colonialism made its own doom unavoidable, chiefly because those who suffered from it learned at the same time how to fight the enemy with his own weapons. This was a natural consequence of the fact that the various colonial administrations, rarely sufficiently interested in the spread of Christian and European culture and of its spiritual values, were spreading instead the knowledge of western technology, including military techniques—they were using the natives for activities which could not be carried out without such a practical knowledge.

How that would turn against Europeans in the event of resistance and revolt against colonial rule was never clearly foreseen until it was too late. There was, however, at least one case in which an extra-European power, strong enough to avoid any colonial penetration, succeeded in obtaining such practical advantages without giving up its cultural tradition and way of life in a fully independent state. This was the case of Japan, which was recognized as one of the great powers of the world— along with the six European ones and the United States of America— at a time when European colonalism was otherwise supreme in all continents. Japan's old rival in the Far East, the much larger Chinese Empire, was too weak to oppose efficiently European political influence in spite of the high level of its culture and of its great power tradition. The establishment of the settlements of almost all colonial powers of Europe on Chinese soil, even if only in the form of temporary concessions, was the clearest evidence that colonialism had really reached a climax at the turn of the nineteenth century, since not even the revolt of the Boxers succeeded in expelling the western foreigners from one of the world's oldest and largest empires. But this is just one more reason to ask whether so-called colonialism with all its shortcomings was really the main reason for the world-wide supremacy which Europe seemed to have definitely reached.

Here we must consider that by the end of the nineteenth century the great powers of Europe already had to share that supremacy with powers which were not, strictly speaking, European, while not all states which were recognized as great powers on the European Continent were at the same time world powers.

As to the first of these two qualifications, it is significant that there appeared in Russia at the turn of the century[10] an interpretation of her historical destiny which even more than that of the anti-western Slavophiles placed the Russian Empire outside Europe and elevated it to a world in itself: a Eurasia which was neither European nor Asiatic but a link or an intermediary area between the two continents, with a claim to supremacy over both of them. At the same time the United States of America, geographically quite outside Europe, followed her example in acquiring through the Spanish War outlying possessions not only in the western hemisphere but also in the Far East. These efforts made that country which originally had revolted against European colonalism another colonial power. Finally, Japan, which had nothing in common with Europe at all, started a colonial expansion not only at the expense of other Asiatic nations but also in the islands of the Pacific.

Of the strictly European powers, Austria-Hungary continued to abstain from any participation in overseas colonial expansion, while Italy, though claiming her share in the colonial division of the world, faced great difficulties in that respect. She was far from attaining the position of a world power similar to that of Britain, France, and Germany, the latter an ambitious newcomer in the rise of colonialism.

The conclusion is clear: the rise of colonialism cannot be simply identified with European supremacy in the world, a supremacy which was challenged and limited by non-European colonial powers. The strongest European power, Great Britain, was already wisely starting the process of transforming parts of her colonial empire, the only one which was really world-wide, into self-governing dominions freely associated with the home country.[11] In spite of that process, which began as early as 1867 in Canada and proved most astonishing in South Africa,[12] where it developed soon after the Boer War, the place of the British Empire, soon to be called a Commonwealth, was a leading one all over the globe and the most striking example of European supremacy in the world. This evolution, completed only in our days, was in the best European tradition, respecting as it did the idea of freedom which old-fashioned colonialism had so badly disregarded, not without serious British responsibilities.

The British case is instructive also for another reason. The outstanding position of an old European nation, significantly enough not a Continental one, was indeed part of European supremacy in the world, but this had nothing to do with a supremacy of the European community as a whole. As a result of her imperial expansion Britain entered into much closer ties with non-European countries which she was leading to nationhood than with the nations of the European Continent which only too frequently were her rivals if not her enemies. Britain's European background, the priceless historical heritage which she continued to share with the whole Continent, made her now share a supremacy of the Europeans which was not necessarily nor even primarily a product of colonialism. It could even be said that the successes of colonialism were only a by-product of more important factors of European supremacy.

One of these factors, certainly not the most attractive one, was the tremendous material power, both strictly military and technological, which some of the European nations had accumulated, particularly in the last century. Since there was no chance for substantial conquests on European soil, these nations, partly in compensation for losses suffered there, were trying to satisfy their ambitions overseas. The case of Japan shows best that a similar development of a non-European nation would lead to the same consequences, the only difference being that the Japanese would make their main conquests in Asia.

Fortunately, there was also a different, much more gratifying factor of European supremacy: the progress of European culture which continued through the whole millennium and reached a climax in the nineteenth century. European culture had always been truly superior to that of so many primitive peoples who unavoidably experienced that superiority by coming in contact with the European. In certain respects, western culture, as it was usually called, became superior to that of other, even older civilized societies. In both cases it was regrettable that cultural superiority was used or rather misused for colonial conquests in connection with the power factor. Even without such conquests and economic exploitations, the spiritual values which Europe represented could have given her a world supremacy which would have been more constructive and much more acceptable to non-Europeans than a control by power politics. And most important, it would have lasted longer.[13]

This leads to the crucial question regarding the causes of the collapse of the supremacy of Europe at the end of her millennium. The evils of colonialism, inviting a violent reaction instead of peaceful cooperation, were only one of these causes. Three others had their roots in Europe herself. One resulted from the fact that some of the great powers violated the right to free and independent development, not only of the peoples in overseas colonies, but of many smaller European nations as well. A second was of a different character: it was the lack of balance between material and spiritual progress which can be traced back to the scientific and industrial revolutions of earlier times, but which reached a climax in the last phase of Europe's millennium. However, the direct cause of the final crisis was the failure to achieve even in that last phase the long overdue organization of the European community in a truly Christian spirit. This could have prevented the wars and revolutions that started in Europe and destroyed her leading position in the world.

CHAPTER XXVIII

The Crisis of Self-Determination inside Europe

IT WAS CERTAINLY REGRETTABLE and must be considered the main evil of colonialism that some European powers disregarded the right of self-determination of the native populations of so many non-European countries. But it ought not to be forgotten that at the same time national self-determination was denied to many millions of Europeans also, a situation which was in sharp contrast with the self-determination then already successfully achieved by the European colonists in most of the western hemisphere. The limitation of national freedom in nineteenth-century Europe was also in contrast with the progress of civic liberties in most European states during the same period. Furthermore, the desire for national independence and sometimes even that for free cultural development was repressed just at a time when national consciousness was progressing everywhere in Europe.[1] In the history of freedom, of that basic idea of the European tradition, inherent in both the Christian and humanistic heritage of Europe, these were indeed dark pages, rather unexpected at the end of Europe's millennium, a period which was so proud of all the progress achieved in the latest centuries.

However, this disappointing situation is not too difficult to explain. It resulted from two developments which were typical of these so-called modern centuries though these all had precedents even in the earlier ones. The first of them which clearly appears to the student of inter-national relations was the predominance of great powers which had little if any respect for the rights of the smaller nations. The other reason, which rarely receives sufficient attention in the usual, realistic interpretation of history, was the growing disregard of moral principles in the conduct of international affairs. In both respects the nineteenth century was far from making any progress.

It is true that the heritage of the age of Enlightenment did not make such progress easier. In the political field the partitions of Poland were a rather embarrassing part of that heritage and a lasting challenge to the idea of self-determination, silenced but not at all eliminated in the later part of the century. The Congress of Vienna had been equally embarrassed by German and Italian claims for self-determination,[2] but these claims received satisfaction through unification in a national body politic half a century later. There remained the serious problem of an Italian *irredenta* in Austria, and the new German Empire included even in its western part dissatisfied minorities after the annexations of Schleswig and particularly of Alsace-Lorraine. However, the violations of the right of self-determination in western Europe cannot be compared, except in the case of Ireland, with the almost general denial of that right in the eastern part of the Continent.

This is a statement which requires far-reaching qualifications, since the situations in the four empires which controlled that part were entirely different. The Ottoman Empire started disintegrating at the very beginning of the century, and on the eve of the Great War which ended the whole period had already lost almost all its European possessions. The national states of the Balkan area, in which the long submerged nations of southeastern Europe regained their freedom and independence, represented an apparent triumph of self-determination[3]—apparent only, because the great powers, after contributing to the liberation of the Christian peoples of the peninsula, continued to interfere with their difficult problems. The troubles which resulted from such a situation were soon used, and still are used, as an argument against national self-determination. The loose talk about a threatening "Balkanization" of Europe by the creation of "new" small states was and is not only unfair to the Balkan nations—some of the oldest of Europe—but an obstacle to any unprejudiced approach to the claims for self-determination in the region north of the Balkans.

For the historian of that region the case of the neighboring Habsburg Monarchy is by far the most instructive. It is with good reason that the historians of the new Austria, almost completely reduced to German-speaking lands, recommend an international cooperation in the study of the multinational Danubian empire which remained one of the great powers until World War I. They emphasize, of course, the importance of the period after 1867, when an interesting, truly unique experiment was made to meet half-way the claims of the ten non-German nationalities of the monarchy without giving up its unity.[4]

The problem is exceptionally instructive, because with each of those nationalities and even with German Austrians the degree of self-determination claimed, as well as the very character of the claim, varied in the course of the century which preceded the fall of the empire. In order to understand the constructive reforms of 1867 and their application, it is necessary to study their background not only from the Congress of Vienna and the proclamation of the Austrian Empire in 1804, but from the origin of each of the ethnic groups, gradually united under Habsburg rule, and of Austria herself. Here again an approach considering the millennium of Europe and of her constituent parts can be helpful. Even those nationalities of Austria-Hungary which misleadingly were called "unhistoric," like the most neglected Slovaks and Slovenes, the Ruthenians and the Serbs, were looking back to historical memories of the tenth or even the ninth century, which remained their inspiration and their living past.[5]

This does not mean that their national revival in the nineteenth century would lead at once to claims for political independence. What they resented, along with the "historic" peoples of the monarchy who had lost their independence at various, well remembered dates, was the refusal of a status of equality with the predominant Germans, who constituted only one fourth of the population but enjoyed political and cultural, economic and social superiority. In the Metternich and in the Bach era, separated only by the "Spring of the Nations" in the abortive revolution of 1848, the centralizing policy of the absolute government favored such predominance for reasons similar to those which had already appeared under Maria Theresa and particularly under Joseph II. The German liberals who, as in 1848, claimed democratic reforms, did not want to include concessions to what they considered a disruptive nationalism of the non-German peoples.

Strangely enough, the German Austrians, though in general the strongest supporters of the unity of the monarchy, were themselves divided regarding the twofold interpretation of Austria's millenary tradition. Practically all of them wanted unity to be based upon a continued German predominance, but there was a significant difference between those who considered themselves an integral part of one German nation and the outpost of the German empire in the Danubian area, and those who took into consideration the long evolution which had made the "eastern march" part of another, multinational empire. The latter were Austrians first, conscious of Austria's specific historical mission and determined to build up their own future within the limits of the Habsburg monarchy, in cultural relations but not in political connection with the other Germans. The former belonged to those ethnic groups which were included only partially in Austria's frontiers, while their majority was living in other states.

Such a distinction is much more important than that between historic nationalities to which the Germans obviously belonged, and peoples to whom that character was rather arbitrarily denied.[6] Only nationalities which were as a whole within the boundaries of the Habsburg Empire could receive a complete and lasting satisfaction of their claims through constitutional reforms. For the others there could not be found any such solution, because they were constantly concerned with the fate of their kin outside these boundaries. In addition, there was a sometimes decisive difference between such divided nationalities, for which the part connected with Austria was in a better situation than the other one, subject to a much more oppressive foreign rule, and others who had independent national states right across the frontier. To make the problem even more involved for the historian, changes inside and outside the Habsburg monarchy were affecting the position and attitude of each individual group. Thus, for example, Serbian and Rumanian nationalism had better chances under the Habsburgs than under the Turks, but as soon as most of these two peoples enjoyed full self-determination after being liberated from Ottoman rule, the situation was reversed and the parts of them which remained in the monarchy were looking towards their national kingdoms—a position similar to that of the Austrian Italians after the unification of Italy.

At the same time, however, the Austrian reforms of the 1860's made the situation of the Galician Poles incomparably better than that of the Poles under Russian or Prussian rule, just as the Ukrainians were much happier under the Habsburgs than under the Tsars. Both were, therefore, ready to support the monarchy, but without giving up their ultimate goal of national unity in an independent state. When after 1866 no parts of Austria were any longer included in the German Confederation, the internal reform of the Habsburg Empire could be carried out before the Hohenzollern Empire was even founded. The solution of 1867 certainly represented progress if compared with the conditions which prevailed after the Congress of Vienna and after the defeat of the revolutionary movements of 1848–1849. But the change was far from satisfying for all the hopes which had been raised in those years and full self-determination—a term not yet used at that time—was not granted to any of the monarchy's nationalities.

In the dualistic system which was established then and lasted until the dissolution of the monarchy, two of these nationalities came very near to that goal. Nearest came the German Austrians, because only very few of them, the Pangermanists, regretted not being included in the new German Empire, and because a close alliance was soon to be concluded between that empire and the old one of the Habsburgs. It is true that the German Austrians now had to share their predominance with the Hungarians, who without reaching complete independence received a status of full equality with Austria for their historic kingdom. They had never been in a more favorable situation since the catastrophe of Mohács. The supplementary compromise, concluded with Croatia in the subsequent year, recognized the state right of another even older kingdom, but restored also its old union with Hungary. This union, even less than in the past, was not based upon equality so that it would be hardly possible to speak of Croatian self-determination.

Though concessions were made at the same time to the other nationalities, in the Hungarian half of the monarchy even the law of 1868, recognizing the rights of their languages, was never strictly respected. In the other half a similar, much more basic recognition, though combined with a large autonomy of the various provinces—historical but rarely ethnic units—disappointed the hopes for the establishment of a real federation. This would have been the only satisfactory substitute for national self-determination. In most cases there were not yet any claims for separation from the monarchy and for independence. The fact that the state rights of the lands of the crown of the St. Václav did not receive recognition like those of the lands of the crown of St. Stephen was resented, though, as well as the fact that the southern Slavs, in spite of a growing feeling of community, were divided among so many administrative units of Austria and Hungary.

The latter problem with its implications of a trialistic reorganization of the whole political body became even more urgent and difficult to solve when Bosnia and Herzegovina were added to the two constituent parts of the monarchy, first through occupation and later through annexation. This explains why the internal nationalities' problems of the Habsburg Empire and the possibilities of their peaceful solution cannot be properly understood without studying at the same time the foreign policy of Austria-Hungary.[7] Her extension in the Balkans, a kind of compensation for her losses in Italy, was not only opposed by a considerable part of the peoples concerned but also by her old Russian rival. For this reason the monarchy had to rely more and more on the German alliance, popular among the Austrian Germans and accepted by the Hungarians as a check of the rising Slavic influence, but contrary to the desires of the other nationalities, including the otherwise rather well satisfied Poles.

Any further concessions to them and to the Slavic nationalities in general were a stumbling block in the relations with the Hohenzollern Empire, so hostile to its Polish subjects. They also hampered relations with Russia, which, though pretending to be the protector of all the other Slavs, did not want them to be satisfied with the Habsburg rule, for Austro-Slavism, according to its Russian interpretation, was regarded as a dangerous rival of Panslavism. This was well realized by Austro-Hungarian diplomacy whenever it wanted to appease Russia, and was used as an excuse for trying to preserve the predominantly German character of the monarchy.[8] At the same time the unnecessary entanglements with international controversies which resulted from the Triple Alliance diverted the attention of Austria-Hungary's political leaders from the most important internal reforms.

Nevertheless the plans for such reforms, which were to implement and improve the solution of 1867, were never given up, in spite of the additional difficulties which resulted from the rivalries and conflicts among the various non-German nationalities and from the uncompromising attitude of the Magyars toward the other peoples of Hungary. In spite of the recurrent governmental crises in both halves of the monarchy, substantial progress was being achieved at least in the Austrian part, though the easy-going ways in dealing with the nationalities problem could not lead to the badly needed reconstruction on federalist grounds, to the formation of what was called by some ambitious planners "The United States of Greater Austria,"[9] which would have been a valuable contribution to a better political organization of Europe as a whole.

Appearing at the end of Europe's millennium in the very center of the Continent, such schemes could even be compared with the vision of a like organization which raised high expectations at the beginning of that millennium around the year 1000. But there is, of course, a striking contrast between the two Catholic emperors who seemed to have a chance for establishing a truly supranational empire, larger or smaller, as a cornerstone for a Europe respecting the rights of all her peoples: between the inspiring Otto III who died too young and the austere Francis Joseph I who was already too old when he tried to adapt the imperial traditions of the past to a new democratic age. Furthermore, there was a prerequisite condition for not only the basic reform but for the very survival of the Habsburg monarchy: the preservation of peace.[10] When, therefore, at the end of an otherwise successful reign some military and diplomatic leaders of the monarchy assumed a heavy share of responsibility for the outbreak of a war that was impossible to localize, they not only sealed the doom of their country but destroyed the opportunity for an evolutionary solution of the problem of self-determination in central Europe. No progress could be made in the field of constitutional reform in the midst of an exhausting war which revealed the irreconcilable aims of the nationalities of Austria-Hungary. When the last Emperor, Charles I, who had good intentions but neither the experience nor the authority of his predecessor, issued his federal declaration of October 1918, it was definitely too little and too late.

However, notwithstanding that ultimate failure, there is a deep contrast between the attitude of Austria-Hungary and that of the other two empires which disappeared at the end of Europe's millennium, as far as the vital problem of national self-determination is concerned. The second Reich of the Hohenzollern, which even more than the first one appeared to all other nations as representative of German imperialism, simply rejected all the claims of its non-German minorities, especially those of the Poles in the eastern provinces of Prussia, the kingdom which practically dominated the empire. That empire itself was supposed to dominate a *Mitteleuropa*[11] in which even the Austrian ally could expect only a secondary place and none of the non-German peoples would be able to determine their future in freedom and independence. But the central Europe controlled by Berlin did not materialize either in times of peace nor as a war aim. The German Empire itself, powerful as it was politically and economically, had no chance of including more non-Germans than those who threatened its national unity during the short period of its existence.

Different and no less instructive than the Austrian case was that of

Russia, which deserved to be called, as the Habsburg monarchy wrongly was, a prison for many nations waiting for a chance of self-determination. The last traces of local autonomy, which replaced to a certain extent a full-fledged federalism in Austria, disappeared in the Russian Empire with the repression of the Polish insurrections of 1830 and 1863, and with the violation of the constitutional rights of Finland, where no revolt had ever taken place, at the end of the century. The claims of those two nations were fairly well known in the West but failed to receive any support. They were eventually recognized as internal questions of Russia. It was hardly realized in Europe that in the Tsarist Empire the Russians, though their percentage was almost twice as high as that of the Germans in the Danubian monarchy, did not constitute an absolute majority, except if the Ukrainians and Byelorussians were included in their number along with the Great Russians.[12]

The national revival of the Ukrainians[13] was making steady progress in the nineteenth century, though the government denied their very existence as a separate nation. Their interpretation of the millennary tradition of the eastern Slavs raised the question whether they or the Muscovite Russians were the legitimate heirs of the old Kievan state, and therefore threatened the very foundations of that nationalism which with orthodoxy and autocracy was officially proclaimed one of the three pillars of the empire. Therefore, even without demanding separation from the empire for the whole territory which they considered their homeland—which would practically cut off Russia from the Black Sea—they constituted a disruptive element and suffered a determined repression even of their cultural development.

Among many of the other non-Russian nationalities this development was on a still rather low level, especially in the Asiatic part of the empire. But even in the European part their treatment was hardly better than that of the colonial peoples, especially since the racial variety among them and the comparatively small number of each of them made any resistance to Russification apparently hopeless. The situation was different only in the Caucasian region—where peoples with traditions as old as that of the Georgians[14] continued an opposition which had for a long time delayed the Russian conquest—and particularly in the Baltic provinces. Lithuania was not included in these provinces in view of her special historical background, and the national movement of the ethnic Lithuanians[15] was strongly repressed in order to maintain the fiction that the whole former Grand Duchy was an essentially Russian land.

But a similar movement was progressing among the closest kin of the Lithuanians: the Latvians of Livonia, and among the Estonians, their neighbors who had always shared the same fate. These peoples had never enjoyed free national statehood, and were now looking for inspiration to the prehistoric past.

Though not always clearly defined in their aspirations, all these national movements proved stronger than expected when the Russian revolution of 1905 gave them an opportunity to raise their claims.[16] That revolution had primarily a social and constitutional character, with the Russians themselves hoping to gain at last political freedom in their own state. Therefore the problem of the non-Russian nationalities rarely receives adequate attention in the study of that new "time of troubles" in Russian history which was to find its continuation in the two revolutions of 1917. However, even these much more violent revolutions cannot be properly understood without realizing that the earlier one, which the Tsarist government succeeded in repressing, had serious nationalistic implications that revealed one of the main weaknesses of the empire.

The trend toward self-determination among the non-Russians had its own weaknesses, which, in addition to the varying degrees of national consciousness, included, as in Austria-Hungary, tensions between the various peoples which were aggravated by the differences in their social structure. Thus in contrast to the Poles, the Lithuanians, Byelorussians, and Ukrainians were turning away from the tradition of the Commonwealth as it existed before the partitions, while in the Baltic provinces Latvians and Estonians were revolting against the German landowners no less than against the Russian administration. Therefore, the reaction which followed those limited concessions the government felt obliged to make to the revolutionary movements could easily check nationalistic aspirations. And when the system of elections to the Duma, the first parliamentary representation of all peoples of the empire, was drastically revised in favor of the conservative elements, the representation of the non-Russians was most severely restricted.[17]

Nevertheless, that first revolution which had been encouraged by Russia's defeat in the war against Japan should have been a warning to those in power that the Tsardom, even more than the Habsburg monarchy, should avoid another war, especially a European one. For the most developed nationalities in the European part of the empire along its exposed western border, such a war would open even better opportunities for claiming self-determination. Yet, it was the Russian Empire which shared with the two others the responsibility for the catastrophe of 1914.

The trend toward self-determination, which was steadily growing among the submerged nationalities of central and eastern Europe, was certainly not a direct cause of that catastrophe. The causes which turned the local conflict between Austria-Hungary and Serbia into a European and eventually a world war had little to do with the issues leading to that conflict and with the unsolved Yugoslav problem within the monarchy. These causes were the rivalries among the great powers and the lack of any international organization of the European state system. But one of the shortcomings of that system was beyond any doubt the lack of consideration which the claims of so many nations, deprived of independence and in most cases even of autonomy, received in the empires, controlled by the privileged nations looking down upon the others with a feeling of superiority.

The governments were aware of the danger which the dissatisfaction of so many of their heterogeneous subjects represented for the administration even in times of peace, but they strangely underestimated the possible rise of that danger in case of war, when it would threaten the continued existence of the great empires. The leaders of these empires blamed the nationalism of the stateless peoples but refused to recognize that the nationalism of those peoples which controlled the empire was an even greater challenge to peace and a permanent obstacle to the establishment of a just and durable European order.

There reappeared, therefore, in the last and decisive phase of Europe's millennium the crucial question which had troubled all the earlier periods of European history: the question of how to secure and to promote the real integration of the European community by giving equal opportunities to all its members. The solution of that question was particularly urgent at a time when all these members reached the full consciousness of their national character, even in cases where the practical continuity of their national development had been interrupted for centuries. But the question was more urgent than before for two additional reasons.

At a time when democracy was progressing in internal national life, at least in most European countries, it was inconsistent to reject democracy in international relations: the equality not only for all states, great and small, but the equal rights to self-determination of all peoples. That the determination of these rights required, more than in the past centuries, the creation of an international authority, was another question, inseparable from the basic one.

Furthermore, at a time when Europe had assumed worldwide responsibilities through her leading powers and had the ambition, if not to dominate, at least to organize, the whole globe, it was deeply disappointing to see that even the organization of Europe had not been achieved nor the elements of unity and diversity reconciled in her structure.

All these problems, though they might seem to be strictly political, could not be settled, as long experience should have taught, by political leaders and through political methods only. While European policies had always been highly controversial, Europe's real greatness remained based upon her Christian and humanistic heritage, which had made possible through all the ages of political turmoil the astonishing progress of European culture. That progress was particularly amazing at the end of Europe's millennium, but the question must be raised, even if only in connection with that of national self-determination—which in most cases began in a cultural vein—whether the cultural progress of the nineteenth century, on the eve of an unforeseen crisis, remained faithful to its twofold heritage. This heritage was typical of European civilization from its earliest origin and had been preserved through all the vicissitudes of the last thousand years, through all the earlier crises of the European conscience. The interpretation of the present one, inseparable from the political decline of Europe in the contemporary world, depends on the answer to that question.

CHAPTER XXIX

European Civilization at the Crossroads

W HILE THE EIGHTEENTH CENTURY ended amidst an unprecedented crisis of revolutions and wars, nothing similar was anticipated at the turn of the nineteenth. There was instead an awareness that something was going wrong with the apparently splendid development of European civilization, and the confusion, disappointment, and even fear of a whole generation found its expression in the loose talk about *fin de siècle* atmosphere.[1] It was perhaps the feeling that it was not only a century, like so many others in European history, that was coming to a close, but that the end of a whole millenary was approaching. For the dualisms of Europe's cultural heritage, which after a thousand years of preparation had troubled the European community through the centuries of its existence, had become more alarming than in any earlier period. Even within the limits of the hundred years from 1815 to 1914, there were so many conflicting fluctuations in European thought that they justified a feeling of alarm at the threshold of the twentieth century.

The rapid change in Europe's intellectual and moral climate in the course of the nineteenth century is best evidenced by the contrast between the realistic positivism of its later part and the idealistic romanticism which molded its first generation. Romanticism, which was much more than a literary trend opposed to classicism, is instructive for the study of the European community for at least two reasons. It was, first, one more proof of Europe's cultural unity in spite of all political divisions. Though not equally strong in all countries, the impact of romanticism was felt very definitely in parts of Europe as different and far away from each other as were England and Poland.[2] But even more significant for the last phase of Europe's millennium was another aspect of the romantic interlude in the history of the modern mind: the revival of the consciousness of uninterrupted continuity in Europe's development.

In the interpretation by the Enlightenment there had appeared, much more than in that by the Renaissance, a long interruption of that continuity in view of the "darkness" of the Middle Ages, which were supposed to separate the ancient and the modern world. The rehabilitation of the mediaeval tradition by Romanticism, uncritical as it was and leading sometimes to glorification, was a sound reaction against such an approach in so far as it restored to its rightful place an important period in the chain of Europe's evolution. In spite of all the exaggeration and mistakes which must be pointed out by the historian in the romantic interpretation of that period, he, more than anybody else, must at the same time be grateful for the trend. It contributed decisively to a better appreciation of historical tradition in general and therefore to the progress in the study of history, a good example of the unquestionable progress in the humanities and social sciences through the nineteenth century.

Such progress should not be overlooked under the impression of the more spectacular progress in the natural sciences and in technology which is considered typical of the nineteenth century and really reached a climax toward its turn. Progress in the field of the historical sciences which—not without the inspiration of Romanticism—started even earlier, was certainly less revolutionary. But independently of its value for specialists, it had far-reaching consequences for the European mind, a mind which always had an interest in history greater than that of other civilized societies. Both the Graeco-Roman and Christian traditions contributed to that interest which, however, for a long time lacked the scholarly precision and objectivity that is taken for granted today. Only as far as the so-called auxiliary sciences of history are concerned, can the progress in that direction be traced back to the seventeenth century, to the age of Mabillon and Montfaucon. It was not before the nineteenth century that in one European country after the other appeared historians who were not only great writers, like those of the age of Voltaire and Gibbon, but great scholars of perfect erudition and penetrating analysis—Ranke being usually given as an example of restless activity through more than half the century—and of universality of interest.[3]

Even Ranke, who wanted so much to find out "what really happened," was not entirely free from a special, well understandable sympathy for his own country and his own Church, as well as for the limited community of Germanic and Romance nations.[4] There was among all his contemporaries, indeed, in Germany and elsewhere, a rather dangerous trend toward idealization of the national past since the historian cannot remain as indifferent to the object of his study as can the chemist or the astronomer, as has been rightly pointed out in opposition to a statement by Taine.[5]

It is even more understandable that some of the most prominent historians, who belonged to nations deprived of political freedom, studied and described their past from the earliest origin with a view to recalling their bygone greatness, encouraging their efforts to regain independence and, if necessary, supporting their national revival. Scholars like Lelewel among the Poles, Palacky among the Czechs, or later Hrushevsky among the Ukrainians,[6] were at the same time political leaders, whose achievements in history-writing influenced the making of history.

It was only natural that their intepretations of the past, of the place of their respective countries in European history and therefore of that history in general, were frequently conflicting. But just for that reason their research and its presentation contributed to the joint effort of historians from all parts of Europe to arrive, though not without stimulating polemics, at a revision of one-sided pictures and thus to a clearer vision of the development of the whole European community.

However, in the midst of so many controversies this vision remained a rather distant goal, and what was called "historicism,"[7] i.e. a dedication to historical tradition and an emphasis of its importance for the present and even the future, proved misleading in many respects. A comprehensive synthesis rarely corresponded to an uncontroversial, truly scientific analysis of the facts, and the perfection of the method failed to result in a systematic philosophy of history. The interest in such a philosophy also increased much beyond the early beginnings in the eighteenth century. Attempts to satisfy it were made, not by professional historians but by philosophers. Even the most elaborate system of Hegel, which influenced European thought for a long time, hardly took into consideration the concrete findings of historical research, and rightly considering the problem of freedom basic for the interpretation of European and even of universal history, interpreted it quite arbitrarily. Hegel's involved interpretation of the historical process, which his Polish admirer Cieszkowski, one of the few philosophers who were also historians, tried in vain to Christianize,[8] did not exercise any widespread lasting influence. Nor can his strange conclusion glorifying the Prussian state be held responsible for the manifestations of extreme nationalism in later German historiography. It so happened, however, that some of Hegel's conceptions and methods were used or rather misused by an economist who wanted to be an authority in philosophy and history too. Through his writings—which could seem rather uninspiring—and even more through his followers, who considered him a political leader and almost a prophet, he succeeded in leaving a truly exceptional impact on European thought and action while many greater minds of his generation are today forgotten: Marx remained for the next one hundred years,[9] right to the end of Europe's millennium, a symbol of the revolutionary trends which brought to a climax all the successive crises of the European conscience, questioning and eventually rejecting the basic values of Europe's historical heritage.

The doctrine which replaced Hegel's pantheistic idealism by atheistic materialism was and is first of all a total rejection of the religious part of that heritage, not only of Christianity but of any religion, including the Judaism of its author's ancestry. Nor was it the dialectical method developed by Hegel which, strangely enough, had its roots in the Christian philosophy of the Middle Ages[10] that made the Marxist attack against religion so much more dangerous than similar materialistic conceptions of isolated, purely abstract philosophers of the nineteenth century. The weaknesses of dialectical materialism—the "Diamat"—have been exposed time and again, most convincingly by outstanding scholars of our generation.[11] But besides the theories of the "Diamat," which might seem almost metaphysical, Marxism includes the "Histomat," historical materialism, something truly new and original, the application of the philosophical theories to the study of history and, most important, to its dogmatically-taught and carefully-planned making.

The scientific falsehood and the practical danger of that philosophy of history, which is indeed more systematic and comprehensive than any other conceived in modern times, have not yet been realized either by the non-Marxist historians or by the political opponents of the movement which was launched by Marx. Some of the specific features of the

"Histomat," especially its emphasis on the problems of chronological periodization, are still dismissed as rather unimportant by the so-called bourgeois scholars, while other aspects continue to exercise upon them a frequently unconscious appeal.[12] A study of Europe's millennium would be most inadequate and deficient if it did not try to point out and to refute the main errors of the Marxist interpretation of history[13] which would result in a distorted picture if applied to any such study.

The picture would necessarily be as one-sided as the periodization which, according to historical materialism, must be used always and everywhere. It is a division based exclusively on the changes in production and therefore on economic criteria. In the days of Marx there was to a large extent a one-sided overemphasis of political, diplomatic and military history with a serious neglect of the social and, even more, the economic factors which were gaining more and more importance. But a revision of such an approach did not require a new philosophy of history. It was being made, as a matter of fact, by historians of very different schools, and, if it went to the opposite extreme, could only lead to another exaggerated treatment of one aspect of history alone, even in the treatment of periods when economics had not the same significance.

Even more arbitrary was the assumption, proclaimed as a scientific discovery of Marx, that in any history there must be a predetermined succession of the same phases of economic development, following the same dialectical pattern. That kind of prophecy, recalling the ancient one which predicted a succession of empires with the Roman as the last and final, included a similar conclusion: the thesis that the socialist phase, realizing the Marxist doctrine in practice, would be the end and climax of the historical process. Never was the question answered why the dialectical evolution would not continue, and an antithesis to socialism result in another synthesis, leading to a progress beyond that, which, according to Marx, socialism represented in comparison with capitalism.

Another objection remains unanswered in regard to this progress. Even if it is admitted that the criterion of social progress is the degree of exploitation of one class by another, an exploitation which is supposed to disappear completely in a classless society, there is no guarantee that in such a society all men, without exception, would not be subject to the particularly oppressive exploitation by the omnipotent state in what Marx himself calls the dictatorship of the proletariat. The prospect that eventually the state would wither away altogether is again nothing but a prophecy, wishful thinking without any scientific foundations.

Since there has to be a total abolition of individual freedom, pending the fulfillment of that prophecy, historical materialism destroys not only the Christian but also the humanistic basis of European civilization. Along with all other spiritual values, such ideas as liberty are reduced to the role of a superstructure, the only basis being the economic one, a complete reversal of the European tradition which stressed the primacy of the spiritual over the material.[14]

What is particularly dangerous in the Marxist antireligion—as dogmatic as any religion could be—is another conclusion of the uncritical belief in the unescapable dialectical process: the certainty of the victory of socialism in its materialistic interpretation, that is of communism, over the doomed capitalistic system, which is supposed to represent all that remains of the tradition of the past. How that victory will be achieved is not determined in all details, but it can be hastened only by a struggle between the still existing classes. This reveals the deepest difference between the Marxist and the non-Marxist, strictly speaking the Christian and the humanistic conception of social progress, since class hatred replaces both Christian charity—the love of neighbor, no matter to what class he belongs—and human solidarity in constructive cooperation.

There remains, however, a question which is decisive for the understanding of the last century of Europe's millennium and which logically arises from all the doubts suggested by any critical analysis of the Marxist doctrine. Why was this doctrine, which exercised such an unusual appeal from the outset, accepted by so many social scientists and by masses of people who were not even able to study the writings of Marx? Why did it lead to the creation of strong political parties and an extreme revolutionary movement which in our time seized power in the largest state of the world with a view to conquering all the others?

The amazing success of a program, which is in opposition to all that most of the Europeans believed in for so many centuries and which means the destruction of the traditional European culture, can be explained only by the specific object which Marx and his followers singled out for their attack. This was indeed the most questionable feature of the contemporary way of life in western society, something comparatively new which itself had very little to do with Europe's historical heritage and which was misleadingly but skillfully presented as the typical feature of the modern period: capitalism. That scapegoat of the Marxist challenge was and is nothing but an economic system of recent date. All those who suffered from it were ready to believe that it was the very essence of an outmoded heritage and the main source of all its short-comings. They became convinced that its destruction was a prerequisite condition for any social progress, so that it was worthwhile to sacrifice the whole set of values which apparently had become inseparable from capitalism, in order to make possible the coming of a golden age on earth as soon as possible.

It is only fair to admit that this practical identification of capitalism with all that is threatened by Marxism, was and is still being made by many of its opponents, as if all the highest values of European culture could be saved only through the preservation of that economic system. At the root of this stands the alarming fact that there was a growing ma-terialism in the otherwise brilliant nineteenth century, especially in its later part,[15] which, without the philosophical implications of Marxism and seeking an entirely different solution of the economic problems of the modern world, recognizes like the Marxists do, the primacy of these problems over the spiritual ones. Such an attitude of those who profit from capitalism helped and continues to help the Marxists to discredit both Christianity, which had not prevented the injustices of that system, and the idea of freedom, which has been defended in the name of unre-stricted economic liberty.

The great spiritual tradition of Europe was thus endangered from two sides by a clash of two economic conceptions, both of which were highly questionable and represented only temporary phases in the mil-lenary evolution of Europe and in the development of one field, by no means the most important. But something else was even more danger-ous. The exaggerated, if not decisive importance given by both sides to material values was to a large extent the result of a progress in technol-ogy which, though welcome in itself, was out of proportion to the much slower and less spectacular progress in other fields. The danger which had started with the scientific revolution of the seventeenth century and especially with the application of its results by the industrial revolution of the eighteenth, reached a climax in the nineteenth and twentieth cen-turies.[16]

The scientific discoveries which were made in the natural sciences, particularly in the fields of physics and chemistry, were now more revo-lutionary than ever before. In rapid succession they were leading to theories and applications which not only satisfied human pride, but gave man a feeling that he had at last dominated nature and was its master. This, however, was a dangerous illusion and a great exaggeration. Unfortunately, it so happened that exactly those manifestations of the power of nature which are most harmful to man proved impossible to control. Hurricanes, floods, and earthquakes continued to plague mankind just as in the past, and nothing could be done even with regard to weather and its impact on agriculture and on health.

Concerning the latter, there was indeed a most gratifying progress in the field of medicine which reduced mortality and human suffering. But medical knowledge and skill remained powerless in the struggle against some of the most terrifying diseases, and it was a special tragedy that discoveries of great scientists, of generous men and women who hoped to be of practical service to health, would eventually lead to consequences which are disastrous for our generation and those to come. Right at the end of Europe's millennium the power to use and to misuse atomic and nuclear energy has cast a shadow on human life in Europe and in the whole world. The end of any security on earth and the possibility of self-destruction of the human race place a truly terrifying responsibility on the admired scientists, which cannot be compensated by the vague prospects of a conquest of outer space and of travels as far as the moon and the planets.[17]

Earlier and uncontroversial improvements in the conditions of daily life and in the various means of communication which the scientific and technical efforts of the western mind have achieved, proved indeed of service to all, and made them, if not better, at least more comfortable. They were, however, achieved at a heavy price which points again at the overestimation of material values, and at the lack of social justice. Besides the shocking contrast between rich and poor countries, even in the richest ones to which those of the major part of Europe and of her transatlantic extension undoubtedly belong, the old contrast between rich and poor individuals and of their respective shares in the amenities and facilities of life is far from being removed. To come back to Marx, his protest against human exploitation, not only in colonial areas but in the leading European countries, was well justified by the situation of the urban proletariat which resulted from an industrialization that outpaced any reform in the conditions of the workers.

The European conscience, confused by the tensions of a machine age which considered more or less dark all ages of the past and questioned all their moral laws, was slow to realize that only a return to those laws, and a respect for them, could save the European heritage from destruction by both the violence of its opponents and the failures of its defenders.

In that vital matter the humanistic tradition inherited from the Graeco-Roman antiquity could be of little help. Its cultivation, which was promoted by the study of the humanities, certainly contributed to a better appreciation of lasting spiritual values. But the progress of these studies, considerable as it was in the nineteenth century, could not possibly touch the masses of the people. And even as far as the intellectuals were concerned, this progress was threatened by a growing trend to limit education in the classics to the advantage of subjects which were considered of more practical use. Furthermore, the moral principles of the ancient world were too vague and inconsistent to satisfy the needs of our entirely different age and thus could only confirm the social scientists in their conviction that ethics were relative both in time and in space.

There remained only the Christian heritage of Europe which could oppose a coherent system of doctrine and morals, the same for all periods of history and for all peoples, to that of Marxism. It could also be opposed to the sceptical relativism of schools of thought which at the end of Europe's millennium were creating in the minds of the intellectual leaders a confusion similar to that in the ancient world two thousand years before.

Christianity entered the nineteenth century in rather critical conditions resulting from the developments of the preceding two hundred years, from the anti-religious attitude of the French Revolution, and from the humiliations of the Papacy by Napoleon. The split into various denominations seemed irreparable and among non-Catholics the impact of state authority and the turn toward the most arbitrary interpretations of the faith were in steady progress. This dark picture changed, however, in the course of the century and particularly toward its end.

In its earlier part, the vindication of the Middle Ages by Romanticism included, of course, a higher appreciation of the traditions of the Christian Commonwealth, but it was too superficial and emotional to be of general, lasting significance. Later the uncritical interpretations of scientific theories and hypotheses, especially those regarding evolution which went far beyond Darwin's own ideas, were another challenge to Christianity. But just as in the sixteenth century, when the disagreements among the religious reformers had strengthened the position of

Catholicism, so in the later nineteenth and early twentieth century there was a turn toward the old Christian ideas, evidenced by the disappointing contradictions among the most outstanding scientists, their inability to answer basic questions of life, and last but not least, the gradual admission that there was an element of relativity and uncertainty in the new scientific conceptions which were supposed to replace religion.

The best evidence of that change favorable to Christianity in general and especially to the Catholic Church, the uncompromising guardian of a tradition of two thousand years, was the rise of papal authority which started during the pontificate of Pius IX, the longest in history.[18] The high hopes raised even among liberals in the early days of that pontificate did not come true. As far as the political role of the pope was concerned, it ended in apparent defeat, when the unification of Italy, achieved not under his leadership but against him, did away with the Papal States after more than a thousand years of existence. But the courage of the Holy See in not accepting that defeat and in making the Vatican an internationally recognized symbol of political independence even without any territorial basis outside its gates, commanded universal respect. And though the first Vatican Council, the twentieth in the history of the Church after the longest interruption in the series of those assemblies, could not complete its work because of the political situation in Italy and in Europe, its proclamation of papal infallibility, criticized by all small oppositions and by practically all the non-Catholic, solved at last an age-old problem and gave to the Catholics a haven of certainty in matters of faith and morals at a time when everything in Europe and in the world was getting uncertain.

Furthermore, there was scarcely ever before an uninterrupted series of popes similar to that from Pius IX to the end of Europe's millennium, whose personal holiness of life and constructive achievements were recognized in all Christendom and gained the respect even of non-Christians. Leo XIII[19] was the first to see the two most urgent needs of his time: the revival of Christian culture and scholarship, and above all social justice. His encyclical *Rerum novarum,* recalled and developed by his successors, was positive evidence that there was a solution of the problems pointed out by Marx in a spirit and through methods entirely different from his. The wise diplomacy of Leo XIII,[20] equal to that of the greatest popes of past ages, took into consideration everything that in the present age could be reconciled with a Christian tradition adapted to new forms of government.

It was made quite clear by Pius X that no compromise with modern trends in the essentials of doctrine was possible. The first pope to be canonized after Pius V answered the challenges of the new age by deepening and sublimating religious life and inspiring it by his own example. Less interested in politics than his predecessor, he was equally aware of the necessity of international peace in a time of spiritual crisis troubling Europe and the world. He died under the shock of the outbreak of a war whose consequences were only too easy to foresee from the moral viewpoint.

It was not the fault of the Church that the papal teachings in social matters and their approach to international relations did not receive sufficient consideration even by Catholics. Both were, however, a revival of the ideas which the Christian Commonwealth had once tried to realize in the interest of the European community. It was the most eloquent appeal to apply Christian principles in social and international life at a time when new dangers appeared in both spheres and were requesting new solutions. All these dangers were tremendously increased in the following years of wars and revolutions, to such an extent that the very existence of the European community and of its culture was at stake after a thousand years of development, which in spite of all imperfections was an outstanding contribution to the progress of mankind. And nobody was more anxious or better qualified to save these high values than the successor of Peter, who from his Roman See watched those tragic events, deeply concerned with the future of Europe, now inseparable from that of the whole world.

CHAPTER XXX

The European Wars and Revolutions of the Twentieth Century

T HE EUROPEAN COMMUNITY, whose millennium is now commemorated, emerged in the later part of the tenth century out of the chaos and trouble of its first half. The major part of the twentieth century, now behind us, has been for Europe a time of even greater trouble and suffering than that which tormented her a thousand years ago. Today, at the end of her millennium, no end of that crisis is yet in sight.

When in the years shortly before 1914 Europe was at the crossroads of her destiny, the situation was not yet hopeless. Atheistic materialism, the greatest danger in the sphere of the spirit, had not yet seized power in any country, not even in the most industrialized ones, and the strongest spiritual force defending Europe's heritage, Christianity, was definitely revitalized. In spite of so many unsolved political problems, nobody expected that the armaments race would lead to a major war in which the weapons accumulated by the great powers would really be used.

However, that was precisely what happened, with all the consequences which Pius X had foreseen on his deathbed, and which made his four successors, different in character but equal in greatness, consider the re-establishment of a real peace, based on justice and charity, the foremost requirement of Europe and of the world.[1] Three of those popes of peace have died, disappointed in that crucial matter. The present pope is repeating their warnings, which after the Second World War are even more urgent than during and after the first one, especially since the totalitarian revolution—its ominous by-product, which was defeated in two countries—triumphed in that largest nation where it started, and hopes to conquer Europe and the world for Marxism in its most extreme communist form.

The origins of the great crisis, which has persisted for more than half a century, with a controversially interpreted interruption of hardly twenty years of precarious peace, have been studied many times in detail, beginning with the question of responsibility for the outbreak of World War I. What seems much more important and constructive is a clear distinction between the consequences of all the wars and revolutions which since 1914 have particularly affected Europe. Only one of these consequences needs no elaboration: the horrible destruction achieved by warfare which became more and more cruel and painful for the civilian populations as technology, especially in the air force, made progress. Under such conditions it is rather surprising that European civilization, whose end was predicted even at the time of the first great war, survived the much greater ordeal of the second one. This gratifying proof of Europe's vitality can, however, lead to the dangerous illusion that, after all, Europe and mankind can also survive a third one in the atomic age.

The outbreak of World War I had one immediate consequence, unexpected by those responsible for the catastrophe, which is extremely instructive for the understanding of European history. Quite independently of the issues which led to the war, there reappeared problems which definitely seemed to belong to the past, but had an immediate influence on the war aims of all the powers in conflict. During the Balkan wars, the prelude to the great one, the continuity of Europe's historical tradition became evident where it had seemed to be most violently interrupted. Dreams of restoring the Greek Empire, which had fallen in 1453, or even the first Bulgarian Empire of the tenth century, of revenge for the defeat of the Serbs at Kossovo in 1389 or for Albania's hardships after the glorious days of Skanderbeg in the later fifteenth century—all such echoes of bygone ages were evidence that the liberation of those peoples, though reviving their ancient rivalries, was no artificial innovation but a rebirth of a millenary past. During the European War of 1914 to 1918 that process was gradually extended from the Balkan through the Danubian to the Baltic region. First to regain its European significance was the Polish question, in direct consequence of the break between the partitioning powers. And one after the other all the claims for self-determination came into the open in the multinational empires.

It was chiefly because of the entrance into the war of a disinterested power, the United States of America, which took that principle seriously, that most of them received satisfaction in the peace settlement.[2]

From the outset United States policy did not favor the disintegration of either the Austro-Hungarian or the Russian Empire,[3] but preferred autonomous developments within their boundaries. In the case of the Habsburg monarchy, its dissolution was soon regretted by many who were alarmed by the emergence in its place of competing successor states. The application of the principle of national self-determination proved more difficult than expected, but if the long-submerged peoples were no longer satisfied with any solution short of full independence, it was because they had been exposed by their masters to all the sufferings of a war, and in the Russian case, of a Bolshevik revolution, for which they were not responsible. If in consequence of the successive defeats of Russia and of the central powers all of these peoples, except the Ukrainians and the Byelorussians forced into the Soviet Union, reached their goal in a belt of larger or smaller states extending from Greece to Finland, this was not something altogether new but a return to traditions which had never been forgotten and to a diversity which corresponded to the old distinctive feature of European history.

There appeared at the same time two trends which could have made it a diversity in unity in the best European tradition. One of them, of local origin, was the idea of regional "ententes," possibly leading to real federations.[4] Unfortunately, neither the Little Entente in the Danubian area nor the Baltic and the Balkan ones in the adjacent areas north and south of it were comprehensive enough nor had the necessary time to develop. The other trend, world-wide in scope but particularly important for Europe, appeared as the most important consequence of America's decisive intervention in the war, but was doomed to failure with America's withdrawal into isolationism: this was the idea of a long overdue international organization for peace and cooperation. Yet, the League of Nations, in spite of its shortcomings and its neglect in the policies of the great powers of Europe, was an achievement of the peace settlement after World War I which even after World War II—a war which the League was unable to prevent—could not be disregarded, a great experiment which had to be tried again by those who wanted to do better than the severely criticized peacemakers of 1919.

These peacemakers had to face a consequence of the war which unfortunately, and contrary to confused wishful thinking, was to be the most lasting one and to appear in all its seriousness when the peace settlement collapsed. That consequence, which preceded by one year the armistice of 1918, was the emergence of the first truly totalitarian power in European history.

It was no accident that such a power came into existence in Russia. While the United States, one of two outsiders whose shifting policies so strongly influenced Europe's destiny was geographically quite extra-European but European through its spiritual heritage,[5] the other one, Russia, while geographically European in her original part, had lost much of that heritage, particularly the dedication to the idea of freedom, through Asiatic influence. In spite of her apparently progressing westernization, she was turning into a separate Eurasian world. Even ideas imported from the European West, as Marxism obviously was, had better chances of being accepted in Russia, in whatever way they differed from the European tradition, and to be developed to their extreme consequences, when combined with specifically Russian features. One of these features was a long experience of despotism, the other one a drive toward unlimited expansion with messianistic implications, more Asiatic than European.[6] Such a background proved more important than the degree of industrialization, so that contrary to the expectations of Marx himself his doctrine was first put into practice, not in the most but in the least industrialized country of Europe.

That country and its peoples had the most disappointing and painful wartime experiences, and this was another reason why a movement which seemed to put an immediate end to the war could attract the masses independently from any purely economic motives. Communism had one more chance, thanks to the despair of those who had suffered too much under the former regime and had no patience to wait for the success of the democratic interlude between Tsardom and Bolshevism. Fascinated by truly maximalistic promises, they were prepared to accept another form of despotism, especially since those who were most violently opposed to such a revolution did not offer any real freedom either. Therefore, the horrors of a civil war right after the international one ended in the bloody victory of the Bolsheviks, and the hesitating attempts of western intervention in favor of the other side,[7] faithful to the alliance with the West, ended in total failure and Russian resentment.

The danger which the strange alliance between international communism and Russian imperialism represented for Europe was fully realized only by the non-Russian peoples who, hardly liberated from Tsarist oppression, had to face the danger of a reconquest by Soviet Russia. For total reconquest, the Red army, the first military force put at the disposal of Marxism by a great power, was not yet strong enough because of the recent defeat in the war with Germany and because of the civil war. But of all the border states only Poland was strong enough to oppose the advance of the new Russia against the West, an advance which started immediately after the armistice on the western front in November 1918 and did not stop until August 1920 at the gates of Warsaw, truly the gates to Europe.[8]

In the decisive battle which saved Poland, the other liberated nations of East Central Europe, and Europe as a whole, rightly called the miracle on the Vistula, the Poles received no assistance,[9] because the West too was exhausted after the great war and even more so because Europe was far from being spiritually united. At the Left there were strange illusions that Communism was perhaps just another form of democracy, contributing to social progress, and that the new Russia could be integrated with Europe better than the Tsarist one. As a reaction against communist influence, there was at the extreme Right an inclination to use another totalitarianism in the struggle against Red totalitarianism with just a different color as its symbol.

Trends of that kind, which soon appeared in various European countries, are usually put together under the common designation of Fascism. As a matter of fact, Fascism, in the specific form which that movement took in Italy, was less extreme than those which preceded it in Russia and followed it in Germany. Though opposed to the idea of freedom, so dear to all Europeans and particularly to the Italians, Fascism tried to avoid an open break with Europe's Christian heritage and even stressed the ancient, Graeco-Roman one. The Roman heritage, nearest to the Italians, was claimed with unprecedented emphasis, but it was claimed as that of the Roman Empire, with its whole program of imperial expansion and conquest inside and outside Europe. At the same time there was an apparent reconciliation between the Rome of Caesar, which was supposed to be restored, and the Rome of Peter, the Papal State being restored too, though limited to the City of the Vatican. But the same Pope Pius XI who accepted that agreement remained strongly opposed to the Fascist ideology, which he never hesitated to denounce, and was deeply worried by the rapprochement between Fascism and the German form of totalitarianism.

That form, called National Socialism, was a challenge to Europe's Christian and humanistic heritage, as violent as was Communism and as ruthless in its methods. One of its most repulsive features was a biological racism, leading to cruel persecution of the Jews. Hostile to any religion, Nazism, best known under this abbreviated name, shared with Fascism an aggressive nationalism which had deeper roots in the German than in the Italian tradition. While not all Italians felt, like the Fascists did, that their country had not received its due after victory in the great war, practically all Germans resented the Versailles Treaty imposed on them after their defeat, and approved its denunciation by the National Socialists. The revisionism which at first pretended that Germany wanted only a peaceful change became an open threat to European peace after the establishment of the totalitarian dictatorship in Germany and her rapid remilitarization. The year 1933 is therefore a much more important turning point in Europe's interwar history than the economic crisis of the preceding years.

Now, with totalitarianism established in three great countries of the Continent there was a growing danger that the peace so painfully gained after World War I would be troubled again. At the same time, the failure of the disarmament conference in Geneva, where Russia and Germany's request for immediate total disarmament had made the project for limitation and gradual reduction of armaments futile, was a decisive blow to the authority of the League of Nations, which in the 1920's had still inspired serious hopes. But the League now depended on the opportunistic policies of the three dictatorships. The promising progress in the field of international organization was doomed, and so were the plans for creating within the universal league a closer union among the European countries, where such an organization had been an urgent need throughout the thousand years of the existence of the European community.

Strangely enough, both western dictatorships claimed to continue and to revive great historical traditions of European unity inspired by imperial ideas. In Italy, the memory of her leading role in the Roman Empire took the nation back almost two thousand years. In Germany, it was proudly predicted that after the first German Empire which, founded almost a thousand years before, had disappeared in 1806, and after the shortlived second one of the Hohenzollern, the Third Reich created by National Socialism would last another thousand years.[10] This was definitely a millennium idea with its threefold implications: commemoration of what happened ten centuries before, continuity of a conception, and anticipation of a glorious future of equal length. But it was at the same time a distortion of the imperial conception, its negative, aggressive aspect intensified, while its constructive traditions were replaced by a "new order" in Europe which was a total negation of her heritage.

It was, however, in the name of the traditions of the first German Empire, that Austria was incorporated with the third one, losing her identity, her own imperial tradition, and her own idea of a special mission in the Danubian area. And so was the inclusion of Bohemia and Moravia, again with a change for the worse if compared with historical memories, since these two mutilated lands were made not a privileged member of the Reich as the old Bohemian Kingdom had been, but its "protectorate" in a deeply humiliating position.

Once these initial successes had been achieved without using armed forces, the new Greater Germany provoked another European war in order to attain the most extreme goals of the old empire, including predominance in Europe. But there were very great differences in the methods of imperial conquest.[11] The conquests outside the territory of the Holy Roman Empire started with that of Poland, as envisaged by emperors of a remote past, but with a view to totally liquidating not only Polish independence but also culture, and turning the persecuted country into a wilderness. Furthermore, this was attempted in a cooperation with the new Soviet Russia, starting with another—the fifth—partition of Poland, but including a partition of all East Central Europe and, for the time being, a joint predominance of the two totalitarian powers in war-torn Europe as a whole.

Without recalling the frequently told story of the collapse of one European country after the other and of the break between the two dictators —that gloomy parody of the Napoleonic Wars—it will suffice again to concentrate on the consequences of the second great European war of the twentieth century. One consequence was similar to what had happened in the first of these wars: it turned from a European into a world war, clear evidence that European history was becoming inseparable from that of all the other parts of the world, and that Europe's predominance in the world, after reaching its climax in the preceding century, was collapsing as were the individual nations of the Continent. Similar, too, but infinitely worse was the destruction of a much larger part of Europe by far more inhuman methods of warfare and occupation. The struggle was similarly decided by the entrance into the war of the United States of America, an indispensable intervention coming from outside Europe.

This time that intervention and assistance in the defeat of a much more dangerous Germany than that of the Hohenzollern came in a much earlier phase of the war. Yet, it came too late. For a half year earlier, Soviet Russia, the latest victim of German aggression, had thus unwillingly become an ally of those powers who were fighting in defense of Europe's freedom against totalitarian tyranny. Soviet Russia was an ally that was equally dangerous to that freedom, an ally that represented a form of tyranny as evil as the common enemy, an ally which was not only extra-European but anti-European.

It was, therefore, the final and decisive consequence of the most horrible war that Europe had experienced in a thousand years, that the peace settlement was an unexpected "defeat in victory"[12] not only for Poland, but for all those who wanted to save Europe's heritage in a free world. That defeat was, as a matter of fact, more than unexpected: it was not even recognized as such in the midst of an enthusiastic relief that the ordeal of war was over.

The same feeling of relief, which prevented mankind from realizing that the war had been ended earlier than expected at the price of the tragedy of Hiroshima and Nagasaki—a tragedy not only for the victims, but for the future of the world—also prevented the realization that the end of the war was a tragedy for Europe, at least for a large part of the Continent. This could happen only because those who were unfairly critical of the peace settlement of 1919 were satisfied in 1945 with no peace settlement at all. The most important issues had been decided when the fighting was not yet over and was expected to continue for quite some time, in the days of a conference, which more than those at the end of August 1939 deserve to be called the last days of Europe.

Before Yalta it still might seem that Europe's liberation from Nazi tyranny, promised in the Atlantic Charter of 1941 and by February 1945 actually certain, would be a return to the great tradition of freedom for all under God, shared by Europe and America. Unfortunately, the conclusion not only of the war but of Europe's millennium was entirely different: there was no vision similar to that of the year 1000, but an attempt to control all "liberated" nations, allies and enemies alike, by three great powers which were to teach them "democracy," even though one of these powers was a communist dictatorship. Two leaders wanted a fair application of the joint "declaration," but one of them came to Yalta as a sick man who died two months later, and the other one, in spite of his knowledge of Europe's great past, failed to oppose the totalitarian partner who wanted to destroy it.

Looking at the tragedy from the viewpoint of Europe's millennium, it would be a mistake to elaborate again on the fate of Poland, considered

a test case and discussed at Yalta more than any other individual problem; it was certainly not out of respect for historical tradition that at
the end of her millennium she received frontiers similar to those she had
at its start. Again, a partition of Poland, the sixth, a poorly disguised subjugation of the whole country by Moscow, influenced the situation of
all East Central Europe, where all nations which had been independent
between the two wars, except for Finland and Greece, shared her fate
through a communist seizure of power.[13] Thus the Soviet Empire
pushed back the frontiers of free Europe as far as they had been at the
time of Charlemagne.

It took ten years before even Austria's freedom was restored, almost
unexpectedly, thanks to an exceptional concession of the Soviet Union.
This happened after an equally unexpected change in the position of
Yugoslavia, another allied country sacrificed at Yalta, which succeeded
in making itself practically independent from Moscow though remaining under communist rule. The historian could be tempted to compare
the present position of Yugoslavia with the role which old Illyricum, the
territory occupied by the southern Slavs more than a thousand years
ago, played as a link and at the same time an object of endless disputes
between Europe's West and East. However, he sees at once the essential
difference between the East of these remote centuries—which was no less
European than the West—and the present one, which has been cut off
from Europe as were the eastern Slavs after their conquest by the
Mongols.

There is some comfort in the fact that none of the nations, which,
after two decades of real independence between the two world wars,
have been made dependent on Moscow in one way or another, has lost
its identity as a separate political body. Even the three unfortunate Baltic
states, which now are included in the Soviet Union just like Byelorussia
and the Ukraine, are constituent republics of the Union under their own
names. But even the "People's republics," which were permitted to remain outside the Union of Soviet Socialist Republics, are subject to Russian control, not only in their foreign relations where that control is
complete, but also in their internal government, which is gradually
sovietized. Their position in Europe—to which they still belong formally
—has been completely reversed: after having been outposts of the West
against the Asiatic or semi-Asiatic East throughout the millennium, they
now have to serve that Eurasian East in its new form, as outposts against
the West.

Even those western powers which participated in the Yalta agreement failed to secure any real victory after the unconditional surrender of the common enemies, despite the heavy price of their concessions to Soviet Russia. The United States of America, indeed, emerged from its second intervention in European as well as Asiatic affairs as the world's strongest power, but power did not give to the American people, who had not desired it at all, any real happiness, nor even a continued feeling of security as they had known it earlier, after the Civil War. In order to defend their own country and the freedom of so many others, the Americans had to enter an armaments race contrary to their tradition and to the desire of their Founding Fathers to avoid entanglements in the affairs of the old world. And as for Britain, in spite of the courage of her people in "their finest hour," far from making any gains comparable to those of Russia, she has not averted, as her war leader had hoped, the liquidation of her empire. As merely one of the members of a Commonwealth which is no longer called British but has become instead a very loose association admitting secession, the United Kingdom is no longer a great power in the traditional meaning of the word.

The same must be said of France, whose predominance on the Continent Britain so wrongly feared after World War I. After the costly colonial wars which followed her tragedy in World War II, France, following the British example, hoped to save her overseas empire at least as a *Communauté,* but she did not succeed. All that she gained in Europe was a reconciliation with Germany after a millenary rivalry. Under the present conditions this means only that she is no stronger than the enemy, which recovered so rapidly after a much worse defeat than in 1918. It is paradoxical that Germany, though limited to her western part, most nearly approaches a great-power position, which her Italian ally has so rapidly lost. But the Federal Republic, too, is no longer what the successive German empires have been before.

The artificial partition of Germany to the obvious disadvantage of the western powers, and the even more artificial division of a Berlin placed in the middle of the Russian zone of occupation, which created an insolvable problem, was one more concession made to the Soviet Union at Yalta. It was made in the interest of peace but, as a matter of fact, made impossible the conclusion of any peace treaty with Germany. The result was, and still is today, seventeen years after "victory," a situation which is "neither war nor peace," a phenomenon not appearing for the first time in Russian history. It preceded the first open aggression of

Muscovite Russia against her western neighbor, in 1492, for a dozen years. It was an experiment which did not succeed for the Soviets before the signature of the Brest Litovsk treaty of 1918.[14] In our days a similar method is part of the "cold war," whose ideological implications, the most dangerous aspect, have not yet received sufficient attention.[15]

The excuse for all the unilateral concessions made before the open outbreak of that strange, still undecided war, was the hope of peaceful cooperation with the Soviet Union in the United Nations organization, that return to the League of Nations idea. The UN, which avoided a name Soviet Russia disliked, was the only constructive consequence of the horrifying experience of World War II. It was the only chance of avoiding World War III, of avoiding the "balance of terror" which replaced the old balance of power as soon as the Soviet Union also had at its disposal the atomic and the hydrogen bombs. In spite of all the well-known disappointments with the United Nations, this organization remains the only instrument for saving the precarious peace of our time. But its very composition is one more evidence that there is no longer any European predominance in the world, but a completely reversed situation.

In conclusion, it might seem that the millennium of a Europe, which has been rightly called "tragic,"[16] is ending in a crisis which is world-wide. But it affects Europe in particular, reminding her historian of the chaotic situation of the tenth century when that millenium started. However, looking back to that remote age of so much confusion and well-justified alarm, the historian finds an almost unexpected reason for looking forward to a better future, by no means a certainty, as the Marxists would make their followers believe, but at least a possibility. History does not repeat itself, but if it proved possible for the last generation of the tenth century to find a solution to the crisis of its time, it is equally possible for the last generation of the twentieth century to achieve a similar success, although the road to follow seems terribly obscure at the present moment.

There is, however, a prerequisite condition. In order to regain an honorable, though certainly not predominant place in the world and to contribute to its salvation, Europe must remain faithful to her heritage and enter the next millennium in the spirit in which the European community came into existence, and with the determination to face new responsibilities and to avoid the mistakes which followed.

At the Threshold of the Next Millennium

CHAPTER XXXI

Toward a United Europe

Two meanings of any millennium—the first, which takes us back into a remote past, and the second, which through a realization of uninterrupted continuity connects that past with the present—obviously open rewarding fields of historical research. It might seem that, on the contrary, historical science has nothing to do with the third meaning, which is merely a speculation about the future, often of a mystical character.

Nevertheless, without donning a prophet's robe, the historian can make scholarly contributions to a better understanding of that last meaning in each specific case, and particularly in the case of the millennium of Europe. He can at least analyze the state of mind which is typical for the end of any millennium. In the case of Europe there are interesting analogies between the end of the tenth and the twentieth centuries. In both of these transition periods from one millennium to another there were, as we know from old history and from contemporary experience, both fears and hopes, suggesting important conclusions as to the experiences of the vanishing millennium and the possibilities of the next.

Fears are much more justified today than they were before the year 1000. This time they are not based, as they were then, on erroneous interpretations of the Holy Scriptures, but on the concrete fact that man, though far from having mastered nature for constructive purposes, has gained the power of putting an end, if not to the world, at least to human history. This means, if not an end in terror, at least terror without end.

Such horrifying perspectives are one more reason for exploring, against the historical background, the hopes which fortunately accompany such fears, just as they did, perhaps more vaguely, a thousand years ago. They cause us to ask what can be done about such dangers. The Europeans have a special reason for doing so, not only because the present crisis originated in Europe, at a time of European predominance in the world, and not even because some Europeans bear a heavy responsibility in that matter, but particularly because it was the European mind whose scientific discoveries and technological inventions have led to such disastrous consequences.

Beginning, therefore, at home, the historians of Europe have first of all to point out again the original mistake, repeated time and again, that the founders and leaders of the European community failed to organize and to unite it for purposes of peace and cooperation. They have to recall that even when that task became so obviously urgent after World War I, all such initiatives, whether they came from private men inspired by a truly crusading spirit or from statesmen who wanted to declare not war but peace,[1] were dismissed by the politicians as utopian dreams, just as in the past.

This time there was an additional obstacle to the realization of the idea of European unity. The rising totalitarian powers either ridiculed that idea or tried to realize it themselves in their own way, which would have resulted in a tragic parody. Fortunately, Nazism has failed to do so and Communism has not yet succeeded, but such ideologies have badly delayed and still are delaying any sound solution of the problem.

After another warning experience the great idea, practically as old as European history, has been taken up with new vigor in the last seventeen years, so that its partial realization already has its history and is being studied by many specialists.[2] They all would agree that the contemporary movement for European integration is developing in the right direction and that it was wise to start it step by step. But the historian considering Europe's millennium must be particularly impressed by the fact that the first of these steps, the creation of a united Europe out of six nations only, the small nucleus composed of France, Italy, West Germany, Belgium, Netherlands, and Luxemburg—the last three more closely united under the name Benelux—corresponds almost exactly to the limited Europe of Charlemagne. If it should be a matter of regret that there is such a regression of more than eleven centuries, or if it should rather suggest a comforting analogy, since the preparatory steps taken at the beginning of the ninth century were followed at the end of the tenth by an integration of Europe which territorially was almost complete—this is a question which no historian can decide.

In any case, the present Europe of the Six is the most concrete object of study for those who hope that it will lead to a more comprehensive unification. It must be noted first that the most satisfactory achievements of this initial group have been made in the economic field. This is quite understandable since in that field the needs of postwar reconstruction were most urgent and the common interests most evident. For similar reasons the example given in that respect attracted the other European countries. The same is true of the obvious necessity to join for a better protection against the common danger of communist aggression.

However, the historical European community was and is much more than a community of coal and steel, a common market, and a community of defense. Even in these fields, particularly in the last one, political problems were to appear, especially since the causes of international unrest and inadequate security were and are so far from being exclusively economic or military. On the other hand, it was precisely in these fields that even a much larger Europe than one of six or fourteen countries could not stand alone, so that the larger issue of American assistance and of the cooperation of the non-European members of the Commonwealth was involved, a question which has to be considered separately. For Europe as such and for her position in the world two other fields were of decisive significance.

The political one remained the most intimately connected with the former, but at the same time it was by far the more delicate. Political were and are the reasons which cause individual European nations to join the movement toward unity or to stay outside in one or more respects. There are still fears, similar to those of the past—though they seem rather secondary if compared with the great general fears of our time—that too much unification will result in the creation, if not of a new "empire"—the name hardly matters—at least of a new kind of supernational authority, possibly with the "predominance," as on much earlier occasions, of one nation over the others. It was in opposition to any such real or illusionary dangers that the claim for a Europe which, in spite of the unavoidable unifying measures, would remain a *Europe des patries* has been raised and has alarmed the leaders of the integration movement.[3]

Once more, as in earlier discussions of nationalism which now seem antiquated, much depends on the interpretation of the terms which are used. Patriotism, in so far as it is the special dedication to one's nation and its tradition, must not be an obstacle to the creation of a larger political body in which, as in federations of the past, various nations would be included; to a return to the unifying ideas which inspired the Christian Commonwealth and the surviving conceptions of a Christian or "great republic" in Europe. Such a well-balanced patriotism can serve as a sound basis for a simultaneous dedication to a larger whole, according to the old truly European principle of diversity in unity. Only if patriotism turns into chauvinism with a refusal to any limitation of exclusive national sovereignty in favor of the common good does it cease to be a constructive force. Then, it makes it impossible to strengthen European unity through common institutions.

Such organs, necessary even for the development of economic cooperation, must include, as far as politics are concerned, a common representation of the various peoples in addition to their national parliaments. Only then will democratic methods prevail, not only in internal affairs but also in international relations, making European unity not an abstract theory nor a scheme in which only the governments are interested, but a direct concern of the people with a strong influence of public opinion. If it is tested within the limits of a European community, the members of which are best prepared for such a development, similar methods will be easier to apply in any universal, world-wide organization, promoting peace and cooperation in all fields.

There remains, last but not least, another field in which the unification of Europe, if well conceived, would serve as an inspiring example. The European community, especially in the period of its greatness, was always primarily a cultural community.[4] Without a special effort to develop that common cultural heritage, neither economic nor political integration will have a solid and lasting base. It is here that it will prove easiest to reconcile the requirements of both diversity and unity, because in contrast to the development of economic or political power, the cultural progress of each individual nation contributes to the progress of all those which are united in the same effort. But once more, in the wake of the experiences of the last two or three centuries and especially of our own time of crisis, a distinction must be made between technical progress, even if it results from the application of pure science, and spiritual progress, stimulated by the humanities, the letters and arts. We know by now how the most admirable achievements of the former can be abused in the service of power-politics and can lead to a dangerous competition, as dangerous as that in economics and politics. It is true that even the so-called moral and social sciences, including history, as well as literary production can be misused by extreme nationalism and have in the past poisoned the relations between so many European nations. But much progress in that respect has been made already and is easier to achieve because no material interests are involved.[5]

At the same time this is a problem of education, first of all on the highest, academic level, where again Europe has a great tradition that goes back to the origin of her oldest universities. There was a time when even these institutions were in many European countries hotbeds of nationalism in the worst sense, and in that respect the centuries proudly called "modern" were a period of regression. But in the decades between the two great wars a significant improvement began, except under the totalitarian regimes. Today there are promising beginnings of an education in the best spirit of European unity, paying due respect to the variety of national tradition. In the thirteen years of its existence, the College of Europe, founded in Bruges, has become the most instructive example of such successful efforts, and projects for establishing one or more European universities of a supranational character in other equally appropriate centers deserve all encouragement.

Such prospects of a progressive unification of Europe, covering all the various spheres of human life, are today unquestionable, stimulating possibilities which, in contrast to equally justified fears, cause Europe's millennium to approach its end not without hopes for a better future. However, that optimistic approach requires two very serious qualifications, which oblige us to look at the other side or rather the *two* other sides of the picture, both equally dark.

If it is true that achievements of even a small Europe—which unites only a very few nations—are attracting the others, it is equally true that many of these others are afraid and unable to move in that direction and to join the emerging free community. Even among countries which are free from Soviet Russia's control and communist rule, there are some[6] who because of their closeness to the Soviet bloc and their commitments to strict neutrality would not dare to enter a European organization which by its very existence is a challenge to Moscow's determination to dominate the world, including all of Europe. It is hardly necessary to emphasize how regrettable it is that any participation in the integration of Europe is absolutely impossible in the political and extremely difficult in the economic field for nations like Finland or Austria, and even a somewhat safer Sweden, whose contributions would be so very desirable and without whom the unification of Europe cannot be considered complete.

They can, of course, to a large extent participate in cultural cooperation with their western neighbors, and this is one more reason why that field is so unusually important today. And to a certain extent such cultural contacts with the free part of Europe are now possible even for nations which are behind the so-called "iron curtain"—an expression which not only for that reason is rather misleading—and which are forced to cooperate, in the cultural field no less than in the others, with the peoples of the Soviet Union first of all.

However, it would be a great illusion to believe that such contacts with the free world—even in the case of a country like Poland[7] which can today establish them more easily than the others—are steps in the direction of their liberation and of their integration with the united Europe that is now in formation. If the Soviet government so strongly resents any reference to the "captive" nations of eastern Europe, it is simply because that adjective corresponds strictly to the truth. They are captive, because they are under totalitarian communist regimes, under the dictatorship of a party which represents only a very small minority of the population and has to follow Moscow's orders not only as to the orientation of the country's foreign policy but also as to the degree of "liberalization" which is permissible at the given moment in each of these submerged countries.

How deeply their life, even spiritually and intellectually, is affected by such a captive situation can be readily observed on the occasion of meetings of their representatives with those of the free countries in discussions on problems of the humanities and social sciences. Far from being free to express their views and thus to contribute to objective research and progress in these fields, in the spirit of the common heritage of all Europeans, they have either to support the orthodox Marxist interpretations or at best to remain silent on controversial issues. The international congresses of historical sciences, in which delegates of the captive nations were permitted to participate only after the adherence of the Soviet Union to that organization, offer a particularly instructive example.[8]

Even more important are the restrictions on freedom in religious life, not an open, violent persecution like the early years of the Bolshevik revolution, except in individual cases, but a relentless, continuous struggle against all religions and especially against Europe's Christian heritage.

The Catholic Church, which is considered particularly dangerous, the main force of spiritual resistance in the captive countries, was rightly called a Church of Silence by Pope Pius XII in his description of its situation in that part of Europe. Only in Poland, where the Catholic tradition is stronger than elsewhere, has that silence been courageously broken on many occasions, particularly after the momentous events of late 1956.

That date must be recalled even in the briefest survey of the postwar fate of East Central Europe, because it proved a decisive turning point as far as the hopes for a real liberation of that part of the Continent are concerned. The unrest which then broke out in the two most important captive countries was indeed the last occasion to assist them in their fight for freedom, a fight which in Hungary took the form of a desperate armed uprising that waited in vain for western intervention.[9] The Poles avoided the tragic ordeal of the Hungarians by trying to obtain concessions from Moscow through pressure exercised by communist leaders who apparently put the vital interests of their nation first. And temporary concessions were made indeed, because the Soviet Union was not prepared to crush two revolutions at one time. But when the opportunity of supporting both movements, different in method as they were, was missed by the West, it became obvious that all that could be expected was a policy of containing Soviet Russia and international Communism within the limits reached in consequence of the Yalta decisions.

To react to these consequences which cut Europe in two would have been comparatively easy immediately after the war, in the years when the intolerable situation created by those decisions became evident in one after the other of the sacrificed East European countries and when the Soviet Union had not yet attained a power comparable to that of the United States. Why nothing was done by the West, either then or in 1956, that is one more question which can be answered only by considering the whole historical background.

It is one of many tragedies of the ten centuries of European history that has to be evoked in this connection: that the West was never sufficiently interested in Europe's eastern areas, which wanted so much to be recognized as an equal and integral part of the European community. Even colonial expansion outside Europe seemed more desirable to the original members of that community than the participation of the younger peoples of eastern Europe in the development of a heritage which those nations so enthusiastically accepted, so frequently defended against the non-European or semi-European East, and enriched on so many occasions within the limits of their possibilities. Western interest in these nations, which seemed to grow at the end of, and after World War I, and which seemed to reappear at the beginning of World War II, disappeared in the course of that war as soon as Soviet Russia was welcomed as a more powerful ally, and even more at its end when continued cooperation with that ally was considered of permanent importance and obtainable at the price of sacrificing once more the peoples between Germany and Russia.

At the end of Europe's millennium, which began when these peoples completed the constitution of an all-inclusive European community, the long-delayed unification of that community is ironically proceeding without them. And neither of them receives the attention which is given, very rightly indeed, to the people of West Berlin. Half of a city, which is recognized as being truly western, seems more important than whole nations with populations of many millions, whose records in the historical development of Europe have never been recognized as significant.

It is, however, only fair to admit that if even the defense of the freedom of West Berlin is now not easy to assure by peaceful means and involves a serious risk of war, the liberation of the nations of East Central Europe is simply impossible in the present conditions without a war which most certainly would be a nuclear war involving all Europe and probably the world. This is well realized by the peoples of these unhappy countries. While under the first shock of disappointment and despair, when they came from domination by one totalitarian power to domination by another, many of them were looking for another war which would at last restore their freedom, they now fear any new war which even in case of a total western victory would first bring them total destruction.

This brings us to the second reason why the hopes inspired by the prospects of a united Europe are unfortunately rather uncertain, even if only western Europe is considered. There is something unreal in all efforts for European integration, as long as the peace of Europe is not really assured. In the present conditions and amidst an armaments race of unprecedented scope and character, a war, a nuclear one at that, can break out not only because of the situation in eastern Europe or because of the question of Berlin and German unification, but for reasons impossible to foresee, in view of the general tension in international relations and of the unexpected crises following each other in all parts of the world.[10] Even if the catastrophe would result from events in faraway regions whose names were until recently unknown to most Europeans, they would be among the first to suffer, because all of Europe, including its western part, would be turned into a battlefield and face total destruction.

The worst, from the European point of view, is that even the complete success of Europe's unification, achieved before the outbreak of a Third World War, would be unable either to prevent such an outbreak or to assure Europe's defense in such a war. This does not mean that a wise, well-coordinated policy of the free European countries cannot contribute very efficiently to prevent a conflict which would mean the end of European civilization, without any prospects of another millennium comparable to the first. But even such a contribution by an at least partly united Europe to plans for disarmament and for establishing in the world a rule of law could not be decisive. The success would depend on two conditions which would have to be met at the threshold of a new millennium if the hopes for a better future are to prevail over the fears of a final collapse.

One of these conditions is the continued and much closer cooperation between a united Europe, comparatively small in area and even in population—if the globe is, as it now must be, considered as a whole—and that new Europe which in the later part of her millennium was founded on the other side of the Atlantic. Such a cooperation was always desirable, but it is particularly urgent today since it would serve as compensation for the losses, even if only temporary, of the old European community in the East, and since the future of the civilization whose foundations are common to Europe and America, is now at stake.

The second condition, decisive not only for both Europe and America but for all mankind, is the full development of the most important part of Europe's heritage, the Christian. This is no longer opposed to the humanistic part, and it should be used at last for a solution for all those problems which have been left behind by the ending millennium and which otherwise have no chance of being settled in the next. Moreover, without the return to the traditions of Christendom, once practically identical with Europe, the Europe of our time could neither be really united nor find an appropriate place in a world to whose extreme limits Christendom has now been spread.[11]

CHAPTER XXXII

Toward an Atlantic Community

A<small>MONG THE VARIOUS NEW IDEAS</small> and conceptions which appeared amidst the confusing turmoil of World War II, the most significant is by far that of the Atlantic community. Never was it better realized than in these critical years of common efforts how much Europe and America have in common; that the old European community had to be enlarged in order to survive in the postwar world; that such a cooperation was also advantageous to America after an experience which proved isolationism impossible; and that to the rising Eurasia east of what remained of a free Europe, corresponded a Euramerica as a new community.

That community was rightly called Atlantic, because just like the Mediterranean Sea in the community which preceded the European, the Atlantic Ocean is the natural center of the new one, and far from separating any longer its two sections, is, in an era of easy communication, a link between them. However, that designation can easily lead to a wrong interpretation which would limit, as is sometimes done, the new community to the countries situated at the Atlantic shores.[1] This would, on the one hand, limit the American interest in the whole conception, since the United States, as well as Canada, extend to the shores of another ocean, the Pacific; and on the other hand, it would limit the European participation to the countries situated along the Atlantic coast, the same being true of South America, if that part of the western hemisphere would, as it should, be considered part of the same community. More important, however, is another danger which ought to be avoided in the building up of a united Euramerica just as in that of a United Europe.

There was in both cases the same initial emphasis on material interests, though in the largest sense of that word. In addition to economics—strictly speaking, to the American aid to a devastated Europe—the equally urgent necessity of a common defense, first against German and then against Russian totalitarianism, decisively contributed to the emergence of a new conception which found its first concrete applications in the Marshall Plan and in the North Atlantic Treaty Organization. As indicated in its name, the latter does not include South America, but, as evidenced in its membership, with good reason avoids excluding European countries far from the Atlantic Ocean.

Both initiatives responded indeed to obvious requirements of the postwar situation; but even in the years of the war, when the new idea was first formulated and discussed, it was an excellent argument in its favor that the two partners, Europe and America, had a common heritage to preserve and to defend in common. Exactly as in the case of Europe's unification, the planned integration on a larger scale could not appeal to its peoples nor lead them from one period of their history into the next, if it were motivated only by temporary expediency and by interests which may turn from integrating to distintegrating forces. Besides the common interests of the given moment, conflicting interests can always appear, particularly in the economic and political fields.

This cannot happen in the spiritual sphere if both sides remain faithful to the ideas which have molded their past and are equally valuable for Europe and for America. In that respect it was helpful that the Atlantic community was conceived when Europeans and Americans were engaged in a hard struggle for freedom, the leading idea in the history of both of them. And thus it was that in the United States the idea of a "melting pot," which was definitely not European, was, at the same time evolving in the direction of a cultural pluralism, similar to that which had always been typical of the European community.[2] Otherwise, the conception of a community even larger, and therefore by no means favoring a complete assimilation of all its members, would have been rather artificial.

There remained, of course, in the great American republic a strong predominance of English culture, in natural consequence of the English origin of so many American institutions and even more because of the role of the English language, which was not only the official one, but the closest cultural bond between all the ethnic groups. Although it is hardly correct to speak of a majority and of minorities of different origin in a country based from the outset on equal rights for all,[3] the people of English ancestry are probably even now, after the settlement of so many other immigrants, by far the most numerous, especially among those in leading positions. But these facts, not easy to ascertain statistically, simply mean that the Americans have more intimate ties with one European nation, the English, than with the others—the term British being perhaps more appropriate in view of the Scotch element which along with the Welsh seems to come next after the purely English and uses the same tongue. In any case, the special community which unites the whole English-speaking world[4] can only contribute to the cultural conditions which are helpful to the constitution of an Atlantic community.

All the non-British peoples of Europe have an increasingly large number of men and women of common origin among the peoples of the United States, and independently of the degree of their assimilation to the English nucleus, and of their unquestionable loyalty to that country, they continue to have cultural ties with their original homelands, which contribute to the natural foundations of the Atlantic community. This is also true of those who immigrated from European countries far from the Atlantic Ocean, but if one of the ethnic groups coming from a specifically Atlantic part of Europe, from the island of Ireland, has made in America, after difficult beginnings, the most remarkable progress, that case only confirms the importance of the English language's role in the whole matter. In spite of the old political opposition to England and a sentimental attachment to the old Gaëlic, English has remained for centuries the language of the Irish. On the other hand, if in the United States the role of those who are of Spanish and French ancestry—and who came, like the equally important Dutch group, from lands situated on the Atlantic—comes next after that of the British and Irish settlers, that fact is parallel to the ties which most of Latin America and French-speaking Canada have with Spain and France, another basic element in the constitution of a comprehensive Atlantic communty.

Everywhere in the Americas, though most particularly in the northern part, the remarkable development of higher education in the last century has certainly prepared to a large extent the emergence of such a community.[5] This results not only from the obvious fact that such a development leads to a better knowledge of the outside world and of Europe in particular, but even more from the role of an institution of

European origin that is intimately connected with Europe's oldest and best traditions: the role of the University. In spite of significant differences in the structure of higher education in Europe and in America (in the latter the college occupies a unique place with no counterpart in the old world), American university life, whether on the undergraduate or graduate level, has so much in common with life in the European countries that it has created one more link between the two parts of the Atlantic community, no similar cultural link existing with the other parts of the world.

This being so, it is not at all surprising that when a few years ago the Rector of the College of Europe returned from a visit to a large number of American universities, he had the impression that America is a *Magna Europa,* just as southern Italy and Sicily were a *Magna Graecia* in ancient times, forming two branches of the same civilization: "two very different branches, but bound by solidarity, not only in the present situation of the world, but by common moral roots."[6]

However, neither is it surprising that when a symposium on the Atlantic community was organized at the College of Europe with the participation of both Americans and Europeans from various countries, their long and lively discussions[7] revealed many areas of disagreement, not only in political, but also in cultural matters, in other words, a psychological difference in the approach from both sides. The impression could arise that to the old dualism within the European community, which resulted from the difference between its Greek and its Roman roots, corresponded now a dualism within the Atlantic community in view of its partly European and partly American character.

For the historian it is interesting that among the various spiritual differences between the European and the American attitude, one is particularly emphasized on all such occasions: it is the difference between the strong impact which history continues to exercise on the European mind and which seems to be, if not non-existent, at least much weaker among the Americans—perhaps not all Americans, because among the intellectuals trained in colleges and universities, there are many, not only the professional historians, who are fully aware and proud of America's historical heritage. Many of them realize that part of that heritage, besides the comparatively brief tradition of the United States, is the heritage which their ancestors brought with them from Europe and which is identical with the whole earlier part of the European one. But it is certainly true that for the average American, history means much less than for the European and that therefore the common roots of the two branches of western culture are not so well remembered west of the Atlantic as they are east of that ocean.

Nevertheless, the consequences of that difference of approach ought not to be overrated, especially since in Europe, too, the peoples at large are no longer historically-minded as were their intellectual leaders in a still recent past. As is usual in similar cases—that of the relations between Latins and Greeks and their descendants being a typical example—the main cultural difficulty in uniting two communities in one results from a feeling of superiority, whether justified or not, on both sides. Two reasons for such a reciprocal feeling in the relations between Europeans and Americans are, consciously or not, connected with their different historical background and therefore deserve attention in a study of Europe's millennium.

The Europeans, proud of their cultural and intellectual achievements in the last ten or more centuries, are obliged to admit that American achievements, reached in a much shorter time, are remarkable too, but particularly as far as material progress is concerned. They are, therefore inclined to conclude that they remain superior in the spiritual field and to blame their new partners in the Atlantic community for their materialistic concerns and interests. Such an impression can easily arise when the United States business world is considered apart from its less spectacular academic life; when concentration is made only on the tremendous power of the trusts or monopolies and the labor unions. That twofold power is indeed a danger to American life itself and is felt by American intellectuals, but it would be unfair not to see a similar growing danger in many European countries also. It is particularly instructive to observe that the frequent criticisms of the Orientals, who blame the West for the materialistic features of its culture, is directed against Europeans no less than against the Americans.[8] This is for both of them a serious warning to revitalize the spiritual elements of their heritage, if they want it to survive and not to be submerged by the machine age.

These issues are, in general, well known, but it is of at least equal significance that if the Europeans claim a superiority in the intellectual field, the Americans reciprocate not only by defending with pride their economic and technical achievements, but also by claiming a superiority for themselves in an entirely different field: in that of government and social structure where their democracy ought to be, in their opinion, a lesson for the Europeans. This is in turn resented by the latter who, with all due respect for the democratic development of the United States in almost two centuries of independence, are not prepared to forget the experience of so many European countries in building up democracy through a much longer period, not only through the millennium of their community but from the early days of ancient Greece.

The trouble is that there have been in the course of history many different forms of democracy, none of which is perfect nor adaptable to all local conditions and all ages. The political philosophy which is the source of American democracy was brought from Europe by the colonists and adapted to a new environment. These conceptions came mostly from England where the tradition of parliamentary government is particularly old and continuous, but also from France where there have been through the centuries so many fluctuations in the conception of freedom which is decisive for the evolution of democracy. But there is hardly any region of Europe, not necessarily in its western part, where the quest for freedom has not produced time and again memorable experiences in democratic progress, even if only as a reaction against autocratic forms of government. All those experiences, along with the American one, which the Europeans are quite prepared to recognize as unusually outstanding and instructive, ought to contribute to the constitution of the Atlantic community.

That constitution can only be a federal one, and considering federalism, so closely associated with democracy, it must be stressed again that instead of a controversy as to whether European or American traditions in that complex matter should prevail, the future of the Atlantic community requires a coordination of the various conceptions of federalism which appeared in the history of its various members.[9] And this is a problem which even more than that of democracy leads from political theory and its application in national life to the practice of international relations and to the determination of the place of the Atlantic community in the world of today.

Here again history, old and recent, has something to say with a view to contributing to an objective interpretation of European and American trends and interests which might sometimes seem conflicting. For Europe the main issue in its relations with the outside world has always been the defense against the recurrent danger threatening her from the East, strictly speaking from western Asia, through the intermediary Eurasian lands. That this danger also threatens America today is obvious, especially as geographical distance has no longer any real significance, and it became apparent even during the last war. But it was also during that war that many Americans were wondering whether for them the tensions on the other side of the Atlantic were not less dangerous than those on the other side of the Pacific, those coming not from western but from eastern Asia,[10] and even more than the Europeans, whose colonial empires are vanishing, the Americans are becoming involved in the crises which trouble every part of the world.

Does this mean that the Atlantic community, while deeply rooted in common cultural traditions, is from the political viewpoint an unrealistic conception, and that approaching the next millennium the European community should be satisfied with a unification of Europe closer than that which has been achieved in the past? Certainly not. On the contrary, such an oversimplified conclusion would be an escape from the realities of our time of transition, as they have developed in the last phase of the outgoing millennium. Europe's predominance in the world, though it lasted only one or two centuries and collapsed before our eyes, has left behind a connection between Europe and the world which is even older than that between America and the other continents. Some at least of the European nations have inherited from their colonial and imperial past associations with the formerly-controlled Asiatic and African countries which cannot be simply liquidated and which create an additional community of political and economic interests with the United States.

Precisely in view of America's world-wide involvements, the danger which more directly threatens Europe from the East is in its present form a problem—one could even say the main problem—which America's policy has to consider everywhere.[11] Old Russian imperialism, as it appeared in the nineteenth century, was even then a problem of the Pacific area, in spite of its withdrawal from the eastern shores of that ocean.[12] Hence the interest of the United States in the Russo-Japanese war at the beginning of the twentieth century. Today Moscow's continued imperialism is intimately connected with Communism's goal of world domination, and the Soviet Union which exercises such strong pressure on the free part of Europe is at the same time behind all the troubles which America has in the other parts of the globe, including those in the western hemisphere itself. Though at present Peking seems even more aggressive, Moscow still is the center of world Communism.

The Atlantic age, which at the threshold of Europe's next millennium replaces the European age, just as the latter once replaced the Mediterranean, differs from both of them because of the larger community which arises. It has not only shifted quite considerably on the map of the globe, but is also, far from being an isolated world in itself, part of a world community which has been very prematurely called "One World." Prematurely, because if the present world seems to be one because of the relations among all its peoples which were established at the end of the European age, it is unfortunately divided to such an extent that the truly universal world history which really begins only now begins as the history of political conflicts, in spite of all the economic and and intellectual ties among the world's various regions.

All these conflicts are dominated by the basic one, as a matter of fact the only one that is a real danger to world peace, the conflict not between the economic systems of capitalism and socialism which could be easily settled by peaceful competition, but between freedom and tyranny, a political conflict intensified by the struggle between two different conceptions of the world and of mankind's destiny. Since the idea of human freedom under God with due respect for each human person has through the centuries been the basic idea of European history, brought from Europe to America and further developed there,[13] it is only natural that Europe and America join in one community which will remain the target of those who threaten freedom and the hope of those outside that community who want to save or to regain their freedom. How the Atlantic community can respond to the challenge of such a responsibility— this is the question which its founders and builders have to face at the present turn of history.

This cannot be achieved by military or economic power alone, even if that power is supported by nuclear energy. Atomic and hydrogen bombs, ready to confront possible aggression with similar methods, may serve as a deterrent for a certain time; but if both sides by continued tests develop these forces of destruction indefinitely, the danger of war increases at the same time, and so does the danger that in the event of such a catastrophe the Atlantic community, united Europe, and most probably civilization in general might cease to exist. Therefore, as long as that community has a chance to develop peaceful relations with the other countries of the world, whether friendly or not, the main objective of its leaders should be to gain the respect of these countries and to attract their peoples by constructive achievements which have nothing to do with power politics.

Taking advantage of the long historical experience of its own peoples, the Atlantic community should try to succeed where the old European one failed in spite of so many endeavors and of its undeniable cultural progress: in discovering a form of government and a social order which could serve not only as a guarantee of its own prosperity and security, but also as an inspiring example for all others. These others would then be convinced of the futility of the totalitarian solutions and of the illusionary character of communist promises and predictions.

In the field of government, ten centuries of experience gained by the European community and almost two more added by America could be used by political scientists for making discoveries and inventions which would contribute much more to the happiness of mankind and to its moral improvement than those made by scientists in the usual sense of that designation. To find at last the most appropriate way for avoiding the misuse of both authority and freedom; for making the people themselves and their well-informed opinion really decide the vital issues of internal and foreign politics; for establishing the most equitable division of power between local and central authorities, and making possible a federation of more than Continental scope—all this could make the next millennium of Europe, in cooperation with America, a hopeful one, with unlimited possibilities for contributing to a similar progress in the whole world.

Inseparable from the problems of government are those of social justice. Here again European and American experiences wisely combined could enable all the theoretical and practical workers in the social field to put before the member-states of the Atlantic community and before the world at large suggestions for evolutionary reforms which would make unnecessary the revolutionary changes which Communism is trying to enforce. The western world is well qualified to work on an economic system which would not be open to the criticism rightly raised regarding capitalism, and on a lasting social order which would sacrifice neither liberty nor equality but secure both of them in a spirit of fraternity.

These are, of course, tremendous tasks but they must be undertaken, if progress in human relations is not to remain far behind the material and technological progress which has been achieved in the last phase of Europe's millennium. Until now only a limited, by no means the most valuable part of the European heritage has been shared with the other continents, not necessarily to the mutual advantage. Europe's next millennium would be a much greater one, if the spiritual values of that heritage would be used for a decisive improvement of international relations inside Europe, of the relations between Europe and America, and of those of both of them with all peoples of good will. This calls for a concluding consideration of the place of the two traditional pillars of European culture in the world of today.

CHAPTER XXXIII

Toward a Christian Humanism

A T THE END OF THE PRESENT STUDY it must be recalled, as it was noted at its beginning, that Europe as a historical community and a civilization rests upon two pillars: the humanism inherited from the ancient Graeco-Roman world and Christianity, the former being of course the older, the latter the more important. It must be repeated, too, that in the past Europe has suffered from the dualism which resulted from such a twofold foundation and heritage. This is no longer so. Fortunately in the present time of crisis and confusion, at least the negative consequences of that dualism have been overcome. Both humanism, which is, strictly speaking, no longer Graeco-Roman but has been enriched by the cultural contributions of so many centuries of Christian Europe's history, and Christianty, which has no longer anything to fear from such a humanism, have now to face the same dangers and the same opposition, and have the same interest, as have Europe and America, in constituting a harmonious community.

Humanism has become Christian, because of a long, though not always harmonious association in the development of a European mind,[1] and even more because the anti-human forces of the machine age and of the totalitarian state make man turn, in Europe even more than elsewhere, toward the one power which, through not one but two millennia, has remained the strongest force of opposition to similar dangers of the past, the most efficient defense of the primacy of spiritual values and of the freedom of the human person. Christianity has become more human than ever before, having given up methods of coercion, which sometimes

[387]

were inhuman, and involvements in power politics which were always detrimental to the Church of Christ. The divisions within Christianity, painful as they are, no longer lead to mutual prejudice or even persecution, and a similar spirit of love has improved the relations with non-Christians, making possible a common struggle when common moral principles are questioned. No humanist would any longer consider Christianity a force of darkness and reaction. No Christian, and that means also the most orthodox Catholic, would deny that any human being, who, according to his best knowledge and honest conviction, follows the precepts of his conscience, belongs spiritually, though not formally, to the mystical body of Christ, His Savior and Redeemer.[2]

In spite of these promising developments at the threshold of what will be Christianity's third millennium, there remains the disturbing question of why over so many years Christ's doctrine of love has not succeeded in making all His followers worthy of their name, not even in the European community where that doctrine prevailed for centuries and not even in the private lives of the individual human beings. Why has moral progress been so slow, especially in social, national and international life, which is the historian's field of study? This question is particularly alarming for the Christian historian who believes in the role of Divine Providence in guiding not only the individuals but also their communities, small or large.

To answer that question, another one must be raised, the old theological problem of the relation between providential guidance and man's free will. The historian, without being qualified to discuss that problem in all its aspects, can, however, make a contribution to its solution. And the historian of the European community—until now, along with its American extension, the only one in the history of the world which was and remained a Christian one—has a special responsibility in that respect.

He will remember that there was at the beginning of Europe's millennium a period of three centuries, that of the Christian Commonwealth, when conditions were extremely favorable to the application of Christian principles in public life. That situation can be considered no less providential than the unification of the Mediterranean world in one Roman Empire, when at the beginning of the first millennium of Christianity the spread of the Gospel was its main task. Unfortunately, the European community which had been formed shortly before, failed to take advantage of that opportunity, and on the contrary, in the next great transition period, the Renaissance, was strongly influenced by the anti-Christian belief that politics had nothing to do with ethics.

However, in that same period it was again providential that in reaction against a worldliness which penetrated even into ecclesiastical life, there was a powerful revival of religious convictions and a full awareness of the necessity of a reform of the Church. Unfortunately, that opportunity was again missed, and far from being used for a consolidation of European unity, actually destroyed it, because equally religious minds did not agree on the ways and means of such a reform, turning it into a revolution and an equally violent reaction against it.

Since Christianity, now divided not only by the earlier schism between West and East but by an even deeper break between Rome and the new Protestant churches, seemed to be a source of trouble instead of peace, the European nations tried to preserve their community and even to achieve world domination without any concern with Christian principles, free from all the limitations which the traditional faith and morals imposed upon Man. Spectacular successes in the so-called Modern Age, and in the century of transition from one millennium to another one, the nineteenth, were, however, combined with another failure to organize Europe in a spirit of peace and cooperation, and ended in a tragic collapse of a European leadership based upon material rather than spiritual force.

After Europe's turning away from her Christian heritage created the wrong impression that this is no longer a Christian but a "post-Christian" society[3] there has been once more a clear appeal to revitalize that heritage and to use it for a solution of otherwise hopeless problems left behind by a thousand years of European history. That appeal is for the believing Christian even more providential than the conditions which developed in the earliest phase of the European community. But whether or not it will be successful depends again on the willingness of the members of that community to follow an appeal which is, of course, addressed not only to them and to their American partners but to all men of good will, in the interest of universal peace, and more than ever before represents the most urgent need if civilization in whatever form is to survive.

This means a return to the Christian philosophy of history, which even in the distant times of its founder—when the prospects for the creation of a European community were as dark as they are today for its further development—had to face similar problems and suggested similar solutions. St. Augustine was certainly not a man to recommend a peace of surrender to evil, a peace at any price. In his standard work *De civitate Dei,* which has to be quoted in the epilogue to the present study as it was in its prologue, since it inspired Pius XII no less than Charlemagne, he pointed out with obvious regret that in general people prefer *qualemcumque pacem* to freedom, expressing his admiration for those "who preferred to perish rather than to serve."[4] But while he admitted in the same chapter that in view of such a weakness of human nature, it is Divine Providence that decides who rules and who is subject, he has other chapters in which he praises peace as the most desirable goal, not only in eternal life but also here on earth; where he regrets the necessity even of just wars and stresses that even *bellantium saevitia* has the establishment of peace as ultimate objective; and tries to give a definition of "universal peace under a just judge." However, a less frequently cited chapter[6] is decisive. There he strongly recommends that those who belong to the *civitas Dei,* which still "wanders on earth," should look for peace and concord with the *terrena civitas* without waiting for God's judgment. That "celestial community," faithful to God,

> calls for citizens out of all peoples and assembles a society wandering in all languages, without caring for differences in customs, laws, and institutions, through which peace on earth is gained and maintained, without cutting off or destroying anything of all this, but on the contrary, saving and following up whatever is different in the various nations, that aims at one and the same end of peace on earth, if it does not hinder religion which teaches to worship one supreme and true God.

These words as well as other passages[7] on the differences in language as a source of conflicts, if any language is imposed by force, or on the consequences of imperial conquests which lead to civil wars and to the necessity of fighting new neighbors, are today, after more than fifteen hundred years, of astonishing actuality. They recommend a new effort to create an international society or community, respecting the traditions and the self-government of all its members and using their heritage for establishing a lasting peace, the only condition being that religion can freely develop.

St. Augustine, writing at a time when only three parts of the world, Europe, Asia, and Africa were distinguished, as they continued to be for the following ten centuries, never claimed any predominance for Europe, his own bishopric being in Africa and the Eastern Christian

Empire extending far into Asia. But since soon after him the non-European parts of Christendom were submerged, Europe having for a long time the privilege of being practically identical with Christendom and the task of propagating the Christian faith in all lands which came under her influence, it so happened that the constitution of an earthly community in peaceful agreement with the celestial one could only come from a European initiative.

The present world crisis results from the fact that Europe used her expansion and predominance all over the world for entirely different ends, for power politics and economic gains, bringing to the non-European peoples material and technological rather than spiritual and moral progress. But the crisis resulted also from the developments inside Europe and of the western society extended far beyond Europe's western limits, for even in that part of the world the various nations were not united for peaceful aims, but fighting each other, some of them being subjugated by the stronger ones without regard for Christian principles.

These principles and all religion are openly denied today in a large part of the world, but if the peoples of that part are to be influenced by those who at least formally remain Christians, the religious life of these happier ones must be deepened and strengthened, adapted to the new conditions without sacrificing any essentials in faith and morals. Faith and morals must penetrate the political life as well as the private life of individuals, respecting in such a spiritual unity the historically developed variety in all other matters. This is certainly no easy task and at the same time only a preparation for an even more difficult one: for convincing, through peaceful means, those who oppose Christian principles that their acceptance and general application would be to the advantage of all those who at present, willing or not, have to follow basically different conceptions.

Such a program for the future is difficult but it does not mean at all that it is utopian and impossible to carry out. It has been rightly said[8] that it only seems so, because the application of Christian principles to public life has never been seriously tried. It has not been tried at all in the later part of the European millennium, the greater part, almost two thirds of its duration; and even at the time of the Christian Commonwealth, when the European community was hardly mature, the efforts in that direction were far from being general and consistent.

It could even be said that at present, contrary to appearances, conditions for such efforts are in many respects more favorable than ever before. First of all, there cannot be any doubt as to their most urgent necessity. Practically all other means for improving the world situation, including the tremendous efforts of two world wars, have been tried and found deficient. Never before have the defenders of the European heritage had to face a program of revolutionary change as systematic and monolithic, as aggressive and untiring, as that of contemporary totalitarianism in its communist form, the first to appear and the last to remain on the battlefield after victory over the others. Without any intention of opposing to that program one which would be equally monolithic and aggressive, a united Europe integrated with the whole Atlantic community which is in the making cannot be satisfied with negative criticism nor with the present spiritual confusion, which is in discouraging contrast with the self-confidence of the other side.

Fortunately, in addition to the alliance between Christianity and humanism, which is so much more natural than the establishment of a "socialist" humanism propagated by some of the most persuasive communist leaders,[9] there is already an evident rebirth of Christianity, providential for the faithful, stimulating for all as an inspiring example and experience. Never before has there been in Christendom such an interest in international peace and organization, not destroying national traditions but reconciling and sublimating them. Never before has the desire for putting an end to all the disagreement among Christians in a spirit of brotherly love and understanding been more generous and determined.

There still remains, it is true, a difference in the interpretation of, and in the approach to that ecumenical movement, started in Europe but already reaching to all corners of the world where there are Christian communities: a difference among those who want Christian unity at any price, accepting the most diverse views of Christ's doctrine and even of His own person, and those who firmly believe that there can be only one truth revealed by God's incarnate Son and that the general acceptance of that truth is a condition for any real unity. But all agree that such a *communis consensus* ought to be reached neither by pressure nor by compromise, but by friendly discussions, study, and prayer.

It is highly significant that Europe's millennium is ending, not with attempts to create a Christian empire as took place in 962, but with the gathering, in 1962, of an ecumenical council of the Catholic Church, the second Vatican Council, continuing the interrupted one of 1870. This council has on its agenda both a study of the requirements of our time which can be met without affecting the God-given character of the Church of Peter, and the study of all possibilities of Christian reunion, wishing with Christ himself *ut omnes unum sint*. Such a unity cannot be achieved immediately. This is unfortunately true, but so is the comforting evidence that Rome's intentions are well understood and appreciated by all other churches. Never have the relations with them been better; an entirely new atmosphere has been created in a Christianity which still remains divided as far as ecclesiastical organization and even essential points of doctrine are concerned, but is already united by a spirit of real charity and the consciousness of common responsibilities in the greatest spiritual crisis the world has ever known.

Such a contribution to religious peace is at the same time a contribution to international peace, since according to the Christian definition, best formulated by St. Augustine many centuries ago, real peace is a tranquility of order in all spheres of life, *pax rerum omnium*. Whether the Council will directly influence and improve international relations, first in what remains of the Christian community, the *res publica Christiana* of the past, and then, since that community is no longer limited to the European one, in the whole world in which, to quote once more St. Augustine, the two *civitates,* the divine and the earthly one are "somehow mixed with each other," is impossible to foresee.[10] Such a result, so highly desirable in our time, would be in the spirit of the great Councils which deliberated with similar intentions squarely in the middle of Europe's millennium, especially since no conflict between papal and conciliary authority confuses the issue today.

Neither is there any conflict between Christianity and humanism, similar to those of the past, inherent in the dualism of the European tradition. The other dualism resulting from the opposition between Roman and Greek elements in Europe's ancient heritage is vanishing more and more. Therefore, the road on which Christian humanism is advancing is a road to both peace and freedom. The progress of that great spiritual movement is the only hope left to those nations, particularly those Christian nations of Europe, which are without freedom. For at the same time they are conscious that freedom cannot and should not be regained at the inhuman price of another world war.

Without those nations which have been sacrificed, after a thousand years of integration with Europe, at the very end of the European millennium, neither a united Europe nor the Atlantic community of the next millennium could possibly be complete and fully satisfactory.

Without their liberation the universal peace which is so rightly desired would not be a peace of justice, but at the best similar to that of the nineteenth century which did not last through the twentieth. To achieve that liberation, as well as the righting of wrongs in the world, without breaking its peace, seems to many nothing but a vicious circle, a utopian dream. But such a dream seems to be the idea of lasting peace itself and, in general, any moral progress in political matters. Yet, such dreams are the only inspiring vision which, similar to that which animated Europe around the year 1000, may animate the world, on the initiative of a truly Christian Europe, at the approach of the year 2000.

That vision includes what is called by the Rome of Peter the conversion of Russia, that is the conversion of the very center of Communism, not only to the Christian faith which even in Russia has not been completely destroyed after more than forty years of Bolshevik rule, not only to reunion with the First Rome which even to the Orthodox believers in the mission of a Third one no longer seems so unacceptable as in the centuries before the experience of the present, but a conversion to a political philosophy which is in complete opposition to that which is now obligatory in the communist-controlled part of the world.

This seems indeed, more than any other expectation, a utopian dream. But if the leaders of the communist world proudly announce with deep conviction that within the lifetime of the next generation they will most certainly convert the free world to their beliefs, the Christians ought to be equally convinced, if not of the certainty, at least of the possibility of reaching a similar goal. After all, it was no less difficult, and two thousand years ago must have seemed a utopian dream, to Christianize the whole of Europe; and yet it was almost completely achieved in the first millennium of Christianity and followed in the course of the next—the first of the European community—by an equally difficult and surprisingly successful missionary expansion in all other parts of the globe. Why should an equally amazing success not be possible in the millennium which now is starting amidst a revival of Christianity supported by all spiritual forces faithful to the great European tradition?

This does not necessarily mean that complete victory in the present struggle of ideas will be gained before the end of this century. Christians do not share the arrogant pride of their opponents. But the last third of the twentieth century can be expected to prove as decisive as was the last third of the tenth. Therefore, the generation which is entering the new millennium of European and universal history will have quite an exceptional responsibility indeed, of which, absorbed as it is by so many material problems, it is not yet sufficiently conscious. This is precisely the reason why an examination of the European conscience, directed by Europe's historical experience, is so badly needed and should be facilitated by the study of European history.

If Marxist materialism pretends to find its vindication in a reinterpretation of the past, those who defend the highest spiritual values, including faith in God and Man's inalienable right to freedom, ought to follow that example by showing to the rising generation the continuity of these ideas in a past which was not predetermined by any inescapable laws but was molded under divine guidance by free human beings. Their efforts in the future ought to be continued in the same spirit.

It would certainly not be in the Christian nor in the humanistic spirit, if the heirs of Europe's millenary tradition would claim any privileged destiny in that respect. But since in their tradition both that universal religion, which they believe to be the true one, and the struggle for human dignity and liberty play such leading roles, it is their duty to make the essentials of that heritage better known to themselves and to the outside world. Europe's millennium in its threefold meaning: an anniversary which so obviously coincides with the beginning of a new period of universal history; a scholarly meditation about ten centuries which have prepared for the present one and made it so momentous; and a legitimate desire to find a solution to the present crisis—such a millennium is an excellent opportunity to fulfill that moral obligation.

That task requires the cooperation not only of many individual historians, each of them a specialist in one of the many fields which have to be explored, but also of many individual nations which commemorate their national millennia. The interest of the Poles in theirs, which raises so many controversial problems, is therefore not only well justified, but a constructive contribution to such a great undertaking, an example which should make other European nations fully aware of their similar obligations in writing and making history.

All historians can thus contribute to that unity of mankind which Pope John XXIII, in the conclusion of his opening address to the Second Vatican Council, on October 11, 1962, has called a necessary basis for making the earthly community similar to the celestial one: *cuius rex veritas, cuius lex caritas, cuius modus aeternitas.*[11]

NOTES TO PREFACE

1. *The Limits and Divisions of European History*, London-New York 1950. To the German translation: *Europa-Grenzen und Gliederung seiner Geschichte*, Darmstadt 1957, I added an epilogue: "Europa-Abendland-Christenheit," pp. 186–201, in which some recent publications dealing with these problems are discussed.

2. This became apparent during the discussions at the Eleventh International Congress of Historical Sciences held in Stockholm in August 1960, especially those which followed the reports of E. Rothacker and E. M. Zhukov on the philosophy and the periodization of history. The reports have been published by the International Committee of Historical Sciences in the series *Rapports*, Stockholm 1960, vol. I; summaries of the discussions in *Actes du Congrès*, pp. 58 f.

3. This interpretation clearly appears in the collective volume *Thousand Years of Polish History*, Warsaw 1960.

4. Briefly summarized by Archbishop J. Gawlina in the introduction to vol. I of the series *Sacrum Poloniae Millennium*, Rome 1954; see the French translation of his statement in vol. IV, Rome 1957, pp. 7–8.

5. See his book *An Historian's Approach to Religion*, London 1956, published soon after vol. VII of his *A Study of History*, Oxford 1954, in which the importance of the religious factor has been so strongly emphasized in part VII: "Universal Churches."

6. See vol. VII (the last) of his *La Formation de l'Europe*, entitled *Le Toit chrétien*, Paris 1957. Quite recently, H. Brugmans, in the introduction to the second part of his survey of European history, *L'Europe prend le large*, Paris 1961 (the first part, *Les origines de la civilisation européenne*, appeared in 1958), has convincingly shown the importance of the religious problems for any such study.

7. See the report on the *Unesco Pax Romana Meeting at Manila*, published in Fribourg 1960, part I: "The Present Impact of the Great Religions of the World upon the Lives of the People in the Orient and Occident." The historical statement by Father H. de la Costa, quoted in the text, is on pp. 124 ff.

8. *On the Philosophy of History*, New York 1959.

9. *The Meaning and Matter of History—A Christian View*, New York 1959

10. See my article "The Moral Laws of History," *The Catholic Historical Review*, XLII (1957), 409–440.

NOTES TO INTRODUCTION

1. This was well realized by Henri Berr who started in 1925 to publish articles in the *Bulletin du centre international de synthèse* (printed as appendix to the *Revue de synthèse historique*, vol. XLII ff.). These articles were written in preparation for a dictionary of historical terminology.

2. The difficulty in defining clearly these terms is obvious in the latest contribution to the problem by Carlton J. H. Hayes, *Nationalism: A Religion*, New York 1960.

3. The date of his visit has been definitely established as the end of 965 or beginning of 966 by H. J. Widajewicz, *Studia nad relacją o Słowianach Ibrahima ibn Jakuba* /Studies concerning the account on the Slavs by Ibrahim ibn Jakub/, Cracow 1946, pp. 16–17.

4. See e.g. G. de Reynold, *La Formation de l'Europe*, VII, Paris 1957, 241, and the remarks by K. Tymieniecki about the formation of Europe in the tenth century in *Przegląd zachodni* /Western Review/, XI (1955), 126.

5. This is the exact translation of L. v. Ranke's frequently quoted words, "Wie es eigentlich gewesen ist."

6. As Berr tried to do in his *La synthèse en histoire*, Paris 1911, in which he outlines a philosophy of history without using the term "discredité."

7. This has been strongly emphasized in E. Rothacker's report, quoted above in n. 2 of the Preface where the "Vor-Urteil" /different from "Vorurteil," i.e. prejudice/, usually made by the historian, is repeatedly mentioned.

8. See my article, "The Place of Christendom in the History of Mankind," *Cahiers d'Histoire mondiale*, UNESCO, I (1954), 927–950.

9. An excellent *Jahrbuch für Universalgeschichte*, under the title of *Saeculum*, was founded by G. Stadtmüller; the first volume appeared in Munich in 1950.

10. See the references to Virgil and Horace in G. Ladner, *The Idea of Reform in the Church Fathers*, Cambridge, Mass. 1960, pp. 12, 26, n. 20. That *saeculum* in the ancient Latin was originally supposed to be the lifetime of one generation only is pointed out in *Lexicon totius Latinitatis*, ed. Fr. Corradini, Patavii 1887, IV, 189 f.

11. *Ibid.;* see also Ladner, *op. cit.,* p. 446 and particularly n. 17.

12. See the quotations by Ladner, *op. cit.,* p. 28.

13. See below, Chapter X, n. 1.

14. J. H. J. Van der Pot, *De Periodisering der Geschiedenia*, Hague 1951, pp. 46–51; see the excellent bibliography of that problem in Ladner, *op. cit.,* p. 29, n.14.

15. Especially in Polish messianism; see Van der Pot, *op. cit.,* pp. 60–64.

NOTES TO CHAPTER I

1. Well shown by de Reynold, *La Formation*, but only as far as the Celtic and Germanic peoples are concerned: V, no. 1, *Le monde barbare-Les Celtes*, Paris 1949, and V, no. 2 *Le monde barbare-Les Germains*, Paris 1953.

2. *L'Eglise, l'Occident, le Monde*, Recherches et débats du Centre catholique des intellectuels français, cahier n. 15, Paris 1954; see in particular the contribution by Henri Daniel-Rops, "L'Eglise est-elle l'Occident?" pp. 42–45.

3. See H. Marrou's polemic with A. Toynbee in *IXe Congrès international des Sciences historiques*, Paris 1950, *Rapports*, especially p. 333.

4. See the latest discussion of the Greek legends in that matter by Denis de Rougemont, *Vingt-huit siècles d'Europe, La conscience européenne à travers les textes d'Hésiode à nos jours*, Paris 1961, pp. 12 ff. I shall refer to this book from which much source material was taken, as: de Rougemont, *Europe*.

5. See the annex, "Asia and Europe: Facts and Fantasies," in Toynbee's *Study*, VIII, 710 ff.

6. The term is used by de Reynold, *La Formation*, III, 35.

7. T. Zieliński, *Helenizm a Judaizm*, 2 vols., Warsaw 1927.

8. De Reynold, *La Formation*, III, "L'Hellénisme et le génie européen," Paris 1944.

9. A. A. Vasiliev, *Histoire de l'Empire byzantin*, II, Paris 1932, 389–433.

10. Hans Kohn, *The Idea of Nationalism*, New York 1944.

11. Vasiliev, *op. cit.*, I, 128, 162; G. Ostrogorsky, *History of the Byzantine State*, Oxford 1956, p. 52, n. 2; p. 95.

12. De Reynold, *La Formation*, III, 74–76; see also R. Andreotti, "Die Weltmonarchie Alexander des Grossen in Überlieferung und geschichtlicher Wirklichkeit," *Saeculum*, VIII (1957), 120–166.

13. Well illustrated by the three maps which were carved on the external walls of the *Forum Romanum* under Mussolini.

14. See the bibliography in Ladner, *op. cit.*, p. 14, n. 31.

15. De Reynold, *La Formation*, VII, on the internal crisis of the ancient world, pp. 37–57, and the influence of the Asiatic religions, p. 144.

16. See F. Engel-Jánosi's essay on "Toynbee and the Tradition of Universal History," in the symposium, *The Intent of Toynbee's Study of History*, ed. E. T. Gargan, Chicago 1961.

17. Though in *De civitate Dei* sometimes also Athens or Rome are called "civitates," lib. 18, cap. 8 and 22.

18. Rightly pointed out by Msgr. L. Cristiani in his study on "La tolérance et l'intolérance de l'Eglise depuis les premiers siècles jusqu'à nos jours," in *Cahiers d'Histoire mondiale*, V (1959); see particularly pp. 75–76.

19. *De civitate Dei*, lib. 4, cap. 4.

20. Much bibliographic information on the recent discussions on the fall of the Roman Empire has been given by F. Cusin in the symposium, *Problemi storici e orientamenti storiografici*, ed. E. Rota, Como 1942, pp. 159 ff.

21. Ladner, *op. cit.*, p. 277.

22. *De civitate Dei*, lib. 18, cap. 13.

23. *Ibid.*, lib. 19, cap. 17; see also de Reynold, *La Formation*, VII, 382, and the last chapter of this book.

24. Halecki, *Pius XII*, London-New York 1954, pp. 9, 21, 237.

25. Christopher Dawson, *The Making of Europe*, London 1932.

NOTES TO CHAPTER II

1. On the significance of Caesar's conquests for the making of Europe see Dawson, *op. cit.*, pp. 27 ff.

2. C. Jullian, *De la Gaule à la France*, Paris 1923.

3. The continuity of Roman tradition in Rumanian history is most eloquently defended by N. Iorga, *Histoire des Roumains et de la romanité orientale*, 10 vols., Paris 1933 ff.

4. On the importance of the Roman period for "the birth of Britain" see Winston S. Churchill, *History of the English Speaking Peoples*, I, London 1956.

5. St. Augustine already wondered whether it was really necessary for the Romans to extend their "imperium tam longe lateque" by continuous wars; see *De civitate Dei,* lib. 3, cap. 10; cf. also lib. 4, cap. 3.

6. Best shown in the political philosophy of Poland's greatest Renaissance statesman, Jan Zamoyski; see W. Sobieski, *Trybun ludu szlacheckiego* /The tribune of the noble people/, Warsaw 1905.

7. G. Vernadsky, *Russia at the Dawn of the Modern Age,* New Haven 1959, p. 168, has shown that such a claim was made earlier by Basil III.

8. Hans Baron, *The Crisis of the Early Italian Renaissance, Civil Humanism and Republican Liberty in an Age of Classicism and Tyranny,* Princeton 1955, I, 38–63; II, 454, 472.

9. W. C. Barck, *Origins of the Medieval World,* Stanford 1958, p. 28.

10. See St. Augustine's remarks, *De civitate Dei,* lib. 2, cap. 19, "De corruptione Romanae rei publicae," after the destruction of Carthage, and particularly lib. 19, cap. 7.

11. See V. Pöschl, "Tacitus und der Untergang des römischen Reiches," *Wiener Studien,* LXIX (1956), 311–320, and also J. Bleicken, "Der Begriff der Freiheit in der letzten Phase der römischen Republik," *Historische Zeitschrift,* CXCV (1962) 1–20.

12. Particularly Toynbee, *Study,* VI, *passim,* and the chart on p. 327.

13. Luke, 19:41.

14. Unfortunately, the series *Histoire des relations internationales,* ed. H. Renouvin, begins only with F. Ganshof's volume on the Middle Ages, Paris 1952.

15. The fallacy of the Roman conviction that their destiny was "parcere subiectis et debellare superbos," is shown by St. Augustine in his "praefatio" to *De civitate Dei* and again in lib. 1, cap. 16.

16. By A. Dopsch and his school; see e.g. E. Patzelt, "Die Kontinuitätsfrage," in *Wirtschaft und Kultur,* Baden 1938, pp. 18–33.

NOTES TO CHAPTER III

1. H. Bergson, *Les deux sources de la morale et de la religion,* Paris 1932.

2. As evidenced in the review *Anthropos,* which began to appear in 1906, and in numerous works of its founder, Rev. P. W. Schmidt.

3. E. Sarkisyanz, *Russland und der Messianismus des Ostens—Sendungsbewusstsein und politischer Chiliasmus des Ostens,* Tübingen 1955.

4. De Reynold, *La Formation,* VII, 27–57; see above, Chapter I, n. 15.

5. De Reynold not only joined them (*ibid.,* VII, 223, 257 f.), but also explained on that occasion the origin of our chronology, based upon the Christian era, and its gradual adoption by the imperial and papal chanceries.

6. See the discussions quoted in note 2 of the Preface.

7. The term is frequently used by J. Maritain.

8. See the comment by J. Lebreton in *Histoire de l'Eglise,* ed. Fliche-Martin, I, Paris 1946, 180–183.

9. See *De civitate Dei,* lib. 18, cap. 2, where the Assyrian and the Roman empires are compared.

10. See the recent discussions on St. Peter's death of Kurt Aland with Karl Heussi in *Historische Zeitschrift*, vols. 183, 186, 191; and also M. Maccarrone, "Cathedra Petri," *Saeculum*, XIII (1962), 278–292, where the reinterpretation of the "Quo vadis" problem also deserves attention (p. 279).

11. See the remarks of J. Zeiller in *Histoire de l'Eglise*, I, 385–388.

12. Recently recalled by A. Bronarski in his study on the apologetical character of H. Sienkiewicz's *Quo Vadis*, published in *Sacrum Poloniae Millennium*, VII (1961).

13. In Toynbee's *Study*.

14. D. M. Gougand, *Christianity in Celtic Lands*, London 1932, pp. 131–146; see also De Paor, *Early Christian Ireland*, London 1958.

15. Dawson, *Making of Europe*, Chapter III: "The Classical Tradition and Christianity."

16. See the excellent chapter on monasticism in Ladner's *Idea of Reform*.

17. See below, Chapter XI, n. 13.

18. Toynbee, *Study*, II, 322–340, 424–433, has pointed out that Ireland had a temporary chance for leadership in the extreme northwest of Europe.

NOTES TO CHAPTER IV

1. See Ch. Diehl, *Justinien et la civilisation byzantine au VIe siècle*, Paris 1901.

2. M. Jugie, *Le schisme byzantin*, Paris 1941.

3. See H. Grégoire's remarks in the symposium, *The Church in the Christian Roman Empire*, New York 1956, p. 86 f., and Ostrogorsky, *op. cit.*, p. 28.

4. By F. Dvornik, *The Photian Schism—History and Legend*, Cambridge 1948, and his report on "The Patriarch Photius in the Light of Recent Research," submitted to the International Congress of Byzantine Studies in Munich, 1958 (*Berichte*, pp. 1–56).

5. Jugie, *op. cit.;* see also his article in the *Dictionnaire de théologie catholique*, XIV/1, Paris 1939, col. 1312 ff.

6. See the remarks in Toynbee's *Study*, VIII, 727, but also my reply in *Europa-Grenzen und Gliederung seiner Geschichte*, Darmstadt 1957, p. 189.

7. S. Runciman, *The Eastern Schism*, Oxford 1955, pp. 29–30, calls this the "triumph of German theology."

8. J. Gill, *The Council of Florence*, Oxford 1959, pp. 231, 240 f.

9. See above, Chapter I, n. 11.

10. See F. Dölger's paper on "The New Rome," submitted to the International Congress of Byzantine Studies in Rome, 1936.

11. Dvornik, *op. cit., passim*.

12. Particularly by Diehl; see his *Byzance, grandeur et décadence*, Paris 1920 (English edition, New Brunswick 1957).

13. By B. Jasinowski, *Wschodnie chrześcijaństwo a Rosja* /Eastern Christianity and Russia/, Wilno 1933.

14. R. Grousset, *Histoire des Croisades*, I, Paris 1934, pp. 1, 628.

15. G. Schlumberger, *L'Epopée byzantine à la fin du Xe siècle*, 3 vols., Paris 1896–1905.

16. A. A. Vasiliev, *The Russian Attack on Constantinople*, Cambridge, Mass. 1946.

17. H. Paszkiewicz, *The Origin of Russia*, London 1954, rightly opposes this theory.

18. The expression is used by Toynbee, *Study, passim.*

19. B. Vernadsky, *Ancient Russia*, New Haven 1943, p. 158 f.

20. A. Spekke, *The Ancient Amber Routes and the Geographical Discovery of the Eastern Baltic*, Stockholm 1957.

21. G. Labuda, *Pierwsze państwo słowiańskie—państwo Samona* /The First Slavic State—the State of Samo/, Poznań 1947.

22. M. H. Serejski, *Idea jedności karolińskiej—studium nad genezą wspólnoty europejskiej w średniowieczu* /The idea of Carolingian Unity—a study of the origin of the European community in the Middle Ages/, Warsaw 1937, p. 15.

23. *Ibid.*, p. 25.

24. See, however, the reservation of E. Amann in *Histoire de l'Eglise*, VI, "L'époque carolingienne," Paris 1947, 162 f.

NOTES TO CHAPTER V

1. These quotations are taken from Serejski, *op. cit.*, pp. 69, 88. See also de Rougemont, *Europe*, pp. 48 ff.

2. *Wirtschaftliche und soziale Grundlagen der europäischen Kulturentwicklung aus der Zeit von Cäsar auf Karl den Grossen*, 2 vols., first published 1918–1920.

3. The latest summary of the endless discussions of Pirenne' thesis was given by Barck, *op. cit.*, pp. 5–28, 115–124.

4. "Charlemagne a formé l'Europe"—this is the conclusion of his detailed inquiry in the matter; see *La Formation*, VII, 405, where Marc Brion's arguments in *De César à Charlemagne*, Paris 1949, were also used.

5. About the decisive role of Alcuin see L. Wallach, *Alcuin and Charlemagne*, Ithaca 1959.

6. De Reynold, *La Formation*, Chapter IV, calls it "La deuxième forme de l'Empire chrétien," the first being that of Constantine the Great.

7. *Ibid.*, p. 373, where he speaks about "le millénarisme impérial." See above, Chapter I, n. 14.

8. Werner Ohnsorge, *Das Zweikaiserproblem im früheren Mittelalter*, Hildesheim 1947; see particularly the introductory remarks on p. 5.

9. F. W. Buckler, *Harun-al-Rashid and Charlemagne*, Cambridge, Mass. 1931.

10. Serejski, *op. cit.*, p. 67.

11. See above, Chapter IV, n. 7.

12. Ostrogorsky, *History* . . . , pp. 162–165; Vasiliev, *Histoire* . . . I, 351–356.

13. *Ibid.*, pp. 175–217.

14. Amann, *Histoire de l'Eglise*, VI, "L'époque carolingienne," pp. 413–445.

15. Dvornik, *The Slavs, Their Origin and Culture*, Cambridge, Mass. 1956, pp. 69 f.

16. Labuda, *op. cit.*

17. See the latest synthesis by Franz Grivec, *Konstantin und Methodius, Lehrer der Slaven*, Wiesbaden 1960. In cooperation with Fr. Tomšić he published *Constantinus et Methodius Thessalonicenses, Fontes*, Zagreb 1962.

18. See Fr. Zagiba, "Die bayrische Slavenmission und ihre Fortsetzung durch Kyrill und Methodius," *Jahrbücher für Geschichte Osteuropa's*, IX (1961), 1–56.

19. K. Lanckorońska, "Studies on the Slavonic Rite in Poland," Rome 1961, *Orientalia Christiana Analecta*, vol. CLXI.

20. Runciman, *A History of the First Bulgarian Empire*, London 1930.

21. Dawson, *Making of Europe*, Chapter XII: "The Restoration of the Western Empire and the Carolingian Renaissance."

NOTES TO CHAPTER VI

1. See, however, the different opinion expressed by Paszkiewicz, *Origin* . . . .

2. See above, Chapter II, n. 15.

3. See the vindication of Charlemagne's Saxon policy in de Reynold, *La Formation*, VII, 397–399, which is, however, hardly convincing.

4. Widajewicz, *Studia nad relacja* . . . , pp. 57–66; A. Gieysztor in *Revue historique*, CCXXVI (1961), 363, n. 5.

5. A. Brackmann, "Die Ostpolitik Otto's des Grossen," *Historische Zeitschrift*, CXXXIV (1926), 246–249, 256.

6. See the account of the Russian Primary Chronicle on Vladimir's conversion.

7. See Gougand, *op. cit.*, p. 182, n. 3; p. 183, n. 2.

8. About St. Bruno of Querfurt see W. Meysztowicz in *Sacrum Poloniae Millennium*, V (1958); and R. Wenskus, *Studien zur historisch-politischen Gedankenwelt Bruno's von Querfurt*, Münster-Köln 1956.

9. H. Holand, *Explorers in America before Columbus*, New York 1956, going back to 986; see also G. M. Gathorne-Hardy, *The Norse Discoverers of America: the Wineland sagas translated and discussed*, Oxford 1921.

10. On Icelandic culture in the century from 930 to 1030 see Dawson, *Making of Europe*, pp. 211–217; K. Gjerset, *History of Iceland*, New York 1924, covers the whole millennium from the tenth to the twentieth century.

11. G. Schnürer, *Kirche und Kultur im Mittelalter*, II, Paderborn 1926, 10–12.

12. On the attempts of the Saxon emperors to subdue Denmark see J. Bryce, *The Holy Roman Empire*, London 1903 (first ed. 1866), app. B, 184–185, 450; also R. Holtzmann, *Geschichte der Sächsischen Kaiserzeit*, München 1943.

13. They are given, among others, by Schnürer, *op. cit.*, II, 140.

14. See Kohn's introduction to *Die Welt der Slaven*, I, Frankfurt 1960, under the title "Einsamkeit und Gemeinsamkeit der Slaven."

15. About J. Peisker's theory in that matter see my *Limits and Divisions of European History*, New York 1950, p. 187 f.

16. Quoted by Vernadsky, *op. cit.*, pp. 158–159.

17. It is difficult to understand how de Reynold, *La Formation*, VII, 488, could include the advance of the Slavs among the "poussées asiatiques" threatening Europe.

18. T. Sulimirski, *Prehistoria Polski* /Poland's Prehistory/, London 1960.

19. Carefully analyzed by K. Tymieniecki, *Ziemie polskie w starożytności* /The Polish Lands in Antiquity/, Poznań 1950.

20. H. Grégoire, "L'origine et le nom des Croates et des Serbes," *Byzantion*, XVII (1944–45).

21. The theory of the northern origin of the Piasts and of their state, presented in its extreme form by Brackmann, "Die Wikinger und die Anfänge Polens," *Abhdl. d. preuss. Akad. d. Wiss.*, Philos.-Hist. Klasse 1942, no. 6, Berlin 1943, was also abandoned by most of the German historians.

22. My remarks on the problem of Russia's relations to Europe in *Limits and Divisions* . . . , pp. 87–101, were supplemented in the German edition, "Europa," pp. 188–190.

NOTES TO CHAPTER VII

1. De Reynold, *La Formation*, VII, 426.

2. A scholarly commemoration of the *renovatio imperii* was organized by the *Società di Studi Romani* in Ravenna as early as November 1961. The proceedings of the discussions, in which many foreign specialists participated, are not yet published. See also H. Beumann in *Histor. Zeitschrift*, CXCV (1962), pp. 529 f.

3. James A. Brundage, "Widukind of Corvey and the Non-Roman Imperial Idea," *Mediaeval Studies*, XXII, Toronto 1960, 15–26; the following quotations are taken from this article.

4. See above, Chapter I, n. 14.

5. Amann in *Histoire de l'Eglise*, VII, "L'Eglise au Pouvoir des laïques," Paris 1949, 45 f., where the restoration of the empire by Otto I and his relations with the papacy are discussed in detail, pp. 44–80.

6. De Reynold, *La Formation*, VII, 420–422, showed best the importance of her marriage to Otto I.

7. See K. J. Conant, "Cluny in the Tenth Century," *Medievalia et Humanistica*, IX (1955), 23–25.

8. See appendix A, "On the Burgundies," to Bryce, *The Holy Roman Empire*, p. 448 f.

9. W. Ohnsorge, "Die Anerkennung des Kaisertums Otto's I durch Byzanz," *Byzantinische Zeitschrift*, LIV (1961), 36.

10. *Ibid.*, pp. 37–50, where the *Legatio Liudprandi* is discussed once more.

11. *Ibid.*, p. 52; the author has pointed out before, p. 49, that Teophano was not really a "porphyrogenita."

12. Vernadsky, *Kievan Russia*, New Haven 1948, p. 41.

13. Best explained by H. Hantsch, *Die Geschichte Österreichs*, I, Graz 1951, 47 ff.

14. Ernst K. Winter, "The Byzantine Millennium of Vienna," *Medievalia et Humanistica*, X (1956), 1–31.

NOTES TO CHAPTER VIII

1. See the "Symposium on the Tenth Century," *Medievalia et Humanistica,* IX (1955), 3–29, especially the excellent contribution by Helen M. Cam on "The Adolescent Nations," pp. 7–9.

2. Jullian, *De la Gaule.* . . .

3. For the whole background see C. Petit-Dutaillis, *La monarchie féodale en France et en Angleterre au Xe et au XIIIe siècle,* Paris 1933.

4. On the significance of the change of the dynasty in 987 see the remarks of A. Luchaire in E. Lavisse, *Histoire de France,* II/2 (1901), 149, 152; see also J. de Pange, *Le roi très chrétien,* Paris 1949, pp. 253–258.

5. De Reynold, *La Formation,* VII, 451 ff.

6. F. M. Stenton, "Anglo-Saxon England," vol. II, of the *Oxford History of England,* London 1947, p. 266, calls him the "most effective ruler in Western Europe after Charlemagne."

7. Athelstan, eldest son and successor of Edward, already called himself "King of the English and ruler of all Britain,"; see *ibid.,* p. 345.

8. In spite of Athelstan's intimate association with the Carolingian and Saxon kings of Germany before the imperial coronation of Otto I, who had been married to his sister; *ibid.,* pp. 339, 342.

9. On the impact of this culture on Spain, see the comments of R. Altamira in *The Cambridge Mediaeval History,* III, 438, and the article of J. M. Millás Vallicroza, "Arab and Hebrew Contributions to Spanish Culture," *Cahiers d'Histoire mondiale,* VI (1961), 732–751.

10. On the idea of the *reconquista* see the remarks of P. Guinard in *Histoire Générale,* ed. G. Glotz, IV/1, Paris 1944, 290–294.

11. On the imperial title in Spain see Altamira, *op. cit.,* VI, 407, and particularly R. Menendez Pidal, *La España del Cid,* Madrid 1929, I, 73–77, 117–120, 262, 344–347.

12. See the symposium on *I problemi comuni dell'Europa postcarolingia,* Spoleto 1955, especially the paper of G. Falco, "La crisi dell' autorità e lo sforzo della ricostruzione in Italia," pp. 39–51.

13. Falco, *loc. cit.,* p. 59, says that "L'asse d'Europa doveva essere formata dalla Germania e dall'Italia."

14. Falco, *loc. cit.,* p. 65; see also L. M. Hartmann, *Geschichte Italiens im Mittelalter,* III, Gotha 1911, 261, with reference to the coronation of Otto I.

15. On the continued existence of the Papal State through more than a thousand years see de Reynold, *La Formation,* 466, 481.

16. Brackmann, "Die Ostpolitik Otto's des Grossen," p. 250, says that John XIII "tritt für uns in die Reihe jener Päpste, die von Leo III über Silvester II zu Gregor VII führt."

17. The decisive importance of Pietro Orseolo at the turn of the century is rightly stressed by R. Cessi, *Storia della Repubblica di Venezia,* I, Milano 1944, pp. 81 ff.; see also his study on "Venezia e l'Oriente," *Problemi storici e orientamenti storiografici,* p. 317 f.

NOTES TO CHAPTER IX

1. This was done in a symposium on the Christianization of Poland and her neighbors, Fordham University, November 1959; the individual contributions were published later in *The Polish Review* and are quoted below.

2. On the millennary of 1929, a short biography of St. Václav /The Life of St. Wenceslas/, Prague 1929, was published by Dvornik who discussed the whole problem in detail in his *The Making of Central and Eastern Europe*, London 1949.

3. A. Florovsky, *Čechy i vostočnye Slaviane*, X-XVIII v. /The Czechs and the Eastern Slavs/, 2 vols., Prague 1935, 1947.

4. Dvornik, "The Role of Bohemia and St. Adalbert in the Spread of Christianity in Poland," *The Polish Review*, V (1960), 15–28; see also his remarks on Bohemia's part in the Christianization of Hungary in his book, *The Making ...*, cited above, pp. 151–156.

5. K. Krofta, *Das Deutschtum in der tschechoslovakischen Geschichte*, Prague 1934; see also S. Harrison Thomson, *Czechoslovakia in European History*, Princeton 1953.

6. See my article on "The Significance of the Christianization of Poland in European History," *The Polish Review*, VI (1961), 2–16, and the interpretations given by T. Manteuffel, "Państwo Mieszka a Europa" /Mieszko's State and Europe/, *Kwartalnik histor.*, LXVII (1960), 1020–1032, and the new hypothesis of J. Dowiat, *Metryka chrztu Mieszka i jej geneza* /The record of Mieszko's baptism and its origin/, Warszawa 1961.

7. Described by Z. Wojciechowski in the symposium *Poland's Place in Europe*, Poznań 1947.

8. See above, Preface, n. 3.

9. See above, Chapter V, n. 19.

10. The controversial interpretations of this problem were recently discussed by Leon Koczy, "Jomsborg," *The Polish Review*, V (1960).

11. See above, Chapter VI, n. 21.

12. See Koczy, "L'Impero e la Polonia, 963–1002," *Antemurale*, IV (1958), 5–26; Ladner, "The Holy Roman Empire of the Tenth Century and East Central Europe," *The Polish Review*, V (1960), 3–14.

13. About all these frontier problems see Gieysztor, "Aspects territoriaux du premier État polonais, IXe-XIe siècle," *Revue historique*, CCXXVI (1961), 357–382.

14. See the bibliography by Z. J. Gasiorowski in *Speculum*, XXX (1955), 555, n. 31; and the recent publications quoted by Gieysztor, *loc. cit.*, 366 n., and Dowiat, *op. cit.*, p. 89, nn. 12 and 13.

15. The unpublished document of the end of the sixteenth century, where this tradition appears, is discussed in my article, "Un écho lointain de Dagome iudex," now in print in the *Portuguese Historical Review;* see also my remarks on the rise of papal power in the second half of the tenth century in the article quoted in n. 6.

16. See Astrik L. Gabriel, "The Conversion of Hungary to Christianity," *The Polish Review*, VI (1961), 31–44.

17. B. Hóman, *Geschichte des Ungarischen Mittelalters*, I, Berlin 1940, 152–157.

18. On occasion of that Millennium a symposium *Sbornik Tomislava,* ed. Mano-jlovič, was published in Zagreb by the Croatian Academy in 1925.

19. See Hóman, *op. cit.,* p. 157; but also R. Grodecki in *Polski Słownik biogra-ficzny* /Polish Biographical Dictionary/, I (1935), 28.

20. Hóman, *op. cit.,* p. 279.

21. Ihor Ševčenko, "The Christianization of Kievan Rus'," *The Polish Review,* V (1960), 29–35; Ludolf Müller, "Die Christianisierung Russlands als Forschungs-problem," *XIe Congrès international des Sciences historiques,* Stockholm 1960, *Résumés des Communications,* pp. 94–95, and the summary of the discussions in *Actes du Congrès,* p. 114.

22. St. Smolka, *Die reussische Welt,* Wien 1916, showed clearly the importance of this problem.

23. Vasiliev, "Was Old Russia a Vassal State of Byzantium?" *Speculum,* VII (1932); but see also Vernadsky, *Kievan Russia,* New Haven 1948, p. 349, n. 87.

24. Vernadsky, *op. cit.,* 214 ff., with reference to the period from 1139 to 1237.

25. On all implications of these questions see Paszkiewicz, *The Origin of Russia;* see also *The Making of the Russian Nation,* London 1962, where the opin-ions of his opponents are discussed.

NOTES TO CHAPTER X

1. Henri Focillon, *L'an mil,* Paris 1952: a brilliant study of the whole back-ground which shows, however, that these fears were far from being general.

2. A. Czajkowski, "The Congress of Gniezno in the Year 1000," *Speculum,* XXIV (1949), 339–356.

3. A symposium *Św. Wojciech* /St. Adalbert/ was published in Gniezno in 1947 on the initiative of the then Primate of Poland, Cardinal Hlond.

4. Paszkiewicz, *Origin . . . ,* appendix VII, 381–404, thinks that this was a metro-politan see of the Slavonic rite, a hypothesis which Lanckorońska has further devel-oped. See Chapter V, n. 19.

5. This is strongly emphasized by R. W. Southern, *The Making of the Middle Ages,* New Haven 1953, pp. 11, 65, 175–178. *The Letters of Gerbert with His Papal Privileges as Sylvester II* was published in English by Harriet Pratt Latin, *Records of Civilization,* no. 60, New York 1961.

6. This is the opinion of Mathilde Uhlirz, developed in her otherwise excellent essay, "Das Werden des Gedankens der 'Renovatio Imperii Romanorum' bei Otto III," pp. 215–218, in *I Problemi comuni dell'Europa post-carolingia,* 201–219 (see there also the inaugural address of Raff. Morghen, pp. 13–35, "L'età di Ottone III Romanorum imperator, servus apostolorum"), and discussed already in her stand-ard work *Jahrbücher des Deutschen Reiches unter Otto II und Otto III,* II, *Otto III,* Berlin 1954, 317–329. See also the appendices XVIII–XX, 538–539.

7. They were examined by Meysztowicz in his study, *"Koronacje pierwszych Piastów* /The Coronations of the first Piasts/, *Sacrum Poloniae Millennium,* III (1956), 283–337, 367–373. His own view, that Bolesław was to be the successor of Otto III, corresponds to the views of Tymieniecki, expressed in *Przegląd zachodni* /Western Review/, XI (1955), 158–160.

8. See e.g. the plates in Dawson, *The Making* . . . , and his comments on p. 14.

9. Percy E. Schramm, *Kaiser, Rom und Renovatio,* Leipzig 1929, p. 118 f., thinks that *Gallia* means "Westdeutschland" and *Germania* "Ostdeutschland," but such an interpretation seems quite arbitrary; interesting, however, is his observation that on an earlier, similar picture *Roma* is called *Italia*.

10. Vernadsky, *op. cit.,* pp. 158 ff.

11. This interpretation, which seems the most acceptable, was among others explained by Brackmann, "Kaiser Otto III und die staatliche Umgestaltung Polens und Ungarns," *Abhdlg, d. preuss. Akad. der Wiss.,* 1939 (Philos.-Hist. Klasse, No. 1), pp. 15–17, in connection with the emperor's title *servus apostolorum* and the situation in Italy and Germany.

12. See the comments of Brackmann, *op. cit.,* p. 25, of Uhlirz, *Jahrbücher,* II, 369–373 and 572–582, and of P. Váczy in *Archivum Europae Centro-Orientalis,* V (1940), 39.

13. Uhlirz, "Das Werden . . . ," pp. 204–205. The same problem is discussed in her paper on the relations between the empire of Otto III and the neighboring states of Poland, Hungary and Venice, at the International Congress of Historical Sciences in Rome, 1955.

14. F. v. Šišić, *Geschichte der Kroaten,* I, Zagreb 1917, pp. 354–384.

15. See Ohnsorge, "Die Anerkennung des Kaisertums Otto's I durch Byzanz," *Byzantinische Zeitschrift,* LIV (1961), especially the concluding remarks on Otto III, pp. 51–52.

16. For Toynbee, *Study,* III, 269, this would be the beginning of the "time of trouble" in the history of the eastern Christian society.

17. Ohnsorge, "Otto's III Legation an Basileios II v. J. 998," *Abendland und Byzanz,* Darmstadt 1958, pp. 288–299.

18. See the article of Meysztowicz quoted in Chapter VI, n. 8.

19. See Schramm, *op. cit.,* II, 96, and the index.

20. The *versus* printed by Schramm, *op. cit.,* II, 63, still belongs to the pontificate of Gregory V, 998.

21. Uhlirz, *loc. cit.,* pp. 201 f. speaks of a "Wiederbelebung des römischen Reichsgedankens im Sinne eines ecclesiastischen Imperium unter der gemeinsamen Leitung von Kaiser und Papst." It is significant that the term *res publica* appears in the time of Otto III, around the year 1000, frequently beside that of *imperium nostrum;* see Schramm, *op. cit.,* I, 101, 130 f.

22. This idea is clearly expressed in his letter which, according to the German chronicler Thietmar, was sent from Kiev to both emperors, Henry II and Basil II, in 1018. See my article, "La Pologne et l'Empire Byzantin," *Byzantion* (1932), pp. 41 ff.

23. Uhlirz, *loc. cit.*

NOTES TO CHAPTER XI

1. Soon after my *Limits and Divisions* . . . , where I discussed the problem at length, there appeared the exhaustive study by Van der Pot, *De Periodisering* . . . , Hague 1951, where the conventional division with the Middle Ages in the center is

criticized on pp. 136–150. See also G. Barraclough, *History in a Changing World,* Oxford 1955, pp. 54–63.

2. The original, Roman meaning of the word was well defined by Alfredo Passerini, "Civiltà ellenica e civiltà romana," *Problemi storici e orientamenti storiografici,* p. 55: "un patrimonio ideale e materiale di tutto il popolo."

3. See the analysis of the concept *Corpus reipublicae mysticum* /Mystical Body of the Commonweal/, as used by Vincent of Beauvais in the twelfth century, given by E. H. Kantorowicz, *The King's Two Bodies, A Study in Mediaeval Political Theology,* Princeton 1957, pp. 207–232.

4. See the rich bibliographical information given by William M. Daly, "Christian Fraternity . . . , the Precarious Survival of an Ideal," *Mediaeval Studies,* XII (Toronto 1960), 47, n. 17; and more recently, de Rougemont, *Europe,* pp. 53 ff.

5. In the important book by Denys Hay, *Europe, the Emergence of an Idea,* Edinburgh 1957.

6. Rightly stressed by A. C. Krey, "Urban's Crusade—Success or Failure?" *American Historical Review,* LIII (1948), 235–250.

7. Dawson, *Making of Europe,* Chapter VI, "The Rise of Mediaeval Unity," pp. 218–238.

8. See e.g. Toynbee, *Study,* IV, 339.

9. Recently discussed by H. Brugmans, *L'Europe prend le large,* Paris 1961; see also L. C. MacKinney, "The People and Public Opinion in the Eleventh Century Peace Movement," *Speculum,* V (1930), 181–206.

10. See J. Levron, *Saint Louis ou l'apogée du Moyen Age,* Paris 1951.

11. It is, therefore, no exaggeration to speak of Cluny's empire, as does André Chagny, *Cluny et son empire,* 2nd ed., Paris 1949.

12. A. Gabriel, the leading authority regarding the international role of the Sorbonne, gave a new example of it in his paper, "The Foreign Students, Members of the English-German Nation, at the University of Paris in the Fifteenth Century," read at the "Colloquium" on the history of the universities during the XIth International Congress of Historical Sciences in Stockholm, 1960; see the summary of the paper in the volume *Communications,* pp. 220–222, and that of the discussion in *Actes du Congrès,* p. 262. See also his earlier books, *Student Life in Ave Maria College in Mediaeval Paris,* Notre Dame 1955, and *Skara House at the Mediaeval University of Paris,* Notre Dame 1960.

13. In spite of the doubts concerning correctness of the term, raised by W. A. Nitze, opposing Ch. H. Haskims in "The So-called Twelfth-Century Renaissance," *Speculum,* XXIII (1948), 464–471, and by R. Sabatino Lopes, "Still Another Renaissance," *American Historical Review,* LVII (1951), 1–21, with reference to the tenth century. The influence of schools and teaching is particularly emphasized in G. Paré, A. Brunel and P. Tremblay, *La Renaissance du XIIe siècle,* Paris-Ottawa 1939, with the subtitle, "Les écoles et l'enseignement."

14. See the article by Millàs Vallicroza, quoted above, Chapter VIII, n. 9, especially its second part, pp. 738–757, and the remarks of Altamira in the *Cambridge Mediaeval History,* VI, 407, as well as those on "The Traffic of Ideas," by R. W. Southern, *Making . . . ,* pp. 63–69.

15. See A. Rubio y Lluch, *La Grecia catalana,* Barcelona 1914.

16. Recently discussed by K. Ślaski, *Podziały terytorialne Pomorza w XII-XIII wieku* /Territorial Divisions of Pomerania in the Twelfth and Thirteenth Centuries/, Poznań 1960.

17. Well shown by A. M. Ammann, "Kirchenpolitische Wandlungen im Ost-Baltikum bis zum Tode Alexander Newski's," *Orientalia Christiana Analecta*, vol. 105, Rome 1936.

18. See B. Spuler, "Die Goldene Horde und Russlands Schicksal," *Saeculum*, VI (1955), 397–406.

19. Even in Soviet historiography the Mongol invasion is considered "le plus grand des malheurs historiques"; see A. M. Sakharov, "Les Mongols et la civilisation russe," *Contributions à l'histoire russe*, a special issue of *Cahiers d'Histoire mondiale* (1958), pp. 77–97 and particularly p. 96.

20. Best described by Paszkiewicz, *Jagiellonowie a Moskwa* /The Jagellonians and Moscow/, I, Warsaw 1933. See also M. Hellmann, "Die geschichtliche Bedeutung des Grossfürstentums Litauen," *Saeculum*, IX (1958), 87–112. The importance of V. T. Pashuto, *Obrazovanie Litovskogo Gosudarstwa* /The Formation of the Lithuanian State/, Moscow 1959, should not be over-estimated as it was in *American Historical Review*, LXVII (1962), 764 f.

NOTES TO CHAPTER XII

1. Bryce, *The Holy Roman Empire*, London 1903, discussing the "Theory of the Mediaeval Empire," Chapter VII, has quoted the contemporary chroniclers, especially Abbot Engelbert of Admont, p. 98, note m, whose interpretation went farthest. The necessity of revision was briefly shown by Daly, "Christian Fraternity . . . ," *op. cit.*, 43–48.

2. See above, Chapter I, n. 14. The most recent interpretation of all European history from the point of view of the "Reichsidee," the succession of world empires, was given by Karl Fürst Schwarzenberg, *Adler und Drache—der Weltherrschaftsgedanke*, Wien 1958; see in particular pp. 6, 267, 280, and the "Monarchenliste" in the appendix, pp. 368–376.

3. See Schramm's subtle distinction between "Weltherrschaft" and "Weltvorherrschaft" in *Rom, Kaisertum, Renovatio*, I, 123 f.

4. So does Brugmans, *Les origines de la civilisation européenne*, Liège 1958.

5. Luchaire, *Innocent III*, vol. V, *Les royautés vassales du Saint-Siège*, Paris 1908.

6. R. Grousset, *Histoire des croisades et du royaume franc de Jérusalem*, III, Paris 1936, p. 289.

7. Particularly by Kantorowicz in his standard work, *Kaiser Friedrich II*, Berlin 1931–1936, 2 vols.; see also his most recent remarks in *The King's Two Bodies*, pp. 97–143, and August Nitschke, "Friedrich II, ein Ritter des hohen Mittelalters," *Historische Zeitschrift*, CXCIV (1962), 1–36.

8. Brugmans, *L'Europe prend.* . . . See also the emphasis of both Kantorowicz and Nitschke on the "altertümlich" character of the policy of Frederick II, who took

his principles as a ruler from a statement which Seneca attributes to Nero, *The King's Two Bodies*, pp. 115–116.

9. On the "Ketzergesetzgebung" of Frederick II, see the appendix of Kantorowicz, *op. cit.*, II, 218 f. See also the remarks of Msgr. Cristiani in *Cahiers d'Histoire mondiale*, V/1 (1959), 80.

10. On the consequences of the interregnum see O. Redlich, *Rudolf von Habsburg; das Deutsche Reich nach dem Untergang des alten Kaisertums*, Innsbruck 1903, and the recent interpretation of Přemysl Otakar's policy by Dvornik, *The Slavs in European History and Civilization*, New Brunswick 1962, pp. 27–29.

11. Gerald Walsh, *Dante Alighieri—Citizen of Christendom*, Milwaukee 1946.

12. See the quotations from "De Monarchia" given by de Rougemont, *Europe*, pp. 56–58, which show that this monarchy was not to be limited to Europe.

13. J. de Lagarde, *La naissance de l'esprit laïque au déclin du Moyen Age, II Marsile de Padoue*, Paris 1948.

14. See its latest discussion with quotations from the most important passages, by de Rougemont, *Europe*, pp. 62 f.

15. Among his various biographers, Walsh in *The Emperor Charles IV, A Study in Holy Roman Imperialism*, London 1924, best showed the supranational aspects of his personality.

16. See my study, "Rome et Byzance au temps du grand schisme d'Occident," *Collectanea theologica*, XVIII (1937), pp. 477–532, and R. Loenertz, *Les recueils de lettres de Demétrius Cydonès*, Vatican City 1947, pp. 93–101.

17. Luchaire, *op. cit.*, vol. VI, *Le Concile du Latran*, Paris 1908.

18. Even Marxist historiography is hesitant as to the dividing line between the feudal and the capitalist period; see Zhukow's report and its discussion at the Stockholm Congress of 1960, quoted in note 2 of the Preface.

19. Basic in this respect is Marc Bloch, *La Société féodale*, 2 vols., Paris 1939–1940. (English edition: *The Feudal Society*, Chicago 1961).

20. In the case of Poland the distinction between fully developed feudalism and processes of feudalization was long ago made clear by Marceli Handelsman, but now Marxist historians try to present almost the whole history of Poland, at least before the partitions, as a period of feudalism.

21. The two problems are particularly well explained by Brugmans, *L'Europe prend* . . .

NOTES TO CHAPTER XIII

1. The studies of Hayes in the matter have been summed up in his book, *Nationalism* . . .

2. See Kohn's *Idea of Nationalism*, Chapters I and II, and his article, "The Dawn of Nationalism in Europe," *American Historical Review*, LII (1947), 265–280.

3. C. Morawski, *Histoire de l'Université de Cracovie*, vol. I, Cracow 1900. For the whole background see L. R. Loomis, "Nationality of the Council of Constance," *American Historical Review*, XLIV (1938–1939), 508–527.

4. Pearl Kibre, *The Nations in the Modern Universities,* Cambridge, Mass. 1948; see also the report of Sven Stelling-Michaud, "L'Histoire des universités au Moyen Age et à la Renaissance," at the XIth International Congress of Historical Sciences, Stockholm 1960, *Rapports* I, and the discussion, *Actes du Congrès,* pp. 257–260.

5. Koczy, "Narody w pierwszej wyprawie krzyżowej" /The nations in the First Crusade/, *Teki historyczne* /Historical Papers/, London 1960–1961, XI, 41–96; the quotations are taken from this article.

6. On the use of the word *patria* in mediaeval sources see Kantorowicz, *op. cit.,* pp. 232–234.

7. See the recent discussions by W. Dworzaczek, *Genealogia,* Warsaw 1959, in the chapter "Ród i rodzina," and my comments in *Teki Historyczne,* XI, 273–274, whether in these cases the common descent is reliable or only symbolized by a common coat-of-arms.

8. See the work of O. Balzer on the restoration of the *regnum Poloniae* in the thirteenth century: *Królestwo polskie,* 3 vols., *Lwów* 1919–1920.

9. See G. Barraclough, *History in a Changing World,* p. 125, n. 2, and de Reynold, *La Formation,* VII, 428, on the final adoption of the name in the fifteenth century.

10. See the remarks of Winter, *Studien zum Severinsproblem,* Klosterneuburg 1959, on "Die babenbergische Staatsräson," pp. 254–284, especially on Austria's patron saint, Duke Leopold III, p. 260.

11. Its position in the empire is well explained by S. Harrison Thomson, *op. cit.,* 2nd ed. See Dvornik, *Slavs in European History,* pp. 21 ff.

12. Dvornik, *op. cit.,* pp. 7, 41 f., and Chapter VII, n. 8 above.

13. See Part II of James W. Thompson, *Feudal Germany,* Chicago 1928.

14. W. Holtzmann, "Imperium und Nationen," *X. Congresso intern. di scienzi storiche,* Rome 1955, *Relazioni* III, 273 f.

15. Cessi, *Storia della Repubblica di Venezia,* II, Milano 1946, pp. 34 f.

16. See above, Chapter VI, n. 12.

17. In a frequently quoted statement by John of Salisbury; see Thompson, *op. cit.,* p. 323, and Barraclough, *op. cit.,* p. 123.

18. See remarks by Altamira, quoted above, Chapter VIII, n. 9, and also Fürst Schwarzenberg, *op. cit.,* pp. 327–329, n. 115, on "Die Spanische Reichsidee."

19. Published in *Lites ac res gestae inter Polonos Ordinemque Cruciferorum,* I, Poznań 1855, pp. 72–353.

20. Discussed along with the League of the Lombard Cities as the earliest examples of federalism by E. A. Freeman, *A History of Federalism in Greece and Italy,* 2nd ed., London 1893. See also W. W. Tarn, "The Constitution of the Achaean League," *The Cambridge Ancient History,* VII (1928), 735–739.

21. See the most recent discussion in de Reynold, *La Formation,* VII, 438 f.

22. Halvdan Koht, "Vereinigte Königreiche des späteren Mittelalters," *Wirtschaft und Kultur,* Baden 1938, pp. 503–511.

23. This has been recently questioned by Dvornik, *op. cit.,* p. 33, but his arguments are not quite convincing.

24. See Halecki, *De Hedvige Andegavensi, Regina Poloniae,* Rome 1953.

NOTES TO CHAPTER XIV

1. See the articles of Ohnsorge quoted above, Chapter X, n. 15, 17.

2. See the symposium, *Après neuf cent ans: L'Eglise et les Eglises, 1054–1954,* Chevetogne 1954; for the general background, particularly the first contribution by Yves M.-J. Congar, published in English, *After Nine Hundred Years,* New York 1959. Anton Michel, one of the contributors to the symposium, discussed the personal responsibilities in his *Humbert und Kerullarios,* 2 vols., Paderborn 1925–1930.

3. This will be explained in an article by I. Ševčenko.

4. See the studies of Meysztowicz on the "Manuscriptum Gertrudae" in *Antemurales,* II (1955), 97–157, and on "L'Union de Kiev avec Rome sous Grégoire VII," *Studi Gregoriani,* V (1956), 83–108.

5. B. Leib, *Rome, Kiev et Byzance à la fin du XIe siècle,* Paris 1924; see also Runciman, *The Eastern Schism,* pp. 104–108.

6. F. Chalandon, *Jean II Comnène et Manuel I Comnène,* Paris 1912; Runciman, *op. cit.,* p. 120 f.

7. See the subtitle of the article by Daly quoted above, Chapter XI, n. 4, and his conclusions, pp. 89–91.

8. See Grégoire, "The Question of the Diversion of the Fourth Crusade," *Byzantion,* XV (1940–41), 152 ff.

9. Alice Gardner, *The Lascarids of Nicaea—Story of an Empire in Exile,* London 1912.

10. Runciman, *History of the Crusades,* II, London 1954, chap. I, *"Outre mer* and its neighbors."

11. W. Norden, *Das Papsttum und Byzanz,* Berlin 1903.

12. See above, Chapter XI, n. 17.

13. As charged by Eduard Winter, *Russland und das Papsttum,* I, Berlin 1960.

14. See my review of Winter's book in *Journal of Central European Affairs,* XXII (1962), 101–104.

15. N. de Baumgarten, *Généalogies et mariages occidentaux des Rurikides russes,* Orientalia Christiana, IX/1, Rome 1927.

16. J. J. Zatko, "The Union of Suzdal," *Journal of Ecclesiastical History,* VIII (1958), 33–52.

17. Vernadsky, The Mongols . . . , p. 148 f.

18. D. J. Geanakoplos, *Emperor Michael Palaeologus and the West, 1258–1282,* Cambridge, Mass. 1959.

19. See the series of articles by H. Evert-Kappesowa in *Byzantinoslavica,* X (1949), XIII (1952), XVI (1955), XVII (1956), on the attitude of Byzantium toward the Latins at the time of the Union of Lyons.

20. Runciman, *The Sicilian Vespers,* Cambridge, Mass. 1958.

21. L. S. Stavrianos, *The Balkans since 1453,* New York 1958; see below, Chapter XXIII, n. 2.

22. M. Viller, "La question de l'Union des Eglises entre Grecs et Latins, 1274–1438," *Revue d'hist. eccl.*, XVII-XVIII (1921–1922).

23. Halecki, *Un Empereur de Byzance à Rome*, Warsaw 1930; see also my article, "Two Paleologi in Venice, 1370–1371," *Byzantion*, XVIII (1944–45), 331–336.

NOTES TO CHAPTER XV

1. This was done at the Xth International Congress of Historical Sciences held in Rome, 1955; see *Relazioni*, III.

2. By L. v. Ranke, *Geschichte der romanischen und germanischen Völker von 1494–1514*, Berlin 1825, p. 1.

3. See the discussion of "L'Estoire d'Eracle," by Grousset, *Histoire des Croisades, I*, pp. 1 and 628, quoted above.

4. See above, Chapter XI, n. 6, and M. W. Baldwin, "Some Recent Interpretations of Pope Urban's Eastern Policy," *The Catholic Historical Review*, XXV (1940), 459–466.

5. See the bulls quoted by G. Rhode, *Die Ostgrenze Polens*, I, Köln-Graz 1955.

6. Such an impression could be created even by the outstanding contributions of Diehl; see his "Byzance et Croisades," in *Choses et gens de Byzance*, Paris 1926, and also Runciman, *Eastern Schism*, pp. 78–101.

7. See Iorga, *Philippe de Mézières et la Croisade au XIVe siècle*, Paris 1896, and *France de Chypre*, Paris 1933.

8. Grousset, *op. cit.*, III, 289.

9. *Ibid.*, II, 609–758; K. M. Setton, ed. *A History of the Crusades*, I, Philadelphia 1955, 591 ff.

10. *Ibid.*, II, 814.

11. Setton, *A History . . .* , I, 262–265, 472 f.

12. Luke, 14:23; see the comments by Msgr. Cristiani in his article cited above, Chapter I, n. 18.

13. Luchaire, *Innocent III*, II, "La croisade des Albigeois," Paris 1905. See now also A. P. Evans in *A History of the Crusades*, II (1962), pp. 277–324.

14. See the article "Inquisition" by E. Vacandard in *Dict. de Théol. cath.* VII/2, Paris 1922, col. 2016–2068.

15. See above, Chapter XII, n. 9.

16. Briefly discussed from another point of view in Chapter XII, n. 14.

17. Iorga, who first used the expression—see above, n. 7—also published six volumes of *Notes et extraits pour servir à l'histoire des croisades au XVe siècle*, Paris 1899–1916. See also S. A. Atiya, *The Crusade in the Later Middle Ages*, London 1938.

18. R. Grodecki, *Kongres Krakowski w. r. 1364* /The Cracow Congress in 1364/, Warsaw 1939.

19. J. Delaville Le Roux, *Les Hospitaliers à Rhodes*, Paris 1913.

20. This congress, though carefully prepared—see Setton, *The Catalan Domination of Athens, 1311–1388*, Cambridge, Mass. 1948—never took place.

21. The seriousness of Christianization questioned by the Teutonic Knights is

evidenced by the documents published in *Codex diplomaticus Ecclesiae Cathedralis necnon Dioceseos Vilnensis,* I, Cracow 1932, particularly nos. 1–13.

22. Rhode quotes statements by historians from different countries on the importance of the Polish-Lithuanian Union in general European history in his *Die Ostgrenze Polens,* I.

NOTES TO CHAPTER XVI

1. For a more detailed discussion see my *Limits and Divisions* . . . , Chapters VIII and IX; Van der Pot, *De Periodisering* . . . , pp. 113–150.

2. E. Joukov, "Des principes d'une histoire universelle," *Cahiers d'Histoire mondiale,* III (1956), 532.

3. See the report by D. Cantimori and A. F. Jacob, "La Periodizzazione dell'età del Rinascimento," at the Xth International Congress of Historical Sciences in Rome, 1955, *Relazioni* IV, particularly pp. 322–336.

4. See e.g. the criticism by S. Nowak of recent American interpretations of the Renaissance in *Kwartalnik historyczny,* LX (1953), 212–227, in the section which is dedicated to "The struggle against hostile ideologies."

5. See above, Chapter XI, n. 13.

6. The famous case of Abélard is typical in that respect; see E. Gilson, *Héloise et Abélard,* Paris 1938, particularly p. 164 and Appendix II. For a Marxist interpretation of the case see N. A. Sidorova, "Abélard et son époque," *Cahiers d'Histoire mondiale,* IV/3 (1958), 541–552, and the discussion of this article, *ibid.,* VI/1 (1960), 175–182.

7. De Reynold, *Le dixseptième siècle: Le classique et le baroque,* Montreal 1944, basic for an understanding of the problem, appeared in a new edition, *Synthèse du dixseptième siècle: France classique et Europe baroque,* Paris 1962.

8. See below, Chapter XXXIII.

9. Ladner, *Idea of Reform;* see also Martin J. Higgins, "The Renaissance of the First Century and the Origin of Standard Late Greek," *Traditio,* III (1945), 49–100.

10. In spite of the Marxist reinterpretations of Polish history, there is a deep interest in Polish historiography in the influence of the Renaissance, as evidenced in the symposium, *Odrodzenie w Polsce* /The Renaissance in Poland/, Warsaw 1953; the proceedings were published in five volumes, 1955 ff.

11. See Dawson, *The Movement of World Revolution,* New York 1959.

12. Recently pointed out by Hay, *Europe—The Emergence of an Idea,* pp. 22 ff., and by de Rougemont, *Europe,* p. 53, who however underestimates considerably the place which the European idea occupied in mediaeval thought. Particularly interesting is the discussion of the problem in Chapter I of Chabod's *Storia dell'idea d'Europa,* Bari 1962, published posthumously, pp. 15–47. But it should be remembered that there *was* a European community even if, and when, it was called *respublica Christiana* or *Christianitas* rather than *Europa.*

13. See below, Chapter XVII.

14. Chabod, who discussed "Il Rinascimento nelle recenti interpretazioni," as far back as 1933 in the *Bulletin of the International Committee of Historical Sci-*

ences, XIX, returned to the problem with special reference to the idea of continuity and to the question of the relations between Renaissance and Middle Ages in his article, "Rinascimento," in *Problemi storici e orientamenti storiografici,* pp. 445–491.

15. Ladner, *op. cit.,* pp. 4, 277, 423 f.

16. Atiya, *op. cit.,* p. 468; see also his remarks in *Cahiers d'Histoire mondiale,* II/2 (1954), 472 f.

NOTES TO CHAPTER XVII

1. Paul Hazard, *La crise de la conscience européenne, 1680–1715,* 2 vols., Paris 1935.

2. K. A. Meissinger, *Der katholische Luther,* München 1952.

3. F. G. Heyman, *Žižka and the Hussite Revolution,* Princeton 1955, and his article "John Rokycana: Church Reform between Hus and Luther," *Church History,* XXVIII (1959), 240–280.

4. Thomson, "Pre-Hussite Heresy in Bohemia," *Engl. Hist. Rev.,* LXVIII (1933), 23–42; see also Dvornik, *The Slavs . . . ,* chap. VIII, "The Czech Reformation."

5. Gill, *The Council of Florence,* p. vii.

6. Noël Valois, *La France et le grand Schisme d'Occident,* I, Paris 1896, 221.

7. Thus, e.g., the Habsburgs' attitude was decisively influenced by their desire to get Urban VI's support for their claims to the Polish crown.

8. Valois, *op. cit.,* IV, 143.

9. The collection *Concilium Florentinum,* started by G. Hofmann, who in 1937–1938 gave the first summary of the "Konzilsarbeit" in Ferrara and Florence, *Orientalia Christiana Periodica,* vols. III and IV, now includes more than twenty volumes edited by the Papal Oriental Institute in Rome since 1940.

10. See L. v. Pastor, *Geschichte der Papste,* I, 325.

11. Halecki, *From Florence to Brest, 1439–1596,* Rome 1958, Part I.

12. It is significant that a special review dedicated to the study of this problem was founded in 1896, titled *Bessarione,* in tribute to the Greek humanist who contributed so much to this cooperation. The review appeared in Rome until 1923. See also Geanakoplos, *Greek Scholars in Venice,* Cambridge, Mass. 1962.

13. See his biography by P. Becker, *Giuliano Cesarini,* Kallmünz 1935.

14. The impact of these conflicting traditions on Czech historiography has been well shown by R. Plaschka, *Von Palacký bis Pekař-Geschichtswissenschaft und Nationalbewusstsein bei den Tschechen,* Graz-Köln 1955.

15. This became apparent in Poland where the Bohemian Brethren could freely develop after being exiled from their homeland by Ferdinand I; see J. Bidlo, *Jednota Bratrská v prvním vyhnanstvi* /The Unity of Brethren in its first exile/, 4 vols., Prague 1900–1932. For the whole background see Dvornik, *The Slavs . . . ,* chapter XVI, "The Reformation and the Slavs."

16. E. M. Wilbur, *A History of Unitarianism,* Cambridge, Mass. 1945. The same author translated into English the work of St. Kot, the Polish historian of the move-

ment, *Socinianism in Poland: The Social and Political Ideas of the Polish Anti-Trinitarians*, Boston 1957.

17. This war raised the special interest of Karl Marx, who wrote a monograph on it.

18. See Msgr. Cristiani, *loc. cit.*, V/4 (1960), 857–878.

19. Brugmans rightly considers the religious wars which started in the sixteenth century a critical turning point; see the conclusions of his *L'Europe prend le large*, which ends with the outbreak of these wars.

20. G. Mattingly, *The Great Armada*, New York 1960, recently showed it in a brilliant way.

21. The Polish case attracted, therefore, the attention of the Protestant historian K. Völker, who was particularly interested in the problem of religious freedom; see his *Toleranz und Intoleranz im Zeitalter der Reformation*, Leipzig 1912, and *Kirchengeschichte Polens*, Berlin-Leipzig 1930.

22. K. Jörgensen, *Ökumenische Bestrebungen unter den polnischen Protestanten bis z. J. 1645*, Copenhagen 1942.

23. G. Stökl, "Das Echo von Renaissance und Reformation im Moskauer Russland," *Jahrb. f. Gesch. Osteuropas*, VII (1959).

24. Halecki, *From Florence . . .*, Part IV.

25. Concerning the latter, rich material was collected by E. Benz, *Die Ostkirche im Lichte der Protestantischen Geschichtsschreibung*, München 1952.

26. Schnürer, *Katholische Kirche und Kultur in der Barockzeit*, Paderborn 1937.

NOTES TO CHAPTER XVIII

1. L. Fueter, *Geschichte des europäischen Staatensystems, 1492–1559*, Berlin 1919, places the Italian wars in the center of the whole development of international relations through the period.

2. K. Brandi, *Kaiser Karl V—Werden und Schicksal einer Persönlichkeit und eines Weltreiches*, 2 vols., 1937–1941; see also the symposium, *Charles Quint et son temps*, Paris 1959.

3. S. Skalweit, "Karl V und die Nationen," *Saeculum*, IX (1958), 379–392, defends the conception of Charles V against "nationalistic" criticism but deals only with the nations which were inside his empire.

4. A. H. Buffington, *The Second Hundred Years' War 1689–1815*, New York 1929.

5. Paszkiewicz, *op. cit.*

6. Interesting sidelights on their attitude at the Council can be found in the exhaustive study by A. Coville, *Jean Petit et la question du tyrannicide au XVe siècle*, Paris 1930.

7. See the latest discussion of his project by de Rougemont, *Europe*, pp. 67–70; see also Dvornik, *The Slavs . . .*, pp. 205 f., on the policy of George of Poděbrady.

8. *Austriae est imperare orbi universo* or *Alles Erdreich ist Oesterreich untertan*. Their matrimonial policy was summed up in the formula, *Bella gerantalii, tu felix Austria nube.*

9. It is surprising that this congress was never studied in detail after the publication of a preliminary study by X. Liske, *Der Wiener Kongress von 1515 und Polen*, Göttingen 1878.

10. See my article, "Die österreichisch-polnischen Beziehungen zur Zeit der Union von Lublin," *Festschrift für P. Th. Michel*, 1963, on the project of another congress to be held in Breslau in 1569, with a view to securing for the Habsburgs the Polish-Lithuanian heritage of the Jagellonians after the Bohemo-Hungarian.

11. A provocative lecture of that title was delivered by A. v. Randa at the *Salzburger Hochschulwochen* of 1959.

12. S. A. Fischer-Galati, *Ottoman Imperialism and German Protestants, 1521-1555*, Cambridge, Mass. 1959.

13. Mattingly, *Renaissance Diplomacy*, Boston 1955.

14. H. Butterfield, *The Statescraft of Machiavelli*, London 1940, defends the traditional interpretation; the whole background is best explained by Chabod, *Machiavelli and the Renaissance*, London 1958, who also describes very well the purely secular character of Machiavelli's conception of Europe in *Storia dell'idea d'Europa*, pp. 48 ff.

15. Mattingly, *Armada*; see above, Chapter XVII, n. 20.

16. Elements of nationalism clearly appear in the war of 1400-1411; see the latest study by S. M. Kuczyński, *Wielka-Wojna 1410-11r.*, 2nd ed., Warsaw 1956, though Rhode in his comments on the sources of trouble in German-Polish relations considers such interpretations of the battle of Grunwald rather artificial.

17. It was replaced by the Hungarian language only by the Diet of 1843–1844.

18. See my chapter on Renaissance culture in *The Cambridge History of Poland*, I (1950).

19. A. Martel, *La langue polonaise dans les pays ruthènes 1569–1667*, Lille 1938.

20. This was pointed out by Dvornik, *The Slavs . . .*, pp. 307, 348, who, however, goes too far in some of his conclusions.

21. G. Szekfü, *Etat et Nation*, Paris 1945.

22. G. Hanotaux, *La France en 1614*, Paris 1913, gave an excellent picture of France during the year when the *Etats généraux* met for the last time.

23. Halecki, *Dzieje Unii jagiellońskiej* /History of the Jagiellonian Union/, 2 vols., Cracow 1919–1920. I tried to supplement this political and constitutional study by discussing some cultural implications in *From Florence . . .*, Part III.

24. On the significance of this turning point in Swiss history see E. Gagliardi, *Der Anteil der Schweiz an den italienischen Kriegen 1494–1516*, Zurich 1919.

25. See my remarks in *Limits and Divisions . . .*, pp. 169–170.

26. See the significant statement quoted by de Rougemont, *Europe*, p. 81.

NOTES TO CHAPTER XIX

1. For the problem discussed in this chapter see my article, "The Defense of Europe in the Renaissance Period," *Didascaliae*, in honor of A. Albareda, Rome 1961, pp. 121–146, where more references are given.

2. On the occasion of the five-hundredth anniversary of that fateful date, the

review *Byzantinoslavica* published a special volume, XIV (1953), under the title of *1453–1953*. It constitutes a most interesting symposium on the consequences of the fall of Constantinople, especially for the Slavs.

3. It was even said with good reason that Byzantium "perpétue l'Antiquité dans le moyen-âge"; see E. Stein in *Traditio*, VII (1949–1951), 99.

4. F. Babinger, *Mehmed der Eroberer und seine Zeit*, München 1953.

5. M. Silberschmidt, *Das orientalische Problem—nach venezianischen Quellen*, Leipzig 1923.

6. Which, however, should not be considered the last crusade, as does Atiya, *The Crusade in the Later Middle Ages*, p. 463.

7. See the latest statement of Gill, *Eugene IV, Pope of Christian Unity*, Westminster, Md. 1961, p. 156, that Varna was "the beginning of the end of Christian Constantinople and of the Union with the Greek."

8. See the series of articles on "Griechische Patriarchen und Römische Päpste," by Hofmann in *Orientalia Christiana*, XIII (1928) to XXXVI (1934).

9. Vernadsky, *op. cit.*, pp. 331 f.

10. Particularly in view of the recent misinterpretation by Winter, *Russland und das Papsttum*, I, Berlin 1960, where the chapter on the Renaissance period, however, gives some new material deserving attention.

11. See Vernadsky, *op. cit.*, Chapter V, pp. 332–390, "The Mongol Impact on Russia."

12. Stressed by Toynbee, *Civilization on Trial*, New York 1948. See also the thorough investigation of "The Growth of Muscovite Autocracy," Dvornik, *The Slavs . . .*, Chapter XV, particularly pp. 374 ff.

13. See the latest discussion of these wars, Dvornik, *op. cit.*, 240 ff., 270 ff. (where the interpretation of the Muscovite aggression against Lithuania, however, raises serious objections), 437 ff.

14. Quoted by de Rougemont, *Europe*, p. 71.

15. W. Kirchner, *The Rise of the Baltic Question*, Newark 1954.

16. The most recent contribution is A. N. Kurat, "The Turkish Expedition to Astrakhan in 1569 and the Problem of the Don-Volga Canal," *The Slavonic and East European Review*, XL (1961), 7–23.

17. The two latest studies of the problem are St. Polčin, "Une tentative d'Union au XVIe siècle: la mission religieuse du Père Antoine Possevino, S. J. en Moscovie, 1581–1582," Rome 1957, *Orientalia Christiana Analecta*, 150, and W. Delius, *Antonio Possevino, S. J. und Ivan Groznyj. Ein Beitrag zu Geschichte der kirchlichen Union und der Gegenreformation des 16. Jahrhunderts*, Berlin 1961.

18. Halecki, "Le projet de ligue anti-ottomane à la fin du XVIe siècle," *Comptes-rendus de l'Académie des Inscriptions et Belles Lettres, 1960*, Paris 1961, pp. 190–200.

19. G. Stökl, *Die Entstehung des Kosakentums*, München 1953. New source material was published by A. G. Welykyj, *Litterae nuntiorum apostolicorum historiam Ukrainae illustrantia*, I–VII (1550–1651), Rome 1959–1962.

20. See C. H. Talbot, *Res Polonicae Elisabetha I Angliae regnante conscripta. Ex Archivis Publicis Londoniarum*, Rome 1961 (vol. IV of the new series *Elementa ad Fontium Editiones*).

NOTES TO CHAPTER XX

1. On the importance of the battle and, in general, the campaigns of Alfonso XI, see the remarks of Altamira in *The Cambridge Mediaeval History*, VII, 574. On the significance of the much earlier victory at Navas de Tolosa (1212) see C. Seco Serrano, "El siglo de los grandes descumbrimentos geograficos," *Cahiers d'Histoire mondiale*, IV/3 (1958), 553–581.

2. A less known chapter of the story was recently studied by F. M. Rogers, *The Travels of the Infante Dom Pedro of Portugal*, Cambridge, Mass. 1961.

3. See R. Barón Castro, "The Discovery of America and the Geographical and Historical Integration of the World," *Cahiers d'Histoire mondiale*, VI/4 (1961), 809–832.

4. On the legendary role of the Irish in even earlier discoveries, see R. Y. Creston, *Journal de bord de Saint Brendan à la recherche du Paradis*, Paris 1957.

5. See H. R. Wagner, *The Rise of F. Cortés*, Los Angeles 1944.

6. See the standard biography of Columbus by S. E. Morrison, *Admiral of the Ocean Sea*, 2 vols., Boston 1942.

7. A. Tovar, "L'incorporation du nouveau monde à la culture occidentale," *Cahiers d'Histoire mondiale*, VI/4 (1961), 833–856.

8. See "Beiträge zur spanischen Kolonialethik," by Juan Friede and Humberto Vasquez Machicado, *Saeculum*, VIII (1957), 372–391, which points out the contributions of the Franciscans in addition to those of the Dominican Las Casas.

9. About the role of Babur on which Toynbee speculated in this connection, see Zeller, *Histoire des relations internationales*, II, Paris 1953, 176 f.

10. The Hakluyt Society re-edited the translation of *The Prester John of the Indies: A True Relation of the Lands of the Prester John, Being the Narrative of the Portuguese Embassy to Ethiopia in 1520 Written by Father Francisco Alvares*, 2 vols., New York 1961.

11. L. v. Pastor, *Geschichte der Päpste*, II, 231 f., particularly n. 2.

12. *Ibid.*, XIII, appendices 67, 69, about such projects by Clement VIII.

13. M. Kluchevsky called it the "osnovnoi fakt" of Russian history; see his *Kurs russkoi istorii*, I, 22–23.

14. See G. V. Lantzeff, *Siberia in the Seventeenth Century: A Study of the Colonial Administration*, Berkeley 1943; and for further developments, F. A. Golder, *Russian Expansion in the Pacific*, Cleveland 1914.

15. R. Kerner, *The Urge to the Sea*, Berkeley 1942.

16. De Rougemont, *Europe*, p. 121.

17. *Ibid.*, as well as in Brugmans' *L'Europe prend* . . . , where that picture is used as a frontispiece.

NOTES TO CHAPTER XXI

1. See Chapter IX, "Modern Contemporary History," in my *Limits and Divisions* . . .

2. R. R. Palmer, *The Age of Democratic Revolution*, Princeton 1959.
3. These implications were best shown by R. J. Hoffman, *The Great Republic*, New York 1942.
4. The most important passages are given by de Rougemont, *Europe*, pp. 94–97.
5. W. Sobieski, *Henryk IV wobec Polski i Szwecji* /Henry IV with regard to Poland and Sweden/, Cracow 1910, with an important appendix on "the great design."
6. De Rougemont, *Europe*, pp. 132 ff. where the project of Crucé is discussed.
7. *Ibid.* See also Chabod, *Storia dell'Idea d'Europa*, pp. 55–59 and 123–142, where he shows very well that the great writers of the Enlightenment, including Voltaire, were mainly interested in the cultural features of Europe in contrast to the newly discovered parts of the world.
8. His contribution to the idea of European unity was rightly emphasized by Brugmans in his opening address of the 1961–62 academic year of the College of Europe—the "promotion of Leibniz."
9. L. H. Schlimgen, "Stanislas Leszczyński, a Reformer in Exile," *Bulletin* of *the Polish Institute of Arts and Sciences in America*, III (1944).
10. See vols. II and III of the *Histoire des relations internationales* (ed. P. Renouvin): G. Zeller, *Les temps modernes I. De Christophe Colomb à Cromwell; II. De Louis XVI à 1789*, Paris 1953.
11. W. Czapliński, "Władysław IV," *The Cambridge History of Poland from the Origins to Sobieski*, Cambridge 1950; see also his paper, "Le problème baltique aux XVIe et XVIIe siècles," *XIe Congrès internationales des Sciences historiques*, Stockholm 1960, *Rapports*, IV, 25–47, and the discussion in *Actes du Congrès*, pp. 149–153.
12. See the articles of F. L. Baumer on the conception of the "Common Corps" of Christendom in *American Historical Review*, L (1944), 26–48; *Journal of Modern History*, XVI (1944), 1–21; *Journal of the History of Ideas*, VI (1945), 131–156.
13. See below, Chapters XXII and XXIII.
14. On the Treaty of the Pyrenees as a turning point in general European history, like the Treaty of Westphalia, see Zeller, *op. cit.*, I, 276.
15. Most recently discussed by W. Leitsch, *Moskau und die Politik des Kaiserhofes im XVII. Jahrhundert*, I, Graz-Köln 1960.
16. Overemphasized by B. F. Porchnev, "Les rapports politiques de l'Europe occidentale et de l'Europe orientale à l'époque de la guerre de trente ans," *XIe Congrès int. des Sciences hist.*, Stockholm 1960, *Rapports*, IV, 136–163, and the discussion in *Actes du Congrès*, pp. 191–199.
17. See the studies on "enlightened despotism" published in the *Bulletin of the International Committee of Historical Sciences* before the war.
18. See the quotation from his work given by de Rougemont, *loc. cit.*

NOTES TO CHAPTER XXII

1. See vols. X–XII of the collection *Peuples et Civilisations*, eds. L. Halphen and P. Sagnac, Paris 1940 ff.

2. See above, Chapters II and VII.

3. Evidenced by the numerous biographies of Gustavus Adolphus and Charles XII, the last by O. Haintz, *König Karl XII von Schweden,* 3 vols., Berlin 1958.

4. Cessi, *Storia* . . . , II.

5. E. Curtis, *A History of Ireland,* 6th ed., London 1950.

6. See above, Chapter III, n. 14.

7. P. H. Brown, *The Legislative Union of England and Scotland,* Oxford 1914.

8. See H. Pirenne, *Histoire de Belgique,* II, Bruxelles 1908, pp. 254 ff.

9. J. Huizinga, "How Holland Became a Nation," *Lectures on Holland for American Students,* 1924, pp. 1–18.

10. This is the title of Huizinga's well-known book, first published in Haarlem, 1919, and translated into many languages.

11. W. Oechsli, *History of Switzerland 1499–1914,* Cambridge 1922.

12. On the international implications of the struggle for control of the Valteline see Zeller, *op. cit.,* I, 230, 253.

13. G. Castella, *Histoire du Canton de Fribourg,* Fribourg 1922, pp. 534 ff., has interesting comments on the origin of the "Sonderbund."

14. De Reynold, *La Suisse une et diverse,* Fribourg 1923.

15. It was recalled in Switzerland in 1962 by the celebration of the 250th anniversary of his birth.

16. In letters XIX and XX of *The Federalist,* ed. E. M. Earle, Princeton 1937; see below, Chapter XXV, n. 11.

17. R. Kann, *The Multinational Empire,* New York 1950, I, particularly the notes.

18. E. Denis, *La fin de l'indépendance de Bohême,* Paris 1890; see also Dvornik, *The Slavs* . . . , pp. 452 ff.

19. R. Kerner, *Bohemia in the Eighteenth Century,* Berkeley 1932.

20. J. Polišenský, "Comenius and His Time," *Cahiers d'Histoire mondiale,* VI/1 (1960), 45–77.

21. H. Marczali, *Hungary in the Eighteenth Century,* London 1910.

NOTES TO CHAPTER XXIII

1. L. Namier, *The Structure of Politics at the Accession of George III,* London 1957.

2. These deplorable consequences of Turkish rule appear even in the rather optimistic interpretation of L. S. Stavrianos, *The Balkans since 1453,* New York 1958.

3. An English translation of the memoirs of St. Zółkiewski, who favored such a peaceful solution, was published under the title *Expedition to Moscow,* London 1959.

4. Pointed out by the Ukrainian historian W. Milkowicz in his synthesis of East European history, published in vol. V of H. Helmolt, *Weltgeschichte,* Leipzig 1906. This contrast appears very clearly in Dvornik, *The Slavs* . . . , Chapters XIV and XV, but his criticism of the Polish constitution, of the *szlachta,* the Union of Lublin

and Brest, etc., was obviously influenced by the Russian and pro-Russian viewpoint in this matter. (See p. 488, n. 13 about Križanić.)

5. A first attempt was made by T. Korzon to establish statistics of the various social groups in Poland before the partitions, *Wewnętrzne dzieje Polski za Stanisława Augusta* /Internal History of Poland under Stanislaus Augustus/, V, Warsaw 1896.

6. Recently stressed by Wojciechowski, *L'Etat polonais au moyen-âge,* Paris 1949.

7. A French translation of the standard work by W. Konopczyński, *Le Liberum Veto,* appeared in Paris in 1930.

8. This publication in nine volumes was initiated by the same writer who was struggling for a basic reform of unanimity rule; see W. J. Rose, *Stanislas Konarski,* London 1929.

9. Evidenced in the interregna of 1572–73, 1575 and 1587.

10. On the recent occasion of its 300th anniversary, studies of this Union were published in various languages, but an exhaustive, fully objective monograph is still missing.

11. Z. Wójcik, *Traktat andruszowski* /The Andrussovo Treaty/, Warsaw 1959, with detailed French summary; see my review in the *Am. Slavic and East Europ. Rev.,* XIX (1960), 308–310.

12. Beginning with the election in 1632, these lists were all published.

13. Both cases have been studied by W. K. Medlin, *Moscow and East Rome,* Geneva 1952; see also Dvornik, *op. cit.,* Chapter XIX: "The Muscovite State under the First Romanov."

14. C. B. O'Brien, *Russia under Two Tsars (1682–1689),* Berkeley 1952.

15. See the extreme interpretation by Toynbee, *Study,* II, 176.

16. M. T. Florinsky, *Russia—A History and an Interpretation,* I, New York, 1953.

17. K. H. Ruffmann, "Russischer Adel als Sondertypus der europäischen Adelswelt," *Jahrb. f. Gesch. Osteur.,* IX (1961), 161–178.

18. G. v. Rauch, *Russland—Staatliche Einheit und Nationale Vielfalt,* München 1953.

19. See C. A. Manning, *The Story of the Ukraine,* New York 1947, pp. 106 ff.; see also Dvornik, *op. cit.,* 511 f., 516, and 523, n. 19.

20. See D. Geyer, "Peter und St. Petersburg," *Jahrb. f. Gesch. Osteur.,* X (1962), 187–200, and the brief discussion of the problem by Stökl in *Die Welt der Slaven,* II, Frankfurt 1962, 52.

21. The contrast between the traditions of the two dynasties continues to be overemphasized in Polish historiography; the continuity appears clearly in the outline by W. and M. Wojciechowski, *Polska Piastów-Polska Jagiellonów,* Poznań 1947.

NOTES TO CHAPTER XXIV

1. For France: de Reynold, *Synthèse du dixseptième siècle,* Paris 1962; for Austria: Kann, *A Study in Austrian Intellectual History from Late Baroque to Romanticism,* New York 1962.

2. Toynbee, *Study*, XII: "Reconsiderations," Oxford 1961, p. 530.

3. See the brief but excellent comments of Chabod, *Storia* . . . , pp. 109 f.

4. G. B. Vico, *Principi di una scienza nuova.*

5. See vols. II (in 2 parts) and IV of the symposium *Odrodzenie w Polsce* /The Renaissance in Poland/, Warsaw 1956.

6. See above, Chapter XXI, n. 8.

7. Pastor, *Päpste*, XII, 203–214, XIII/2, 616–630.

8. See the study by Engel-Janosi, cited in Chapter I, n. 16.

9. First pointed out by H. Bergson, *Les deux sources de la morale* . . . , 334 ff.

10. P. Mantoux, *The Industrial Revolution in the Eighteenth Century*, New York 1928.

11. See the report by Zhukov, quoted in the Preface.

12. See the comments by W. F. Reddaway in *Cambridge History of Poland from Augustus II to Pilsudski*, Cambridge 1941.

13. See above, Chapter XXI.

14. De Reynold, *L'Europe tragique*, Paris 1935, Introduction.

NOTES TO CHAPTER XXV

1. Palmer, "Recent Interpretations of the Influence of the French Revolution," *Cahiers d'Histoire mondiale*, II/1 (1954), 173–195.

2. J. Bainville, *Histoire de France*, Paris 1924; Charles Seignobos, *Histoire sincère de la nation française*, Paris 1933.

3. S. Neumann, *Permanent Revolution*, New York 1942.

4. G. Bruun, "The Heritage of Jacobinism," *Fordham University Studies*, New York 1946.

5. R. Aron, *Histoire de Vichy*, Paris 1954.

6. G. Hanotaux, *Jeanne d'Arc*, Paris 1911.

7. Palmer, *Age of Democratic Revolution*, vol. I, *The Challenge, 1760–1791.*

8. See on the "émeute populaire" of 1790 and the actual reunion of 1791 the article by J. Girard on "Avignon," in the *Dict. d'Hist. et de la Géogr. ecclesiast.*, V (1930), col. 1128.

9. M. Lerner, *America as a Civilization*, New York 1957.

10. This new term, much more appropriate, is frequently used by Fr. John Courtney Murray, S. J.

11. *The Federalist*, letters XVII–XX (by Hamilton and Madison).

12. Kohn, *The Swiss Constitution*, New York 1948, showed it on the occasion of the centennial.

13. See W. S. Robertson, *Rise of the Spanish-American Republics*, New York 1918.

14. See J. B. Brebner, *North Atlantic Triangle: The Interplay of Canada, the United States and Britain*, New Haven 1945.

15. See R. Dow, "Proctor: a Geopolitical Study of Russia and the United States," *The Russian Review*, I (1941), 6–19.

16. As R. H. Lord did in his excellent work on *The Second Partition of Poland*, Cambridge, Mass. 1915, and Palmer, *op. cit.*, Chapter XIII.

17. J. Lukacs, "Poland's Place in the European State System," *The Polish Review*, VI (1961), showed very well that the partitions of Poland were a revolution in eastern Europe comparable to the French Revolution in western Europe.

18. Recently studied by H. H. Kaplan, *The First Partition of Poland*, New York 1962.

19. R. Hoffman, *Edmund Burke—New York Agent*, Philadelphia 1956.

20. M. Haiman, *Kościuszko in the American Revolution*, New York 1942; *Kościuszko—Leader and Exile*, New York 1944.

21. As done by Reddaway, *op. cit.*

22. Haiman, *The Fall of Poland in Contemporary American Opinion*, Chicago 1935.

23. Lord, *op. cit.*, pp. 153–191.

24. De Rougemont, *Europe*, pp. 111, 120.

NOTES TO CHAPTER XXVI

1. This is the title of G. Ferrero's wartime study of the Congress of Vienna, New York 1940.

2. Especially in England and America; German historiography is much more critical; see K. Griewank, *Der Wiener Kongress*, 2nd ed., Leipzig 1954.

3. This is the title of R. Kissinger's postwar study of the Congress of Vienna, Cambridge, Mass. 1960.

4. H. Nicolson, *The Congress of Vienna*, New York 1946.

5. Published in *Les Partages de la Pologne et les luttes pour l'indépendance*, ed. K. Lutostański, Lausanne 1918, pp. 345–346 (Aug. 1814).

6. C. Waliszewski, *Le règne d'Alexandre Ier*, III, Paris 1925.

7. M. Kukiel, *Czartoryski and European Unity*, Princeton 1953.

8. H. A. Strauss, *The Attitude of the Congress of Vienna toward Nationalism in Germany, Italy and Poland*, New York 1945.

9. R. F. Leslie, *Polish Politics and the Revolution of November 1830*, London 1956, underestimated its importance in this and other respects.

10. "L'extension intérieure," wrongly translated in the English text submitted to the British Parliament, which was used by D. Montgomery Hyde in *The Cambridge History of Poland*, II, 270 /"interior development" instead of "extension"/.

11. C. Black examined this possibility in *The Journal of Central European Affairs*, VI (1948).

12. See the recent bibliography by E. Hösch in *Jahrb. f. Gesch. Osteur.*, IX (1961), 399–434.

13. Bóbr-Tylingo, "Un congrès international manqué," *The Polish Review*, IV (1960).

14. Bryce, *op. cit.*, in the supplement to the 1903 edition, pp. 399 f. wrongly sees in the new Hohenzollern Empire the "representative" and "offspring" of the old Holy Roman Empire.

15. L. Eisenmann, *Le compromis austro-hongrois*, Paris 1904, still remains the most exhaustive study.

16. George H. Rupp's *A Wavering Friendship*, Cambridge, Mass. 1941, is a discussion of the relations between Austria-Hungary and Russia after the Congress of Berlin.

17. R. Kjellén, *Die Grossmächte der Gegenwart*, Leipzig 1914.

NOTES TO CHAPTER XXVII

1. For details see O. Hoetzsch, *Russland—Eine Einführung auf Grund seiner Geschichte 1904–1912*, Berlin 1913.

2. See H. A. Wieschhoff, *Colonial Policies in Africa*, Philadelphia 1944.

3. See above, Chapter XX, n. 9.

4. See my article, "The Place of Christendom in the History of Mankind," *Cahiers d'Histoire mondiale*, I (1954), 927–950.

5. Thompson, *Feudal Germany*, Part II.

6. G. H. Dunne, *Generation of Giants: The Story of the Jesuits in the Last Decade of the Ming Dynasty*, Notre Dame 1962.

7. H. Jedin, "Weltmission und Kolonialismus," *Saeculum*, IX (1958), 393–404.

8. The case of Albert Schweitzer must be recalled as a shining exception.

9. This quotation, like the preceding one, is taken from E. V. Mittlebeeler, *European Colonization in Africa*, Washington, Institute for Ethnic Studies, Georgetown University, 1961, where the case against (pp. 5–7) and for colonialism (pp. 7–12) is clearly stated.

10. See Hoetzsch, *op. cit.*, about the origin of the Eurasian conception in the time of Nicolas II.

11. Alfred Zimmern, *The Third British Empire*, London 1934.

12. Lord Cecil, as delegate of South Africa to the first Assembly of the League of Nations in 1920, could recall in one of his speeches that his father, Lord Salisbury, had conducted the Boer War.

13. See the conclusion of Jedin's article, quoted above, n. 7: "Der Kolonialismus ist tot und wird nicht mehr auferstehen; die Weltmission der Kirche muss und wird weiterbestehen" (p. 404).

NOTES TO CHAPTER XXVIII

1. This appears clearly in G. Weill's *L'Europe du XIXe siècle et l'idée de nationalité*, Paris 1938, which is still the best survey of the problem.

2. See the study by Strauss quoted in Chapter XXVI, n. 8.

3. W. M. Gewehr, *The Rise of Nationalism in the Balkans*, New York 1931.

4. See the resolution adopted at the XIth International Congress of Historical Sciences, Stockholm 1960, after a thorough discussion of the report by F. Zwitter, J. Sidak and V. Bogdanov on "Les problèmes nationaux dans la monarchie des Habsbourg," *Rapports*, V, 163–190, also published separately in enlarged form.

5. See Thomson's remarks about the Slovaks in his *Czechoslovakia in European History*, Princeton 1953.

6. Strongly emphasized by Kann, *Multinational Empire*, I; but see also the analysis of the various other classifications of the nationalities of Austria-Hungary in his book, *The Habsburg Monarchy*, Princeton 1958.

7. This was rightly stressed by Hantsch in the discussion quoted above, n. 4.

8. E. Walters, "Austro-Russian Relations under Goluchowski, 1895–1906," *The Slavonic and East Europ. Review*, XXXII (1953–1954), gives documentary evidence in that matter; see particularly Aehrenthal's report of December 31, 1898, pp. 198–200.

9. This is the title of a book published in 1908 by A. Popovici, *Die Vereinigten Staaten von Grossösterreich.*

10. See the statement of K. Badeni quoted by Kann, *op. cit.*, II (conclusion).

11. This is the title of a well-known and influential book by F. Naumann which appeared in Berlin in 1915. For the conflicting interpretations of the German concept of *Mitteleuropa* see the books by H. C. Meyer, *Mitteleuropa in German Thought and Action 1815–1945*, The Hague 1955, and J. Pajewski, *"Mitteleuropa." Studia z dziejów imperializmu niemieckiego w dobie pierwszej wojny światowej* /Studies on the History of German Imperialism at the Time of the First World War/, Poznań 1959, particularly pp. 112–137.

12. See the most recent discussion of the problem in *Die Welt der Slaven*, II, Frankfurt 1962, where Kohn, pp. 84–88, writes on Russia in the nineteenth century regarding the nationalities policy; on the statistics, p. 103; and Scheibert, pp. 209–264, on Byelorussians and Ukrainians.

13. See the introduction to J. S. Reshetar, *The Ukrainian Revolution 1917–1920*, Princeton 1952.

14. W. E. D. Allen, *A History of the Georgian People*, London 1932.

15. Briefly discussed in the introduction to A. E. Senn, *The Emergence of Modern Lithuania*, New York 1959.

16. The case of the Byelorussians deserves further study since it is not too clearly presented in N. P. Vakar, *Belorussia—The Making of a Nation*, Cambridge, Mass. 1956.

17. See the statistics given by Hoetzsch in the book cited in Chapter XXVII, n. 1.

NOTES TO CHAPTER XXIX

1. Recently discussed, as far as Austria was concerned, by V. C. E. Schorske, "Politics and the Psyche in 'Fin de siècle' Vienna," *American Historical Review*, LXVI (1961), 930–946.

2. The symposium, *Mickiewicz in World Literature*, ed. W. Lednicki, Berkeley 1956, contains rich material on the international relations promoted by Romanticism.

3. Th. von Laue, *Leopold Ranke, the Formative Years*, Princeton 1950.

4. On the persistence of the limitation of the European community in modern historiography, see the remarks by F. Seibt in *Hist. Zeitschr.*, CXCV (1962), 57.

5. In the introduction to his work *Les Origines de la France contemporaine.*

6. On Hrushevsky see e.g. the introduction to the reprint of his *Istorija Ukrainy-Rusy,* 11 vols. (up to 1660), which was published in New York 1954–1958; see also my review in *American Historical Review,* LXIV (1959), 995–998.

7. E. Troeltsch, *Der Historismus und seine Probleme,* Berlin 1922, presents a valuable introduction to that problem.

8. Cieszkowski's main work, *Ojcze nasz* /Our Father/, appeared in an English translation by W. J. Rose. See also A. Żoltowski, *Adam Cieszkowski-eine Philosophie der Tat.*

9. On his place in nineteenth-century thought see J. Barzun, *Darwin, Marx, Wagner,* Boston 1941, and S. Hook, *From Hegel to Marx,* New York 1936.

10. De Reynold, *La Formation,* VII, 275 f.

11. Particularly the works of J. Bocheński and G. A. Wetter.

12. See the discussion of Zhukov's report at the Stockholm Congress of 1960, *Actes du Congrès,* pp. 58 f.

13. In addition to M. M. Bober's *Karl Marx's Interpretation of History,* Cambridge, Mass. 1948, the comprehensive symposium published by *Saeculum,* XI (1960), on the occasion of the Stockholm Congress is of special value; see also in an earlier volume of the same journal, IX, 425–445, V. Piroschkow, "Einige Probleme des historischen Materialismus."

14. Maritain, *La primauté du spirituel,* Paris 1927.

15. Hayes, *A Generation of Materialism, 1871–1900,* New York 1941, has a very appropriate title for the history of the whole period.

16. Well stressed in the introduction of Toynbee's *Study,* I. J. Lukacs, in *A History of the Cold War,* New York 1961, raised very pertinent questions as to the consequences of industry and technology for "the transformation of human societies in a totalitarian direction" (p. 168), and of the overestimation of "the economic interpretation of any historical or the scientific interpretation of any human phenomenon" (p. 204, n. 9).

17. Lukacs, *op. cit.,* pp. 147 f., is rightly skeptical in this respect and in recalling that "history still concerns men on this earth."

18. E. E. Y. Hales, *Pio Nono,* New York 1954.

19. E. Soderini, *Il pontificato di Leone XIII,* 3 vols., Milano 1932–1933.

20. See also R. A. Graham, *Vatican Diplomacy,* Princeton 1959, and P. Droulers, "Le catholicisme dans le monde au XIXe siècle," *Cahiers d'Histoire mondiale,* V/2 (1959), 375–401.

NOTES TO CHAPTER XXX

1. Their most important statements in the matter of peace up to 1942 were collected by H. C. Koenig, *Principles for Peace—Selections from Papal Documents,* Washington 1943.

2. B. Newman, *The New Europe,* New York 1943, gives a general picture of the striking consequences of World War I.

3. V. S. Mamatey, *The United States and East Central Europe 1914–1918,*

Princeton 1957, and G. Kennan, *Soviet American Relations*, I: *Russia Leaves the War*, Princeton 1956.

4. The deeper reasons why the idea of a comprehensive federal system in East Central Europe did not materialize are well explained in P. Wandycz, *France and Her Eastern Allies 1919–1925*, Minneapolis 1962.

5. The contrast between Russia's and America's role in the crucial year of 1917 was well described by E. Hölzle in "Formverwandlung der Geschichte—Das Jahre 1917," *Saeculum*, VI (1955), 329–344, and "Europa und die beiden Weltmächte," *ibid.*, IX (1958), 176–188.

6. E. Sarkisyanz, *Russland und der Messianismus des Ostens—Sendungsbewusstsein und politischer Chiliasmus des Ostens*, Tübingen 1955.

7. Kennan, *op. cit.*, II: *The Decision to Intervene*, Princeton 1958.

8. T. Komarnicki, *The Rebirth of the Polish Republic 1914–1920*, London 1957.

9. R. Debicki, *Foreign Policy of Poland 1919-1939*, New York 1962, p. 32 f.

10. W. L. Shirer, *The Rise and Fall of the Third Reich*, New York 1960.

11. See my article, "The Two World Wars—a Comparison," *Thought*, XXI (1946), 21-24.

12. J. Ciechanowski, *Defeat in Victory*, New York 1947, has a title not too different from that of Churchill's memoirs, VI: *Triumph and Tragedy*, London 1954.

13. See the symposium edited by S. D. Kertesz, *The Fate of East Central Europe*, Notre Dame 1956.

14. J. Wheeler-Bennett, *The Forgotten Peace—March 1918*, New York 1938.

15. Not even in Lukacs' book, quoted in Chapter XXIX, n. 16; in the conclusion of his earlier work, *The Great Powers and Eastern Europe*, New York 1949, he explained very well the situation at the end of the armed conflict which had "the cold war" as its consequence.

16. De Reynold, as quoted in Chapter XXIV, n. 14.

NOTES TO CHAPTER XXXI

1. R. Coudenhove-Calergi, *Crusade for Europe*, New York 1958, where the founder of the Pan-European movement gives due attention to the initiative of Aristide Briand, who made his "declaration of peace" at the Assembly of the League of Nations.

2. Many contributions and helpful bibliographies appear in *Les Cahiers de Bruges*, the review published since 1951 by the College of Europe which is mentioned below.

3. By General de Gaulle who, however, now seems to favor a predominance of two powers, France and Germany, in the European community, an approach which is much more alarming. Particularly dangerous is the possibility that the whole world could move in the direction of "a new era of Empires," as stressed by J. Pirenne, *Les grands courants de l'histoire universelle*, vol. VII, Paris 1956, pp. 957 ff.

4. This was recalled by Pope Pius XII in an address to the professors and stu-

dents of the College of Europe when he received them in audience in February 1953.

5. A special effort is being made, as far as history is concerned, by UNESCO's Commission for a Cultural and Scientific History of Mankind. The first volumes are already in print and many interesting articles—some of them quoted in the preceding chapters—have appeared in the *Cahiers d'Histoire mondiale,* the review which has been collecting material in preparation for the project ever since 1954.

6. The present situation of these countries as well as those under Soviet control is discussed in the symposium, *East Central Europe and the World–Developments in the Post-Stalin Era,* ed. Kertesz, Notre Dame 1962, as a sequel to the volume quoted above, Chapter XXX, n. 13.

7. See my contribution to the volume cited above; a comprehensive study was published by R. F. Staar, *Poland 1944–1962,* Baton Rouge 1962.

8. Particularly the Congress held in Rome in 1955; see the report on the discussions *X Congresso internazionale di scienze storiche.*

9. See the rich material collected by P. E. Zinner, *National Communism and Popular Revolt,* New York 1956, and his recent book, *Revolution in Hungary,* New York 1962.

10. This was written before the Cuban crisis of October 1962.

11. See the sometimes paradoxical but provocative conclusions of F. Heer, *Das Experiment Europa. Tausend Jahre Christenheit,* Einsiedeln 1952, pp. 74–78.

NOTES TO CHAPTER XXXII

1. This danger was already pointed out in my *Limits and Divisions . . . ,* Chapter III, n: 32.

2. See above, Chapter XXV, n. 10.

3. This mistake appears in the subtitle of the highly controversial book by L. Gerson, *Woodrow Wilson and the Rebirth of Poland, A Study in the Influence on American Policy of Minority Groups of Foreign Origin,* New Haven 1953.

4. Best shown in Churchill's *History of the English Speaking Peoples,* IV, London 1959.

5. See the memoirs of the founder of the Institute of International Education, S. P. Duggan, *Professor at Large,* New York 1943.

6. See the conclusion of Brugmans, "Magna Europa," *Les Cahiers de Bruges,* V (1955), 115.

7. *Ibid.,* VII (1957), no. 3–4: "Communauté atlantique," with a comprehensive bibliography entitled "Éléments d'une bibliographie atlantique," 162–188.

8. See e.g. the report on the Manila Conference of 1960, quoted above, Preface, n. 7.

9. See M. V. Millar, "American Federalism and European Peace," *Thought,* XVIII (1949).

10. It is interesting to note in this connection that F. J. Turner's ideas have not at all lost their influence on American thinking; see R. E. Riegel, "American Frontier Theory," *Cahiers d'Histoire mondiale* III (1956), 356–380.

11. The problems which the United States has to face in that part of the world received special attention in the symposium quoted above, Chapter XXX, n. 13. See also H. L. Roberts, *Russia and America—Dangers and Prospects,* New York 1956.

12. Hölzle, *Russland und Amerika,* I (to 1867), München 1953.

13. See R. Konetzke, "Forschungsprobleme zur Geschichte der Religion und ihrer Bedeutung in den Kolonisationen Amerikas," *Saeculum,* X (1959), 82–102.

NOTES TO CHAPTER XXXIII

1. See de Reynold, *La Formation,* VII, 170 f., where the origin of Christian humanism is traced back to St. Paul.

2. All this clearly results from the deliberations of the Second Vatican Council and especially from the opening address by Pope John XXIII on October 11, 1962.

3. The expression is frequently used by Toynbee, *Study.*

4. *De civitate Dei,* lib. XVIII, cap. 2.

5. *Ibid.,* lib. XVIII, cap. 11, 12, 13.

6. *Ibid.,* lib. XIX, cap. 17.

7. *Ibid.,* lib. XIX, cap. 7; on the three parts of the world see lib. XVI, cap. 17.

8. By G. K. Chesterton.

9. By the Polish philosopher A. Schaff, who propagated his idea at the "Rencontres de Genève" of 1961.

10. A specific project in the matter of international peace was submitted by a group of bishops during the first session of the Council in the fall of 1962. These expectations have been fulfilled by the encyclical, *Pacem in terris,* issued when production of this book was underway.

11. These last Latin words are a quotation from a letter of St. Augustine (Ep. CXXXVIII, 9).

Index